D1258070

Read this book online today:

With SAP PRESS BooksOnline we offer you online access to knowledge from the leading SAP experts. Whether you use it as a beneficial supplement or as an alternative to the printed book, with SAP PRESS BooksOnline you can:

- Access your book anywhere, at any time. All you need is an Internet connection.
- Perform full text searches on your book and on the entire SAP PRESS library.
- Build your own personalized SAP library.

The SAP PRESS customer advantage:

Register this book today at *www.sap-press.com* and obtain exclusive free trial access to its online version. If you like it (and we think you will), you can choose to purchase permanent, unrestricted access to the online edition at a very special price!

Here's how to get started:

1. Visit *www.sap-press.com*.
2. Click on the link for SAP PRESS BooksOnline and login (or create an account).
3. Enter your free trial license key, shown below in the corner of the page.
4. Try out your online book with full, unrestricted access for a limited time!

Your personal free trial **license key**
for this online book is:

qgjm-ntph-xe6a-s5f4

SAP® BusinessObjects Web Intelligence

 PRESS

SAP PRESS is a joint initiative of SAP and Galileo Press. The know-how offered by SAP specialists combined with the expertise of the Galileo Press publishing house offers the reader expert books in the field. SAP PRESS features first-hand information and expert advice, and provides useful skills for professional decision-making.

SAP PRESS offers a variety of books on technical and business related topics for the SAP user. For further information, please visit our website: *www.sap-press.com*.

Ingo Hilgefort
Inside SAP BusinessObjects Advanced Analysis
2011, 343 pp.
978-1-59229-371-1

Ingo Hilgefort
Inside SAP BusinessObjects Explorer
2010, 307 pp.
978-1-59229-340-7

Ingo Hilgefort
Reporting and Analytics with SAP BusinessObjects
2009, 655 pp.
978-1-59229-310-0

Larry Sackett
MDX Reporting and Analytics with SAP NetWeaver BW
2009, 380 pp.
978-1-59229-249-3

Jim Brogden, Heather Sinkwitz, and Mac Holden

SAP® BusinessObjects Web Intelligence

Galileo Press

Bonn • Boston

Galileo Press is named after the Italian physicist, mathematician and philosopher Galileo Galilei (1564–1642). He is known as one of the founders of modern science and an advocate of our contemporary, heliocentric worldview. His words *Eppur se muove* (And yet it moves) have become legendary. The Galileo Press logo depicts Jupiter orbited by the four Galilean moons, which were discovered by Galileo in 1610.

Editor Erik Herman
Technical Reviewer Coy Yonce
Copyeditor Julie McNamee
Cover Design Jill Winitzer
Photo Credit Image Copyright MikLav. Used under license from Shutterstock.com.
Layout Design Vera Brauner
Production Editor Kelly O'Callaghan
Assistant Production Editor Graham Geary
Typesetting Publishers' Design and Production Services, Inc.
Printed and bound in Canada

ISBN 978-1-59229-322-3
© 2012 by Galileo Press Inc., Boston (MA)
1st edition 2010, 1st reprint 2012

Library of Congress Cataloging-in-Publication Data
SAP BusinessObjects Web intelligence / Jim Brogden ... [et al.]. — 1st ed.
       p. cm.
   Includes bibliographical references and index.
   ISBN-13: 978-1-59229-322-3 (alk. paper)
   ISBN-10: 1-59229-322-0 (alk. paper)
   1. BusinessObjects.   2. Business intelligence — Data processing.
3. Management information systems.   I. Brogden, Jim, 1972–
   HD38.7.S265 2010
   658.4'038028553 — dc22
                                        2010002060

FSC
www.fsc.org
MIX
Paper from
responsible sources
FSC® C011825

Contents at a Glance

Contents

3 Creating a Web Intelligence XI 3.x Query 67

7   Formatting Web Intelligence Reports 185

10 Displaying Data with Charts 269

11 Working Within InfoView 297

14 Advanced Universe Design Topics 365

15 Linking in Web Intelligence Reports 387

Foreword

Business Intelligence (BI) is a conundrum; it is (in my opinion at least) the single most valuable technology available to organizations, bar none. It is a universally applicable technology which, when applied well, can transform corporate performance, drive innovation and help save lives, to mention just a few of its almost infinite array of uses (it has even been used to catch bank robbers and track the movements of a poisoned spy, believe it or not).

None of this should be a surprise. All of these things are the obvious result of the good use of information and, if it is about anything, BI is about making better use of information.

Further proof comes from the annual Gartner survey, which has ranked BI the number one technology priority for CIOs for each of the last four years (ahead of ERP, CRM, Virtualization, Collaboration, Security and SOA amongst others).

But despite all this, BI is one of the least recognized technologies both inside and outside IT. I bet that a general survey of business people would place all of the other technologies listed above higher than BI in terms of both visibility and importance. In fact I suspect that outside of IT (and often inside it) people would not recognize BI as a category in the way they would the others.

After almost twenty years in the BI industry, this still puzzles me, why does BI not stand out as a must-have, must-implement, cannot-do-without-it technology? I can see three possible reasons:

❶ The ability to access and understand information in systems across the organization is just taken for granted.

❷ It is possible (despite being hugely expensive in hidden costs) to achieve similar using a lot of manual labor and spreadsheets or other ad-hoc technologies

❸ The benefits of BI are too often passed off as "largely intangible" whereas other technologies are easier to tie to "real" cost savings.

❶ is so rarely the case that it must be a combination of ❷ and ❸. In fact I have to say that I have rarely seen a really compelling business case made for BI in advance of its implementation. Although time and again after-the-fact analyses often reveal three figure ROIs (the most extreme case I saw was a $750k project which only just scraped together the case to go ahead but returned over $22M in savings in its first year of operation).

So what does all this mean to you? It means that in some ways the book you are holding is the key to a secret garden of opportunity. If BI is a universally applicable technology then Web Intelligence is as close as you can get to a universally applicable BI tool. Amongst the hundreds (possibly thousands) of BI tools available on the market, there are many which are more suited to specific parts of the BI spectrum (my particular favorite is Xcelsius, also from SAP BusinessObjects) but arguably none which have the overall breadth and depth of Web Intelligence. If you could only choose one BI tool then Web Intelligence would make the shortlist every time.

However, there is a price to pay. With great power and flexibility comes a steep learning curve. Web Intelligence is not a tool you can master in a week; in fact I think it is safe to say that however long you have been working with Web Intelligence you will find something new within these pages. But this is not just a book for the long-time WebI user, it also provides a grounding in the underlying principles to help even those who are new to BI to get started quickly and easily.

If you are new to the BI community, I would like to welcome you to a new view of the world, a view which opens up a remarkable opportunity to change the status quo, change the way you and your colleagues do business, to make a difference in just about any field of business. As the BusinessObjects marketing used to say, "to transform the way the world works."

Donald MacCormick
December 2009
Ross, CA

Acknowledgments

I would like to begin by thanking the publishing team at Galileo Press and especially Erik Herman for being a driving force behind this book from the inception of the table of contents. Erik was extremely helpful throughout the entire process and answered all 947 of my questions quickly and positively.

This book could not have been possible if it weren't for an excellent team of co-authors. Special thanks to Heather Sinkwitz and Mac Holden for their dedication to this project and writing contributions. I would also like to recognize Coy Yonce for providing information on Web Intelligence XI 3.1 SP2 and for his valuable contributions as the technical editor.

I would like to recognize AJ Smith for playing a very important role in helping me to become a more insightful data analyst and business intelligence specialist. AJ has been a mentor and "data coach" to me for the last couple of years and a positive influence on my career. Thank you also goes out to Doug Miller for his continued day to day support and encouragement.

I would be remiss if I did not recognize a group of talented developers that I had the good fortune of working with early in my IT career. These people introduced me to the world of business intelligence and provided countless hours of assistance along the way. They are: Mary Long, John Delbeau, Wendy Dorsey, and Clay Elrod.

Lastly, I would like to express many thanks to my wife Christi for her unyielding support and patience while enduring several months and countless evening hours of me being glued to the laptop working on this book. In addition, I would like to extend a very special appreciation to my sons Jamie and Hunter for providing the motivation to work hard every day.

Jim Brogden

There are so many people that I have met along my career path that have given me knowledge and support along the way. Since there are too many to list, I want to send a warm thank you to everyone that I have had the pleasure of working with in the past and present who have given me the experience necessary to write this book. I want to a make special mention of my InfoSol family and my Rural/Metro colleagues as well. Most importantly, I want to thank my family and friends for their kind words, support, and understanding while I worked on this book – Chris, Payton, Zen, and Max – thank you!

Heather Sinkwitz

I would like to thank the SAP staff members from various offices around the world for the help, examples and even program code they provided when putting together these chapters. Of course, the online SAP developer library at *http://www. sdn.sap.com/irj/boc/sdklibrary* also offers a wealth of advice and examples.

Mac Holden

SAP® BusinessObjects™ Web Intelligence® XI 3.1 is the industry's most powerful ad hoc query, reporting, and analysis solution on the market today. Create, analyze, publish, and share enterprise-wide reports in minutes with Web Intelligence XI 3.1.

1   SAP BusinessObjects Web Intelligence XI 3.1

SAP BusinessObjects Web Intelligence is a best-in-class ad hoc query, reporting, and analysis tool designed with the business user in mind. With Web Intelligence XI 3.1, users have self-service access to company data through an easy-to-use web-based portal interface known as InfoView.

Web Intelligence provides business users with the tools to make better decisions and offer deeper insight into company data. The major benefits include the ability to drill, pivot, chart, track changes, publish, schedule, and share business information online and within a single online portal.

There are many aspects to developing Web Intelligence documents, and this book will explain every detail in creating highly functional and analytical reports. The features available in Web Intelligence allow you to analyze company data in a way that you have never done before. By learning to use the rich set of functions available out of the box (OOB), you'll be able to make more informed and accurate business decisions.

This chapter introduces you to the key features and core functionality of the Web Intelligence reporting tool. We'll also discuss the steps for setting up the report viewing properties and introduce the reporting analysis environments.

1.1   Features of Web Intelligence

Web Intelligence has been known for many years by report developers as "WebI" (pronounced "webby"). It's best known as a highly intuitive, web-based query and analysis tool that provides business users with the capability of creating and modifying queries without having to write a single line of SQL.

By reducing the level of complexity in report building, business users have unprecedented opportunities to analyze and leverage company information. The InfoView portal makes sharing reports across the enterprise a breeze.

The architecture of the SAP BusinessObjects Enterprise solution allows Web Intelligence reports to operate purely within the web browser. This architecture significantly reduces deployment costs and complexity, making it easier for small to midsize companies to use the SAP BusinessObjects reporting suite.

Enterprise reporting is no longer just for executives. Business users leverage the strengths of Web Intelligence to interact with and analyze data on a daily basis. Web Intelligence plays a very important role in extending analysis across the enterprise to a large audience of casual users and power users, in addition to executives.

Key Advantages of SAP BusinessObjects Web Intelligence XI 3.1

- ▶ Generate SQL without knowledge of underlying data structures
- ▶ Develop and analyze reports in a zero-client online portal structure
- ▶ Self-service access to company data for business users
- ▶ Merge dimensions of multiple data providers for more robust reports
- ▶ Drill-down functionality in reports
- ▶ Extensive set of out-of-the-box (OOB) report section functions
- ▶ Ease-of-use in creating analytical documents with a variety of chart types
- ▶ Capability of adding functionality with Web Intelligence Extension Points
- ▶ Integration with Microsoft Office via SAP BusinessObjects Live Office
- ▶ Integration with SAP NetWeaver BW and SAP NetWeaver
- ▶ Customization through the SDK and with creating BI widgets
- ▶ Multidimensional reporting through OLAP universes

In the following sections, we'll discuss the six primary functions of Web Intelligence: query, report, analyze, share, customize, and integrate.

1.1.1 Core Functionality

The primary function of Web Intelligence XI 3.1 is to provide the capability of querying a set of data without any knowledge of the SQL language and interactively analyzing data to further restrict, expand, and modify the way information is displayed and delivered. After data is retrieved, formatting is easily applied to present results in a variety of customized formats.

The data retrieved with Web Intelligence is displayed in the report section by using report element templates. The available templates include data tables, charts, and free-hand cells to meet a wide variety of reporting requirements. After your query has been refreshed and results are returned, the data is easily visualized by inserting report templates and result objects into your reports.

Reports can be quickly organized by inserting breaks to group the data and by applying block- or report-level filters. These actions can be completed with just a couple clicks of the mouse. An extensive set of shortcut icons are available to assist with frequently used customizations. These icons are located at the top of the screen within Web Intelligence and grouped into three toolbars.

When you're ready to share your work, you can easily publish your documents to the InfoView portal. Users across the enterprise will then have the opportunity to view and interact with your reports by logging into InfoView through a web browser without any installation requirements. Extended interaction is available to users by right-clicking on a report or report element for on-the-fly interaction and customization.

Primary Web Intelligence Functions

Following are descriptions of the primary Web Intelligence functions:

▸ **Query:** Building queries in Web Intelligence XI 3.1 has been significantly improved compared to previous versions. In Web Intelligence XI 3.1, you now have the capability of connecting to multiple universes within the same document and synchronizing your data through merged dimensions. In addition, you can quickly and graphically generate complex SQL statements within the Web Intelligence query panel that contain subqueries and unions (referred to as combined queries).

▸ **Report:** Over the course of this book, you'll learn to create everything from simple reports to complex analysis documents with multiple report tabs. Unlock the full potential of Web Intelligence XI 3.1 by using the built-in editing and formatting features available for presenting data quickly and accurately. Reporting with Web Intelligence is also very flexible and intuitive. Never again let your reporting solution cause the bottleneck in your business intelligence solution.

► **Analyze:** Use drill filters, report filters, block filters, and built-in report functions to provide detailed, laser-targeted analysis. Discover the extensive list of report functions and contexts available for creating precise variables and formulas.

Provide deep analysis and deliver valuable analytical reports to the user community with the functionality of Web Intelligence XI 3.1 and become a more insightful analyst and subject matter expert (SME) with your clients' data. Perform on-the-fly modifications to reports with an extensive set of options available when you right-click on a report.

► **Share:** Publish your Web Intelligence report documents to the InfoView portal for collaborative analysis. The documents can then be scheduled to execute the generated SQL statements and distribute the data to enterprise user inboxes or emailed externally.

InfoView delivers Web Intelligence reports within the default folder structure or within a folder-like structure known as categories. Reports can also be delivered in SAP BusinessObjects Dashboard Builder XI 3.1.

► **Customize:** Ever wonder how to make modifications to the "look and feel" of Web Intelligence? Take your SAP BusinessObjects installation to the next level by editing the provided SDK to produce customized business intelligence reporting solutions.

Use Web Intelligence extension points to extend the functionality of Web Intelligence. Produce additional customizations by developing BI widgets with Web Intelligence data.

► **Integrate:** Discover the capabilities of integrating Web Intelligence with Microsoft Office by using SAP BusinessObjects LiveOffice for flexible and portable reporting documents. The rich set of SAP BusinessObjects reporting tools now lends itself to integration.

1.1.2 Web Intelligence Offline

Operating remotely in offline mode is no longer an aberration of report developers. As of mid-2008, Web Intelligence report development is now possible in offline mode with the SAP BusinessObjects XI 3.1 client tool called Web Intelligence Rich Client.

This portable version of Web Intelligence provides report developers with the capability to disconnect from the Central Management Server (CMS) and work outside of InfoView. Web Intelligence Rich Client also provides the capability of using a local data source. You can import a TXT, CSV, or XLS as a local data source to create Web Intelligence documents.

Figure 1.1 shows the screen that appears when you launch Web Intelligence Rich Client. Click the Create a New Document icon to create a new Rich Client report. The two choices available are to create a new document that uses either a Universe or Local Data Source as the access type.

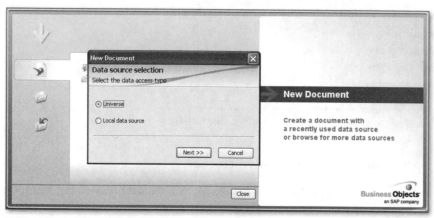

Figure 1.1 Create a New Document in Web Intelligence Rich Client

1.1.3 Launching Web Intelligence Rich Client

Figure 1.2 shows the full list of SAP BusinessObjects XI 3.1 client tools currently available. The highlighted tool, Web Intelligence Rich Client, can be launched to connect to the SAP BusinessObjects Enterprise system or used in offline mode.

Web Intelligence Rich Client can be launched as your editing tool of choice by selecting Desktop as the default creation tool in the Preferences section.

If Web Intelligence Rich Client doesn't already exist on your PC, you can install it by going to the Default Creation/Editing Tool section located in the Web Intelligence settings on the Preferences page. This information will be discussed in detail over the next several pages.

Figure 1.2 Full List of SAP BusinessObjects XI 3.1 Client Tools

1.1.4   Web Intelligence and the Microcube

After a query has been refreshed in Web Intelligence, the data is stored in memory in an unseen microcube. The *microcube* is a data storage structure existing within each report to store the query results behind the scenes. This structure provides the capability of displaying the data within any reporting block type, chart type, or combination of interactions while also providing the ability to drill down.

By storing the result data of each document for the last query that was successfully executed, the microcube allows you to analyze data using different dimensions in separate report tabs and report blocks while only revealing the data that you request.

Until the data becomes visible on a report, it remains stored behind the scenes in the microcube.

1.2 Web Intelligence InfoView Preferences

InfoView is the centralized web portal designed to provide access to all of your business intelligence content, securely and within a single platform. InfoView allows you to create, modify, save, share, and analyze valuable company data from a single location.

By deploying SAP BusinessObjects XI 3.1, you'll enable business users to make better and more informed decisions. The built-in structures of Web Intelligence work seamlessly within InfoView, providing the capability to analyze data with ease.

Web Intelligence now allows you to create and modify reports conveniently through an Internet browser or by working locally with Web Intelligence Rich Client.

Working in offline mode allows report developers to disconnect from the CMS and work locally with saved Web Intelligence documents. This new functionality fulfills the frequently requested task of saving and editing Web Intelligence documents outside of InfoView.

Figure 1.3 shows a custom-formatted Web Intelligence report with drill filters being viewed within InfoView and opened in a new window.

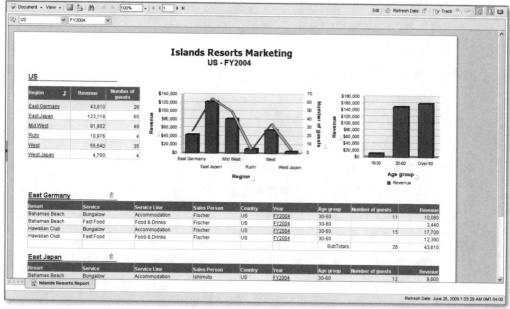

Figure 1.3 Web Intelligence Report Viewed in InfoView

1.3   Setting Web Intelligence Preferences in InfoView

A number of configurable settings are available to enhance the user experience when viewing and interacting with Web Intelligence reports in InfoView. To begin adjusting settings for viewing and interacting with SAP BusinessObjects reporting objects, click the Preferences button located in the upper-right corner of InfoView (see Figure 1.4).

Figure 1.4   Locating the Preferences Button in InfoView

Depending on your security rights, the Preferences page allows you to modify several General Settings and to modify the default settings for viewing and interacting with reporting documents created with the following products:

▸ Set Reporting Tool Preferences

   ▸ Web Intelligence

   ▸ Desktop Intelligence

   ▸ Crystal Reports

   ▸ Dashboard and Analytics

   ▸ Voyager Client

▸ Web Intelligence Preferences

   ▸ Default View Format

   ▸ Creation/Editing Tool

   ▸ Select Default Universe (optional)

   ▸ Drill Options

   ▸ Start Drill Session

   ▸ Priority for Saving Report Data to Microsoft Excel

1.3.1 Setting the Default View Format

When setting the default view format, you have three options: Web, Interactive, and PDF (see Figure 1.5). We discuss each of these options in the sections that follow.

▼ **Web Intelligence**

Select a default view format:

◉ Web (no downloading required)

○ Interactive (no downloading required)

○ PDF (Adobe AcrobatReader required)

Figure 1.5 Web Intelligence Default View Formats

Web View Format

The Web view format allows you to perform all of the basic functions of viewing and analyzing a report such as saving a document to the repository; saving files locally in either PDF, XLS, or CSV format; or viewing a report in one of the four view modes.

In the Web view format, only the report filter toolbar is available when viewing a Web Intelligence report in InfoView. This toolbar provides the same functionality as drill mode.

Drill Mode with the Web View Format

When viewing a report in InfoView, click the magnifying glass shortcut icon in the upper-right corner of a Web Intelligence report to start drill mode (see Figure 1.6).

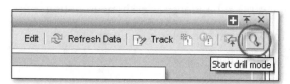

Figure 1.6 Start Drill Mode in a Web Intelligence Document

The report filter toolbar allows users to perform drilling analysis on a report by either selecting a value from an existing prompt or adding a report filter object.

> **Tip**
>
> Report filters provide the capability of filtering report data similar to the way data is restricted in the Where clause of a SQL statement. However, because the data has already been returned from the query and stored in the microcube, drill filters can limit your report data on the fly by only displaying filtered data.

Interactive View Format

The Interactive view format provides the greatest level of interaction for report consumers. When selecting Interactive as the default view format, Web Intelligence users have access to the four toolbars shown in Figure 1.7.

This viewing format is most commonly reserved for power users or advanced report consumers that benefit from the additional report functionality.

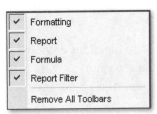

Figure 1.7 Report Toolbars Available in Interactive Viewing Mode

In addition to the Formatting, Report, Formula, and Report Filter toolbars becoming available when viewing Web Intelligence documents with the Interactive View Format, every object on a report has an extensive list of additional features when right-clicking on a report element.

Figure 1.8 shows the menu options available after right-clicking on a measure column in a vertical table while viewing a report in the Interactive view format in InfoView, and the following list gives the suboptions for each menu option.

- **Insert:** New Row or Column Above/Below the Selected Column
- **Format:** Cell, All Table Cells, Table, Section, Report
- **Filter:** Add Filter or Remove Filter
- **Turn Table To:** Turn the selected data table to any of the following available Chart and Table Types:
  - Four Data Tables
  - Nine Bar Charts

- Eight Line Charts
- Eight Area Charts
- Four Pie Charts
- Four Radar Charts

Figure 1.8 Features Available When Right-Clicking on a Vertical Table

- **Break:** Insert/Remove, Properties
- **Sort:** None, Ascending, Descending, (Custom Sort and Remove Sort available for dimensional objects), Properties
- **Calculation:** Sum, Count, Average, Min, Max, Percentage, Default
- **Hyperlink:** New, Edit, Remove, Read Contents as Hyperlink
- **Order:** Bring to Front, Send to Back, Bring Forward, Send Backward
- **Align:** Align Left, Center, Right, Top, Middle, Bottom, Relative Position
- **Remove:** Row, Column, Table

> **Note**
>
> The Add Input Control feature is only available in SAP BusinessObjects Web Intelligence XI 3.1 SP 2. This powerful analysis feature provides a variety of components to filter result data. This selection is very easy to use and extremely helpful.

PDF View Format

The PDF view format has very little interactive functionality. The primary feature of this viewing format is to open the Web Intelligence report in a PDF. After the document opens, you can print or save the PDF report.

You can view the report in Web view by clicking the View in HTML Format button located in the upper-left toolbar of the report. Figure 1.9 shows this button in PDF view.

PDF reports can be easily shared with users across the enterprise, emailed, posted to an FTP site, or published to the SAP BusinessObjects XI 3.1 InfoView portal.

Figure 1.9 Web Intelligence Report Viewed in PDF View

1.3.2   Locale When Viewing a Document

When viewing a Web Intelligence document, the data can be formatted by either the document locale or preferred viewing locale. To set the preferred viewing locale to be different from the default browser locale, follow these steps:

1. Click the Use My Preferred Viewing Locale to Format the Data option under the Web Intelligence preferences.

2. Open the General Preferences section.

3. Scroll down to Preferred Viewing Locale, and change the default from Use Browser Locale to the locale of your choice.

1.3.3   Select the Default Creation/Editing Tool

Four editing tools are available to be used with Web Intelligence documents. Following is a list of those tools with an explanation of each:

▶ **Advanced:** The Advanced editing tool launches a Java applet to provide you with a Java report panel for developing and editing reports. This setting requires Java 2 and provides the most comprehensive set of functions.

▶ **Interactive:** The Interactive editing tool is a standalone HTML-based editor that doesn't require Java 2 or other external technologies.

▶ **Desktop:** The Desktop setting requires the Web Intelligence Rich Client. This is where you can download the Rich Client tool if it isn't already installed. When the Desktop tool is selected as your editing tool of choice, Web Intelligence Rich Client is launched any time you edit or create a Web Intelligence document. The basic viewing of a report within InfoView is unaffected by this setting. This setting also requires that Java is installed on your PC for it to launch.

▶ **Web Accessibility:** This editing tool doesn't require Java 2 or any other external technology and is best known for being 508 compliant.

Figure 1.10 shows the editing tool choices available for creating/editing a Web Intelligence document.

Figure 1.10 Selecting a Default Creation/Editing Tool for Web Intelligence

1.3.4 Drill Option Preferences

In addition to providing drill filters in drill mode, many data tables and charts provide the capability of drilling down with a single click. This type of drilling is available when drill mode is activated and when dimension objects in report elements don't contain formulas.

Three settings are available for selection under Drill Options when setting Web Intelligence preferences. Any combination of these settings can be selected. The recommended combination is to select Prompt When Drill Requires Additional Data and Synchronize Drill on Report Blocks. You also have the choice of either showing or hiding the drill toolbar when opening a report.

The three drill options are listed here:

▶ Prompt When Drill Requires Additional Data

▶ Synchronize Drill on Report Blocks

▶ Hide Drill Toolbar on Startup

You also have the choice of defining where a drill session starts. Just beneath the Drill Options selections are two option buttons that allow you to start drill sessions on a duplicate or existing report. The default selection is On Existing Report. Figure 1.11 shows the available options as they appear in the Web Intelligence Preferences menu.

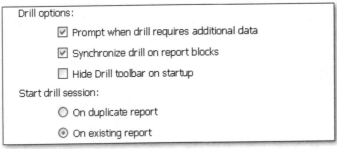

Figure 1.11 Drill Options Settings and Drill Session Start Type

1.3.5 Saving to Microsoft Excel Priority

The final setting in Web Intelligence Preferences is to assign the priority for saving reports to Excel. The default setting is to prioritize easy data processing in Excel.

Following are the two choices:

▶ Prioritize the Formatting of the Documents

▶ Prioritize Easy Data Processing in Excel

1.4 Reporting Analysis Environments

Web Intelligence reporting is delivered to business users in either a zero-client or thin-client method. Reporting documents are accessed through a web browser by logging on to the InfoView portal or opened in the locally installed Web Intelligence Rich Client tool.

1.4.1   Zero-Client Online Analysis

You don't have to install SAP BusinessObjects software to experience the benefits of Web Intelligence. With just a web browser, you can log on to InfoView to view, create, edit, analyze, schedule, or interact with Web Intelligence reporting documents.

1.4.2   Thin-Client Development

Since the addition of the Web Intelligence Rich Client, analysis has been extended to power users who need to analyze data while being disconnected from the CMS or enterprise portal.

When connected to the CMS, documents can be exported directly to the enterprise system for online analysis. Once published, reports created in Rich Client are easily shared with other enterprise users.

1.5   Viewing and Saving Reports

Web Intelligence reports can be viewed in InfoView with four different viewing modes. Each mode displays data differently and can be easily switched.

Figure 1.12 shows the four modes for viewing a report in Web Intelligence. To change formats, click the small down arrow to the right of the View button to reveal the full list of view modes. Page mode allows you to view the report the way it fits on a page while also having the luxury of drilling into the data.

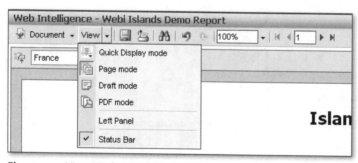

Figure 1.12   View Modes Available in Web Intelligence

1.5.1 Report Viewing Modes

Quick Display mode and Draft mode are very similar when viewing reports and show the data in the report elements the way they exist on the screen rather than optimized for printing. These two sections are very useful when analyzing data that will be either exported to Excel or just viewed.

Quick Display mode shows report headers and footers while Draft mode displays on the report body.

PDF mode is very convenient for viewing data that needs to be formatted for printing in a professional style. Is this mode, reports are converted to PDF within the same window. The drawback of PDF mode is that drill filters are no longer present.

Other functions available in Web view are the options to Edit (if proper permissions have been granted), Refresh Data, and Track Changes. If you edit a report, you'll have the opportunity to modify the SQL in the Query Panel and access many features and properties in the Report Panel. Both panels will be discussed in detail over the course of this book.

To close, edit, save, or access the properties of a reporting document, click the Document button in the upper-left corner of the Web Intelligence default toolbar. Figure 1.13 shows the list of actions available when you click the Document button.

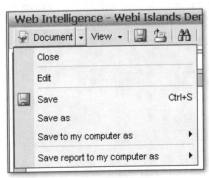

Figure 1.13 Actions Available for an Opened Web Intelligence Document

1.5.2 Saving Web Intelligence Reports

Web Intelligence documents can be saved to the repository of the CMS by clicking Save As in the Document menu. Click Save to My Computer As to export the data to your PC as one of the following file types: XLS, CSV, or PDF.

By clicking Save, you'll overwrite the existing version. Depending on your rights, you can update Web Intelligence documents that reside in the folder structure within InfoView.

1.6 Summary

Web Intelligence provides an extensive set of mature features that combine complex query building with detailed analytical reporting capabilities. This best-in-class reporting tool introduced in 1997 has evolved to become the standard ad hoc analysis and reporting tool for many corporations around the world.

The core functionality of Web Intelligence contains an extensive list of valuable features. Developing complex queries visually without knowledge of the underlying SQL makes report building much easier for business users. The ability to query multiple data sources within the same document and linking the results by merging dimensions is an extremely valuable analytical report development feature.

Web Intelligence reports are easily viewed and analyzed by using only a web browser connected to the InfoView portal. Reporting documents can be shared with selected users across the enterprise and then scheduled to be refreshed and delivered to a user inbox or external email address.

You can take analysis offline with Web Intelligence Rich Client. Report developers now have the capability of saving Web Intelligence documents locally and analyzing data without being connected to the CMS. This functionality is similar to Desktop Intelligence but with all of the advantages of Web Intelligence.

Chapter 2 will introduce you to the patented SAP BusinessObjects semantic layer known as the SAP BusinessObjects Universe.

The SAP BusinessObjects universe is a key factor in solving business problems and creating a successful SAP BusinessObjects enterprise reporting solution.

2 The SAP BusinessObjects Universe

The SAP BusinessObjects universe is the secure layer between your database and reporting solution. The universe shields business users from the complexities of the database and provides a reliable and consistent data retrieval experience across all of the SAP BusinessObjects reporting tools. The universe is a secure window into the database or data warehouse in your organization.

Universes allow you to graphically visualize selected database tables and views and then create joins to match table relationships in the database schema. Objects can be created and categorized for the fields that business users need to solve business problems. Universes also allow you to incorporate business logic into objects with case statements and other types of calculations.

2.1 What Is a Universe?

The SAP BusinessObjects universe is the patented semantic layer that allows report designers to access the database without having to know any information about the underlying data structure. Being able to build reports without writing SQL statements highlights the ease-of-use of the SAP BusinessObjects Enterprise suite of reporting tools.

The Importance of the Universe

Each universe is a single file that contains a connection to your database and business "objects" aliases to database fields. An unlimited number of Web Intelligence reports are then sourced from a single universe. As the database evolves and structures change, updates flow through seamlessly to reports by making corrections in one place: the universe.

The success of your Web Intelligence reports, Desktop Intelligence reports, Crystal Reports® (when using a universe as a data source), and even Web Service Description Language (WSDL) files generated by Query as a Web Service, depend heavily on the careful creation of this foundational layer.

It's important to note that universes should be created by experienced developers with extensive knowledge of the business and the SQL language. Understanding the structure of the database schema and table relationships is critical in developing a functional universe.

Although the concepts are fairly simple and straightforward, your universes should be carefully designed and tested. Errors in universe design can have profound negative effects on reports that lead to long running queries and worst of all, inaccurate results.

2.1.1 Design with the Business User in Mind

When creating classes and objects, it's important to keep in mind the audience that will be using the universe to build Web Intelligence reports. Database field names are often quite different from business terms and should always be translated to appropriate aliases with commonly known business terminology. Also, whenever possible, incorporate business logic into field objects to allow for consistent report development across the user community.

By adding objects containing business logic into the universe, objects can be created to contain case statements and other calculations that meet business requirements. This can help to minimize the number of report level variables needed by report developers and allow for the same variables to be used in many reports without having to re-create them in each report.

The client tool used to develop and maintain universes is called Designer. Throughout the sections in this chapter, we'll discuss the steps required to create a basic universe.

The full-client *Designer* tool is installed on a developer, administrator, or power user's PC and is commonly accompanied by an array of other client tools, including *Web Intelligence Rich Client* and *Desktop Intelligence*.

2.1.2 Primary Elements in a Universe

Following are the primary elements in a universe:

- ▸ Classes
- ▸ Objects
- ▸ Database tables (when mapped to a relational database)
- ▸ Joins

Classes

Classes appear as folders and serve as a grouping structure for aliased database fields and calculations known as *objects*.

A "best practice" is to create separate classes for date fields, measures, filters, and other descriptive categories unique to your specific warehouse or schema.

The primary goal in building a useful class structure is to organize objects into logical folder groupings that can be easily understood by users when creating Web Intelligence, Desktop Intelligence, or Crystal Reports.

Objects

As mentioned earlier, *objects* are simply aliased database fields. It's very common for database tables and views to contain a large number of fields with cryptic naming conventions not easily understood by a business user. It's also common for tables to contain several fields with little value to a business user.

By requiring a universe designer to create the objects that will ultimately be used in reports, any fields not used for reporting can simply be ignored. Users are then shielded from using any unnecessary fields and from deciphering cryptic naming conventions. However, objects should be created for any field that will potentially be used. Aliases (or object names) should always be created with commonly used business terminology.

Objects also go a step further with the ability to embed business logic and calculations that appear as nothing more than a field to a report developer. This syntax will be discussed in detail later in the book.

Inserting Database Tables and Views

Database fact tables, dimension tables, and views are inserted into the universe and then joined according to their relationship in the database schema.

The following are three procedures for inserting database objects into the universe:

► Click INSERT • TABLES, and then double-click a table name, drag and drop objects into the structure pane, or select a table and click Insert.

► A second way of inserting tables is by double-clicking in the structure pane to show the Table Browser.

► A third way of opening the Table Browser is to click the shortcut icon in Designer, which is available within the Editing toolbar.

After your tables have been inserted into the universe, it's time to begin identifying the fields used to join the tables. We'll talk more about join types and the procedure for joining tables later in the chapter.

Which Tables Can Be Inserted?

► The tables available to be inserted depend on the database credentials of the developer logged on to the Designer tool.

► To revise the database connection after a universe has been created, click FILE • PARAMETERS, and select Edit to revise the current connection.

► To use the commonly used ODBC connection type, create an ODBC system data source to connect to your database, open the administrative tool called Data Sources (ODBC), click the System DSN tab, and then add a System Data Source.

2.1.3 Creating a New Universe

To create a new universe, open Designer, and then log on to the SAP BusinessObjects Enterprise system. You'll be prompted to enter the following information:

► **System:** SAP BusinessObjects Enterprise or Edge Series system

► **User Name:** Valid username previously set up in the CMC (Central Management Console)

► **Password:** Valid password

► **Authentication Type:** Enterprise, LDAP, Windows AD, or Windows NT

After you've successfully logged on to Designer, click FILE • NEW or click the blank page icon to begin creating a new universe. The Universe Parameters box will open, and you'll need to enter a Name and select a Connection to proceed.

If you select New, the New Connection Wizard guides you through a simple process of creating a new connection. The first step in defining a new connection is to select your database middleware.

Available Database Middleware Selections

- Apache
- Business Objects
- Generic
- Hewlett Packard
- HSQLDB
- Hyperion
- IBM
- Informix
- Microsoft
- NCR
- Netezza
- Open Edge
- Oracle
- SalesForce.com
- SAP
- Sun
- Sybase

Figure 2.1 shows the Universe Parameters screen that appears when you're creating a new universe. Seven tabs are available on the Universe Parameters settings window, but the two most commonly revised tabs are the Definition tab and the Controls tab.

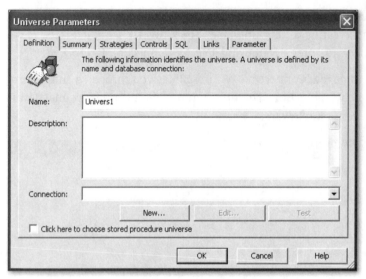

Figure 2.1 Setting Universe Parameters When Creating a Universe

2.1.4   Setting Query Limits

Two important settings can be found on the Controls tab: Limit the Size of the Result Set and Limit the Execution Time.

The default settings are 5,000 rows for the result set and 10 minutes for the execution time. Depending on your data warehouse environment and SAP BusinessObjects reporting solution, these levels may be inadequate, and you'll almost certainly need to adjust the size limit of your result set.

It's best not to uncheck the Limit Size of Result Set To box to protect your database from potentially huge sets of data returned by a user. In most cases, your database administrator (DBA) can provide you with a maximum number of rows to retrieve in a single query. The maximum result set is commonly set between 100,000 and 500,000 rows. Figure 2.2 shows the Query Limits settings.

It's also not recommended to remove the Limit Execution Time To checkbox to protect your database from potentially long-running queries created by Web Intelligence report consumers. The default limit for execution time is set at 10 minutes but can be easily adjusted up or down.

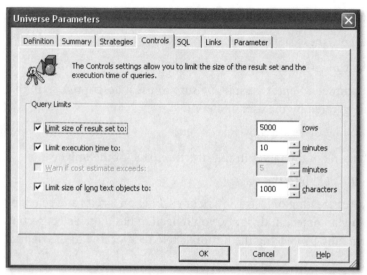

Figure 2.2 Default Universe Settings Located on the Controls Tab

Now that universe controls have been put into place for query limits, the next section will discuss the types of objects to be created in a universe.

2.1.5 Object Types

Objects are created in the universe and defined as one of three object types:

▶ **Dimension:** Objects used to provide the basis for analysis. Dimension objects usually consist of geographic information, date information, products, and other descriptive fields.

▶ **Detail:** (optional) Very similar to dimension object types but provide supporting details rather than data used as the primary basis of analysis. Examples are ZIP code and addresses.

▶ **Measure:** Numeric values used to quantify and calculate data. Aggregations and counts are the two most common types of measures.

Now that you understand the basic types of objects that are created in a universe, the next section provides instructions for creating classes and objects.

2.1.6 Creating Classes and Objects

To create a class, follow these steps:

1. Right-click in the Universe pane, and then select Class.
2. When you're prompted to enter a name, be sure to use a descriptive term that will be easily interpreted by the user audience.

To create objects, follow these steps:

1. Click on a field in one of the tables in the structure pane of the universe.
2. Drag and drop the field into the class.
3. A secondary way of creating objects is by right-clicking on a class and selecting Object. By creating an object in this way, you'll need to build the Select section of the object manually by clicking the button labeled >> located to the right of the Select box.

The Where section in the Definition tab of an object can be a valuable method of creating objects that meet business requirements. This section is commonly used to hard code a value associated with an object. The benefit is to remove the burden of the Web Intelligence report developer from adding a required filter when building ad hoc reports.

It's important to note that a variety of built-in functions are available for creating complex custom fields.

After creating your formula, be sure to click Parse to validate the formula.

2.1.7 Object Properties Described

Figure 2.3 shows a close-up look at the properties of the Number of Guests object in the Island Resorts Marketing universe. There are several important areas available to be modified when editing or creating an object. The Island Resorts Marketing universe is a demo universe that installs with SAP BusinessObjects and the Designer tool. To locate the universe, launch Designer, and click FILE • OPEN. A window opens to a folder of default universes.

The options in this screen are described in the following list:

▶ Beginning in the top left, the Name is the object alias that will be visible to Web Intelligence users when creating reports.

▶ Type is the data type of the field in the Select section.

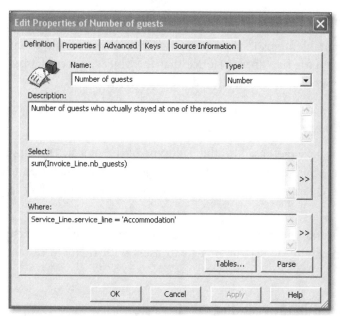

Figure 2.3 Object Properties for the Number of Guests Object

▶ The Description section is optional but can be very helpful to a user when developing reports. The description is displayed on mouseover in Web Intelligence.

▶ The Select section is where the field name is inserted. You'll notice in Figure 2.3 that the field is identified as *table_name.field_name*. To select a field, click the >> button to the right of the Select box. You'll then have the opportunity to simply select a table and column, class and object, or use a built-in function to further customize your object.

▶ The Where section is most commonly used to hard code a filter to be applied anytime the object is included in a report.

Parse Before Completing an Object

Be sure to click Parse before clicking OK when creating or editing your object. This will help to ensure that your syntax is correct if you manually entered any information, including a formula or calculation, or changed the data type of the object.

2.1.8 Object Definition Properties

Figure 2.3 shows the editable items in the Definition tab and an example of the aggregated field INVOICE_LINE.NB_GUESTS. Notice that the object also contains a filter included in the Where section as described previously.

Each object contains five tabs used for customizing object properties. The Properties tab allows you to change the qualification of the object.

A default qualification is selected based on the data type of the object. The most common reason to revise this setting is to change an object from a Dimension to a Detail. To change the Qualification, click the Properties tab as shown later in Figure 2.4.

The Advanced tab is very important in highly secure deployments. Here, universe designers have the opportunity to restrict objects to users with rights to certain security access levels.

Grant or Revoke Privileges to the Following Roles

Also in the Advanced tab, objects can be restricted to a certain role in a report. Checkboxes are provided to allow or grant the capability of three role types:

▶ **Result:** Allows an object to be used in a query.

▶ **Condition:** Allows an object to be used as a condition or query filter.

▶ **Sort:** Allows returned values of the object to be sorted in the report.

Security Access Levels

The Security Access Level setting allows you to set the requirement for a certain level of privileges to access the object. Following is a list of the available access levels. This setting is helpful in advanced and secure deployments of SAP BusinessObjects that contain data and objects that range from public to confidential and private access rights.

▶ Public

▶ Controlled

▶ Restricted

► Confidential

► Private

Identifying Object Types

Figure 2.4 shows the icons that represent the three qualification types used in the universe. These symbols provide an easy way of identifying object types when creating Web Intelligence reports.

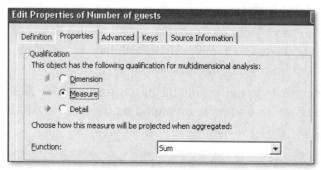

Figure 2.4 Universe Objects and Qualification Icons

Object Qualification

Also, notice in Figure 2.4 that the object function can be revised on this tab. This selection appears when the Measure qualification is selected.

2.1.9 Table Joins in the Universe

To create a cohesive set of related objects, a successful SAP BusinessObjects universe design should contain a collection of correctly joined tables. A universe can range from a very large to a very small number of dimension tables.

The number of objects in a universe can also range from very few to several. However, one thing all successful universe designs include is a series of joins that mimic the ones in the database schema.

Whether the database design is a star schema, snowflake, or a hybrid of the two (usually referred to as a star-flake), it's important to maintain the integrity of the database by joining the fields properly. In most cases, a *fact* table (usually containing

Measures) is located at the center of the universe, and *dimension* tables join to it by using one of five different join types.

2.1.10 Join Types

Traditional join types are inner join, left join, right join, and full outer join. Other joins include the following:

▶ **Equi-joins:** Two tables are linked when the values in both fields are equal. This type of join is also considered a simple join.

▶ **Theta joins:** Theta joins are most commonly used in warehouses that don't contain keys and when an equivalent field doesn't exist in both the fact and dimension table. The operator can be anything except equal.

▶ **Outer joins:** It's important that you understand the data before applying these types of joins. Outer joins can have a significant impact on the speed at which a query is returned. This is especially true when views are used.

> **Note**
>
> Outer joins occur when one table contains rows that don't exist in the other table. Right outer joins, left outer joins, or full outer joins can be selected.

2.1.11 How to Join Tables

After you add the tables to the universe, identify keys and join fields, and select join types, it's time to create the joins.

Select the first field in a table used to create the join. This will most likely be a key if you're working in a relational database. Then drag it to the table you're joining to, and drop it on top of the Join To field.

As an example, if you're joining field1 in Table1 to field1 in Table2, click on field1 in Table1, and then drag and drop it on top of field1 in Table2. The join is now complete. You can then edit the join by right-clicking on it and selecting the Join Properties.

Figure 2.5 shows the tables in the Island Resort Marketing universe that ships with SAP BusinessObjects Enterprise (BOE) XI 3.1.

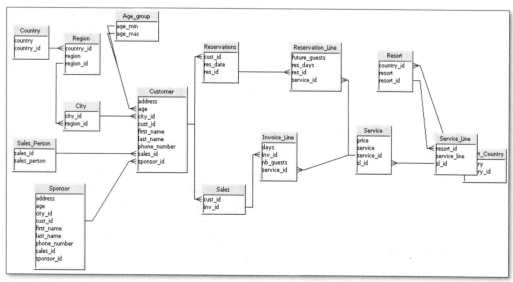

Figure 2.5 Tables with Joins in the Island Resorts Marketing Universe

2.1.12 Editing Joins

To edit the properties of a join, double-click the line (or join) connecting two tables in your universe to open the Edit Join properties window.

Within this window, you can revise a variety of join settings. The following is a list of available join settings that can be edited.

- **Cardinality:** Explicitly force the join to a one-to-one, one-to-many, or many-to-many relationship. By selecting a one-to-many or many-to-many relationship, a crows-foot is added to the join line connecting the two tables.

- **Detect Cardinality:** This button is used to detect the type of relationship that exists between the two tables.

- **Set Outer Joins:** Two checkboxes labeled Outer Join are located just beneath each table. Check the box just beneath the table that requires all fields to be returned. If both boxes are checked, a full-outer join will be created.

- **Setting Join Conditions:** There are six default conditions available in a simple equi-join. These conditions are: =, !=, >, <, >=, and <=.

- **Between Condition:** If two fields are selected from one of the tables, then the Between condition is set by default. This is very useful when joining to a table

53

that doesn't contain a key or field to join to with an equi-join. An example of this type of join is available in the demo Island Resorts Marketing universe connecting the Customer table to the Age_group table.

▸ **Complex Join Condition:** If your join requires additional modification to duplicate the business rules in the universe, a Complex condition can be used to further customize the join.

▸ **Advanced:** If you click the Advanced tab, an Advanced Join Properties window will open stating that ANSI 92 must be supported to edit these properties.

> **Note**
>
> To enable ANSI 92 mode, click FILE • PARAMETERS to open the Universe Parameters properties window. Select the Parameter tab, and select the Parameter Name ANSI92. The default value is No, but when selected, the value can be changed to Yes. Click Replace and then OK to accept.

Right-clicking on a join gives you several additional modification options. Among the most significant are the Context, Number of Rows in Table, and Options. Figure 2.6 shows the options presented when right-clicking on a join.

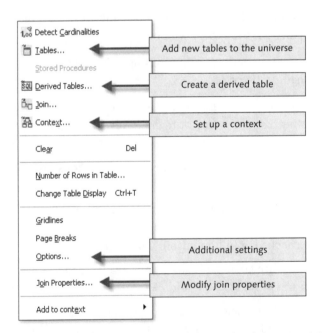

Figure 2.6 Option Menu Presented When Right-Clicking on a Join

Contexts are used when more than one fact table exists within a universe or when a loop exists when joining dimensional tables. Contexts need to be set up to define the correct join path in the universe. Contexts can become complex especially to business users developing ad hoc Web Intelligence reports. Contexts should only be used when necessary. In most cases, a new universe should be created to accommodate the additional join path.

The Options selection allows you to modify many aspects of the visual representation of the tables and joins in the structure view, including modification choices of changing the join shape, column alignment, print settings, default universe folder location, and checking universe integrity.

2.1.13 Right-Click on a Join to Edit Join Properties

You also can right-click on a single table in the universe to view specific table information. Two common reasons for right-clicking on a table are to view associated objects and to view table values.

As your database evolves, new dimension tables are often created that take the place of existing dimensions. The View Associated Objects feature is very valuable because it quickly identifies all objects created by using the selected table. This allows the universe designer to revise the object definitions created from the associated table. Table replacement is seamless to the user.

2.1.14 Options

Right-clicking on a join and then selecting Options shows the default universe folder (see Figure 2.7). This option allows you to set the location on your PC where universes will be saved.

Another way to access the set of menu options shown in Figure 2.7 is to click TOOLS • OPTIONS.

The Graphics tab shows the drawing options for representing the database structure in the universe. Join shapes, column properties, and table appearances are also modified in the Graphics tab.

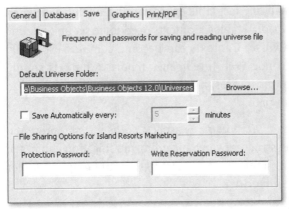

Figure 2.7 Set the Location to Save Universes Locally

The Print/PDF tab shows the printing options available when printing a universe. The metadata associated with a universe can be printed for documentation purposes by clicking FILE • PRINT.

To see how the universe table schema will appear if printed, right-click anywhere in the structure pane of the universe, and then select Page Breaks. This allows you to modify the positioning of tables to print the table schema on a single screen.

Grid Lines is also a selection on the right-click menu to help with alignment.

2.1.15 Edit Join Properties

Figure 2.8 shows the Edit Join window used to customize a join between two tables or views in a universe.

> **Tip**
>
> Join properties should only be created or edited by an administrator, database developer, or subject matter expert (SME) with database knowledge. Take the time to consult with the data warehouse architect to understand the relationship of the tables before creating or editing joins.
>
> The universe is the foundational layer of any successful SAP BusinessObjects reporting solution and must be free of errors and in line with the database.

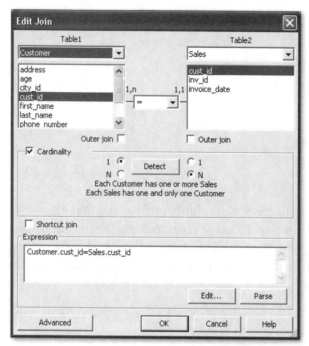

Figure 2.8 Join Property Settings Available for Editing

2.2 Publish a Universe to SAP BusinessObjects Enterprise

After inserting database tables in your universe and creating classes and objects, you'll be ready to publish the universe to the SAP BusinessObjects Enterprise system and begin creating Web Intelligence reports in InfoView.

By publishing a universe to SAP BusinessObjects Enterprise, several SAP Business-Objects reporting tools can use the universe as the data source for creating queries and building reports. Next, we'll discuss how to test and publish a universe.

2.2.1 Run an Integrity Check on Your Universe

Before publishing a universe to the SAP BusinessObjects repository, be sure to check the integrity of all of the objects and conditions within the universe.

An icon with a green checkmark is available within the Editing toolbar in Designer. Click this shortcut icon to see a quick list of checks and tests to run before publishing a universe to a SAP BusinessObjects test or production repository.

The following is a list of the items in the Integrity Check menu:

- Check All
- Check Universe Structure
- Parse Objects
- Parse Joins
- Parse Conditions
- Check for Loops
- Check for Context

An eighth item is also available to check the cardinality of the joins in the universe. The Check All box selects the top seven check types, but the Check Cardinalities option requires manual selection. Depending on the size of your universe and the number of rows within the tables, Designer may take an exceedingly large amount of time to detect the cardinality of every join in the universe.

If loops are detected, you'll need to resolve these before exporting or publishing. This can be resolved by creating contexts or aliased tables.

The parsing of objects, joins, and conditions can be done at the time of creation or while editing each item individually. The Integrity Check provides a method of verifying that the syntax and properties are configured properly.

> **Note**
>
> Integrity Check can also be accessed by clicking TOOLS • CHECK INTEGRITY.

Be sure that your universe is well tested before publishing or exporting to your SAP BusinessObjects production repository. Many organizations require some type of review or analysis by a project manager or team lead before approving a universe to be published to the repository.

2.2.2 Save and Export

When a universe is ready to be submitted to the repository, the first step is to save it locally. A saved version must exist before exporting a universe. As mentioned earlier, this location can be set by right-clicking in the structure pane and choosing Options and then the Save tab. You can also revise the location by clicking TOOLS • OPTIONS.

Click FILE • EXPORT to publish the universe to the SAP BusinessObjects repository of your choice. Before clicking OK, you must select a Domain and Group. This allows you to place the universe in the domain of your choice while selecting the group access at the same time.

Figure 2.9 shows the Export Universe screen. Notice the Domain drop-down and the list box of available Groups.

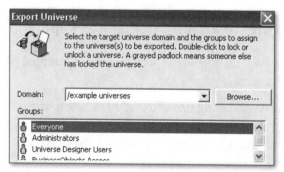

Figure 2.9 Selections Available When Exporting a Universe

2.2.3   Importing a Universe

To import a universe in Designer, click FILE • IMPORT. Select the Folder and the Universe Name that you would like to import, and then click OK (see Figure 2.10). Multiple universes can be imported at the same time.

You can toggle between two open universes within a single instance of Designer by clicking FILE • WINDOW and selecting the unchecked universe.

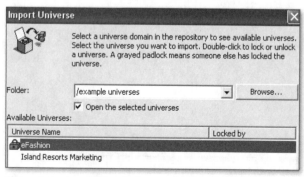

Figure 2.10 Importing a Universe with the eFashion Universe Locked

Be aware that if you double-click a universe from the Available Universes list before importing, a lock will appear to the left of the universe name. This will prevent any other developers from importing the universe until the lock is removed.

When a universe has been imported and edited, the changes aren't available to Web Intelligence report writers and report consumers until it has been exported to the CMS.

2.3   Using a Universe to Create a Web Intelligence Report

When you attempt to create a new Web Intelligence report, you'll be prompted to select a universe to serve as the data source.

Figure 2.11 shows the Island Resorts Marketing universe, ready to be exported to the SAP BusinessObjects Enterprise. Notice on the left side of the figure is a full list of classes and objects. When a Web Intelligence report is created, only the classes and objects will be visible to users.

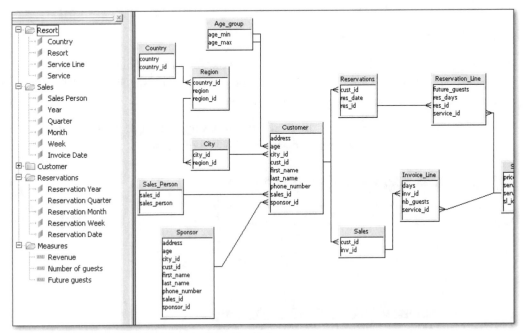

Figure 2.11   The Island Resorts Marketing Universe

Universe Classes, Objects, Tables and Joins

Web Intelligence report developers are shielded from the table structure in the universe. Only object names with appropriate aliases and the logical class structure are viewable at the time of report creation.

When creating ad hoc queries, users never have to scroll through tables in search of fields to include in a report. Objects and filters created with business terminology play a key role in producing highly functional data-rich reports that are easy to use. Accurate data and user acceptance are two important elements in a business intelligence reporting solution.

2.4   Getting to Know the Designer Toolbars

Three toolbars exist within Designer to provide quick access to many tasks involved in universe design and development. These toolbars are the Standard toolbar, Editing toolbar, and Formula Bar, and they can be viewed or hidden by right-clicking in the area near the File menu.

Figure 2.12 show the toolbars available within Designer followed by a listing of the tasks within each toolbar.

The Editing toolbar provides quick access to inserting, parsing, and detecting potential issues within a universe. The Check Integrity shortcut icon is available on the Editing toolbar as well as shortcut icons to insert a class, object, and condition.

The *Editing* toolbar contains two new icons that were previously unavailable in legacy instances of Designer. These buttons provide a quick way to evaluate security settings.

The first button is used to manage access restrictions; the second new button allows you to preview the net access *restrictions applied to a user or group.*

Figure 2.12   Standard Toolbar Shortcut Icons

Standard Toolbar Tasks			
New Universe	Open	Save	Print
Print Preview	Cut	Copy	Paste
Find	Find Again	Undo	Parameters
Quick Design Wizard	Hierarchies	Connections View List Mode	
Universe Window	Arrange Tables PCT Zoom Adjuster		

Figure 2.13 shows the shortcut icons available within the Editing toolbar.

Figure 2.13 Editing Toolbar with Shortcut Icons

Editing Toolbar Tasks			
Insert Class	Insert Object	Insert Condition	Show/Hide
Table Browser	Insert Join	Insert Alias	Insert Context
Detect Cardinalities	Detect Joins	Detect Loop	Detect Aliases
Detect Contexts	Detect Keys	Check Integrity	
Create, modify, or delete, or apply access restrictions			
View net result of all access restrictions applied to a user or group			

The Formula bar provides quick access to the object definitions. You can save time by revising object definitions in the Formula bar.

In the example in Figure 2.14, the Revenue object is selected, and the object definition appears in the Edit Formula box. This toolbar provides the universe designer with easy access to editing object formulas.

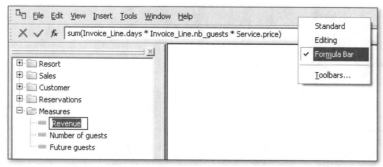

Figure 2.14   Formula Bar Showing the Definition of the Revenue Object

Formula Bar			
Formula bar	Validate	Join Properties	Cancel

2.5   OLAP Universes

As the title of this section indicates, universes aren't limited to connecting to relational database schemas. Designer has the capability of connecting to an OLAP data source such as SAP NetWeaver and SAP NetWeaver Business Warehouse (SAP NetWeaver BW), Microsoft Analysis Services, and Hyperion Essbase.

Designer connects to an OLAP provider in the database middleware section when defining universe parameters (see Figure 2.15). Just select your cube, and Designer does the rest, building the universe for you.

The structure pane is empty, but classes and objects are created based on the metadata in the multidimensional data source.

After successfully connecting to your cube or multidimensional data source, save the universe locally and then export it as you would a standard universe.

After the universe has been exported to the repository, and proper permissions have been granted, business users will have the opportunity to create Web Intelligence queries and reports, Crystal Reports, and even Query as a Web Service WSDLs from multidimensional data by accessing a universe.

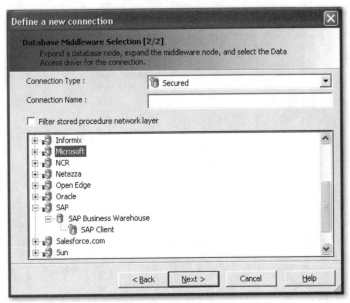

Figure 2.15 Database Middleware Selections

Improvements to OLAP universes appear in SAP BusinessObjects XI 3.1 SP2 to include a dictionary of MDX (multidimensional expressions) elements that can be inserted into objects. The MDX elements available depend on the data source or cube.

2.6 Summary

The SAP BusinessObjects universe is the backbone of a Web Intelligence and SAP BusinessObjects reporting solution. The universe is the patented semantic layer connecting reports to databases. When databases evolve, universe structures can be refreshed and updated to incorporate the changes without effecting reports.

Classes and objects are created to shield users from the complexities of the database. These classes are aliased with business terminology to increase the ease-of-use for business users.

Universes can be sourced from either relational databases or multidimensional cubes. If relational databases are used, tables or views should be inserted and then joined according to the database schema to maintain database integrity.

When creating or editing a universe, several options and settings are available for editing. Toolbars with shortcut icons provide single-click access to many different functions, including integrity checks, revising parameters, and defining hierarchies.

Chapter 3 describes the details for using universe objects to create queries in a Web Intelligence document and retrieve results to be used in reports.

You can create queries graphically with SAP BusinessObjects Web Intelligence XI 3.x using the highly intuitive Query Panel. Using the Result Objects and Query Filter panes allows you to access the data you need from your universes and databases.

3   Creating a Web Intelligence XI 3.x Query

The Query Panel in Web Intelligence lets you generate SQL statements that are submitted to your database to retrieve the data you need. This is achieved by inserting universe objects into the Result Objects pane and then constraining the query by adding objects to the Query Filters pane.

The objects inserted into the Result Objects pane translate to the Select section in the generated SQL statement. Web Intelligence gets its information for the where clause from the objects included in the Query Filters pane. Query filters can be hard-coded conditions created in the universe or dimension objects inserted into the Query Filters pane with assigned values. When defining query filters, more than 15 different operators are available to help you limit your query to return only the data you need.

After a query has completed successfully, the retrieved data is stored within each Web Intelligence document in an unseen *microcube*. At this point, the data is ready to be formatted and presented in a report.

This chapter takes you through every aspect of creating a Web Intelligence query from within the InfoView portal. Chapter 17, Web Intelligence Rich Client, will discuss the steps to building queries using the Web Intelligence Rich Client.

Web Intelligence Rich Client provides the capability of accessing a universe as a data source and also connecting to an Excel file as a *local data source*. A common purpose for accessing a local data source is to use an existing Excel file to create a document with all of the powerful features available in SAP BusinessObjects Web Intelligence XI 3.x.

3.1 Tour of the Query Panel

We will begin this discussion of building Web Intelligence queries in InfoView with a tour of the Query Panel.

To get started, log on to InfoView and launch Web Intelligence by following these steps:

1. Locate the New button located in the upper-left portion of InfoView.

2. Click the small down arrow to reveal the available reporting tools.

3. Select Web Intelligence Document from this list to begin creating your first report.

Figure 3.1 gives you an idea of the reporting types available when the New button in InfoView is selected.

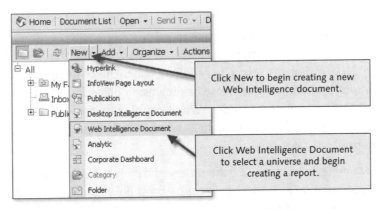

Figure 3.1 Creating a Web Intelligence Document in InfoView

After selecting Web Intelligence Document from the list of tools, you will be prompted to select a universe as the data source for your report. SAP BusinessObjects XI 3.1 ships with a few demo universes, including the Island Resorts Marketing universe.

This chapter will use the Island Resorts Marketing universe to create example queries that can be easily reconstructed on your instance of SAP BusinessObjects XI 3.1.

The examples in this chapter describe the creation of reports using the Java Report Panel. This setting is listed as the Advanced (Java 2 required) tool when selecting the default creation/editing tool in Web Intelligence Preferences. The default view format has been set to Interactive.

After you have chosen to create a new Web Intelligence Document and have selected Island Resorts Marketing as your universe, Web Intelligence will open within InfoView to reveal the Query Panel. At this point, you are ready to begin the query-building process by using the objects in the Query Manager pane.

Figure 3.2 gives you a glimpse of the full Query Panel at the beginning of the query-building process after a universe has been selected.

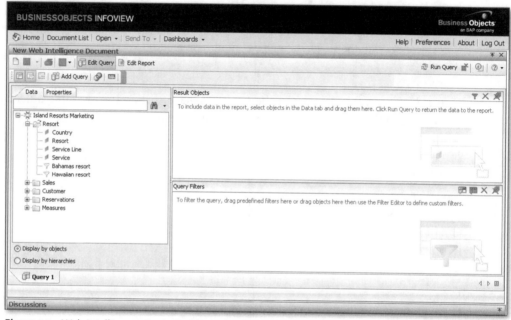

Figure 3.2 Web Intelligence Query Panel in InfoView

The Query Panel consists of three panes:

▶ Query Manager pane

▶ Result Objects pane

▶ Query Filters pane

Now let's explore the Query Manager pane.

3.1.1 The Query Manager Pane

The Query Manager pane is located on the left side of the document and provides two primary functions. These functions are presented separately in two tabs: the Data tab and the Properties tab. The purpose of the Query Manager pane is to provide data and modify properties.

The Data tab contains the classes and objects that were previously setup in the universe. This is when object aliasing in universe design begins to play an important role in report development.

Tip

The objects in your universes should be consistently named with business terms to provide users with the simplest and most intuitive approach to retrieving the data they need.

Figure 3.3 shows the Data tab in the Query Manager listing the available objects and classes in the Island Resorts Marketing universe.

Figure 3.3 Classes and Objects in the Data Tab of the Query Manager Pane

The Properties tab in the Query Manager is used to set properties for eight different categories in the current query. By default, these properties are presented in expanded mode to allow for quick updates.

The first property to be updated is the query name. This setting becomes very useful when multiple queries are added to a single Web Intelligence document.

The following section includes a list of all eight properties that can be modified in the Query Manager.

3.1.2 Query Manager Properties

Let's take a look at the eight properties that can be modified in the Query Manager:

► **Name:** This property allows you to revise the name of any query in the document or query panel.

► **Universe:** Click the small button located to the right of the universe name to change the universe. Before the universe can be changed, at least one object must be included in the Result Objects pane in the Query Panel.

► **Limits:** Apply the Max Rows Retrieved setting and Max Retrieval Time setting to restrict the result size and retrieval duration of the query by clicking the checkbox beside the desired setting and then revising the associated number to your preference (see Figure 3.4).

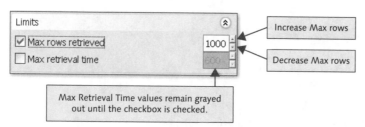

Figure 3.4 Setting the Max Rows Retrieved Limit in the Query Manager

► **Sample:** Sampling enables you to retrieve a fixed or random sample of the data when querying databases that support sampling. Random sampling is applied by default unless Fixed is selected. Sampling is only available in the Advanced creation/editing tool or Java Report Panel and is disabled if your database doesn't support sampling.

► **Data:** This query property provides the option of retrieving duplicate rows or unique rows when refreshing queries that contain dimensional objects only. Retrieve Duplicate Rows is checked by default. Uncheck this setting to force the query to retrieve a unique set of dimension object rows.

▶ **Security:** The Security section provides the option to allow other users to edit all queries and is checked by default. If unchecked, only the report developer can make revisions to the current document.

▶ **Prompt Order:** This section allows you to change the order of the prompts if multiple prompted filter objects exist in the Query Filters pane.

▶ **Context:** The Context setting provides the option to reset contexts on refresh (checked by default). A button is provided to clear contexts before the next refresh.

Figure 3.5 shows the Properties tab in the Query Manager with all eight of the property categories collapsed.

Figure 3.5 Properties Tab in the Query Manager Pane

3.1.3 Display Universe Objects by Hierarchies

In the lower-left corner of the Data tab, two options are available to determine how the objects are displayed in the pane:

▶ Display by Objects
▶ Display by Hierarchies

The default selection is to display the objects as they were created in the universe. This means that the objects appear within a series of classes. An example of this appears in Figure 3.3 earlier.

If the second selection is made, Display by Hierarchies, the objects will be displayed in the Query Manager by the *hierarchies* that were set up in the universe. This means that only dimensions will appear in the Query Manager.

Figure 3.6 shows how the objects are displayed in the data manager when being viewed by hierarchies rather than classes.

> **Tip**
>
> Choosing to display the objects by hierarchies gives you an opportunity to see the relationship of the dimension objects in the universe. This is useful when setting up drillable report filters with cascading values.

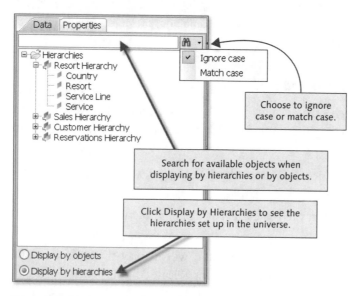

Figure 3.6 Display Universe Object by Hierarchies

Accessing Help

Click Help in the lower-right corner of the Properties tab of the Query Manager to launch the Java Report Panel Online Help web page. This web page is only available when using the Advanced report creation/editing tool, also known as the Java Report Panel.

3.2   Query Basics

Building queries in SAP BusinessObjects Web Intelligence XI 3.x is achieved by performing the following actions:

- ► Add data objects to the Result Objects pane
- ► Add data objects to the Query Filters pane

Objects can be moved to these panes by dragging them from the Query Manager and then dropping them in the desired pane. The same result can be accomplished by double-clicking objects in the Query Manager.

> **Tip**
>
> When double-clicking an object predefined as a condition, the object will be inserted into the Query Filters pane only.

3.2.1   Evaluating Generated SQL

After a query has been created, you have the opportunity to review and edit the SQL generated by the Query Panel. This can be achieved by following these steps:

1. Click the SQL shortcut icon to launch the SQL Viewer window and display the generated SQL statement.

2. In the SQL Viewer, select the *Use Custom SQL option* to edit the generated SQL statement.

3. The *View SQL* button becomes clickable and will display the generated SQL statement if at least one object is added to the Result Objects pane.

> **Tip**
>
> The Report Panel is displayed after a query has been refreshed. Click Edit Query to return to the Query Panel to edit the Result Objects pane, edit the Filter Objects pane, or modify custom SQL.

Figure 3.7 shows the options available when reviewing the generated SQL statement. The default selection is to *Use the SQL Generated by Your Query*.

Figure 3.7   View SQL Statement Generated by the Query Panel

Figure 3.8 shows the default selection in the SQL Viewer using the SQL generated by the Query Panel. Click Use Custom SQL to make revisions.

Modifying the generated SQL statement should only be attempted if you understand SQL syntax and have a legitimate business reason for manually overriding the generated SQL statement.

When the `Select` section of the generated SQL statement is modified, the number of objects, data types of result objects, and the order of the data types must match the items in the Result Objects section.

Figure 3.8   Customize Generated SQL Statement

When the Use Custom SQL option is selected, the grayed-out SQL statement becomes modifiable. Editing the SQL statement will enable the Undo button located at the bottom of the SQL Viewer. You also have the option of clicking Copy to copy the SQL statement. This is helpful if you need to paste the SQL statement into another window to edit it or email it to a colleague.

A Validate SQL button is also present when modifying the generated SQL statement. This is a very handy feature that protects you from submitting a custom SQL statement that contains errors to the database.

Figure 3.9 shows the buttons located at the bottom of the SQL Viewer window.

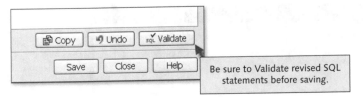

Figure 3.9 Validate Revised SQL Statements

Restricting the Modification of Generated SQL

From an administrative perspective, the rights to view SQL and edit SQL can be denied in the Central Management Console (CMC). This is accomplished by modifying the included rights of an access level. Locate the application collection and Web Intelligence type for a full list of specific modifiable rights in the CMC.

3.2.2 Adding Additional Queries

New queries can be added containing result objects that have absolutely nothing in common with the result objects in the original query. This is common if reporting requirements call for elements from both unrelated data sets to be presented on the same report or within the same document.

Figure 3.10 shows a Web Intelligence document being created in InfoView. The Add Query button is located above the Query Manager pane and located within the Query toolbar.

> **Tip**
>
> In the Query Panel, locate and click the Add Query button in the upper-left portion of the document. You will then be prompted to select a universe from the list of available universes.

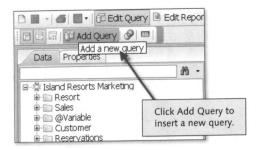

Figure 3.10 Add a New Query to an Existing Web Intelligence Document

3.2.3   Merging Dimensions

The Merge Dimensions function is used to tie the results of two or more queries together if they contain one or more common dimensions.

Merging dimensions allows you to synchronize result data from two separate sources. This functionality was added to Web Intelligence in version XI R2, but similar functionality was previously available in earlier versions of Desktop Intelligence when linking objects in the Data Manager.

Figure 3.11 shows the Merge Dimensions shortcut icon used to launch the Merge Dimensions dialog window.

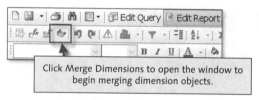

Figure 3.11   Click the Merge Dimensions Icon to Merge Dimension Objects

The dimensions available to be merged from all queries are listed in the top section of the *Merge Dimensions* dialog window (see Figure 3.12).

Steps to Merging Dimensions

Begin this process by launching the Merge Dimensions dialog window shown in Figure 3.12:

1. Click the dimension to be merged in the Query 1 section.
2. Click the dimension in the Query 2 section to be merged to the object selected in the Query 1 section.
3. Click the Merge button.
4. After clicking Merge, the Edit Merged Dimension window is launched.
5. Provide a Merged Dimension Name and Description for the newly created dimension object.
6. Click OK to accept your changes.
7. Click *Values* to review the values of the dimensions being merged.
8. Click OK to accept the creation of the new merged dimension.

Tips

▶ When two dimensions have been merged, both dimensions will be moved from the Available Dimensions section to the Merge Dimensions section.

▶ Any time a new query is added to an existing document, you will have the opportunity to refresh all queries at once or run a selected single query.

▶ When refreshing the new query for the first time, you will be prompted to choose how to include the data in the report.

▶ If a Web Intelligence document contains two or more queries, merging dimensions isn't required unless your plan is to include results from both queries to appear within the same report element.

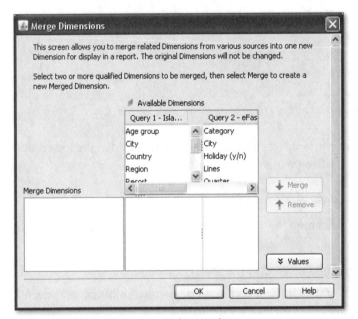

Figure 3.12 Merge Dimensions Dialog Window

The Merge Dimensions dialog window shows all of the available dimensions within the Web Intelligence document that can be merged. The dimensions are identified by the source query from where they originated.

The example in Figure 3.12 shows the available dimensions coming from two queries: Query 1 and Query 2. If the window were expanded, you would also see the names of the universes that were used to generate the two queries.

All available dimensions existing in every query in the document will appear on this screen when the Merge Dimensions icon is selected.

Figure 3.12 shows the two available sets of objects (or queries) that exist in the document. Many additional queries can also be added to a single Web Intelligence document, and the dimensions can also be merged to produce a large set of linked results data from disparate sources.

Including New Result Data

After a new query has been added to a Web Intelligence document and the query is refreshed for the first time, you will be prompted to choose how the new results are to be displayed. Figure 3.13 shows the three available choices as described here:

- **Insert a Table in a New Report:** This selection adds the results from the new query to a new Report tab.

- **Insert a Table in the Current Report:** A data table containing the results from the new query will be added to the previously existing report.

- **Include the Result Objects in the Document Without Generating a Table:** Includes the data in the microcube but doesn't add it to a report.

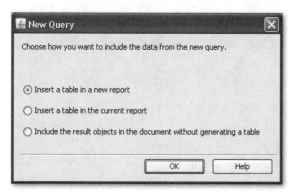

Figure 3.13 Choose How Data from the New Query Is Displayed

Data Synchronization Properties

Web Intelligence can merge your dimensions automatically if the Auto-Merge Dimensions checkbox is checked in the document properties.

To access the document properties, right-click in the Report Panel outside of the charts and tables, and then select Document Properties from the menu. By default, the document properties will appear on the right side of your Web Intelligence document.

Document Properties Assigned in the Report Panel

The previous instructions have all dealt with modifying properties in the Query Panel. But to modify the Document Properties in a reporting document, you must access the Report Panel.

Figure 3.14 shows the four categories of Document Properties available for modification in each Web Intelligence report.

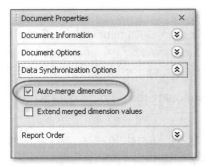

Figure 3.14 Document Properties in a Web Intelligence Report

Accessing the Document Properties

▸ View the Report Panel.

▸ Right-click anywhere in the report, and select Document Properties.

These four Document Property categories are described next:

▸ Document Information

▸ Document Options

▸ Data Synchronization Options

▸ Report Order

Document Information

The Document Information category is an informational set of properties that provides the following information:

▸ **Created By:** Report author.

▸ **Last Modified By:** The last user to save the document.

▸ **Creation Date:** Date of creation.

- **Name:** Name of the document.
- **Description:** Description of the document (optional).
- **Keywords:** Keywords associated with the document (optional).
- **Locale:** The document's formatting type.
- **Data Tracking:** Boolean value; on or off.

Document Options

The Document Options category contains a couple of very important property settings to enhance the effectiveness of particular reports:

- **Refresh on Open:** Forces the query to be refreshed when the report is opened. This feature is useful in prompted reports and when the data is restricted to the user logged on to InfoView. Reports set to Refresh on Open often also include the Purge Data setting in the report.
- **Enhanced Viewing:** Applies the page definition with page margins set by the system administrator or report developer.
- **Use Query Drill:** Modifies the underlying query when drilling down or drilling up in a report. Dimensions are added or removed to the Result Objects section of the query, and query filters are added dynamically based on the drill selection. The scope of analysis is also modified dynamically. The query drill feature is most commonly used when reports contain aggregate measures calculated at the database level.
- **Permanent Regional Formatting:** Permanently sets the locale or regional formatting of the document.

Data Synchronization Options

Data Synchronization Options allow for dimensions to be merged automatically if multiple queries are used. Web Intelligence can merge your dimensions for you if the Auto-Merge Dimensions checkbox is checked in the Document Properties dialog box.

- **Auto-Merge Dimensions:** Automatically merges dimensions when more than one query is added to the document that contains objects with the same name, same data type, and from the same universe.

▶ **Extend Merged Dimension Values:** Shows all of the data in a report that contains synchronized or merged dimension objects, not just the values relating to the merged objects.

Report Order

The Report Order category in Document Properties enables you to change the order of the report tabs within a document if multiple tabs exist.

3.2.4 Setting Up a Combined Query

The idea behind combined queries is to return a single set of data that would otherwise be impossible to retrieve with a single query. Combined queries are created in the Query Panel and merged at the database level to compare the rows in one query to the rows retrieved by an additional query.

Combined queries are created in the Query Panel, and the returned values can be displayed in one of three different relationship types:

▶ **Union:** Includes the rows from both queries.

▶ **Intersection:** Includes the rows common to both queries.

▶ **Minus:** Includes the rows from the first query minus the rows from the second query.

Combined Query Requirements
The primary rules required for creating a combined query: ▶ Result objects in each query must contain the same number of objects or the query won't refresh. ▶ The order of the objects in both queries must have matching data types. If the data types don't match, the query won't refresh.

Unions

Unions are most commonly used when you are attempting to build a result set with incompatible objects that can't be include in the same block in a report because of database or universe configurations.

In many cases, all of the result objects will be exactly the same in both queries except for minor differences in result objects or query filters.

The results from both queries are pushed to the database to complete the merging, and a single set of results is returned.

The first query in a union is created like any other query. To add a union query, click the Combined Query shortcut icon located in the Query panel when editing a document (see Figure 3.15).

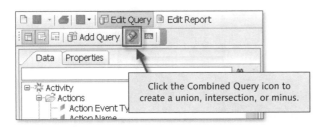

Figure 3.15 Locating the Icon Used to Create a Combined Query

After a combined query has been added, Query 1 changes names to become *Combined Query 1*, and a *Combined Query 2* is inserted. You can toggle back and forth from these two queries by clicking the buttons that include the new query names located in the lower half of the Query Manager.

Tip

The default combined query type is Union. To change from Union to an Intersection or Minus, double-click the word "Union" in the Query Manager pane located to the left of the combined query names (as shown in Figure 3.16).

Figure 3.16 shows the Query Manager after a combined query is inserted.

Intersection

Intersections are added when the goal is to produce a combined query that returns only the values that appear in both queries. The purpose of this type of query is to cut away any nonintersecting data.

Minus

The Minus combined query is used to remove everything in the results of the first query from the results of the second query. The purpose of this type of combined query is to find the results in the first query that aren't in the results of the second.

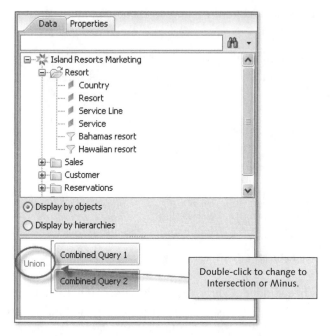

Figure 3.16 Combined Query Added to the Query Manager

Remove a Combined Query

To remove a combined query, right-click on a combined query button, as shown in Figure 3.16, and then select Remove.

3.3   Result Objects

The Result Objects pane is one of the most basic and most important sections required for creating queries in Web Intelligence.

The Result Objects pane is located in the Query Panel of a Web Intelligence document and is displayed when a new query is created or an existing query is edited. Figure 3.17 shows the Query Panel in the beginning stages of the query-building process.

Objects are added to the Results Objects pane in two ways:

▶ Drag and drop
▶ Double-clicking

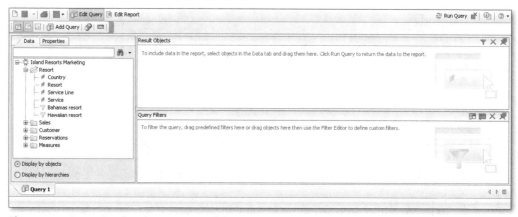

Figure 3.17 Query Panel at the Beginning of the Query-Building Processes

The Results Objects pane includes the following statement in light gray to guide and remind report developers every time a new query is created: "To include data in the report, select objects in the Data tab and drag them here. Click Run Query to return the data to the report." The message is removed when a dimension or measure object is added to the Result Objects pane.

To begin analyzing the data and building reports for these dimensions and measures, the objects must be included in the Result Objects pane to start the query-building process and SQL-generation process.

The objects displayed in the Results Objects section are used to generate a SQL statement that is submitted to the database.

Removing Result Objects

Figure 3.18 shows the options available in the top-right corner of the Result Objects pane that allow you to remove objects or apply a quick filter to a dimension object. The Quick Filter icon is only available if a dimension is selected.

To remove objects from the Result Objects pane, use any of these methods:

▶ Drag and drop objects from the Result Objects pane to anywhere inside the Query Manager pane.

▶ Select the object, and then click the X located in the upper-right corner of the pane to remove the selected object.

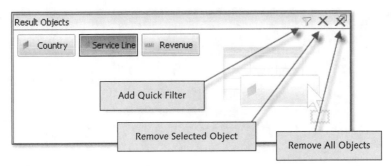

Figure 3.18 Shortcuts to Applying a Quick Filter and Removing Objects

▶ To remove all objects from the Result Objects pane, click the X located in the far right corner of the pane.

▶ Select the object to be removed, and press the ⌈Delete⌋ key.

3.4 Query Filters

Query filters are used to generate the where clause for the SQL statement that is submitted to the database. These objects work very closely with the Result Objects pane to provide a simple and intuitive interface for retrieving and restricting data.

Query filters allow you to minimize the amount of data returned from the query by restricting the query to specific criteria.

For example, you can add the Month dimension to the Query Filters pane and set it to July, and then add the Year dimension and set it to 2009. This will retrieve the total *Number of guests* for July 2009.

The benefits of query filters include the following:

▶ Return only the data you need to fulfill reporting requirements.

▶ Restrict confidential data from being displayed in reports or being returned to the microcube.

▶ Retrieve manageable result sets that can be exported to Excel, exported as a PDF, or printed.

Filter objects are identified by two major categories:

▶ Predefined filters (or conditions)

▶ Custom filters

3.4.1 Predefined Filters

Predefined filters are created by a developer or administrator and saved in the universe as *conditions*. These predefined conditions are easily recognizable in the Query Panel because a yellow filter icon appears to the left of the condition name.

An example of a very simple predefined filter is the Bahamas Resort condition predefined in the Island Resorts Marketing universe. The following line of code was added to the Where section in the properties of the condition.

```
Resort.resort = 'Bahamas Beach'
```

The importance of this example is to show the potential confusion from a user's perspective in trying to produce a report with Bahamas *resort* data and not knowing that it appears in the database as Bahamas Beach. This confusion has been removed from the user with the predefined condition.

Predefined filters can be set up in the universe to contain a variety of complex SQL syntax.

Condition Segments

Universe developers can create conditions containing any of the following segments:

▶ **Case statements:** Provide If/Else/Then logic to a condition or object.

▶ **And/or logic:** Multiple filters can be applied within a single condition.

▶ **In list:** Allows a condition to be created for many items in a list.

3.4.2 Custom Filters

Custom filters are conditions that are created on the fly by report developers. These types of filters are created when dimension objects are dragged and dropped into the Query Filters pane.

After a dimension object has been added to the Query Filters pane, you can choose how to set up the filter.

A dimension object can be set up with one of the following five query filter types:

- **Constant:** Manually enter a custom value.
- **Value(s) from list:** Provides a list of values for one or more selections.
- **Prompt:** Prompts the user to enter or select a value when the query is refreshed.
- **Result from another query:** Allows filters to be created using a result object retrieved by a different query within the same document. This filter type is only available in SP 2.
- **Object:** Provides the capability of selecting a predefined object or variable as the dimension value (can't use the `In List` or `Not In List` operators).

Figure 3.19 shows the button to change the assignment type from *Constant* to *Value(s) from List*, *Prompt*, or *Object*.

The default operator type when a dimension is added to the Query Filters pane is In List, and the default assignment type is Constant.

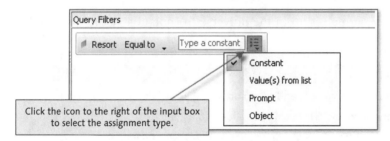

Figure 3.19   Select the Conditions Assignment Type

The operators available when creating a condition are as follows:

- **Equal To:** Obtains data equal to a selected or entered value.

  Example: `Resort = French Riviera`
- **Not Equal To:** Obtains data not equal to a selected or entered value.

  Example: `Resort <> French Riviera`
- **Greater Than:** Retrieves only the data greater than an entered value.

  Example: `Number of guests > 1500`

▶ **Greater Than or Equal To:** Retrieves only the data greater than or equal to a selected or entered value.

Example: `Number of guests >= 1500`

▶ **Less Than:** Retrieves only the data less than a selected or entered value.

Example: `Number of guests < 1500`

▶ **Less Than or Equal To:** Retrieves only the data less than or equal to a selected or entered value.

Example: `Number of guests <= 1500`

▶ **Between:** Retrieves only the data between two values.

Example: `Number of guests BETWEEN 1500 and 2000`

▶ **Not Between:** Retrieves only the data not between two values.

Example: `Number of guests NOT BETWEEN 1500 and 2000`

▶ **In List:** Retrieves the data for one or more selected or entered values.

Example: `City IN ('Belfast','Paris','London','Mobile')`

▶ **Not in List:** Restricts the query from returning data for one or more selected or entered values.

Example: `City NOT IN ('Belfast','Paris','London','Mobile')`

▶ **Is Null:** Retrieves only the values that don't have data- (have a null value).

Example: `City IS NULL`

▶ **Is Not Null:** Retrieves only the values that have data.

Example: `City IS NOT NULL`

▶ **Matches Pattern:** Retrieves the data that matches the pattern of a selected or entered value. This operator is translated as `Like` when the SQL statement is generated. In the example, all cities beginning with A will be returned.

Example: `City LIKE 'A%'`

Note

The wildcard character, %, is used to represent an indefinite number of characters. The underscore symbol, _, is used to represent a single character. An example of using this wildcard character is `City = 'G_neva'`.

▶ **Different from Pattern:** Retrieves the data that doesn't match the pattern of a selected or entered value. This operator is translated as Not Like when the SQL statement is generated. The following example returns all cities that don't begin with A.

Example: City NOT LIKE 'A%'

▶ **Both:** Retrieves data that corresponds to two values. If the Both filter is used with a dimension object, an intersection is generated.

▶ **Except:** Retrieves the data for other values in the dimension while restricting a selected or entered value. A minus query is generated when this operator is used.

Figure 3.20 shows the full list of operators available when the small down arrow is selected when creating a condition.

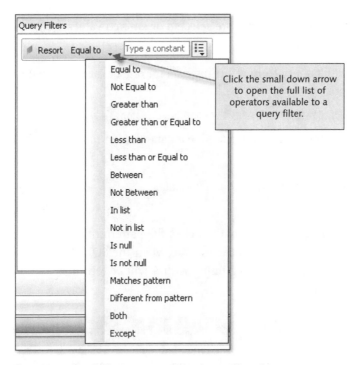

Figure 3.20 Available Operators in the Query Filters Pane

Retrieve exactly the data you need with this extensive list of query filter operators. Figure 3.20 shows the list of operators available when a dimension object is being filtered. If a measure is added to the Query Filters pane, then the following operator types aren't available:

▶ Matches Pattern

▶ Different from Pattern

3.4.3 Quick Filters

Quick filters are created when a dimensional result object is selected and the filter icon located in the upper-right corner of the Result Objects pane is clicked. This procedure opens the *Add Quick Filter* dialog box to allow you to quickly define the new condition or filter.

Figure 3.21 shows the *Add Quick Filter* dialog box that opens when a quick filter is added for the *Country* object. The operator is set to *Equal To* if a single value is selected, but if multiple values are selected from the displayed values, the operator will be set to *In List*.

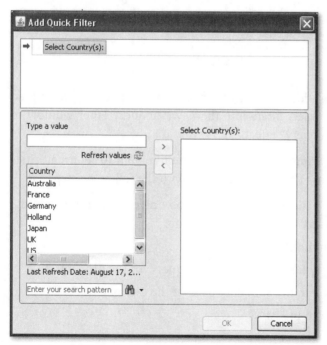

Figure 3.21 Adding a Quick Filter to a Result Object

3.4.4 Creating a Subquery

Subqueries are used in Web Intelligence to produce a query within a query. This type of document is used when the primary query needs to be filtered by the inner query or subquery. When a query containing a subquery is refreshed, the subquery runs first and then returns the values to be filtered in the main query.

This type of query is used when the main query needs to be filtered by a value that isn't known at the time of refresh.

Figure 3.22 shows how to add a subquery to an existing filter by simply clicking the Add Subquery button located in the upper-right corner of the Query Filters panel.

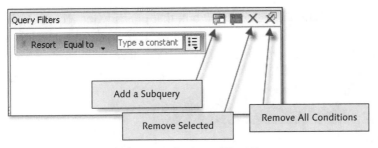

Figure 3.22 Insert a Subquery into the Query Filters Pane

After a subquery has been added to your document, you need to drag predefined filters or custom-defined object filters into the new Subquery Filter window to create the "query within a query" effect.

An example scenario for using a subquery is the requirement to return all cities within two selected regions. This is accomplished with the following steps:

1. Create a query from the Island Resorts Marketing universe, and then add the City and Region objects to the Result Objects pane.

2. Select the City object in the Data tab.

3. Click the Add a Subquery button to create a subquery for the City object.

4. Drag the Region object into the Subquery pane of the City object.

5. Set the Region operator to In List.

6. Select Value(s) from List, and then select East Germany and Mid West as the Region values.

7. Run the query.

The results returned will include only cities within the East Germany and Mid West region.

3.4.5 Creating Nested Conditions

Query filter conditions can be grouped by using AND and OR to perform extended business logic with conditions.

Figure 3.23 shows a Query Filter pane with four predefined and grouped conditions. These conditions are grouped to provide a more customized filtering technique. Rather than just dragging all four conditions into the pane, they are added as condition pairs or groups.

Grouping filters is accomplished with the following steps:

1. Drop an object or predefined condition onto the very bottom of the condition that you want to group it with.

   By default, the objects will appear in an And group.

2. If Or is required, double-click the new And group operator, and the group operator will become Or.

3. The example in Figure 3.23 will return only the values associated with the Bahamas Resort for 2008 OR the Hawaiian Resort for 2009.

Figure 3.23 Nested Predefined Query Filter Conditions

3.5 Prompted Queries

Prompted queries are used to require report consumers to make selections before a Web Intelligence document is opened. This is achieved by following these steps:

1. Create prompted query filters.

2. Set the document to Refresh on Open.

Saving a Report to Refresh on Open

To save a report so that it refreshes on open, follow these steps:

1. Begin the process by editing a report and viewing the Report Panel.

2. In the Report Panel, right-click and then select *Document Properties*.

3. Check the *Refresh on Open* option under *Document Options*. Figure 3.24 shows the Document Properties window and the Refresh on Open selection.

4. When saving a document with the Save As method, click the Advanced button, and then check the Refresh on Open box.

Either checkbox will refresh a query when the document is opened. If prompted conditions are present, the user will be prompted for input before proceeding.

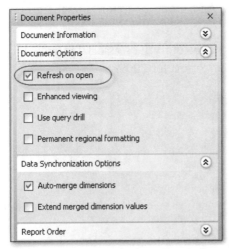

Figure 3.24 Setting Refresh on Open in Document Properties

Figure 3.25 shows the buttons to create a prompted custom filter. The button on the far right should be changed to Prompt to reveal the button immediately to its left. By clicking the button on Step 2 in the screenshot, the Prompt Properties dialog window is launched.

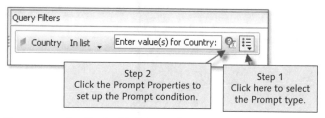

Figure 3.25 Set Up the Prompt Condition

Create a Prompted Filter

To create a prompted filter, follow these steps:

1. Click the button on the far right of the condition object to reveal five condition types if Service Pack 2 is installed (four condition types if not).

2. Select Prompt as the condition type.

3. Click the Prompt Properties button located immediately to the left to set up the properties for the prompted condition.

> **Tip**
>
> The *Prompt Properties* button in Figure 3.25 is only visible when Prompt has been selected as the condition type. Select *Prompt* with Step 1 in Figure 3.25.

Figure 3.26 shows the Prompt properties dialog window. Several settings can be modified for the prompted condition object.

Setting Prompt Properties

Following is a listing of properties that can be set up for a prompted filter object:

▶ **Prompt Text:** This text box is used to allow report developers to create a customized and appropriate message for business users when they are prompted to enter or select values.

▶ **Prompt with List of Values:** Provides the user with a distinct list of values for the prompted dimension (check or uncheck).

▶ **Keep Last Values Selected:** Maintains the values of the previous refresh. This setting shouldn't be selected when the data being queried is of a sensitive nature (check or uncheck).

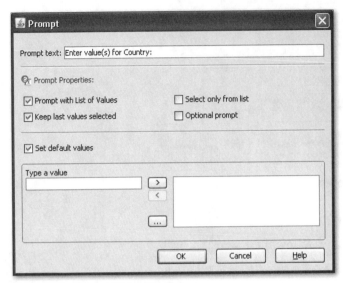

Figure 3.26 Prompt Dialog Window

▸ **Select Only from List:** Prohibits the users from entering values and requires that they only select from the list of values (check or uncheck).

▸ **Optional Prompt:** Sets the prompt to be optional (check or uncheck).

▸ **Set Default Values:** Enter one or more default values (check or uncheck).

> **Note**
>
> If *Set Default Values* has been checked, the button labeled with three ellipses to the right of the setting becomes enabled. Click this button to select multiple values.

3.6   Summary

You can use the highly intuitive Query Panel in Web Intelligence for self-service access to company data. Ad hoc report building is painless with the extensive set of query features available for business users in the zero-client web-based version of SAP BusinessObjects Web Intelligence XI 3.x.

With InfoView, documents are shared quickly and securely to users across the Enterprise in minutes rather than days.

Key Strengths of the Web Intelligence Query Panel

▸ Intuitive self-service access to company data

▸ Graphically generate SQL statements with universe objects

▸ Drag-and-drop web-based interface

▸ Include multiple data sources in a single document

▸ Merge dimensions to combine results from different sources

▸ More than 15 different condition types available when filtering objects

▸ Produce combined queries: union, intersection, minus

▸ Create a query within a query with subqueries

▸ Use custom SQL by modifying generated SQL statements

▸ Apply condition groupings with AND and OR

▸ Limit the query retrieval time and row counts with query properties

▸ Change universes in existing report documents

▸ Prompt users for input when reports are refreshed when opened

Using the drag-and-drop interface of the Query Panel, you can create queries to graphically transform prebuilt universe objects into analytical reports. The objects added to the Result Objects and Query Filter panes generate SQL statements without users having to write a single line of code. Report developers of all experience levels benefit from the ease-of-use of Web Intelligence.

You can also take your queries even deeper by retrieving data from multiple data sources. Once only available in Desktop Intelligence, dimensions from different data sources can now be merged within the same document to provide a robust set of data for analytical report building.

Also, with just a few clicks of the mouse, you can create complex documents with combined queries and subqueries, and by modifying generated SQL statements.

Precise results are returned by constraining values at the database level with a rich set of operators for query filtering. You can group your conditions in nested pairings with the AND and OR operators for more complex filtering.

You can control your row counts by limiting the maximum number of rows retrieved. Your DBAs will also appreciate the reduced stress on the database when you set a maximum retrieval time on your queries.

The combination of an extensive set of query features and an intuitive web-based report development interface makes Web Intelligence XI 3.x a best-in-class query and analysis solution for any data warehouse, data mart, or business intelligence reporting environment.

Chapter 4 will discuss the process of creating a Web Intelligence report.

Web Intelligence XI 3.x reports are used to analyze, present, and interact with highly formatted company data to enable accurate and more informed decisions. You can use drill filters, input controls, charts, data tables, block filters, and a lengthy set of report functions to produce custom reports.

4   Creating a Web Intelligence XI 3.x Report

Reports in SAP BusinessObjects Web Intelligence XI 3.x are used for viewing, analyzing, and sharing company data in a secure, customized, and drillable web-based delivery format. Reports are saved to the file repository server and delivered to the user with InfoView — the SAP BusinessObjects business intelligence reporting portal.

Web Intelligence enables you to present company data in your reports by adding data blocks and charts to the Report Panel through the use of several provided report templates. Data can be grouped by adding multiple sections and breaks to produce analytical documents by including sorts and drill filters.

After creating a Web Intelligence reporting document, users can quickly share their findings with other users across the enterprise by saving reports in the file repository and folder structure storage area accessed with InfoView. Depending on permissions, users are either granted or denied access to view, schedule, or even edit documents while working within InfoView.

The application also enables users to identify significant values by including *alerters* in your reports. Alerters can be applied to many columns in a report, can be assigned to every column or row in a data table, or can be applied to single columns and headers of data table reporting elements. Data changes can also be easily identified and tracked in reports by activating *data tracking*.

Web Intelligence also allows users to create precisely designed reports with the aid of a *report grid* and *snap to grid* functionality. In addition, you can maintain defined formatting and object placement relationships by assigning *relative position* attributes to report elements.

The broad set of features available in the Web Intelligence Report Panel allows report developers to produce highly customized free-form presentations for better insight into company data.

This chapter begins by describing the different Report Panels available to report developers, then introduces the various sections in the Java Report Panel, and takes you through the process of presenting data in a report.

4.1 The Web Intelligence Report Panel

The Web Intelligence Report Panel is available in four different formatting tool types. As discussed in Chapter 1, SAP BusinessObjects Web Intelligence XI 3.1, the Report Panel is selected by clicking Preferences in InfoView and then choosing a Web Intelligence default creation/editing tool. Following are the four choices available when setting the default creation/editing tool and the associated Report Panel:

- **Advanced (Java 2 required), also known as the Web Intelligence Java Report Panel:** The Advanced (Java) Report Panel provides the greatest flexibility for creating advanced reports within InfoView. This panel includes a formula editor for quick access to creating and editing variables and formulas, and requires the installation of a Java applet before opening, creating, or editing a document.

- **Interactive (no downloading required), also known as the Web Intelligence Query – HTML panel:** This panel is designed for users that require a pure HTML installation without installing Java applets. This panel provides a complete reporting solution with a slightly different look and feel than in the Java Report Panel. While the appearance is slightly different, the panel still allows users to develop reports with all of the same features available in the Java Report Panel.

- **Desktop or Web Intelligence Rich Client:** The newest and most significant improvement in Web Intelligence reporting over the past couple of years is the availability of the Web Intelligence Rich Client. This tool must be installed on a PC, and, once installed, reporting can be done in offline mode similar to Desktop Intelligence reports but with all of the features of Web Intelligence.

- **Web Accessibility (508 compliant), also known as the Web Intelligence HTML Report Panel:** This panel is available for users who only need to create very basic reports. This panel isn't commonly used because of the strength of the Java and Query-HTML Panels. Web Intelligence must be deployed in JSP mode for the HTML Report Panel to be available.

4.1.1 Working in the Report Panel

The Report Panel contains several areas that can be modified when creating or editing Web Intelligence reports. The full Report Panel is shown in Figure 4.1.

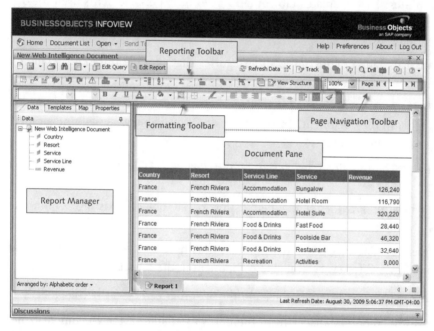

Figure 4.1 Web Intelligence Report Edited in the Java Report Panel

Following are the primary sections in the Report Panel:

► Report Manager
► Document pane
► Toolbars
  ► Reporting
  ► Formatting
  ► Page navigation

The Four Tabs in the Report Manager

The Report Manager contains four tabs and is required for creating Web Intelligence XI 3.x reporting documents. The Report Manager also plays a critical role in editing existing documents.

▸ **Data:** This tab contains the fields included in the Result Objects pane in the Query Panel and locally created formulas and variables. All objects in the Data tab are available to be displayed in reports.

▸ **Templates:** The Templates tab contains a set of Report Elements used for displaying data in reports. Report Elements include data tables, charts, and freestanding cells.

▸ **Map:** This tab contains three subcategories that provide different details on how components are displayed in the report:

  ▸ **Map:** Provides a linked list of the reports and section values within each report in the document. This section is only available when editing a report and viewing results.

  ▸ **Filters:** Shows filters that exist on report elements and data blocks within the reports.

  ▸ **Structure:** Provides a detailed listing of all objects existing within the document.

▸ **Properties:** The Properties tab provides a comprehensive list of settings that can be revised for every available component in the report.

The Report Manager is redockable, and the tab order can be easily changed.

To move the Report Manager from the default left side of the Document pane, click the symbol to the left of the tab name, and then drag and drop the panel to the right of the Document pane.

Properties are also editable for the report itself, allowing changes to be made to the page orientation, margins, header and footer height, and background color, just to name a few.

> **Note**
>
> If Service Pack 2 has been installed on your server, a fifth tab will be added to the Report Manager called Input Controls.
>
> Input Controls allow both report developers and users to include a variety of components to filter report data.

Figure 4.2 shows the Report Manager and the result objects from the Query Panel in the Data tab. An example query was created using the Islands Resort Marketing universe that included four dimension result objects and one measure result object. The data for the fields displayed in the Data tab has been retrieved from the database and exists within the document's microcube.

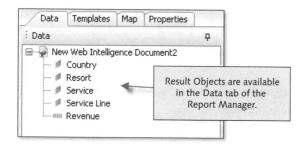

Figure 4.2 Web Intelligence Report Being Edited in the Java Report Panel

Click the Templates tab to reveal the report elements available for reporting. After adding a report element to the Document pane, drag and drop the result objects from the Data tab into the report elements to visualize the data.

The Document Pane

The Document pane is the primary section in the report panel of a Web Intelligence document and can also be considered the reporting canvas. This panel is used to display data and produce the actual Web Intelligence report.

The Document pane contains three sections:

▶ Report Header (not required)

▶ Report Body

▶ Report Footer (not required)

> **Tip**
>
> When a query is refreshed for the first time, the result objects will appear in the Document pane in a report titled Report 1. All result objects will also appear in the Report Manager. For any additional refreshes after the initial refresh, the Report Manager will be updated with the latest list of result objects, but the objects appearing on the Document pane won't change unless revised by the developer.

Rename, Insert, Duplicate, or Delete a Report Tab

The default report names are shown in Figure 4.3.

Figure 4.3 Default Report Names in the Document Pane

However, you can make changes to the report tab names. To rename, insert, duplicate, or delete report tabs, use these methods:

▶ Right-click on the report name tab located in the lower left of the report.

▶ Select Rename Report to change the name of the report tab.

▶ Select Insert Report to add a new report tab.

▶ Select Duplicate Report to make a duplicate copy of the current report.

▶ Select Delete Report to remove the current report tab.

Report Options

Figure 4.4 shows the actions available when right-clicking on the report name tab located at the lower left of the Document pane. The option to Move Report is only enabled when two or more reports exist within the document.

Figure 4.4 List of Actions Available When Right-Clicking on the Report Tab

Formatting Toolbar

The formatting toolbar can be hidden or shown by right-clicking in the gray panel above the Document pane. This toolbar becomes very valuable when editing data tables. Figure 4.5 shows the formatting toolbar.

Whether updating a horizontal table, vertical table, crosstab, form, or free-standing cell, the formatting toolbar allows you to instantly revise the format of entire columns with only a couple clicks.

Two new items in the formatting toolbar are the *Wrap Text* and *Format Painter* shortcut icons. Both items are very handy additions to the toolbar.

▶ **Wrap Text:** Allows a word wrap style of formatting to be applied to the selected column or columns so that a carriage return takes place within the cell rather than extending the value horizontally.

▶ **Format Painter:** This shortcut icon is used to quickly copy the format of an existing cell or column then apply it to an additional cell or column. This is accomplished by first selecting a cell that contains the preferred formatting, clicking the Format Painter icon, then clicking the text that you would like to apply the formatting to.

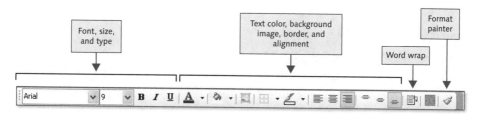

Figure 4.5 Formatting Toolbar

Reporting Toolbar

The reporting toolbar contains many important shortcut icons. The first three will likely be used very frequently. The first icon displays the Report Filter panel to allow filtering on selected blocks or the entire report.

The next two icons are used for editing and creating formulas and variables. Commonly used formatting functions available in this toolbar include creating and editing alerters, applying ranking, sorting, and inserting/removing breaks.

Developers also have quick access to adding aggregations (Sum, Count, Average, Min, Max, and Percentage); inserting rows and columns, layer objects, and report elements; aligning blocks; and toggling from page view to quick display view. Figure 4.6 shows the icons in the reporting toolbar with icon names.

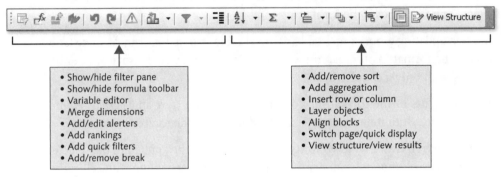

Figure 4.6   Reporting Toolbar

One of the most important items in the reporting toolbar is the View Structure button. The View Structure button allows you to access the document structure of a report, a step necessary for adding optional dimensions to charts and when editing the size of sections.

After clicking the View Structure button, the label changes to read View Results.

Page Navigation Toolbar

The page navigation toolbar allows you to change the size of the report being viewed and scroll from the current page being viewed to the next page, last page, previous page, and first page. Figure 4.7 shows the page navigation toolbar.

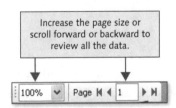

Figure 4.7   Page Navigation Toolbar

Default or Main Toolbars

There are two other toolbars that are displayed by default. The first toolbar is shown in Figure 4.8 with the icons listed in order. This toolbar allows you to create a new document or save a document either locally as a PDF, XLS, CSV, or to the CMS and file repository.

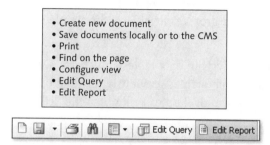

Figure 4.8 Default or Main Toolbar Icons

The printer icon provides one-click report printing, and the binoculars icon allows you to search report data for any length of characters.

If you need to revise a query while editing a report, this toolbar located in the upper-left corner of the Report Panel gives you the opportunity to return to the Query Panel by clicking Edit Query.

The second default toolbar is shown in Figure 4.9. This toolbar is located in the upper-right portion of the Report Panel and provides a couple very important and fundamental functions: refreshing data and purging data.

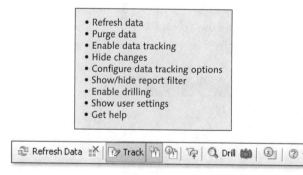

Figure 4.9 Default or Main Toolbar #2

Being able to refresh data is the primary function when generating reports. You also can purge report data with this set of tools by using the icon immediately to the right of the Refresh Data button. This is important when publishing reports to the file repository with restricted data.

Drilling versus Report Filtering

It's important to recognize the difference in report filtering and enabling drill mode. The Drill icon presented in the main toolbar in Figure 4.9 is used to enable drill mode. It also provides a Drill pane to drop result objects for simple report filtering.

Drill mode is provided for single-click analysis in data tables and charts. Drilling takes place along drill paths defined in the hierarchies previously set up in the universe. Drill mode allows report consumers to drill up or drill down the drill path for deeper and quicker analysis.

The show/hide report filter toolbar, activated by clicking the filter icon (to the left of the Drill button) only provides the Drill pane for report filtering without activating drill mode.

All of the result objects retrieved from the Query Panel can be dropped into the Drill pane for report filtering.

Activate Data Tracking

Activating data tracking is a recent addition to Web Intelligence and has become a valuable analysis feature. To activate data tracking in a report, click Track in the main toolbar located in the upper-right corner of the Report Panel. You are immediately prompted to set the reference point for data tracking.

The reference point selections are displayed in Figure 4.10. The first selection resets the reference after each refresh, while the second selection uses the current data as the reference point for all future refreshes.

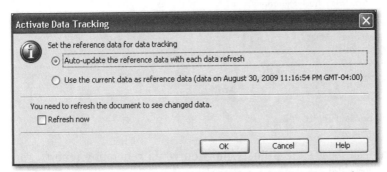

Figure 4.10   Setting the Data Reference Point When Activating Data Tracking

A variety of data tracking options are available when tracking has been enabled. These options include font formatting for dimension insertions and deletions, detail changes, and increased/decreased values for measures.

The default selection is to Auto-Update the Reference Data with Each Data Refresh.

4.1.2 Viewing Web Intelligence Reports

From a business user perspective, Web Intelligence reports can be viewed in four different viewing modes:

▶ **Quick Display mode:** This is the default display mode. The maximum displayed vertical and horizontal records can be defined in the Properties tab.

▶ **Page mode:** Displays reports as they would appear if printed.

▶ **Draft mode:** Displays only the report elements (charts, tables, free-standing cells). Primarily used for analysis.

▶ **PDF mode:** Launches the report data in PDF within the InfoView Panel.

The next section focuses on the report elements and components available in Web Intelligence for creating reports.

4.2 Report Elements and Properties

Report elements are the components used by Web Intelligence to display data in reports. These elements are available within the Templates tab located in the Report Manager. Report elements include the following items:

▶ **Tables**

　▶ **Horizontal Table:** Displays header cells to the left of the table.

　▶ **Vertical Table:** Displays header cells at the top of the table.

　▶ **Crosstab:** Display dimensions across the top and along the left side of the table while displaying measures in the body of the table.

　▶ **Form:** Display categorized dimension descriptions or mailing addresses.

▶ **Charts**

　▶ **Bar:** Graphically present values in vertical or horizontal charts.

　▶ **Line:** Display data graphically with connected data points.

　▶ **Area:** Display quantitative data graphically across time.

　▶ **Pie:** Display data as a percentage of the whole with pie slices.

　▶ **Radar:** Graphically display multivariate data.

▶ **Free-Standing Cells**

　▶ **Formula and Text Cells:** Single value cells used for formulas or headings.

　▶ **Page Number Cells:** Allows page numbers to be applied to reports.

The first Report Element listed in the Templates tab is titled "Report." Use this template to insert a new report tab into your existing document. Drag and drop the Report element template into the Document pane, and a new reporting tab is added to your existing Web Intelligence document.

Figure 4.11 shows the Report Elements available in the Templates tab.

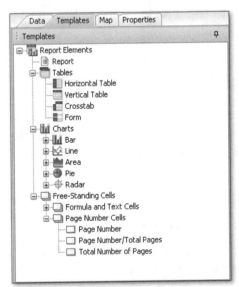

Figure 4.11 Report Elements Available in the Template Tab

Bar Charts

▸ **Vertical Grouped:** Chart data with vertical bars with the option to include a secondary dimension for grouping within the chart.

▸ **Horizontal Grouped:** Chart data with horizontal bars with the option to include a secondary dimension for grouping within the chart.

▸ **Vertical Stacked:** Chart data with vertical bars with the option to include a secondary dimension for stacking values vertically.

▸ **Horizontal Stacked:** Chart data with horizontal bars with the option to include a secondary dimension for stacking values horizontally.

▸ **Vertical Percent:** Used to vertically display the percent of each charted dimension object and optional secondary dimension object by percentage.

▸ **Horizontal Percent:** Used to horizontally display the percent of each charted dimension object and optional secondary dimension object by percentage.

▸ **3D Bar:** Three-dimensional vertical display of measures by dimension.

▸ **Vertical Bar and Line:** Provides the capability of charting two measures within a single chart to display one set of values with a vertical bar while presenting the second set of values with a line.

▸ **Horizontal Bar and Line:** Provides the capability of charting two measures within a single chart to display one set of values with a horizontal bar while presenting the second set of values with a line.

Line Charts

▸ Vertical Mixed

▸ Horizontal Mixed

▸ Vertical Stacked

▸ Horizontal Stacked

▸ Vertical Percent

▸ Horizontal Percent

▸ 3D Line

▸ 3D Surface

Area Charts

- ▶ Vertical Absolute
- ▶ Horizontal Absolute
- ▶ Vertical Stacked
- ▶ Horizontal Stacked
- ▶ Vertical Percent
- ▶ Horizontal Percent
- ▶ 3D Area
- ▶ 3D Surface

Pie Charts

- ▶ **Pie:** Pie charts are used to display each part as a portion of the whole.
- ▶ **Doughnut:** Pie chart display resembling a doughnut.
- ▶ **3D Pie:** Standard pie presented three-dimensionally.
- ▶ **3D Doughnut:** Three-dimensional representation of doughnut chart.

Radar Charts

- ▶ **Radar Line:** Connects the X-axis and Y-axis at the chart center. Data points are connected with lines.
- ▶ **Stacked Area Radar:** Connects the X-axis and Y-axis at the chart center. Presents data for many factors related to a single dimension item. Data points are connected with lines and then filled similar to area charts.
- ▶ **Polar:** Requires two measures and a dimension object. Plotted XY values are displayed on a circular grid.
- ▶ **Scatter:** Requires two measures and a dimension object. Plots a series of points where the values on the X-axis and Y-axis meet.

Formula and Text Cells

- ▶ **Blank cell:** Blank cells can be used for custom headings or subheadings, or to display information that should appear in a data table.
- ▶ **Drill Filters:** Adds the formula =DrillFilters() to a single cell when added to a report. This formula is used to display the drill filter values from the report filters. A common use of this function is to edit the formula to the following when multiple drill filters are used: =DrillFilters("/").

- ▶ **Last Refresh Date:** Drag and drop this cell onto a report to display the last time the report has been refreshed. Adding it to the report adds a cell with the following formula: `=LastExecutionDate()`.
- ▶ **Document Name:** Adds the document name to the report. Uses the following formula: `=DocumentName()`.
- ▶ **Query Summary:** Includes several details about the existing document, including universe name, last refresh date and time, last execution duration in minutes, number of rows, if duplicate row retrieval was off/on, and the query definition. Formula: `=QuerySummary()`.
- ▶ **Prompt Summary:** Provides a list of the values selected if a prompt filter was used in the query filters in the Query Panel. Formula: `=PromptSummary()`.
- ▶ **Report Filter Summary:** Displays all report filters existing within any of the reports in the current document. Formula: `=ReportFilterSummary()`.

Page Number Cells

- ▶ **Page Number:** Used to include the page number in a report.
- ▶ **Page Number/Total Pages:** Displays the page number followed by the total number of pages within the document. Example: 1/30.
- ▶ **Total Number of Pages:** Displays only the total number of report pages.

The Properties Tab

The Properties tab allows report developers to set and revise the properties on every element and object in the Report Panel (see Figure 4.12).

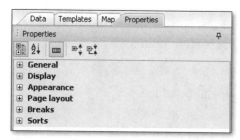

Figure 4.12   Properties Tab with Collapsed Categories

Properties can be displayed in two different formats: categorized or alphabetical. A description of the selected property can be shown or hidden and all property categories can be expanded or collapsed with a single click.

These property viewing formats are described in the following section.

Five Property Formats

The five property formats are described here:

▶ **Categorized:** Groups report object properties into categories.

▶ **Alphabetical:** Removes categories and displays all properties alphabetically.

▶ **Show/Hide Description Area:** Displays a description of the selected property at the bottom of the Report Manager window.

▶ **Expand (all):** Shows all categorized properties (only available while viewing categorized properties).

▶ **Collapse (all):** Hides all categorized properties, showing only the categories (only available while viewing categorized properties).

The next section describes how to add charts and data tables to a report and the steps required for adding result objects to the report elements.

4.3   Adding Data to Report Elements

Data is added to reports by including any of the report elements described in the previous section.

Following are the steps for adding a report element to the Document pane of a Web Intelligence report after your query has been refreshed:

1. Click the Templates tab in the Report Manager.

2. Locate and expand the report element type to be added.

3. Select a specific element.

4. Drag and drop the element onto the Document pane.

5. Click View Structure to add the result objects to the report elements. (View Structure is automatically selected when a chart is dropped onto the report canvas.)

> **Note**
>
> Viewing the structure of the Document pane will allow you to build the report elements without actually seeing the data, which is very useful when working with large sets of data.

Populate a Crosstab

Drag result objects from the Data tab in the Report Manager, and then drop them to the appropriate section in the crosstab. Figure 4.13 shows where to drop dimension and measure objects in a crosstab table.

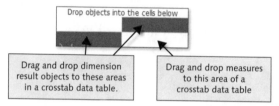

Figure 4.13   Crosstab in Structure View

Figure 4.14 shows a crosstab table and a horizontal grouped bar chart in Structure View.

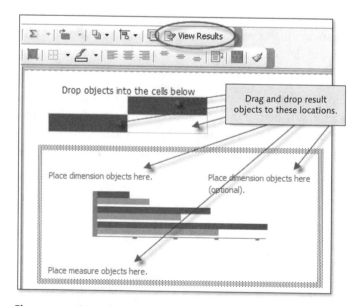

Figure 4.14   Crosstab and Horizontal Grouped Bar Chart in Structure View

Populate a Chart

To populate a chart, click View Structure to display the areas in the chart to drop the dimension and measure objects from the Data tab in the Report Manager. Simply drag and drop your result objects to the correct location on the chart and then you'll be ready to view the results.

> **Note**
>
> A chart must include at least one dimension object and one measure.

Click View Results to return to the report and see the data populated in the charts and tables.

The next section discusses how sections and breaks can be used to enhance the readability and functionality of a report.

4.4   Sections and Breaks

Sections are used to group data into visually separated segments. *Breaks* provide the capability of quickly inserting subtotals into data tables.

4.4.1   Sections

A section gives the appearance that a new block of data has been added under each section heading. Report elements can be added either before or after a section has been added.

When a section has been added to a report, a *section master cell* is generated to appear as a section header and is placed directly above existing report elements. Figure 4.15 shows the results of setting a country field as a section. Two section master cells appear, and data are grouped by values relating to France and the US.

Figure 4.15 Country Section in the Document Pane

Adding a Section

To add a section, follow these steps:

1. Drag a table report element, results object, or multiple result objects to the Document pane in the report. If a table was added, drag and drop result objects from the Data tab to the appropriate section of the table.

2. After adding result objects to the Document pane in your report, be sure that you're working in Results View.

3. Right-click on a dimension, and then select Set as Section.

Adding a section allows any existing tables or charts in the report to become visually separated and grouped by the result object set as the section.

4.4.2 Breaks

Breaks are used to produce grouped data while giving the appearance of subgroupings or subtotals. Breaks are different from sections because if a break is added in a report element table, the table is grouped by the break object, the result object remains in the table, and no master cell heading is added to the report.

Multiple breaks can exist within a single section to provide grouped subtotals. An example of including a break within a section was shown earlier in Figure 4.15. In this example, the `country` result object has been set as the section, and a break has been added to the `service line` result object. By setting `country` as a section, the data block becomes separated into two manageable blocks of data: one block for France and the other block for the US.

Figure 4.16 shows the icon used to add or remove a break. Before clicking the break icon, you need to select the row or column containing the object to add the break to.

Figure 4.16 Add/Remove Break Icon Located in the Reporting Toolbar

A break has also been added to the entire data block for the Service Line field. This allows for Service Line subtotals to be generated within each section block as shown in Figure 4.17.

France		Section	Break
Resort	Service Line	Service	Revenue
French Riviera	Accommodation	Bungalow	126,240
French Riviera		Hotel Room	116,790
French Riviera		Hotel Suite	320,220
	Accommodation		**563,250**
Resort	Service Line	Service	Revenue
French Riviera	Food & Drinks	Fast Food	28,440
French Riviera		Poolside Bar	46,320
French Riviera		Restaurant	32,640
	Food & Drinks		**107,400**

Figure 4.17 Breaks and Sorts Added to a Data Table

The following section describes how to insert sorting and ranking in a report.

4.5   Sorting and Ranking

Sorting and ranking data is a simple technique that increases report readability and displays the most significant information to report consumers in the shortest amount of time.

4.5.1   Sorting

Sorting can be applied to tables or charts in a report and on either dimension objects or measures. Sorting is always applied within breaks and sections.

Four sort types are available while viewing a report in InfoView or when editing a Web Intelligence document:

▶ **Default:** Natural sorting occurs based on the type of data in the columns.

▶ **Ascending:** Begins with the smallest value at the top, for example, A, B, C, or 2, 4, 6.

▶ **Descending:** Ends with the smallest value at the top, for example, C, B, A, or 6, 4, 2.

▶ **Custom:** Defined by the user; often applies to character names, but doesn't apply to measures.

Apply a Sort in a Table

To apply a sort in a table, follow these steps:

1. Select the column or result object to be sorted.

2. Click the down arrow located immediately to the right of the sort icon.

3. Select the sort type.

4. Click the sort icon to remove applied sorting and return to default.

Figure 4.18 shows a measure column sorted in descending order in a table.

Apply Sorting within a Chart

To apply sorting within a chart, follow these steps:

1. Click View Structure located in the main toolbar to switch from Results View to Structure View.

2. Click the object in the chart to be sorted.

3. Click the down arrow located immediately to the right of the sort icon.

4. Select the sort type.

5. Click View Results to return to the Result View in the Document pane.

6. Return to the Structure View, and add, remove, or edit an existing sort.

7. Click the sort icon again to remove the sort.

Custom Sorting

Custom sorting is only available for dimension objects and while either editing or viewing a document in the Java Report Panel.

When the Custom Sort Type has been selected, the dimension values of the object will be displayed in natural or descending order.

You can re-sort the item values by selecting values individually and clicking the up or down arrows until the values are in the order that you prefer.

You also can include temporary values to fulfill future sorting requirements.

An example of this is when a month name object sorts alphabetically rather than chronologically. For months to appear in chronological order, you need to create a custom sort to reorder the values. If you only have data through June, then July through December values won't appear in the list.

This is when to include *temporary values*. Enter the month names from July to December, add them to the existing list, and then order them chronologically rather than alphabetically. This will keep the month data sorted correctly for all future refreshes.

Figure 4.18 shows a data table with the month abbreviation field. The only way to sort the months correctly is to apply a Custom Sort.

Custom Sort Dialog Box

Figure 4.19 shows the Custom Sort dialog box used to sort the month name abbreviations. Click the values in the provided list box, and then use the arrows to the right to move them up or down the list.

The left side of the Custom Sort screen allows you to add temporary values for items that don't currently appear within the list of values.

	France	US
Apr	43,900	244,976
Aug	79,200	152,140
Dec	68,360	217,482
Feb	70,835	128,940
Jan	32,850	234,853
Jul	37,185	281,392
Jun	119,280	212,046
Mar	104,880	218,258
May	78,985	122,630
Nov	45,710	137,620
Oct	44,495	275,727
Sep	109,740	225,040

Sorted Alphabetically

Figure 4.18 Default or Natural Sorting Applied to the Month Abbreviation

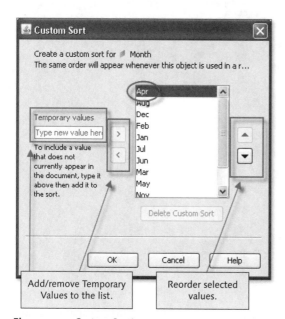

Add/remove Temporary Values to the list.

Reorder selected values.

Figure 4.19 Custom Sorting

Remove Custom Sort Value

If a custom sort has been added but needs to be removed, click the Temporary Value in the list of values, and the Delete Custom Sort button becomes enable. Click the button to permanently remove the custom value from the list.

Figure 4.20 shows sorting being set on a measure within a data table and within a section.

> **Note**
>
> Notice that Custom Sort isn't an option when sorting on a measure object. Custom sorting is only available for dimension objects.

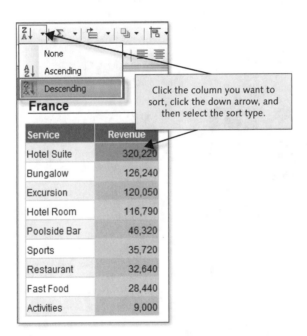

Figure 4.20　Revenue Sorted in Descending Order within a Section

Sorting in Charts

Figure 4.21 shows a vertical bar chart in Structure View with a descending sort applied to the revenue measure object. The purpose of this type of sort is to show the service dimension items displayed from high to low by revenue.

Note

Chart sorting can only be applied in Structure View.

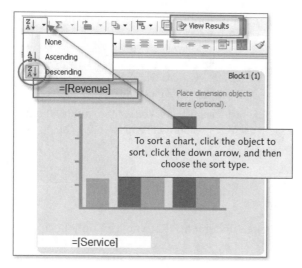

Figure 4.21   Working in Structure View to Apply a Sort in a Chart

4.5.2   Ranking

Ranking is used to display the top or bottom number of objects within a block. Values are ranked by dimensions and are based on measures of several different types and calculation modes.

▶ **Top or Bottom number of values:** Select either Top, Bottom, or both, and then use the up and down arrows or text box to set the values.

▶ **Based on: [measure]:** Select a measure to use for ranking.

▶ **Ranked By:** (optional) The selected dimension object used by the ranking to create the top or bottom values.

▶ **Calculation Mode:**

  ▶ **Count:** Returns the top or bottom n records of the Based On selection.

  ▶ **Percentage:** Returns the top or bottom n% records of the total number of records and the Based On selection.

▶ **Cumulative Sum:** Returns the top or bottom records for the cumulative sum of the measure selected and (optionally) the Based On selected; doesn't exceed n.

▶ **Cumulative Percentage:** Returns the top or bottom records for the cumulative sum of the measure selected and (optionally) the Based On selected; doesn't exceed n%.

> **Note**
>
> Ranking takes precedence over any previously setup sorts in a report block.
>
> Web Intelligence includes *tied rankings*, which means that if you want to display the top 10 values, and 3 records have the same value, 13 records will appear in the top 10 list.

Add a Ranking

To add a ranking, follow these steps:

1. Modify or edit your Web Intelligence document. (Ranking can only be applied in edit mode.)

2. Select a table or chart to be ranked.

3. Click the Apply/Remove Ranking button located in the reporting toolbar.

4. Select the Ranking Properties available in the Rank dialog box.

Figure 4.22 shows the options available when clicking the small down arrow located immediately to the right of the Apply/Remove Ranking button.

Two options will be available if a ranking has already been added to a report element: Edit Ranking and Remove Ranking.

Only one ranking can be added to a report element.

Figure 4.23 shows the Rank dialog box opened when Add Ranking or Edit Ranking is selected.

This dialog box allows you to configure the ranking properties by checking the Top, Bottom, or both ranking property types followed by selecting the Based On, Ranked By, and Calculation Mode to create or edit a ranking.

Figure 4.22 Add Ranking to a Vertical Table

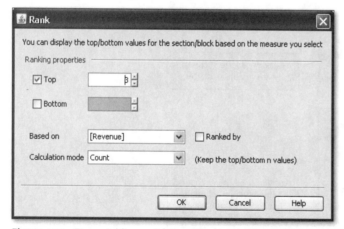

Figure 4.23 Figure Adding or Editing a Ranking in the Rank Dialog Box

The next section discusses alerters and how they can be used to enhance Web Intelligence reports.

4.6 Alerters

Alerters are used in Web Intelligence reports to highlight values that meet a specified set of criteria. When a set of criteria has been met, values can be displayed with customized formatting. This includes the capability to modify the following areas:

- **Text:** Font, type, size, color, underline, strikethrough.
- **Background:** Color, skin, image from URL, image from file.
- **Border:** One or more sides, border size, color.

Figure 4.24 shows the Alerter shortcut icon available in the reporting toolbar. The following are some of the major limitations of applying alerters in a report:

- Up to 30 alerters can be applied to a single Web Intelligence reporting document.
- Alerters can be applied to a maximum of 20 different rows or columns in a table report element.
- Up to 10 different alerts can be applied to a single column.
- A single alerter can contain up to 6 conditions.

Figure 4.24 Alerter Icon in the Reporting Tool – Add/Remove Alerter

The Alerter dialog window is launched when you click the Alerter shortcut icon on the reporting toolbar. You can then create a new alerter or edit, duplicate, or remove an existing alerter.

Figure 4.25 shows the Alerters dialog window for adding or editing an alerter.

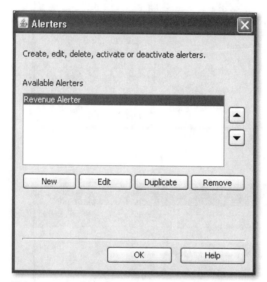

Figure 4.25 Alerters Dialog Box – Creating a New Alerter

Click New or Edit to launch the Alerter Editor window. From this window, revise the following items to create the criteria for the alerter:

▶ **Filtered Object or Cell:** Select the field or result object to be evaluated.

▶ **Operator:** Select the operator to be used, for example, Equal to, Greater than, and so on.

▶ **Operands:** Type in a value for the alerter.

After configuring these three settings, click the Format button to launch the Alerter Display window. Figure 4.26 shows the Alerter Editor window and the items required to create an alerter.

Figure 4.27 shows the Alerter Display window that is launched when clicking the Format button in the Alerter Editor window.

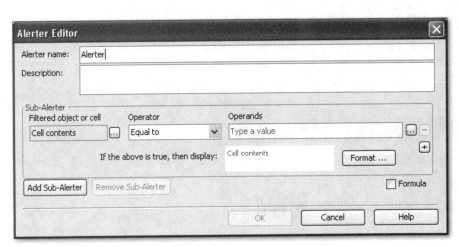

Figure 4.26 Alerter Editor

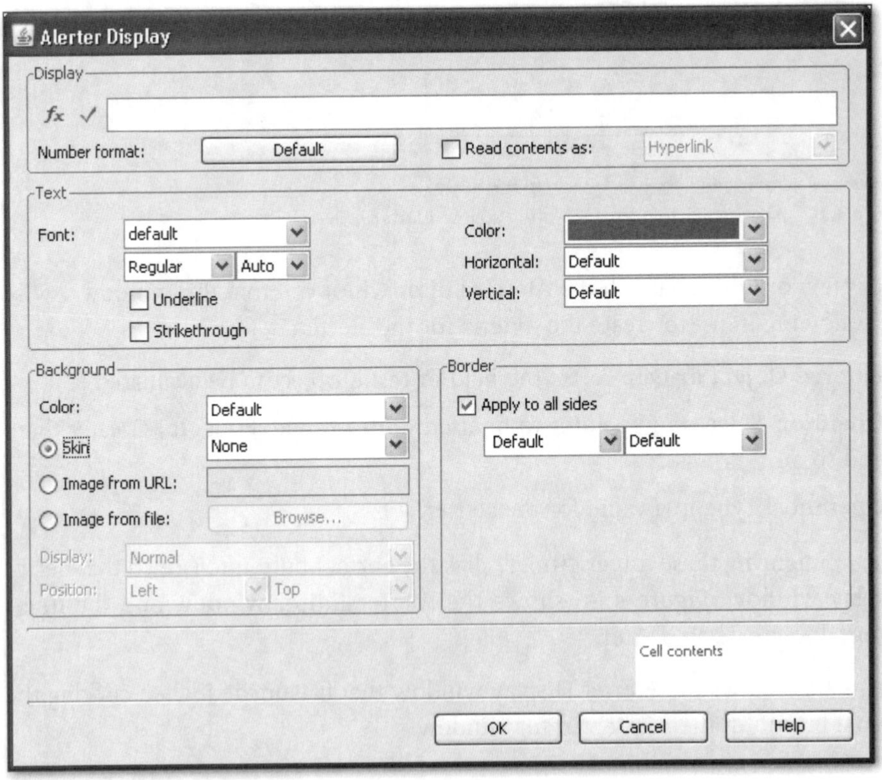

Figure 4.27 Alerter Display

After an alerter has been created, select a column or table heading, and then click the Alerters icon in the reporting toolbar to launch the Alerters window. All available alerters will have an open checkbox located to the left of the alerter name.

Check the Alerter that you want to apply to the selected column, and click OK. Figure 4.28 shows an alerter being applied with these three steps:

1. Select the column to apply the alerter to.

2. Click the Alerter icon.

3. Check the alerter(s) to be applied to the selected column(s).

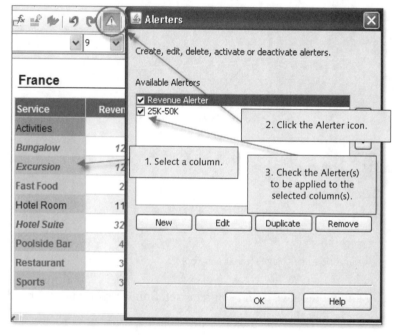

Figure 4.28 Alerters Dialog Box – Applying Alerters

The next section explains how to modify report headers and footers and also describes the method for including background images in reports.

4.7 Headers, Footers, and Background Images

The header and footer sections in a Web Intelligence document can be hidden or displayed depending on your preference or business requirement.

Click the header or footer section in the Document pane to view the Page Layout properties in the Properties tab of the Report Manager. Figure 4.29 shows the Page Layout properties with the page header selected.

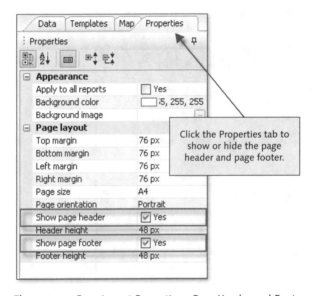

Figure 4.29   Page Layout Properties – Page Header and Footers

If the page header and footer have both been removed from a report and you need to add them back in, follow these steps:

1. Click the Properties tab in the Report Manager.
2. Click Edit Query.
3. Click Edit Report to return to the Report Panel, and the Show Page Header and Show Page Footer properties will be available to be checked.

4.7.1 Background Images

Quite often, report developers need to include background images or company logos in Web Intelligence reporting documents. This is easily achieved by following just a few steps:

1. Go to the Templates tab, and drag a Blank Cell from the Free-Standing Cells category onto the Document pane of your report.
2. After the Blank Cell has been added, click the cell, and then view the properties relating to it in the Properties tab. Figure 4.30 shows the properties available to the blank cell.
3. Click the ellipsis icon located to the right of the Background Image property.

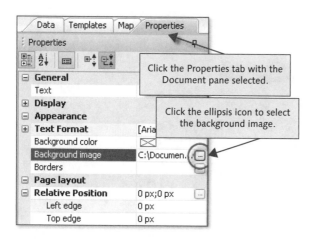

Figure 4.30 Setting a Background Image

The Background Image dialog box opens to provide four options:

▸ **None:** Default selection.
▸ **Skin:** Choose from five predefined photos.
▸ **Image from URL:** Opens a dialog box for manual URL entry.
▸ **Image from File:** Enables Browse to locate and select a local image.

Background images can be created with the following file types: PNG, BMP, GIF, JPG, or JPEG.

Figure 4.31 shows the Background Image dialog box used for selecting or pointing to a background image.

Images are presented with five different Display types:

► Normal

► Stretch (not supported in HTML)

► Tile

► Horizontal Tile

► Vertical Tile

The position of the images can be displayed in any of these combinations:

► Top, Center, Bottom

► Left, Center, Right

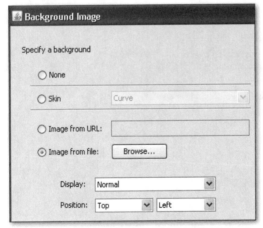

Figure 4.31 Background Image Dialog Box

Page layouts play an important role in the way reports are displayed and printed. The next section describes the steps for modifying report page layouts.

4.8 Adjusting Page Layouts

Page margins in a Web Intelligence report can be modified to fit business requirements or standards. The default margins in a report are as follows:

- ▶ Top margin: 76 px

- ▶ Bottom margin: 76 px

- ▶ Left margin: 76 px

- ▶ Right margin: 76 px

Margins are adjusted by accessing the Page Layout properties of the Document pane. Locate the margin properties under Page layout in the Properties tab of the Report Manager, and then use the up or down arrows to change the size.

The changes take effect when you click off of the size adjustment arrows. Figure 4.32 shows the Page Layout properties and highlights the Top Margin adjustment arrows for modifying the margin sizes.

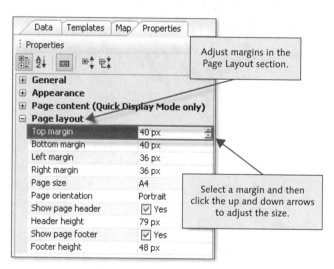

Figure 4.32 Adjusting Page Margins

The next section describes how reporting components can be aligned in a report and positioned in relation to each other.

4.9 Align and Relative Position

Proper report element alignment and relative positioning will improve the overall attractiveness and effectiveness of your Web Intelligence reports. When business users view reports that contain unusually aligned charts and data tables, the reports aren't usually as convincing as well designed and properly formatted reporting documents.

Use the Align functions to format the placement of report elements and the Relative Position feature to maintain consistent spacing and alignment when one or more blocks or report elements exist on a report.

Figure 4.33 shows the alignment types available when two or more report elements are selected. With two components selected, right-click to reveal the following four options:

▶ **Remove:** Deletes both report elements.

▶ **Format:** Highlights the Properties tab in the Report Manager.

▶ **Align:** Reveals several options for aligning report elements.

▶ **Document Properties:** Opens the Document Properties dialog box.

Mouse over the Align option to display the following alignment options:

▶ Align Left

▶ Align Center

▶ Align Right

▶ Align Top

▶ Align Middle

▶ Align Bottom

▶ Relative Position

▶ Show Grid

▶ Snap to Grid

▶ Grid Settings

The Relative Position setting allows two report elements to be tied together and spaced by a selected number of pixels.

To set up relative positioning, select a secondary report element, and then locate the Relative Position setting in the Properties tab in the Report Manager. Figure 4.34 shows the Relative Position properties of a bar chart in a report.

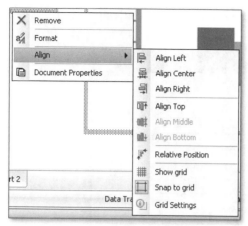

Figure 4.33 Aligning Objects When Selecting Multiple Report Elements

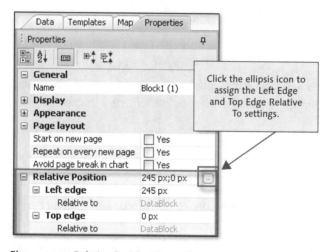

Figure 4.34 Relative Position Properties

The next step is to click the ellipsis button located to the right of the Relative Position property. When this button is selected, the Relative Position dialog box is launched. After this window is opened, follow the steps below.

1. Select either Left Edge, Right Edge, or None from the first box at the top, and then either select: Top Edge, Bottom Edge, or None from the bottom setting.

2. Select the object(s) to assign the relative distance to.

3. Choose the relative distance for both the top section and the bottom section.

Figure 4.35 shows the options available when assigning relative position.

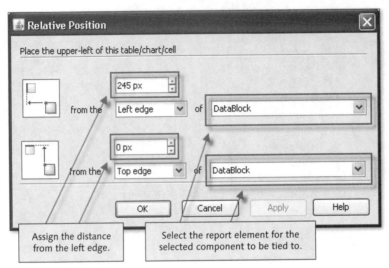

Figure 4.35 Assigning Relative Position

Relative positioning of charts and data tables gives reports the flexibility to present data in a similar format when the amount of data being reported fluctuates.

4.10 Summary

Reports in SAP BusinessObjects Web Intelligence XI 3.x are created for viewing, analyzing, and sharing company data in a secure, customized, and drillable web-based delivery format.

Reports are created by using the result objects and report elements, and by setting properties in the tabs provided by the Report Manager. Reports are physically presented in the Document pane and easily enhanced with the extensive list of shortcut icons in five provided toolbars.

Web Intelligence allows you to present multiple reports within a single reporting document that contain a variety of data visualization component types. You also have the ability to create drillable and highly formatted reports that include sections, breaks, sorting, ranking, and report filters to produce effective analytical documents.

Changes in report data can be easily identified when data tracking is enabled and when detailed alerters have been created.

Web Intelligence XI 3.x provides a full spectrum of reporting components for displaying data. This includes data tables, free-hand cells, and more than 30 different types of charts.

The Report Panel provides a highly intuitive development canvas that allows business users to create, edit, and share reports with ease.

Chapter 5 describes the variety of ways to filter data in a Web Intelligence query or report.

SAP BusinessObjects Web Intelligence XI 3.x provides a number of ways to filter data and present specific information for solving business problems. Whether restricting data in the Query Panel or filtering results in the Report Panel, business users have many options for displaying filtered company information.

5   Filtering Data

Filtering and restricting data is used to produce reporting documents that provide business users with pertinent and contextually relevant information.

You can restrict the amount of information returned to your report by applying query filters in the Query Panel. Query filters translate to the where clause of the generated SQL statement and help you minimize the amount of information returned to the *microcube* in a Web Intelligence XI 3.x document.

After running or refreshing a query in a Web Intelligence document and retrieving data, you can filter your results to produce reports, data tables, and charts with specific information.

The Filter pane in the Report Panel allows users to apply distinct sets of filters to different blocks within a single report or apply filters to entire reports. You can use the report filter toolbar to quickly and easily add filtered dimensions to entire reporting tabs.

With the addition of SP2, report consumers and developers now have access to an extensive set of new filtering components.

5.1   Query Filtering

Query filtering is used to restrict the amount of information retrieved from the database when a query is refreshed. Query filtering is achieved by including any of three filter types when creating a query.

▸ **Predefined filters:** Filter objects created in the universe.

▸ **User-defined filters:** Filters defined in the Query Panel.

▸ **Prompted filters:** Filter objects that prompt users for input.

5.1.1 Predefined Filters

Predefined filters are objects that have been previously setup in the universe. These filter types are symbolized with a yellow funnel icon and contain SQL syntax that assigns a value to a dimension object or contains a CASE statement.

Figure 5.1 shows the predefined filters in the demo Island Resorts Marketing universe. This example shows that the predefined filter objects have been added to their associated classes. Another common practice is to create a separate class designated specifically for predefined filter objects.

In the event that several predefined filters are required in the universe, subclasses should be created within the designated *filters* class for intuitive report filtering for business users.

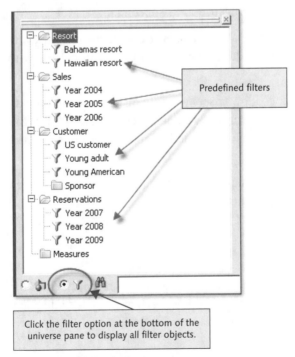

Figure 5.1 Predefined Filters

The contents of a predefined filter generally contain the assignment of a specific value or set of values. Figure 5.2 shows the filter object definition for the Bahamas Resort object in the Island Resorts Marketing universe.

The key element in a predefined filter is the Where section in the filter definition. Figure 5.2 assigns the `Bahamas Beach` value to the `Resort.resort` dimension.

Anytime this object is used in your query, the data returned will only be related to the Bahamas beach resort.

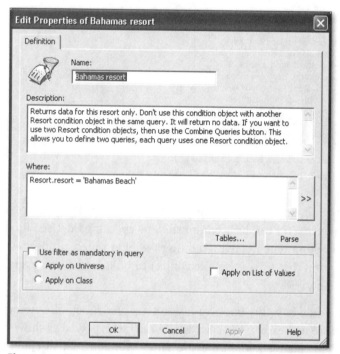

Figure 5.2 Properties of the Predefined Bahamas Resort Filter

A predefined filter object also contains a Description area for documenting the details around the object. The biggest advantage of adding a description to a predefined filter object is being able to see those notes when creating a Web Intelligence XI 3.x report.

Pictured in Figure 5.3 is the Query Manager pane with the predefined Bahamas Resort filter selected. In the lower-right corner of the dialog box is a pop-up text window displaying the description of the Bahamas resort filter.

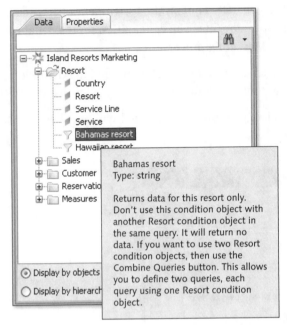

Figure 5.3 Visualize Predefined Filter Descriptions While Creating a Report

In many cases, predefined filters need to be applied by default to every query created from a specific universe. This can be accomplished by checking the Use Filter as Mandatory in Query option when viewing/editing the filter object properties. Figure 5.4 shows the option that forces the filter object to be inserted into every query created from the universe.

As a universe designer, you'll have the opportunity to set a predefined filter to be applied on either the entire universe or the class where the filter is saved as shown in Figure 5.4. They become enabled when the Use Filter as Mandatory in Query checkbox is checked.

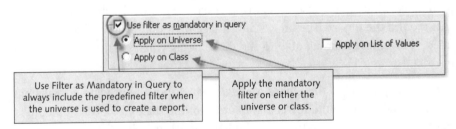

Figure 5.4 Apply Filter as Mandatory Query

A single predefined filter can include the assignment of values to multiple objects within the same filter. A simple example of this can be seen in Figure 5.5. This example contains two-dimensional filters within the same filter object. The syntax used in the filter is as follows:

```
Customer.age <=30 AND Country.country = 'US'
```

By adding a predefined filter to a Web Intelligence query, the data returned to the microcube will be restricted by the conditions defined in the filter.

When creating a predefined filter object, be sure to name the object with a term or short phrase that clearly describes the purpose of the filter.

The filter in Figure 5.5 adequately describes the conditions defined in the Where section of the object.

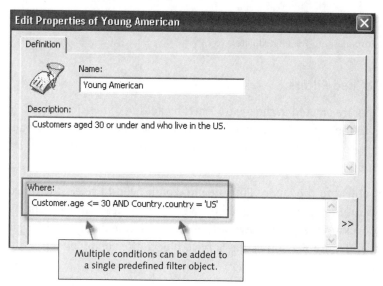

Figure 5.5 Multiple Conditions in a Single Predefined Filter Object

Predefined filters can also contain a variety of formulas. Figure 5.6 shows a predefined filter containing a formula that extracts the year from a date field and assigns it to 2009.

The purpose of this object is to provide a filter that restricts the data to the year 2009 when a year field isn't available.

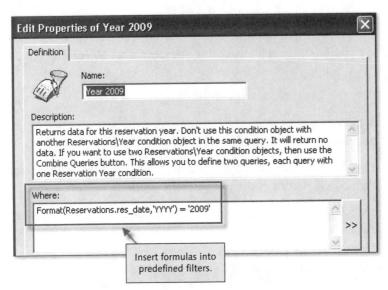

Figure 5.6 Insert Formulas into Predefined Filters

5.1.2   User-Defined Filters

User-defined filters are created in the Query Panel by adding dimension, detail, or measure objects to the Query Filters pane. Add objects to the Query Filters pane by dragging them from the Query Manager and then dropping the objects in the Query Filters pane.

After adding an object to the Query Filters pane, you'll need to select the object operator. By default, the operator assigned by Web Intelligence is In List. Change the operator by clicking the small down arrow located immediately to the right of the In List label. Figure 5.7 shows the Service object after being added to the Query Filters pane.

Figure 5.8 shows the different operators available for creating filters with measure, detail, and dimension objects.

After the operator has been selected, click the icon to the right of the input box to select the assignment type. Figure 5.9 shows the assignment type choices available in Web Intelligence 3.1 when creating a user-defined filter.

The default assignment type selection is Constant.

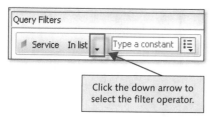

Click the down arrow to
select the filter operator.

Figure 5.7 Service Dimension Object Added to the Query Filters Pane

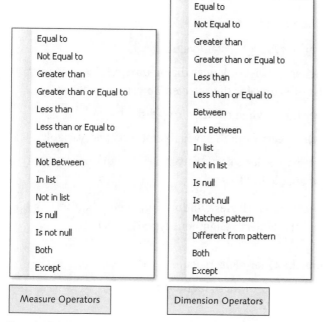

Figure 5.8 Operators Available for Measure and Dimension Objects

SP2 includes an additional option to select the results from another query residing in the same document.

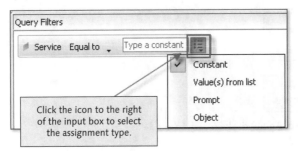

Figure 5.9 User-Defined Filter Assignment Types

The filter assignment types are listed here:

▶ **Constant:** Allows the user to type a constant value.

▶ **Value(s) from list:** Launches the List of Values dialog box to select one or more values from a distinct list of values for the selected object.

▶ **Prompt:** Prompts for user input when a query is refreshed.

▶ **Object (from this query):** Selects from the available objects and variables.

▶ **Results (from another query):** Selects a value from a different query within the same document. (Only available in SP2.)

Figure 5.10 shows the Objects and Variables window launched when setting up a user-defined query filter and the Object assignment type is selected.

Remove Filter Objects from the Query Filters Pane

To remove filter objects, choose any of these methods:

▶ Select the filter, and press `Delete`.

▶ Drag the filter from the Query Filter pane, and drop it in the Query Manager with the Data tab selected.

▶ Select the filter, and then click the X in the upper-right corner of the pane.

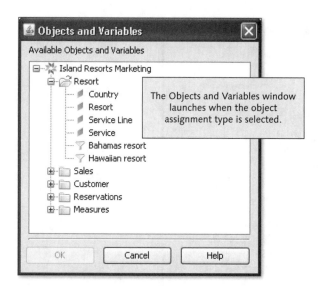

Figure 5.10 Objects and Variables Window

5.1.3 Prompted Filters

Use prompted filters to ask report consumers for input when a report is refreshed.

When a Web Intelligence XI 3.x reporting document is saved with the setting to Refresh on Open, and the document includes prompted filters, business users will be required to answer the prompt(s) when the report is refreshed.

▶ Figure 5.11 shows the Prompt Properties icon for the Prompt assignment type.

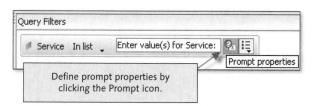

Figure 5.11 Prompt Properties Icon

Figure 5.12 shows the List of Values dialog box when the selected filter assignment type is Value(s) from List.

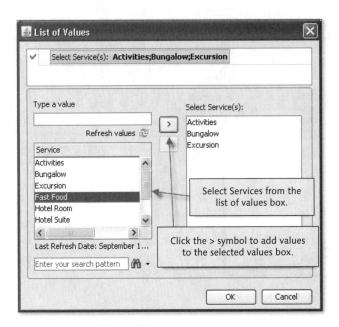

Figure 5.12 List of Values Dialog Box

By choosing Value(s) from List when setting the properties of a prompted filter, report consumers will be shown a full distinct list of the values that belong to the object being filtered when the report is refreshed.

List of values (LOVs) are either enabled or disabled when the objects are created in the universe. Custom LOVs can also be created in the universe to provide cascading prompted filtering to report consumers.

To select values from the List of Values dialog box, follow these steps:

1. Select values from the list of distinct values to be included.

2. Click the > button to add the values to the Selected Services box.

3. Selected values will be displayed at the top of the window. Click OK to accept

Prompt Filter Properties

When a prompted filter object is included in a query, report developers have the opportunity to revise a variety of properties for each filter object.

Figure 5.13 shows the Prompt properties window launched when defining a prompt. The properties are described here:

▶ **Prompt Text:** A prompt text is added by default.

▶ **Prompt with List of Values:** Displays a distinct list of values for the object being filtered.

▶ **Keep Last Values Selected:** Defaults to the last value selected.

▶ **Select Only from List:** Requires the selection of list value(s).

▶ **Optional Prompt:** Sets the prompt to be optional rather than required.

▶ **Set Default Values:** Allows a default value to be added to the filter.

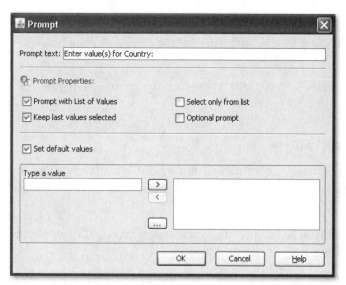

Figure 5.13 Prompt Dialog Box for Configuring Prompted Filters

The next section describes the process of applying filters in reports.

5.2   Report Filtering

Report filtering provides business users with the capability of displaying a small subset of data in a report rather than everything returned from the query and stored locally in the microcube.

It's very common for business requirements to call for Web Intelligence reports that contain charts for specific values in a data set along with additional charts or data table elements that display different values.

This type of functionality is possible in Web Intelligence XI 3.x by applying different report filters to each report element or block component within a report.

When values are filtered in a report, the data is only hidden from the user and still available within the microcube stored within the document. This allows business users to insert new report tabs and set up new filters without affecting other reports in the same document.

Filtering report data can be achieved by performing the following actions:

▶ Add standard report filters to entire reports by assigning values to objects in the Filter pane.

▶ Add standard report filters to specific blocks by assigning values to objects in the Filter pane.

▶ Add simple report filters by assigning values to objects in the report filter toolbar.

5.2.1 Standard Report Filters

Standard report filters are easily added to a reporting document by clicking the report filter shortcut icon in the reporting toolbar. This capability is available when editing or viewing a Web Intelligence XI 3.x report.

The standard report filter icon has a different appearance when creating or editing a report compared to when a report is being viewed.

Figure 5.14 shows the show/hide report filter pane shortcut icon when a report is being edited or created. Figure 5.15 shows the filter icon available when a report is being viewed.

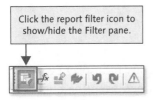

Figure 5.14 Show/Hide Filter Pane Icon

The Add Filter icon in Figure 5.15, visible when viewing a report, differs from the show/hide filter pane icon when a document is being edited or created.

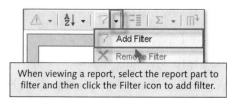

When viewing a report, select the report part to filter and then click the Filter icon to add filter.

Figure 5.15 Add Filters While Viewing Reports

> **Note**
>
> The primary difference between adding a standard filter when editing a report compared to adding a filter while viewing a report is the use of the Filter pane.
>
> The Filter pane is available when editing or creating a document, allowing you to drag and drop objects into the Filter pane.

The Report Filter Pane – Editing or Creating a Report

To edit or create a report, follow these steps:

1. Click the show/hide filter pane icon shown Figure 5.14.

2. Select the report part to apply the filter to, and then drag objects into the pane.

3. Select the operator, add a value, and click OK to accept.

Figure 5.16 shows the Filter pane used to create report or block filters in a reporting document.

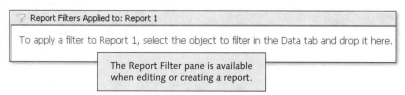

The Report Filter pane is available when editing or creating a report.

Figure 5.16 Report Filter Pane - Editing or Creating a Report

Filtering When Viewing Reports

The first step of filtering reports or reporting elements (blocks, charts, or tables) while viewing reports is to select a report part and then click the filter icon. Three types of filtering can be set up while viewing a report.

Launch the following editing tools to create on-the-fly filtering:

▶ **Report Filter Editor:** Select the report itself and click the filter icon.

▶ **Section Filter Editor:** Select a report section before clicking the filter icon.

▶ **Block Filter Editor:** Select a report element or block (table or chart) to launch this filter editor.

Figure 5.17 shows the Block Filter Editor that is launched when a chart is selected and the filter icon is clicked.

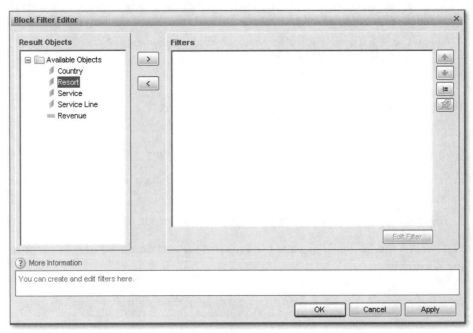

Figure 5.17 Block Filter Editor

After the Block Filter Editor is opened, select from the available result objects, and click the > symbol to begin creating the filter. The Filter window is launched, and you can select from the list of values and also set the operator.

Figure 5.18 shows the list of values for the Service result object being filtered and the list of available operators in the drop-down box.

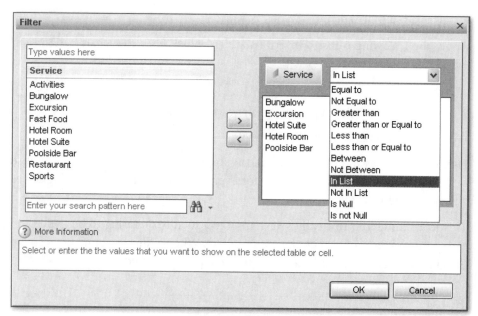

Figure 5.18 Assigning Values and Operator to the Filtered Object

Simple Report Filter Versus Report Filter

Simple report filters are added by dragging and dropping result objects onto the report filter toolbar. Distinct lists of the object values will be displayed in a drop-down component and provide a flexible method of filtering to the entire report. Simple filtering can be toggled OFF or ON by selecting the report filter toolbar icon located on one of the default toolbars.

Report filters are added by selecting a report part (or the entire report) and clicking the filter icon. The Filter Editor is then launched to walk you through the process of setting up your filter. These filters restrict data and function similar to a hard-coded filter. These filters remain in a report until they are manually changed.

5.2.2 Standard Block Filters

Standard block filters are very similar to standard report filters, but they apply to single blocks rather than entire reports. Block filters can be applied when reports are being viewed, edited, or created.

Apply Block Filters When Viewing a Report

Apply the following steps to insert a standard block filter to a chart or Data tab while viewing a report:

1. Mouse over a chart or data block.

2. Select the icon in the upper-left corner of the block.

3. Click the filter icon in the Report Panel.

Figure 5.19 shows the icon located in the upper left of a chart when you mouse over the object. This icon is available for every object in a report, including tables and free-standing cells.

This icon allows you to clearly select an object to allow filtering to be applied to the specific object rather than the entire report. When a filter is applied to a single data block in a report, only that block in the report is filtered.

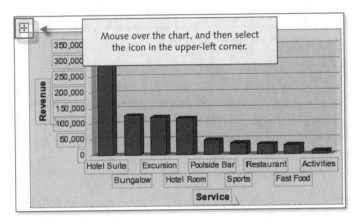

Figure 5.19   Selecting a Chart Object When Viewing a Report

After a block has been selected, click the filter icon in the reporting toolbar to launch the Block Filter Editor. Figure 5.20 shows the filter icon present in the reporting toolbar when viewing a report.

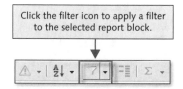

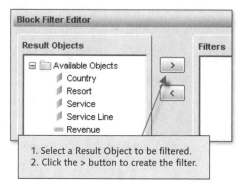

Figure 5.20 Filter Icons Available for Block Filtering When Viewing a Report

The filter icon will launch the Block Filter Editor as shown in Figure 5.21. The Block Filter Editor works exactly like report filtering as previously displayed in Figure 5.18 and discussed in Section 5.2.1, Standard Report Filters.

Figure 5.21 Block Filter Editor – Creating Result Object Filters

Apply Block Filters When Editing or Creating a Report

Begin by selecting the show/hide filter pane icon located in the reporting toolbar to open the Filter pane. This pane will open directly above the report to display all the result filters for the selected report element.

With the Filter pane opened, you can select each report element (charts, data tables, free-standing cells) in a report and then drag result objects from the Data tab in the Report Manager and drop them into the Filter pane. Once in the Filter pane, select an operator and value to define the filter.

The flexibility of applying filters to selected report elements in a single Web Intelligence report allows you to apply a variety of different filters to every object in your report for highly customized presentations.

Figure 5.22 shows the Filter pane when a report is being edited or created.

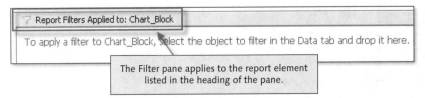

Figure 5.22 Filter Pane Applied When Editing or Creating a Report

When a result object is dropped into the Filter pane, the Filter Editor window is immediately opened to assist you with setting up the filter. The name of the block or reporting being filtered is displayed in the upper-left section of the Filter Editor dialog box.

The Filter Editor window is used to set the following properties:

▸ **Operator:** Selected from the provided list box.

▸ **Operand Type:** Constant (entered by developer) or Value(s) from List.

▸ **Value or Values Selected:** Entered by the developer or selected when viewing the values from the list.

Figure 5.23 shows the Filter Editor as it appears when filtering the Service result object.

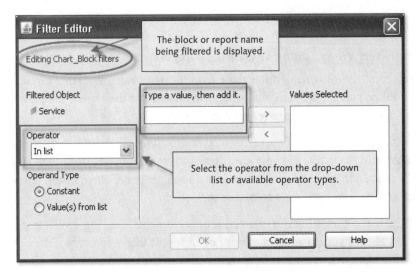

Figure 5.23 Filter Editor Settings

5.2.3   Simple Report Filters

Simple report filters are used to provide filtering to an entire Web Intelligence XI 3.x report. Each Report tab in a document can contain a different series of simple report filters.

Simple report filters are located in the filter toolbar directly above the report. The filter toolbar is enabled by clicking the show/hide report filter toolbar icon located in the main toolbar in the upper left of a report. Figure 5.24 shows the icon used to toggle from showing or hiding the filter toolbar.

Figure 5.24   Show or Hide the Report Filter Toolbar

When the filter toolbar is enabled, a message is displayed in the toolbar to lead report developers to the location where the drop result objects should be filtered.

The message displayed is "Drop objects here to add simple report filters" as shown in Figure 5.25.

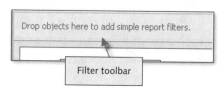

Figure 5.25   Filter Toolbar – No Filters Added

Dimension and detail objects can be dropped to the filter toolbar to instantly create drop-down report filtering. Figure 5.26 shows the filter toolbar with three dimension objects added.

Result dimension objects added
to the filter toolbar.

Figure 5.26 Result Objects Added to the Filter Toolbar

Removing Filter Objects

Follow these steps to remove objects from the filter toolbar:

1. Click the icon located to the left of the object to be removed.

2. Drag and drop the object to the Report Manager with the Data tab selected.

Add Report Filters While Viewing a Report

Report filters can be easily added when viewing reports by following a couple of simple steps:

1. Click the show/hide report filter toolbar icon located in the main toolbar in the upper right of the report. Figure 5.27 shows the shortcut icon.

2. After the report filter toolbar is opened, click the icon on the far left of the toolbar to view a list of available dimension or detail objects. This report filter is shown in Figure 5.28.

3. Click the add simple report filter icon to display available dimension or detail objects.

4. Mouse over available hierarchies, and then click a result object to add it to the report filter. Figure 5.29 shows the result objects that can be added to the report filter toolbar.

Click the show/hide report filter toolbar
icon located in the main toolbar.

Figure 5.27 Show/Hide Report Filter Toolbar Icon While Viewing a Report

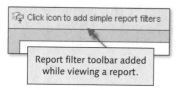

Figure 5.28   Report Filter Toolbar Added While Viewing a Report

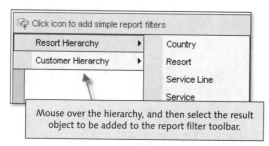

Figure 5.29   Add Simple Report Filter from Available Result Objects

Section 5.3 introduces the new report filtering controls in SP2.

5.3   Filtering Reports with Input Controls

Input controls are report filtering components added to Web Intelligence XI 3.1 with the release of SP2.

These new filtering tools are provided in their own tab in the Report Manager on the Report Panel. Figure 5.30 shows the Report Manager with the Input Controls tab included.

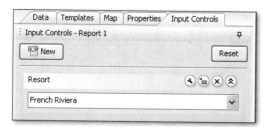

Figure 5.30   Report Manager Featuring the Input Controls Tab

Add a new input control to your Web Intelligence report by clicking the New button on the Input Controls tab in the Report Manager (see Figure 5.31).

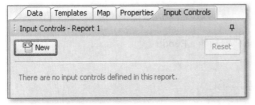

Figure 5.31 Add New Input Control

When you click the New button, the Define Input Control dialog window opens to allow you to select a result object as a basis for the input control.

After you select a result object, click Next to open the Define Input Control window. This is where you can choose the control type used as the filter component. Following are the lists of available control types.

The first two groups are the control types available for dimension or detail result objects.

▸ Single value control types:

  ▸ Entry Field

  ▸ Combo Box

  ▸ Radio Buttons

  ▸ List Box

▸ Multiple value control types

  ▸ Check Boxes

  ▸ List Box

The following groups are the control types available for measure objects.

▸ Single value control types

  ▸ Entry Field

  ▸ Spinner

  ▸ Simple Slider

▶ Multiple value control types

  ▶ Double Slider

Figure 5.32 displays the control type components available for dimension or detail objects in a report.

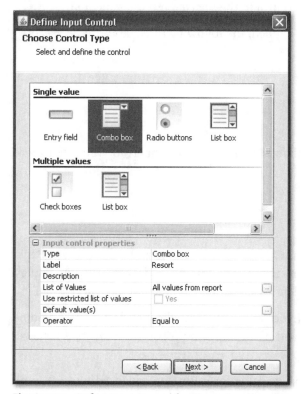

Figure 5.32 Define Input Control for Dimension Objects

After selecting a control type, you can modify the label and description of the control type component. You can also select the operator used in the filter, from the following list of operators:

▶ Equal to

▶ Not equal to

▶ Less than

▶ Less than or equal to

- ▸ Greater than

- ▸ Greater than or equal to

After you've selected the control type and operator, the next window prompts you to select the report elements to assign the input control to.

Click Finish to apply the input control to the selected report element(s).

After an input control has been applied, the following three tasks can be executed on the input control:

- ▸ Edit

- ▸ Show Dependencies

- ▸ Remove

Appendix B contains additional details on the enhancements to Web Intelligence introduced in SP2.

5.4 Summary

Filtering data in Web Intelligence XI 3.x is both flexible and easy to apply. Begin filtering your documents with restricting the amount of data returned in a query by including predefined, user-defined, or prompted filters in the Query Panel.

After data is returned to the microcube in a Web Intelligence document, fine-tune your reports by adding report and block filters to precisely display data for business users.

An extensive list of operators is available for setting up advanced filters in both the Query Panel and Report Panel. Whether filtering the available data in your data source or limiting data from being displayed in the Report Panel, report developers have many choices for meeting business requirements with reporting documents.

Take filtering to an even finer level by applying block filters to specific charts and data tables within a report. As a report developer or report consumer, use the filter toolbar to provide dimension and detail values in selectable drop-down lists to quickly filter entire reports.

The next chapter will discuss the different formats available for displaying and presenting data in a report.

Using the features in SAP BusinessObjects Web Intelligence XI 3.1 to display data transforms business information into analytical data-rich reports. Strategically group, break, and position data tables and free-hand cells in the Report Panel to convey information to the user in the most meaningful way.

6 Displaying Data with Tables

Displaying data in Web Intelligence XI 3.1 is achieved by inserting result objects into more than 33 different chart types and 4 different data table types, which are known in Web Intelligence as report elements.

This chapter focuses on presenting data by using the four report element tables and the use of free-standing cells located in the Templates tab in the Report Panel.

Figure 6.1 shows the tables available in the Report Panel used by Web Intelligence to display data. Each table contains an extensive set of properties that can be modified to allow for detailed reporting customizations.

The four table types are Horizontal Table, Vertical Table, Crosstab, and Form.

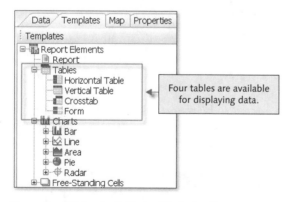

Figure 6.1 Tables Available for Displaying Data

After refreshing a query for the first time in a new document, the full list of result objects will be displayed in a vertical table in the Report Panel by default.

Any subsequent refreshes that include additions to the Result Objects pane in the Query Panel won't automatically include the additional fields to the report. However, the result objects will appear in the Data tab in the Report Manager.

> **Tip**
>
> The Data tab is used to maintain the list of result objects and variables available to be added to report element tables and charts.

Figure 6.2 shows the default appearance of data as it appears in the Report Panel if five result objects are added to the Query Panel in the initial refresh of a document.

A report title will be added by default in a text cell, given the title "Report Title," and contain a bottom border making it easy to locate.

Country	Resort	Service Line	Service	Revenue
France	French Riviera	Accommodation	Bungalow	126,240
France	French Riviera	Accommodation	Hotel Room	116,790
France	French Riviera	Accommodation	Hotel Suite	320,220
France	French Riviera	Food & Drinks	Fast Food	28,440
France	French Riviera	Food & Drinks	Poolside Bar	46,320
France	French Riviera	Food & Drinks	Restaurant	32,640
France	French Riviera	Recreation	Activities	9,000
France	French Riviera	Recreation	Excursion	120,050
France	French Riviera	Recreation	Sports	35,720
US	Bahamas Beach	Accommodation	Bungalow	142,720

Figure 6.2 Default Display in the Report Panel

Formulas and result objects can be added to the report title of a report to provide a dynamic title based on user interactions. An example of a dynamic report title can be created by using one of the following formulas:

> **Formula Examples for Report Titles**
>
> ```
> =DrillFilters(" / ")
> =If(Count([Resort])=1;[Resort];"All "+Count([Resort])+" Resorts")
> ```

Both formulas require objects to be added to the report filter toolbar. The second formula requires the Resort object to be added to the report filter.

Chapter 8, Using Formulas and Variables, will focus on writing formulas and variables to solve business problems. Many examples will be provided and syntax explained to give you the tools to create your own set of valuable and creative calculations.

6.1 Using Tables

Tables are the Web Intelligence XI 3.1 reporting components used to present information to business users. Tables provide many customizable properties to help you quickly format and design useful reports and display the data in a style that best fits your requirements.

These properties are available in six primary categories:

▶ **General:** Edit the report element display name.

▶ **Display:** Depending on the table type, provides up to nine checkboxes that allow for various features to be displayed or hidden.

▶ **Appearance:** Modify the background color, header cells, body cells, footer cells, alternate row/column colors, and borders, or provide a background image.

▶ **Page Layout:** Define relative positioning to force objects to be displayed within a specified number of pixels. Also choose to repeat the header or footer on every page, force an object to start on a new page, or avoid page breaks.

▶ **Breaks:** Modify up to five break properties when a break is added to a table. Set the break priority if more than one break exists.

▶ **Sorts:** Manage sort settings if columns or rows have been sorted.

6.1.1 Add Report Elements While Viewing Reports

Click the chart and table types shortcut icon located at the bottom of the Report Panel while viewing a report to access the complete list of Web Intelligence report elements.

To add a report element to a report, simply drag an element from the Chart and Table Types tab in the Report Manager and drop it onto the Report Panel. Being able to add data tables or charts while viewing reports is very useful to ad hoc report consumers and developers.

Report Manager Shortcut Icons – Viewing Reports

Figure 6.3 shows the shortcut icons used to access the different functional categories of a report viewed in InfoView.

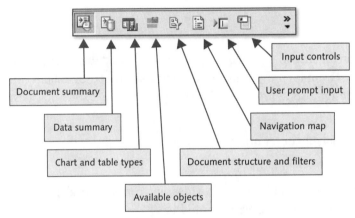

Figure 6.3 Report Panel Shortcut Icons – Viewing a Report

Figure 6.4 shows the *chart and table types* available to be added to a Web Intelligence report while viewing a report. These report elements are the exact same table types and cells available when editing or creating a report.

> **Note**
>
> While viewing a report, report elements are accessed by clicking the chart and table types shortcut icon. While editing or creating a report, click the Templates tab to access the report elements.

After dropping a report element into the Report Panel of your document, you can begin adding result objects to your report and populating the new table by clicking the Available Objects button at the bottom of the Report Manager and then dragging available objects and dropping them onto the table element recently added.

Figure 6.5 shows the Country result object being added to an empty crosstab table while viewing a report.

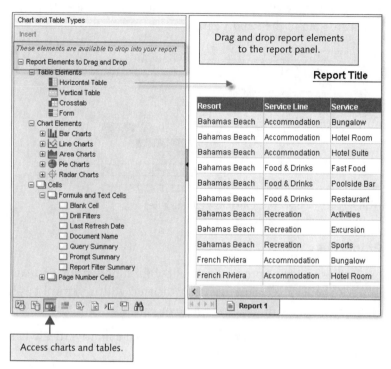

Figure 6.4   Chart and Table Types Tab – Viewing a Report

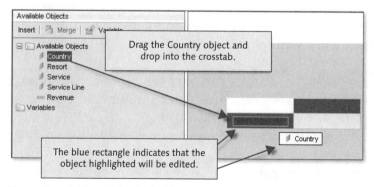

Figure 6.5   Adding an Available Object to a Crosstab – Viewing a Report

6.1.2 Adding Objects to Data Tables When Editing or Creating a Report

Figure 6.6 shows the Country result object being moved from the Data tab in the Report Manager to a crosstab in the Report Panel.

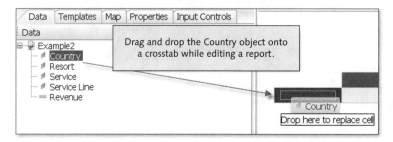

Figure 6.6 Adding an Available Object to a Crosstab – Editing a Report

6.1.3 Table Properties

Every table has an extensive list of properties to allow for modification and customization. Figure 6.7 shows the Properties tab associated with a vertical table. Additionally, specific elements within tables can be modified.

Not pictured in the screenshot in Figure 6.7 are additional subproperties when expanding: Text Format, Relative Position, Breaks, and Sorts.

General Property

The General property contains a Name setting that allows you to rename the selected block. Figure 6.7 shows the name as "Block1." Click the name to replace the default name with a new name of your choice.

Tip
If relative positioning will be included in your reports, it's a best practice to rename your table and chart blocks to a descriptive or meaningful name.
Web Intelligence will name all blocks Block followed by a number for the order the object was added to a report.
Setting up relative positioning can become quite confusing without descriptive or meaningful name assigned to each block.

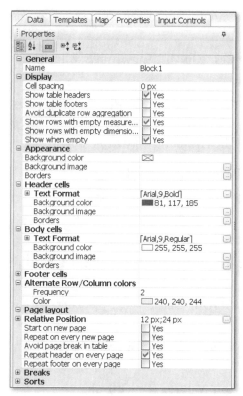

Figure 6.7 Properties of a Vertical Table

Display Property

Depending on the table type selected, up to nine Display properties are available for modification. The crosstab table type allows for the greatest number of Display properties with nine. The horizontal and vertical table types provide seven display property settings, while the form table provides five display properties.

The vertical table display properties include the following:

▶ **Cell Spacing:** Modify the cell spacing of a table. The default spacing value is set at 0 pixels.

▶ **Show Table Headers:** (On/Off) Show or hide column headings.

▶ **Show Table Footers:** (On/Off) Show or hide the row that contains the measure column sum values.

▸ **Avoid Duplicate Row Aggregation:** (On/Off) Unchecked by default; avoids duplicate row aggregation.

▸ **Show Rows with Empty Measure Values:** (On/Off) Shows rows where measures have null values.

▸ **Show Rows with Empty Dimension Values:** (On/Off) Shows rows where dimensions have null values.

▸ **Show When Empty:** (On/Off) Displays the element even when empty.

The horizontal table display properties include the following:

▸ **Cell Spacing:** Modify the cell spacing of a table. The default spacing value is set at 0 pixels.

▸ **Show Table Header:** (On/Off) Show or hide column headings.

▸ **Show Table Footer:** (On/Off) Show or hide the row that contains the measure column sum values.

▸ **Avoid Duplicate Row Aggregation:** (On/Off) Unchecked by default; avoids duplicate row aggregation.

▸ **Show Columns with Empty Measure Values:** (On/Off) Shows columns where measures have null values.

▸ **Show Columns with Empty Dimension Values:** (On/Off) Shows columns where dimensions have null values.

▸ **Show When Empty:** (On/Off) Displays the element even when empty.

The crosstab display properties include the following:

▸ **Cell Spacing:** Modify the cell spacing of a table. The default spacing value is set at 0 pixels.

▸ **Show Object Name:** (On/Off) Show crosstab object name.

▸ **Show Top Header:** (On/Off) Show crosstab vertical (top) header.

▸ **Show Left Header:** (On/Off) Show crosstab horizontal (top) header.

▸ **Show Table Footer:** (On/Off) Show or hide table footers.

▸ **Avoid Duplicate Row Aggregation:** (On/Off) Avoid duplicate row aggregation on the table.

▸ **Show Rows/Columns with Empty Measure Values:** (On/Off) Shows rows/columns where measures have null values.

▶ **Show Rows/Columns with Empty Dimension Values:** (On/Off) Shows rows/columns where dimensions have null values.

▶ **Show When Empty:** (On/Off) Displays the element even when empty.

The form display properties include the following:

▶ **Cell Spacing:** Modify the cell spacing of a table. The default spacing value is set at 2 pixels.

▶ **Show Table Header:** (On/Off) Show or hide column headings.

▶ **Avoid Duplicate Row Aggregation:** (On/Off) Avoid duplicate row aggregation on the table.

▶ **Show Columns with Empty Measure Values:** (On/Off) Shows columns where measures have null values.

▶ **Show Columns with Empty Dimension Values:** (On/Off) Shows columns where dimensions have null values.

▶ **Show When Empty:** (On/Off) Displays the element even when empty.

Appearance Property

The Appearance property allows you to modify many visual aspects of a table:

▶ **Background Color:** Change the background color of headers, rows, columns, or cell spacing if the spacing is set to 1 pixel or greater.

▶ **Background Image:** Apply a background image to selected table section. Choose from the following four choices

  ▶ None.

  ▶ Skin: Curve, Business Objects, Dots, Draft, Final Copy.

  ▶ Image from URL: Choose display and position of image after entering URL.

  ▶ Image from File: Browse for a local or network image.

▶ **Borders:** Apply border through the use of the Border Editor.

▶ **Header, Body, and Footer Cells:** Change the text format of the cells by modifying the following settings:

  ▶ Font Name: 14 available fonts

  ▶ Size: 6 to 44

  ▶ Style: Regular, Bold, Italic, Bold Italic

  ▶ Underline: (On/Off)

- ▶ Strikethrough: (On/Off)
- ▶ Text Color
- ▶ Wrap Text: (On/Off) Wraps text to a second line within the cell
- ▶ Vertical Text Alignment: Default, top, center, bottom
- ▶ Horizontal Text Alignment: Default, left, center, right
- ▶ **Alternate Row/Column Colors:** Adjust the frequency and color of the alternate row or column coloring.

Page Layout Property

The Page Layout properties allow you to assign a variety of positioning settings to report elements in a report. Following is a complete list of Page Layout properties:

- ▶ **Start on a New Page:** Sets the block to start on a new page.
- ▶ **Repeat on Every New Page:** Sets the cell to repeat on every new page.
- ▶ **Avoid Page Break in Table:** Fits the table onto one page where possible.
- ▶ **Repeat Header on Every Page:** Repeats the table header on every page.
- ▶ **Repeat Footer on Every Page:** Repeats the table footer on every page.

Relative Position

You can Assign the upper-left corner of a table, chart, or cell to another block by choosing two settings:

- ▶ Left edge
- ▶ Top edge

The next section discusses the types of data tables available to be used in the Report Panel of a Web Intelligence reporting document.

6.2   Table Types

The four table types available in Web Intelligence XI 3.1 are listed next. The two most commonly used tables are the vertical table and the crosstab.

- ▶ **Horizontal table:** Header cells listed on the left of the table.
- ▶ **Vertical table:** Header cells listed on the top of the table.

▸ **Crosstab:** Dimensions are listed across the top and along the left side of the table. Measures are displayed in the body as a cross section of the charted dimensions.

▸ **Form:** Commonly used to display small groups of related information such as addresses or employee information.

6.2.1 Horizontal Table

Figure 6.8 shows a horizontal table populated with three result objects.

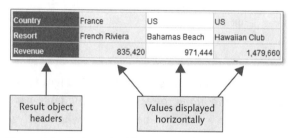

Country	France	US	US
Resort	French Riviera	Bahamas Beach	Hawaiian Club
Revenue	835,420	971,444	1,479,660

Result object headers — Values displayed horizontally

Figure 6.8   Horizontal Table Displayed with Three Result Objects

6.2.2 Vertical Table

Figure 6.9 displays a vertical table with the same result objects as Figure 6.9.

Country	Resort	Revenue
France	French Riviera	835,420
US	Bahamas Beach	971,444
US	Hawaiian Club	1,479,660

Result object headings appear across the top. — Values appear in columns.

Figure 6.9   Vertical Table Displayed with Three Result Objects

> **Note**
>
> Vertical tables are easily added to a report by selecting multiple result objects in the Data tab of the Report Manager and then dragging and dropping them into the Report Panel.

6.2.3 Crosstab Table

Figure 6.10 shows a crosstab table with two dimension objects and a measure.

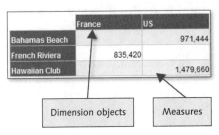

Figure 6.10 Crosstab Displayed with Three Result Objects

Pivot a Crosstab

Figure 6.11 displays a crosstab table that contains the same fields as in Figure 6.10 but the dimension objects across the top and along the left side of the table have switched positions to provide the user with a different perspective when analyzing the data.

Crosstab tables are often referred to as pivot tables because of their ability to pivot or switch the dimension objects from the top and left sides of the table.

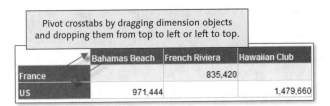

Figure 6.11 Crosstab Displayed with Three Result Objects

6.2.4 Form Table

A form table is most commonly used to display information relating to customers, employees, or other sets of closely related fields and objects.

An ideal situation is to add a dimension object at the top of the form table with detail objects added beneath the related dimension item.

Figure 6.12 shows where to drop an object in a form table so it appears as the second dimension in the table.

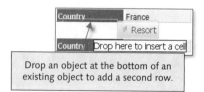

Drop an object at the bottom of an existing object to add a second row.

Figure 6.12   Dimension Added to an Existing Form Table

Figure 6.13 shows the finished result of the action displayed in Figure 6.12.

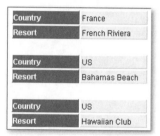

Figure 6.13   Form Table Displayed with Two Result Objects

The procedure for grouping data in a report is discussed in the next section.

6.3   Grouping Data

Grouping data in Web Intelligence is accomplished by setting sections for dimension objects or applying breaks to columns displayed in tables.

Multiple sections can be added to a single report, and subsequently added sections display data in subsections. One restriction of a section is that it can't be a measure object.

6.3.1   Set as Section

Figure 6.14 shows the Resort object in a vertical table being set as a section.

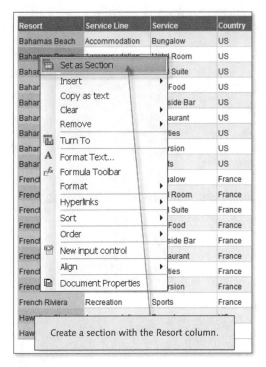

Figure 6.14   Resort Object Being Set as Section

Steps for Adding Sections to a Data Table

To add a section to a report, follow these steps:

1. Use an existing data table containing result objects. After you have inserted a table into your report and populated it with result objects, identify an object to set as the section.

2. Right-click on the object, and select Set as Section. This will split the rows into groups based on the values of the dimension defined as the section.

After an object has been set as a section, it will be removed from the table and added as a table header. The remaining values in the table will be separated by the values of the dimension section.

Figure 6.15 shows the outcome of setting the existing result object Resort column to a section. The Resort object has been added as a block header and the object is no longer a column in the table.

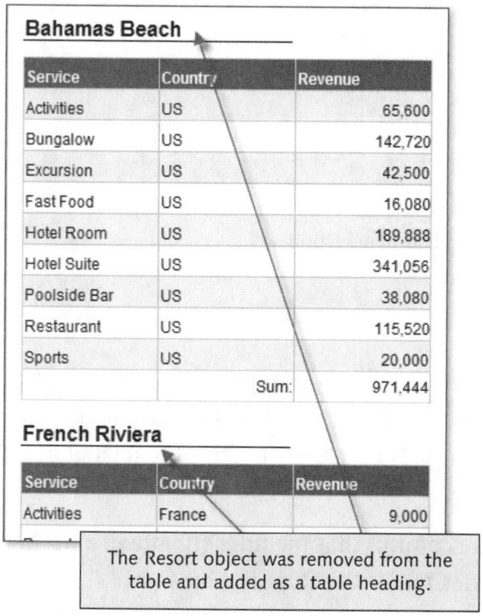

Bahamas Beach

Service	Country		Revenue
Activities	US		65,600
Bungalow	US		142,720
Excursion	US		42,500
Fast Food	US		16,080
Hotel Room	US		189,888
Hotel Suite	US		341,056
Poolside Bar	US		38,080
Restaurant	US		115,520
Sports	US		20,000
		Sum:	971,444

French Riviera

Service	Country		Revenue
Activities	France		9,000

The Resort object was removed from the table and added as a table heading.

Figure 6.15 Resort Dimension Object - Set as Section

After a section has been added, additional report elements can be added to the section. The values in any additional elements are grouped by the same values in the section heading.

To view the size of a section(s) and structure of a report, click the View Structure button located at the top of the document. View the report structure to resize the height of the section.

Figure 6.16 shows the Structure View of the report that contains the section added in the previous step.

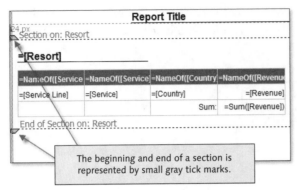

Figure 6.16 Structure of a Report – Beginning and End of a Section

6.3.2 Grouping Data with Breaks

Another way of grouping table data in a Web Intelligence report is by using breaks. *Breaks* are similar to sections but when added, they don't include block headings. When a break is added, a new set of break properties become available for customization.

To edit the properties of a break, click the column that includes the break and then locate the break property in the Properties tab of the Report Manager.

Figure 6.17 shows the break properties available when editing/creating a report.

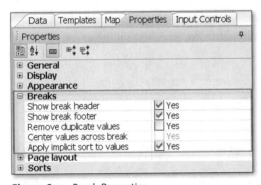

Figure 6.17 Break Properties

The next section discusses the process of converting or turning existing report elements into different display types. Turn charts to crosstabs or crosstabs to charts in just a couple clicks.

6.4 Converting Table Formats and Types

Tables can be quickly converted to other table types or report element types by right-clicking on a table and selecting Turn To. Figure 6.18 shows a selected vertical table with the right-click menu displayed.

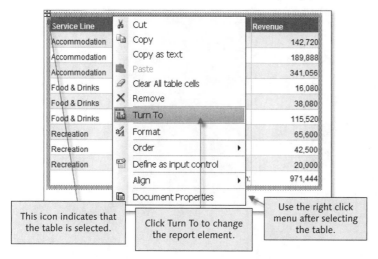

Figure 6.18 Right-Click Menu with a Vertical Table Selected

When a report is being edited and Turn To is selected by right-clicking on a table or chart, a Turn To window is launched. This window allows you to change the data table to a different type or chart with just one click.

If a report is being viewed in InfoView, right-click on a table or chart, and select Turn Chart To or Turn Table To from the menu of options to launch the Turn To window.

Figure 6.19 shows the Turn To window that allows you to convert the current report element to a different element or component type.

The current report element type is labeled in the window, and a visual representation of the element type appears depressed as in Figure 6.19.

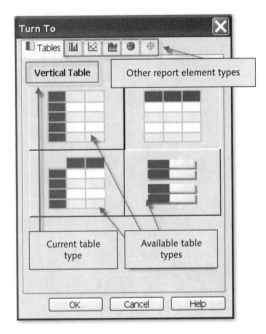

Figure 6.19 Turn To Options

The next section discusses the use of single free-standing cells in a report.

6.5 Free-Standing Cells

Free-standing cells can be used to enhance reports by providing a variety of functionality. Free-standing cells can be used for a variety of purposes, including titles, subtitles, refresh dates, drill filter selections, page numbers, single values, and many more (see Figure 6.20).

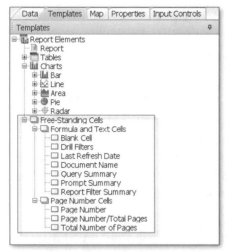

Figure 6.20 Free-Standing Cells Available in the Templates Tab

The following list describes each of the free-standing cells available in the Templates tab of the Report Manager:

▶ **Blank Cell:** A single empty cell used for inserting headings, text labels, single values, formulas, or calculations.

▶ **Drill Filters:** A single cell object containing the `DrillFilters()` function. This function becomes useful when dynamic headings or subheadings are required to display the dimensional selections made by users when objects are added to the report filter toolbar.

▶ **Last Refresh Date:** Object used to display the last refresh date of the query in a Web Intelligence document. If two or more queries exist in the document, a Data Provider window will prompt you to select the query to identify the last refresh. The `LastExecutionDate()` formula is used in this object. Figure 6.21 shows the Data Provider window that appears when the Last Refresh Date cell is added when multiple queries exist within a single document.

▶ **Document Name:** Displays the name of the Web Intelligence document. Uses the `DocumentName()` formula.

▶ **Query Summary:** Provides many details relating to the query or queries in the document, including query name, universe name, last refresh date, execution duration, number of rows retrieved, and result objects returned. Uses the `Query Summary()` function.

▶ **Prompt Summary:** Displays the details of prompted filters. Uses the `Prompt-Summary()` function.

▶ **Report Filter Summary:** Provides details on the filters used in the Report Panel of a document. Uses the function `ReportFilterSummary()`.

▶ **Page Number:** Uses the function `Page()` to display the page number.

▶ **Page Number/Total Pages:** This cell uses the following functions concatenated together to display the current page number followed by the total number of pages in the document: `Page()+"/"+NumberOfPages()`. The end result will be displayed as 1/16 for page 1 of 16. This formula can be modified to display Page 1 of 16 rather than 1/16 by using the following formula: `="Page "+Page()+" of "+NumberOfPages()`.

▶ **Total Number of Pages:** Displays the total number of pages in a report. Uses the function `NumberOfPages()`.

The blank cell is the most flexible free-standing cell report element. Use this cell to strategically place text labels, headings, or single calculations on a report.

Also use the blank cell element to create a hyperlink to another reporting document, link to an Xcelsius flash object, or link to a website within the InfoView portal. More details about hyperlinking will be discussed in Chapter 15, Linking in Web Intelligence Reports.

If two queries exist in the same Web Intelligence document and the Last Refresh Date free-standing cell is added to a report, the Data Provider window will pop up to allow you to choose the query for the Last Refresh Date (see Figure 6.21).

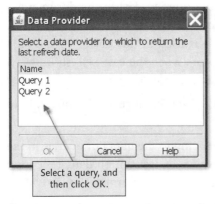

Figure 6.21 Select a Query When Using the Last Refresh Date Cell

Blank free-standing cells give report developers and consumers the option to include custom labels, individual calculations, and report functions.

6.6   Summary

Tables are the components used by Web Intelligence to visually deliver data in a reporting document. Table data can be presented by using four different table types, and properties can be adjusted to modify every aspect of a table report element.

Tables offer the convenience of adding report element tables and populating the table structures with result objects or variables while editing, creating, or viewing a Web Intelligence XI 3.1 document.

Table data can be grouped into sections or include breaks to create visual separate groups — all with a single table report element.

Tables enable users to quickly convert table objects into charts with as few as two clicks and use free-standing cells to enhance reports with single value calculations, dynamic headings, hyperlinks, or page numbers.

Chapter 7 will provide an in-depth discussion of the various settings that can be modified to use advanced formatting techniques in a Web Intelligence reporting document.

Learn how to format and customize Web Intelligence reporting documents by modifying the properties of reports, report elements, sections, breaks, and free-standing cells. This chapter discusses how to design and format reporting documents for online analysis, exporting to Microsoft Excel, or viewing in PDF format for high-quality printing and distribution.

7   Formatting Web Intelligence Reports

Every organization has unique requirements for displaying and presenting data to business users. To meet the requirements of organizations around the world, SAP BusinessObjects Web Intelligence XI 3.1 provides a lengthy set of editable properties for report modification and customization.

Report customization is simple, and your formatting updates are immediately displayed to report developers. The Report Panel in Web Intelligence XI 3.1 provides the capability to customize just about every aspect of a report. Use the Properties tab in the Report Manager to modify the default properties of every section and object used in a report.

Whether developing a report in edit mode or viewing a report through the Info-View portal, a rich set of features are available when right-clicking on a section or report element. Quickly format, sort, align, filter, layer, or turn objects by right-clicking on items selecting the functionality of choice.

Formatting can be applied to every object in a Web Intelligence report, including the report itself. You can apply custom formatting to each segment in a report's structure. This includes the report header, report footer, and report body.

The entire collection of report elements in the Templates tab of the Report Manager are customizable by editing each object's unique set of properties or by using the formatting toolbar in the Report Panel as shown in Figure 7.1.

Figure 7.1   The Formatting Toolbar in the Report Panel

7.1   Report Formatting

One of the most basic types of formatting involves customizing the properties of the entire report. To assign the correct and most appropriate property values to your reports, you must first have an idea of the primary use of the reporting document being developed.

7.1.1   Primary Uses of Web Intelligence Reporting Documents

Web Intelligence reporting documents can be loosely grouped into three major categories. These categories include ad hoc reporting analysis, report printing, and report exporting:

- Ad hoc reporting used for online interactive analysis, includes report drilling and filtering
- Enterprise reports designed for printing and exporting to PDF files
- Data retrieval documents used for exporting data to XLS or CSV files

Web Intelligence is widely known and accepted for its strengths in ad hoc reporting and analysis. This is due in part to its ease-of-use, intuitive interface, and numerous modifiable properties of data display objects.

Figure 7.2 shows the four property categories available for revising the report itself. To access these properties, click the outer edges of the Report Panel or the portion of the report that doesn't contain a report element, and then select the Properties tab in the Report Manager. If more than one report exists in a document, click the Properties tab, and then toggle from report to report.

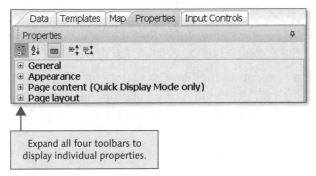

Figure 7.2 Collapsed List of Report Properties

Figure 7.3 shows the full list of the individual properties in an expanded mode. Expand the property categories by clicking the plus symbols beside each category.

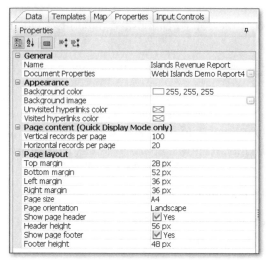

Figure 7.3 Expanded List of Report Properties

Following are the four main property categories of a report:

▶ General

▶ Appearance

▶ Page Content

▶ Page Layout

The General set of properties includes the following two individual properties:

▶ **Name:** Change the name of the selected reporting tab by editing the Name property. The report name can also be revised by right-clicking on the tab and selecting Rename Report.

▶ **Document Properties:** Launch the Document Properties by clicking the ellipsis button located to the right of the reporting document name. Document Properties are used to display document information, revise document options, set data synchronization options, and assign report Order.

The set of Appearance properties include the following four properties.

- **Background Color:** Select an alternate background color to change the default color.

- **Background Image:** Click the ellipsis button to select an image to use as a background image.

- **Unvisited Hyperlinks Color:** Modify the color of unvisited hyperlinks when they are included in a report.

- **Visited Hyperlinks Color:** Modify the color of visited hyperlinks when they are included in a report.

The number of records per page can be modified by revising the properties in the Page Content section. This setting allows reports to be created that display data in a style comfortable for the user community. It allows reports to be created that are easy to use and in a standard format.

The Page Content properties include the following settings:

- **Vertical Records per Page:** The default setting equals 100.

- **Horizontal Records per Page:** The default setting equals 20.

One of the most important sets of report properties is found in the Page Layout properties. Ten properties can be modified to revise the default reporting page settings:

- **Top Margin:** The default setting is 76 pixels. Type over the existing number setting, or click the up or down arrows to raise or decrease the number of pixels. The up or down arrows become visible when clicking in the object label.

- **Bottom Margin:** The default setting equals 76 pixels.

- **Left Margin:** The default setting equals 76 pixels.

- **Right Margin:** The default setting equals 76 pixels.

- **Page Size:** The default page size is A4. There are 24 different page sizes available.

- **Page Orientation:** Portrait is the default. Landscape is also available.

- **Show Page Header:** Checked by default. Uncheck to hide the page header.

- **Header Height:** The default setting equals 48 pixels.

- **Show Page Footer:** Checked by default. Uncheck to hide the page footer.

- **Footer Height:** The default setting equals 48 pixels.

Property Viewing Preferences

Properties can be viewed differently by clicking the icons located immediately beneath the Properties heading.

▶ Alphabetic

▶ Categorized

▶ Show/Hide Description Area

▶ Expand

▶ Collapse

Figure 7.4 shows the five preferences for viewing properties.

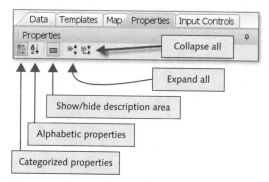

Figure 7.4 Viewing Preferences of Properties

7.1.2 Preparing Reports for the Three Primary Report Functions

Reports should be prepared differently based on their intended use. Following are the major report uses followed by the formatting preferences of each use:

▶ **Ad hoc reporting for interactive analysis**
Interactive analysis should be done in the default report viewing setting of quick display mode. Page mode and draft mode are also acceptable, but PDF mode isn't recommended for reporting documents intended for interactive filtering and analysis.

▶ **Reports designed for printing**
Page mode and PDF mode are two commonly used report viewing formats when reports are intended for printing. The PDF viewing mode provides quick

access to printing, but the report filter toolbar is unavailable. Page mode allows for report filtering and also displays the report as it will appear if printed.

▶ **Exporting data to XLS or CSV files**
When Web Intelligence reports are intended as data retrieval documents to be exported and saved as XLS or CSV files, set the data blocks in the report to the left edge and top edge of the object to 0. This allows the data to appear in the Excel file beginning in cell A1.

7.2 Formatting Sections and Breaks

Sections and breaks were introduced briefly in Chapter 4, Creating a Web Intelligence XI 3.x Report, as methods to group data visually in a Web Intelligence report. In addition to grouping data, sections and breaks can be formatted to add increased viewing flexibility.

Sections and breaks are both very useful when adding aggregate measures to produce subtotals in a report. Sections allow you to split table data into groups based on a selected section object. Breaks provide the functionality to produce subtotals within a section when displaying data in tables.

The most significant difference between sections and breaks is that charts can be dropped into sections to graphically display subtotal or sectioned data. The next several pages will discuss formatting for sections and breaks.

7.2.1 Formatting Sections

Section properties are modified by editing the attributes of five primary property categories. These properties can be modified to accomplish formatting tasks such as changing the background color of a section, forcing each section to display values on a new page, or avoiding page breaks within a section.

Figure 7.5 shows the properties of an existing section in a report. This example shows the default properties for the Age Group section.

The five property categories for a section — General, Display, Appearance, Page Layout, and Sorts — are described in the following list:

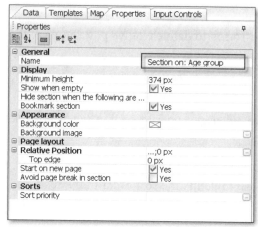

Figure 7.5 Section Properties

▶ **General property category**

  ▶ **Name:** The Name of a section is located in the General category and can be modified by double-clicking on the default name and then typing over the existing name.

▶ **Display property category**

  ▶ **Minimum Height:** The default pixel setting is based on the objects that exist within the section.

  ▶ **Show When Empty:** Sections can be hidden or displayed when report elements are empty (checked by default).

  ▶ **Hide Section When the Following Are Empty:** Provides a drop-down checkbox list of the objects within the selected section. Use this option when you want to hide the section if a selected block is empty.

  ▶ **Bookmark Section:** Sets a bookmark to the current section. This setting is used to include the section as a hyperlink in the navigation map.

▶ **Appearance property category**

  ▶ **Background Color:** Apply a nondefault color to the selected section.

  ▶ **Background Image:** Select a background image to appear as the background of the section.

- **Page Layout property category**
  - **Relative Position:** Select the ellipsis icon to define relative positioning of the selected section.
  - **Start On a New Page:** Display each set of section values on a new page (check or uncheck).
  - **Avoid Page Break in Section:** Avoid page break in section when possible (check or uncheck).
- **Sorts property category**
  - **Sort Priority:** Click the ellipsis icon to define the sort order in the section.

Adding Report Elements to a Section

Sections are clearly visible when viewing the structure of a report. Click View Structure at the top of the report, and look for the beginning and end section separators.

Figure 7.6 shows the identifiable beginning and ending lines of a section. Click anywhere inside the section while viewing the report in structure mode. Click the Properties tab in the Report Manager to begin modifying the default property settings.

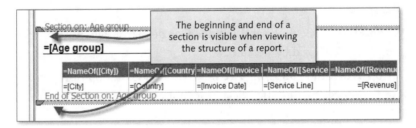

Figure 7.6 Section Viewed in Structure Mode of a Report

Removing a Section

Use the following two steps to quickly remove a section from a report:

1. Click anywhere within the section.

2. Right-click, and then select Remove.

3. If viewing a report, select Remove Section.

Removing a Section Master Cell

By default, a section master cell is added to a report when a dimension object is set as a section. In most cases, the section master cell label is a very convenient way to identify and describe the contents of the section. But, in some cases, you'll want to remove a section master cell while keeping the section.

To remove a section master cell but keep the section, simply select the section master cell, right-click, and choose Remove.

Figure 7.7 shows the message you'll receive when removing a section master cell while viewing a report in InfoView. The wording will be slightly different if you remove a section master cell while editing or creating a report.

The message gives you the choice of removing the associated section of the associated section master cell.

Figure 7.7 Removing a Section Master Cell While Viewing a Report

7.2.2 Formatting Breaks

Breaks provide a quick way of grouping data visually and displaying subtotals in a report. Groups are added to a report by selecting a result object in a table element and then clicking the break button located in the reporting toolbar.

After a break has been added to a report, you can format the break object by checking or unchecking a series of five break properties.

These properties provide the capability of displaying breaks in a number of ways. Following are the five break properties that can be turned on or off.

> **Note**
>
> To access the break properties, a break must exist in a report and be selected. After selecting the object that includes the break, the Breaks property category will be displayed in the Properties tab.
>
> Click the + symbol to the left of the Breaks property category to expand the property and access the individual properties listed next.

- ▶ Show Break Header

- ▶ Show Break Footer

- ▶ Remove Duplicate Values

- ▶ Center Values Across Break

- ▶ Apply Implicit Sort to Values

Figure 7.8 shows a small vertical table with a single break object added for the Country field. In this example, four properties are checked by default.

Country	Region	Resort	Sales Person	Revenue
France	East Germany	French Riviera	Fischer	69,240
	East Japan	French Riviera	Ishimoto	226,275
	Mid West	French Riviera	Galagers	141,300
	West	French Riviera	Galagers	105,095
France				

Country	Region	Resort	Sales Person	Revenue
US	East Germany	Bahamas Beach	Fischer	58,720
	East Germany	Hawaiian Club	Fischer	94,950
	East Japan	Bahamas Beach	Ishimoto	180,348
	East Japan	Hawaiian Club	Ishimoto	238,260
	Mid West	Bahamas Beach	Galagers	141,584
	Mid West	Hawaiian Club	Galagers	158,710
	Ruhr	Bahamas Beach	Fischer	10,976
	West	Bahamas Beach	Galagers	66,200
	West	Hawaiian Club	Galagers	130,250
	West Japan	Bahamas Beach	Nagata	4,700
US				

| Remove duplicate values | Implicit sort applied | Break header | | Break footer |

Figure 7.8 Break Added to a Vertical Table

The break added to the Country object adds column headers and column footers known as break headers and footers to each group of data. By default, duplicates are removed, and groups are sorted. This is why only the first row in each group contains a value in the first column.

All four of these properties can be changed by unchecking the associated properties in the Break category of the Property tab in the Report Manager.

Figure 7.9 displays the editable properties of a break added to a data table.

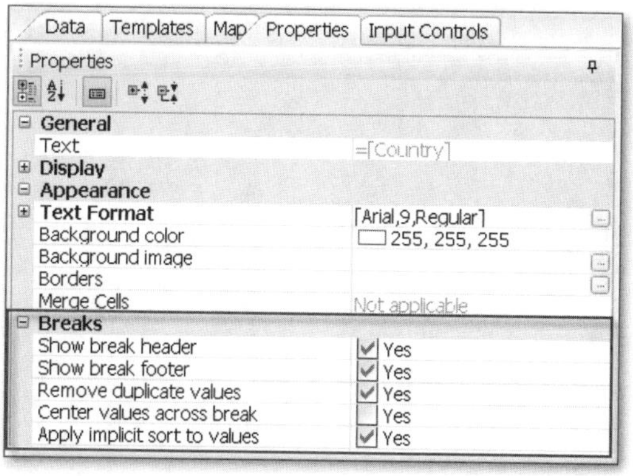

Figure 7.9 Break Properties

Figure 7.10 shows a vertical table with Center Values Across Break selected.

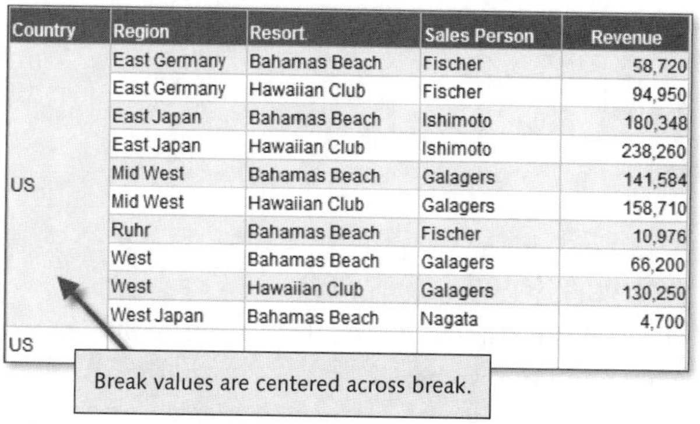

Figure 7.10 Vertical Table with Values Centered Across Break

7.2.3 Adding Charts to Sections

Add a single chart to a section in the Report Panel to display charted data for every section master cell value. Figure 7.11 shows two bar charts with values associated to each chart's section master cell.

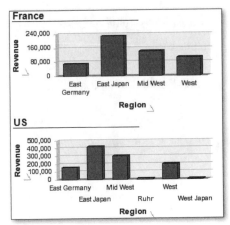

Figure 7.11   Vertical Grouped Bar Chart

Figure 7.12 show the bar chart in Figure 7.11 in structure mode.

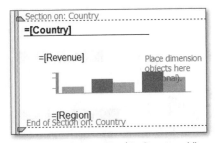

Figure 7.12   Report Panel in Structure View
Showing a Chart in a Section

Formatting Sections While Viewing a Report

Sections can be easily modified or adjusted on the fly in InfoView without entering edit mode by completing the following two steps:

1. Right-click on a report section in InfoView.

2. Mouse over Format, and then click Section to launch the Format Section window.

7.3   Formatting Data Tables

Chapter 6, Displaying Data with Tables, discusses the process of adding and populating a data table in a report. We'll pick up where Chapter 6 leaves off by providing details on formatting the rows and columns in a data table and describing the features available when right-clicking on a row or column in a data table.

The primary method of displaying data in a Web Intelligence report is achieved by adding result objects to one or more of the four available data tables.

As stated earlier, the table types are listed as follows:

- ▸ Horizontal Table
- ▸ Vertical Table
- ▸ Crosstab
- ▸ Form

Tables are accessed by selecting the Templates tab in the Report Manager. You insert tables, also known as report elements, onto the Report Panel by dragging them from the Templates tab and then dropping them onto the canvas of the Report Panel.

After a table has been added to the report canvas, you drop result objects onto the various sections of the table to begin viewing your result data.

After adding and populating table elements in your report, you're ready to begin formatting your tables to meet business requirements and convey your information to the user in the best way possible. The next several pages will describe how to format the individual sections in each type of data table.

7.3.1   Formatting a Vertical Table

Vertical tables consist of a series of columns used to vertically display dimensions, details, and measures. Result object names are listed in the header section, and the values are displayed vertically in columns.

Aggregates can be applied to columns in a table containing measures. This allows the report developer to display break totals, section totals, or block totals with as few as three clicks.

Adding Aggregate Values to a Table

Select the column in a data table containing the measure object to be aggregated, and then click the small down arrow immediately to the right of the Insert Sum shortcut icon in the reporting toolbar. This will display the full list of shortcut aggregates. Figure 7.13 shows the icon used to insert an aggregate value.

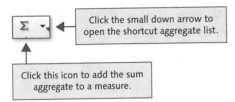

Figure 7.13 Insert a Sum or Other Aggregate Value into a Table

Figure 7.14 shows the full list of aggregates available when clicking the small down arrow located to the right of the insert sum shortcut icon.

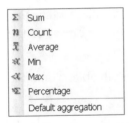

Figure 7.14 Aggregate Values Available for Quick Insert

Aggregates are commonly added to the break footer section of a table. Following are the three most frequently used ways to add aggregates to a break footer:

▶ Select a column containing a measure object, and click Insert Sum.

▶ Drag a measure object from the Data tab, and drop it into the desired cell in the break footer of a table.

▶ Use the Formula Editor to create a formula or variable for the footer cell.

Figure 7.15 shows the result of dropping the [Revenue] result object into the revenue break footer cell. It also shows the break footer cell selected in the Sales Person column. This was done to illustrate that the formula toolbar become enabled and is available for input. Use this toolbar if you have a very short formula, hard-coded value, or want to add a simple result object reference.

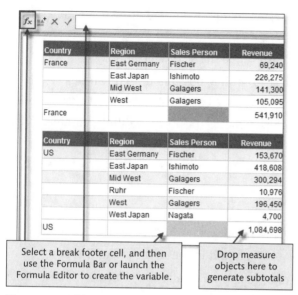

Figure 7.15 Adding Aggregate Values to a Break Footer

Click the *fx* icon to launch the Formula Editor to assist you with building the variable or formula. Chapter 8, Using Formulas and Variables, discusses the formula editor in detail.

Property Categories of Columns or Rows in a Vertical or Horizontal Table

The two primary property categories in vertical and horizontal tables are in the Display and Appearance property categories. Twenty properties are available for editing a selected column in a vertical table or row in a horizontal table.

7.3.2 Column and Row Properties of a Table

Following are the column and row properties for a table:

▶ **General**

▸ Text: Contains the name of the result object, formula, or variable.

▶ **Display**

▸ Autofit Width: Width of selected column is auto-adjusted if checked. Width is manually adjusted by report developer if unchecked.

▸ Width: Cell width in pixels of the selected column.

▶ Autofit Height: Height of selected column is auto-adjusted if checked. Height is manually adjusted by report developer if unchecked.

▶ Height: Height in pixels of each cell in the selected column.

▶ Read Cell Contents As: Select from four possible drop-down object values: Text, Hyperlink, HTML, or Image URL. The default selection is Text.

▶ Horizontal Padding: Used to pad spaces (in pixels) to the beginning of the column.

▶ Vertical Padding: Used to pad spaces (in pixels) vertically to the selected column.

▶ **Appearance**

▶ Background Color: Apply a background color to the selected column.

▶ Background Image: Apply a background image to the selected column.

▶ Borders: Use the Border Editor to apply a border to one or more sides of the cells in the selected column.

▶ Merge Cells: Becomes enabled when two columns are selected. Once enabled, this property becomes a checkbox that allows you to merge the two columns if checked. Be careful when using this feature because if the selected cells contain multiple values, only the contents of the first selected cell will be kept.

▶ Number Format: Only available for columns with measure objects.

▶ **Text Format** (located inside the Appearance property)

▶ Font Name: Select a font from the 14 fonts available.

▶ Size: Select a font size between 6 and 44. Auto is also available.

▶ Style: Regular, Bold, Italic, Bold Italic.

▶ Underline: Underlines the values in the selected column.

▶ Strikethrough: Strikes through the values of the selected column.

▶ Text Color: Modify the text color of the values in the selected column.

▶ Wrap Text: Allows for multi-word values to wrap to the next line. This property is commonly used in report headings.

> ► Vertical Text Alignment: Default, Top, Center, Bottom.

> ► Horizontal Text Alignment: Default, Left, Center, Right.

► **Sorts**

> ► Sort: Applies only when a sort has been added for the selected column.

Figure 7.16 shows the display, appearance, and text format properties.

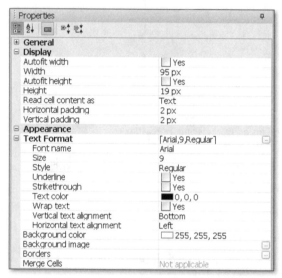

Figure 7.16 Properties of a Dimension Objects in a Vertical Table

7.3.3 Formatting a Crosstab

Crosstabs provide the capability of displaying data when more than one dimension is required in a table or data block. Often referred to as a pivot table, a crosstab is created by dropping a dimension or detail object onto the top axis of the table and also along the left axis of the data table.

Measures are added to the body of the table and display the values corresponding to the dimensions along the top and down the left side.

Crosstabs aren't limited to a single dimension object placed along the top and left side of the table. It's very common to include between two and five dimensions objects along the left side and two dimension objects across the top.

Figure 7.17 displays a crosstab with the [Sales Person] dimension across the top, and three dimension objects charted along the left of the table.

			Fischer	Galagers	Ishimoto	Nagata
France	East Germany	French Riviera	69,240			
France	East Japan	French Riviera			226,275	
France	Mid West	French Riviera		141,300		
France	West	French Riviera		105,095		
US	East Germany	Bahamas Beach	58,720			
US	East Germany	Hawaiian Club	94,950			
US	East Japan	Bahamas Beach			180,348	
US	East Japan	Hawaiian Club			238,260	
US	Mid West	Bahamas Beach		141,584		
US	Mid West	Hawaiian Club		158,710		
US	Ruhr	Bahamas Beach	10,976			
US	West	Bahamas Beach		66,200		
US	West	Hawaiian Club		130,250		
US	West Japan	Bahamas Beach				4,700

Figure 7.17 Crosstab Containing Four Dimension Objects and a Measure

Crosstabs can be easily modified to include many common features, such as the following:

► The addition of breaks for dimension objects

► Inclusion of column headings for dimension objects located on the left

► Aggregates added to the measure values displayed in the body of the table

► Subtotals added for break objects

Crosstab Aggregates

To add aggregates to a crosstab, click the measure object, and then click the insert sum shortcut icon in the reporting toolbar. A new column will be added to the right side of the table with row totals, and a new row will be added at the bottom of the table with column totals.

Formatted Crosstabs

Figure 7.18 shows a crosstab with a break added to the Country object, dimension column headings, background color, and text color revised for the vertical dimension objects, break totals, and a block total. The break object includes the break property of Center Values Across Break.

Country	Region	Fischer	Galagers	Ishimoto	Nagata
France	East Germany	69,240			
	East Japan			226,275	
	Mid West		141,300		
	West		105,095		
	France Totals:	*69,240*	*246,395*	*226,275*	
US	East Germany	153,670			
	East Japan			418,608	
	Mid West		300,294		
	Ruhr	10,976			
	West		196,450		
	West Japan				4,700
	US Totals:	*164,646*	*496,744*	*418,608*	*4,700*
	TOTALS:	**233,886**	**743,139**	**644,883**	**4,700**

Figure 7.18 Formatted Crosstab

Adding and Removing Objects to a Table

To remove an object from a crosstab or other table type, right-click on the object, and select Remove. You'll have the opportunity to choose Remove Column or Remove Row.

To add a result object to an existing table, drag an object from the Data tab of the Report Manager, and drop it onto the right edge, left edge, top, bottom, or center of an existing object in a table.

Layering Report Elements with the Order Function

On occasion, a need may arise to layer or slightly overlap tables, charts, and free-standing cells in a report. This can be achieved while viewing a report, editing an existing report, or creating a new report.

Layering objects helps report developers maximize the space available in a report and overlap the margins of multiple charts without interference.

To layer an object, begin by right-clicking on the report element to layer. Mouse over the Order selection to display the four ordering options after the menu of options appears:

- Bring to Front
- Send to Back

- Bring Forward

- Send Backward

The Bring Forward and Send Backward options move the selected report element either forward or backward by one position.

Figure 7.19 displays the right-click menu and the ordering options for the selected crosstab table.

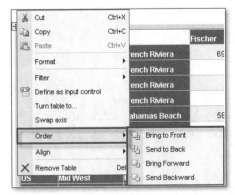

Figure 7.19 Order Setting for Layering Report Elements

7.4   Formatting Numbers and Dates

Numbers and date values can be formatted in a table to accommodate a wide variety of reporting requirements.

This section refers to creating or editing an existing Web Intelligence report using the Java Report Panel. To begin assigning a nondefault format to a column or row in a table, right-click on the row or column that you want to revise and click Format Number.

Figure 7.20 shows the right-click menu after selecting a measure object. Click Format Number to launch the Number Format dialog box. The default format type is Default unless the format type has been changed.

Figure 7.20   Right-Click on a Measure Object to Revise the Number Format

Measure objects and date dimensions can be formatted by selecting one of five different nondefault format types in the Number Format window:

▸ Number

▸ Currency

▸ Date/Time

▸ Boolean

▸ Custom

Figure 7.21 shows the Number Format window with the default type selected.

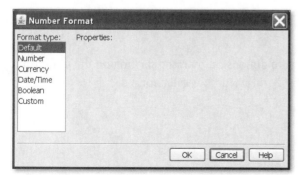

Figure 7.21   Number Format Window Used for Selecting the Format Type

7.4.1 Number Format

To change the number format, click Number in the Format Type list. By default, eight number properties will be listed in the Properties window.

The number Properties are available to provide the most commonly used measure formats.

Figure 7.22 shows the number format Properties for a selected measure object.

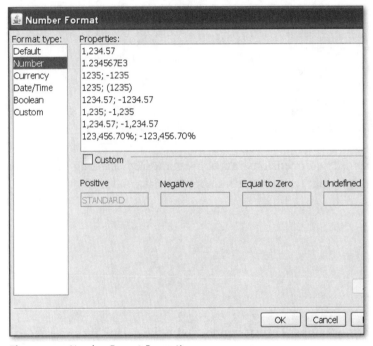

Figure 7.22 Number Format Properties

7.4.2 Date/Time Format

Modify the default format of a date dimension by right-clicking on the dimension object in a table and clicking the Format Number selection.

It might seem a little unusual to select Format Number when your intention is to format a date. But after Format Number has been selected, the Number Format window allows you to select the Date/Time format type.

Twelve frequently used date/time properties are available in the Properties window after selecting the Date/Time format type.

Figure 7.23 shows the Date/Time Properties available in the Number Format window. Click the property that matches your date or time formatting requirement, and click OK.

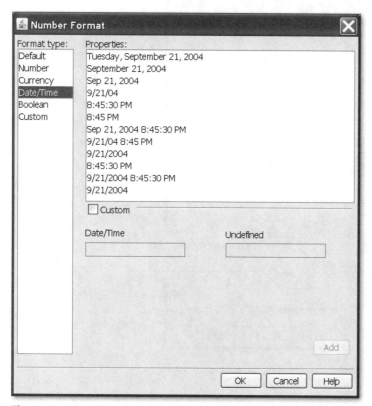

Figure 7.23 Date/Time Properties

Creating a Custom Property

If your date format requirement isn't shown in the Properties window, select the date/time property that most closely matches your requirement, and check the Custom checkbox.

By clicking the Custom checkbox, the Date/Time and Undefined text boxes become enabled. This provides you with the capability of modifying the selected property and then adding it to the set of Custom properties (see Figure 7.24).

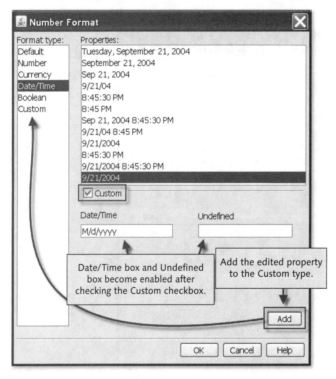

Figure 7.24 Customize and Add an Existing Date/Time Format Property

Table 7.1 provides a reference for characters that can be used to create custom number properties.

Character(s)	Display(s)	Example(s)
#	Represents a corresponding digit.	Use the #,##0 to convert '12345' to '12345'.
0	Includes leading digits if a value has less digits than listed in the format.	Using the format #0,000 converts the value of '123' to '0,123'.
,	Grouping separator.	'123456789' converts to '123,456,789' with the format #,##0.
.	Decimal separator.	Convert '12.34556756' to '12.34' with the format #,###.#0.
[%]%	Displays a percentage sign after the value. Multiplies the value by 100.	'.445' is displayed as '44.5%'.
%	Adds a % sign immediately after the value. Doesn't multiply by 100.	'.445' is displayed as '.445%'.
	Nonbreaking space.	'12345' is displayed as '12 345' when using the format # ##0.
a, b, c, 1, 2, 3, $, (etc.)	Alphanumeric characters.	The format '$#.#0' converts '123.45' to '$123.45'.
[Red], [Dark Red], [Green], [Yellow], [Gray], [White], [Blue], [Dark Blue], [Dark Green]	Changes the value to the specified color.	Use the format #,##0[Blue] to display positive values in blue. Use -#,##0[Red] to display negative values in red.

Table 7.1 Number Formatting Reference

Table 7.2 provides a reference to characters that can be used to modify and create custom date properties.

Character(s)	Display(s)	Example(s)
d	Number of the day of the month	The 12th is displayed as '12'; the 5th is displayed as '5'.
dd	Two-digit number of the day of the month	The 12th is displayed as '12'; the 5th is displayed as '05'.
ddd	Abbreviated name of the day with the first letter capitalized	Monday converts to 'Mon' when using the ddd format.
dddd	Full name of the day with the first letter capitalized	Monday is displayed as 'Monday' with the format dddd.
dddd dd	Day of the week followed by a space then the two-digit number of the day	Monday is converted to 'Monday 01' with the format dddd dd.
M	The number of the month with no leading zeros	January is converted to '1', October is converted to '10'.
MM	Two-digit month number	January is converted to '01', October is converted to '10'.
mmm	The name of the month abbreviated, first letter capitalized	January is converted to 'Jan'.
mmmm	The full name of the month	January is displayed when using the mmmm format.
yy	The last two digits of the year	'2010' is converted to '10'.
yyyy	All four digits of the year	'2010' is displayed as 2010 when using yyyy.

Table 7.2 Date Formatting Reference

Table 7.3 provides a reference to characters that can be used to modify and create custom properties with time values.

Character(s)	Display(s)	Example(s)
h:mm:ss a	Hour with no leading zeros; seconds and minutes with leading zeros; AM or PM is displayed after the time	'22:10:42' converts to '10:10:42 PM' with the format h:mm:ss a.
HH	Hour according to the 24-hour clock	'22:43' converts to 22 with the HH format.
hh	Hour according to the 12-hour clock	'22:43' converts to 10 with the hh format.
HH:mm	Hour and minutes with leading zeros	'9:04' converts to '09:04:00' with the format HH:mm.
HH:mm:ss	Hour, minutes, and seconds with leading zeros	'9:04:07' converts to '09:04:07' with the format HH:mm:ss.
mm:ss	Minutes and seconds with leading zeros	'9:04:07' converts to '04:07' with the format mm:ss.

Table 7.3 Time Formatting Reference

7.5   Formatting Table Values While Viewing Reports

Formatting can be applied to data tables while viewing a report in InfoView. Right-click on the column or row that you want to format, mouse over the format selection, and then choose from the following list of selections:

▶ Cell

▶ All Table Cells

▶ Table

▶ Report

Figure 7.25 shows the formatting choices available when right-clicking on a table column while viewing a report.

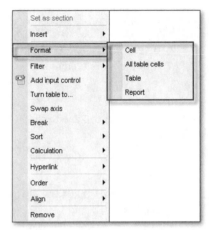

Figure 7.25 Formatting a Column in a Table While Viewing a Report

When right-clicking on a measure, select Cell as the object type to launch a window containing six modifiable tabs.

Figure 7.26 shows the Format Cell property window to modify a variety of cell attributes while viewing a report.

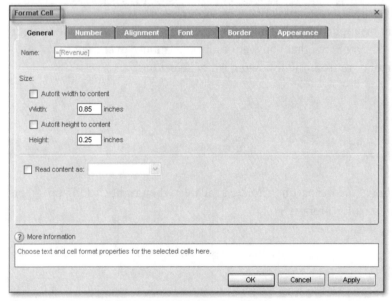

Figure 7.26 Format Cell Window While Viewing a Report

Formatting Properties When Viewing a Report

Report consumers can modify the following properties while viewing a report:

- General
  - Size
  - Read Content As: Hyperlink, HTML, Image URL
- Number Format
  - Only existing formats can be used. Custom formatting can't be added while viewing a report.
- Alignment
  - Three Horizontal Alignment types
  - Three Vertical Alignment types
  - Vertical and Horizontal Cell Padding (in inches)
  - Wrap Text option
- Font
  - Font Name
  - Font Style
  - Font Size
  - Font Color
  - Font Effects
- Border
  - Apply borders to one or more sides
- Appearance
  - Background Color
  - Background Pattern
  - Skin
  - Image from URL
  - Image from File

Note

If you right-click on a dimension object in a table and select Format Cell, only five tabs will be displayed in the Format Cell editing window. The Number tab won't appear when applying formatting to a dimension or detail object.

7.6 Summary

The development of customized reports is easier than ever with the features available in the Properties tab of the Report Manager in the Web Intelligence Report Panel. Use the Properties tab to modify every object included in a report. Apply additional formatting to your reports by changing the format of specific parts of a data table or specific sections of a report. Columns, rows, and table headings can all be formatted to include different settings.

The process of formatting reports isn't limited to the editing or creating phases of report development. Formatting can also be applied while viewing a report in InfoView. By right-clicking on a report section, table, or chart, an extensive set of formatting features become available to report writers or consumers.

Use breaks and sections to split or visually separate data in a report. Then check the option to include break footers to create the structure for adding break aggregates. Drag and drop measures to the break footer section to produce subtotals of the data in your reports.

Dates and numbers can be formatted to meet the needs of any business or reporting requirements. If a preferred format isn't available in the list of available format type properties, create a custom format for displaying number, currency, dates, or time values.

Chapter 8 describes how to use formulas and variables to produce values derived from data retrieved by result objects in the Query Panel.

Create complex calculations by using data objects retrieved from your database along with more than 145 built-in reporting functions and nearly 40 operators in the Formula Editor. By using formulas and variables to transform data into analytical information, you'll be able to make better business decisions.

8 Using Formulas and Variables

Formulas and variables are commonly used structures that allow you to create calculations using the data retrieved from a query. Variables are used to store the calculation syntax of a formula into reusable objects that are saved in Web Intelligence reporting documents.

Variables can be used in a report to simplify formula calculations and to display your data in a different way than was retrieved by your query from the database.

Variables can be used to insert If-Then-Else logic into a column or chart type reporting element, produce standard calculations, or create custom calculations — all within a single object that can be used throughout a reporting document.

The *formula toolbar* provides the capability to quickly revise the definition of an object in a toolbar similar to Microsoft Excel. The *Variable Editor* can be used to create complex and detailed formulas with the convenience of viewing all available data elements, functions, and operator types in the same window.

The next several sections will introduce you to the Variable Editor, explain the syntax used in creating formulas and variables, and provide examples to help you get the most out of the Variable Editor.

8.1   Formulas and Variables

The first step in creating a variable in a Web Intelligence report is to locate the editor tools needed to build the formula. The second step is to understand the Web Intelligence formula syntax of the statement that will become the variable.

We'll begin by editing an existing report and pointing out the Variable Editor located on the reporting toolbar in the Report Panel.

There are 17 shortcut icons in the reporting toolbar; the Variable Editor icon is located near the left edge in the reporting toolbar as shown in Figure 8.1.

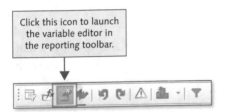

Figure 8.1   Accessing the Variable Editor – Editing/Creating Report

> **Note**
>
> The Variable Editor is only available in the Advanced Java editor and Web Intelligence Rich Client.

8.1.1   Creating Formulas

Formulas are calculations used in a variable or result object calculations that are included in data tables or charts.

Every object added to a table or chart in a report contains a formula definition, even if the object added comes directly from the Data tab in the report. Figure 8.2 shows the dimension object selected in a crosstab with the formula toolbar displayed. Notice the formula for the selected object is =[Service].

The formula or definition of a selected object in a table can be edited by changing the definition in the formula toolbar. An example of a revision that can be applied to the selected object is displayed in Figure 8.3. In Figure 8.3, the [Service] object was replaced with an IF-THEN statement by modifying the object definition in the formula toolbar.

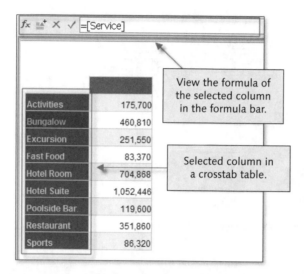

Figure 8.2 Formula of the Selected Object in a Crosstab Table

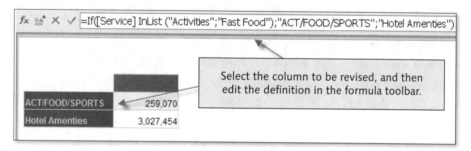

Figure 8.3 Revising the Formula of a Selected Object in a Crosstab

To modify a formula in a chart, follow these steps:

1. Click View Structure to view the report in structure mode.

2. Select the object in the chart to be modified.

3. Revise the statement in the formula toolbar as shown in Figure 8.4.

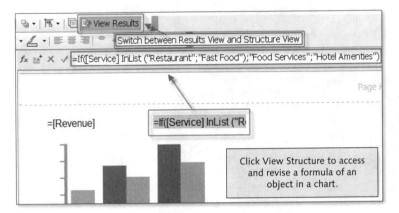

Figure 8.4 Revising the Formula of a Selected Object in a Crosstab

---

Tip

To create a more complex formula for an object in a table or chart, click the *Formula Editor* icon located to the left of the formula toolbar to launch the Formula Editor. This icon is shown in Figure 8.5 along with the three other commands to use when editing an object definition or formula:

▶ **Formula Editor:** Launch the Formula Editor by clicking the *fx* icon.

▶ **Create Variable:** Transform the existing formula into a reusable variable.

▶ **Cancel:** Cancel the revisions made to a calculation in the formula toolbar.

▶ **Validate:** Validate the formula by clicking the green check icon.

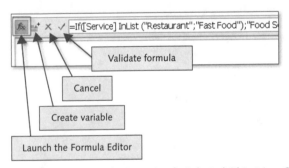

Figure 8.5 Revising the Formula of a Selected Object in a Crosstab

8.1.2   Exploring the Formula Editor

After launching the Formula Editor, you can graphically build or edit your formula by using elements from the three categories of objects or elements used in a formula.

Following are the three categories used in the Formula Editor for advanced formula creation:

▸ **Data:** All result objects and variables that exist within the document.

▸ **Functions:** More than 140 functions are available to be used in formulas.

▸ **Operators:** Nearly 40 operators are available to be used in formulas.

Figure 8.6 shows the Formula Editor window, a tool that allows you to create and edit formulas graphically, write free-hand syntax, or do a combination of both.

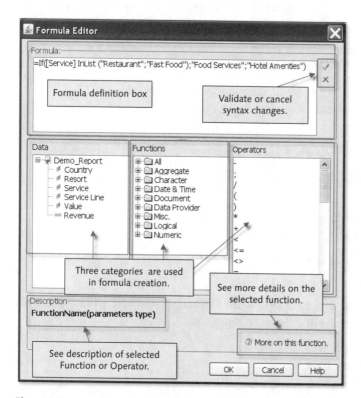

Figure 8.6   Formula Editor

The formula can be edited manually or modified by dragging and dropping objects from the three formula categories. Click the green checkmark to the right of the formula window to validate the syntax of the formula.

A brief description is provided at the bottom of the Formula Editor showing the proper syntax of the function selected. Click More On This Function when a function or operator is selected to launch a help page with detailed information.

Functions in the Formula Editor are presented in 8 different categories. A ninth category is also provided that contains all 140+ functions. These function groups are listed here:

- **Aggregate:** Contains 23 functions, including Average(), Min(), Max(), Sum(), Median(), Percentage(), RunningSum().
- **Character:** Contains 24 functions, including Char(), FormatNumber(), Concatenation(), LeftTrim(), Pos().
- **Date & Time:** Contains 17 functions, including CurrentDate(), CurrentTime(), LastDayOfMonth(), Year(), Month().
- **Document:** Contains 12 functions, including DocumentAuthor(), ReportFilter(), DrillFilters(), PromptSummary().
- **Data Provider:** Contains 16 functions, including UserResponse(), Connection(), UniverseName(), NumberOfRows().
- **Misc.:** Contains 24 functions, including If(), Else, Then, BlockName, CurrentUser(), ForceMerge(), NameOf().
- **Logical:** Contains 9 functions, including Even(), IsDate(), IsNull(), IsNumber(), IsString, IsTime(), Odd().
- **Numeric:** Contains 23 functions, including Abs(), Ceil(), Cos(), Floor(), Power(), Rank(), ToNumber().

Additional information and examples of the formulas listed here will be discussed in Section 8.2, Reporting Functions and Operators.

8.1.3 Creating Variables

Variables are formulas that have been converted into objects. By promoting a calculation or formula into a variable, you're creating a local result object that can be used throughout a reporting document.

To turn a formula into a variable, click the create variable icon located to the left of the formula toolbar as shown in Figure 8.7.

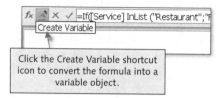

Click the Create Variable shortcut icon to convert the formula into a variable object.

Figure 8.7 Launch the Create Variable Window to Convert the Formula into a Variable

After you click the create variable shortcut icon, the Create Variable window opens to display the current variable definition.

The Create Variable window allows you to perform the following actions before clicking OK and creating the new variable:

▸ **Name:** Name the variable to a descriptive and user-friendly term or short phrase.

▸ **Qualification:** Select Dimension, Measure, or Detail as the variable qualification type.

▸ **Formula:** Review the syntax of the formula to be used in the variable.

Figure 8.8 shows the Create Variable window used to name and set the qualification of a new variable object being converted from a formula.

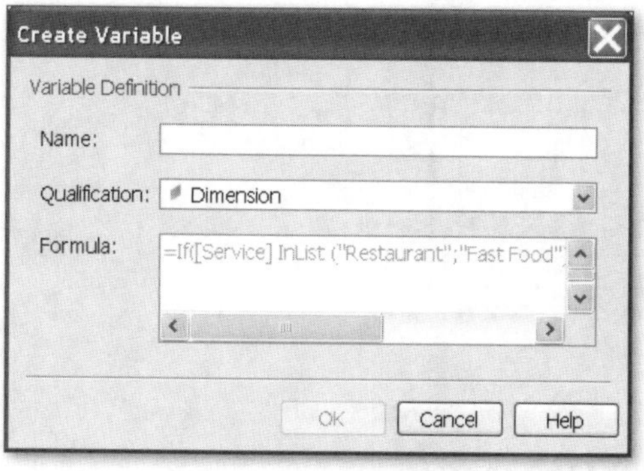

Figure 8.8 Create Variable Window

8.1.4 Using the Variable Editor

Locate and click on the variable editor shortcut icon in the reporting toolbar while editing or creating a report to launch the Variable Editor, which works almost identically to the Formula Editor discussed earlier in this chapter. The primary difference between the Formula Editor and the Variable Editor is that the Variable Editor contains a Variable Definition section. This section allows you to name variables being created and also to select the variable qualification.

Figure 8.9 shows the Variable Editor used for creating calculations in your report. Manually enter a formula, or use the items available in the Data, Functions, and Operators boxes to assist you with building a formula.

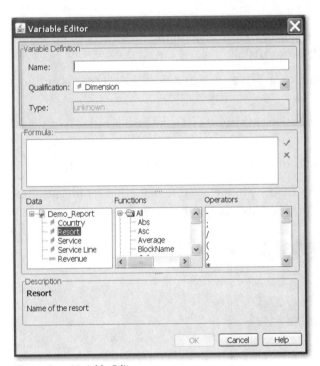

Figure 8.9 Variable Editor

8.2 Reporting Functions and Operators

Web Intelligence provides an extensive set of reporting functions that allow you to create very detailed and complex formulas for producing advanced reporting documents.

This section introduces you to the full list of reporting functions available for creating formulas and variables in the Report Panel. More than 140 reporting functions can be easily located within 8 functional categories.

The broad collection of operators used in formulas and variables are also described in the coming section. With more than 40 operators available, report developers can create precise formulas that leverage the full set of built-in reporting functions.

The eight function categories in the Formula and Variable Editors are listed here:

▶ **Aggregate:** Aggregate measures.

▶ **Character:** Functions that interact with character data.

▶ **Date & Time:** Functions created with date data.

▶ **Document:** Identify information about the current document.

▶ **Data Provider:** Functions available to identify information relating to the data provider in the current document.

▶ **Misc.:** Functions covering a variety of topics not included in the other categories.

▶ **Logical:** Logical Boolean functions.

▶ **Numeric:** Numerical related functions.

8.2.1 Aggregate Functions

Aggregate functions are used for returning numeric calculations for creating commonly used formulas with measure objects. They are described in Table 8.1.

Function	Description
`Average(measure;IncludeEmpty)`	Returns the average value of a measure
`Count(dimension|measure;IncludeEmpty;Distinct|All)`	Returns the number of values in a dimension or measure
`First(dimension|measure)`	Returns the first value in a data set
`Interpolation(measure;PointToPoint|Linear;NotOnBreak;Row|Column)`	Calculates empty measure values by interpolation
`Last(dimension|measure)`	Returns the last value in a dimension or measure

Table 8.1 Aggregate Functions

Function	Description
`Max(dimension|measure)`	Returns the largest value in a dimension or measure
`Median(measure)`	Returns the median (middle value) of a measure
`Min(dimension|measure)`	Returns the smallest value in a dimension or measure
`Mode(dimension|measure)`	Returns the most frequently occurring value in a data set
`Percentage(measure;break;row|col)`	Expresses a measure value as a percentage of its embedding context
`Percentile(measure;percentile)`	Returns the nth percentile of a measure
`Product(measure)`	Multiplies the values of a measure
`RunningAverage(measure;Row|Col;IncludeEmpty;reset_dims)`	Returns the running average of a measure
`RunningCount(dimension|measure;Row|Col;IncludeEmpty;reset_dims)`	Returns the running count of a number set
`RunningMax(dimension|measure;Row|Col;reset_dims)`	Returns the running maximum of a dimension or measure
`RunningMin(dimension|measure;Row|Col;reset_dims)`	Returns the running minimum of a dimension or measure
`RunningProduct(dimension|measure;Row|Col;reset_dims)`	Returns the running product of a measure
`RunningSum(dimension|measure;Row|Col;reset_dims)`	Returns the running sum of a measure
`StdDev(measure)`	Returns the standard deviation of a measure
`StdDevP(measure)`	Returns the population standard deviation of a measure
`Sum(measure)`	Returns the sum of a measure
`Var(measure)`	Returns the variance of a measure
`VarP(measure)`	Returns the population variance of a measure

Table 8.1 Aggregate Functions (Cont.)

8.2.2 Character Functions

Character functions are primarily used for performing tasks that manipulate dimension objects (see Table 8.2).

Function	Description
`Asc(string)`	Returns the ASCII value of a character
`Char(ascii_code)`	Returns the character associated with an ASCII code
`Concatenation(first_string;second_string)`	Concatenates (joins) two character strings
`Fill(repeating_string;num_repeats)`	Builds a string by repeating a string *n* times
`FormatDate(date;format_string)`	Formats a date according to a specified format
`FormatNumber(number;format_string)`	Formats a number according to a specified format
`HTMLEncode(html)`	Applies HTML encoding rules to a string
`InitCap(string)`	Capitalizes the first letter of a string
`Left(string;num_chars)`	Returns the leftmost characters of a string
`LeftPad(padded_string;length;left_string)`	Pads a string on its left with another string
`LeftTrim(trimmed_string)`	Trims the leading spaces from a string
`Length(string)`	Returns the number of characters in a string
`Lower(string)`	Converts a string to lowercase
`Match(string;pattern)`	Determines whether a string matches a pattern
`Pos(string;pattern)`	Returns the starting position of a text pattern in a string
`Replace(replace_in;replaced_string;replace_with)`	Replaces part of a string with another string
`Right(string;num_chars)`	Returns the rightmost characters of a string

Table 8.2 Character Functions

Function	Description
`RightPad(padded_string;length;right_string)`	Pads a string on its right with another string
`RightTrim(trimmed_string)`	Trims the trailing spaces from a string
`Substr(string;start;length)`	Returns part of a string
`Trim(trimmed_string)`	Trims the leading and trailing spaces from a string
`Upper(string)`	Converts a string to uppercase
`URLEncode(html)`	Applies URL encoding rules to a string
`WordCap(string)`	Capitalizes the first letter of all of the words in a string

Table 8.2 Character Functions (Cont.)

8.2.3 Date & Time Functions

Date & Time functions provide developers with the capability of extracting date elements from date objects and calculating date differences (see Table 8.3).

Function	Description
`CurrentDate()`	Returns the current date formatted according to the regional settings
`CurrentTime()`	Returns the current time formatted according to the regional settings
`DayName(date)`	Returns the day name in a date
`DayNumberOfMonth(date)`	Returns the day number in a month
`DayNumberOfWeek(date)`	Returns the day number in a week
`DayNumberOfYear(date)`	Returns the day number in a year
`DaysBetween(first_date;last_date)`	Returns the number of days between two dates
`LastDayOfMonth(date)`	Returns the date of the last day in a month
`LastDayOfWeek(date)`	Returns the date of the last day in a week
`Month(date)`	Returns the month name in a date

Table 8.3 Date and Time Functions

Function	Description
MonthNumberOfYear(date)	Returns the month number in a date
MonthsBetween(first_date;last_date)	Returns the number of months between two dates
Quarter(date)	Returns the quarter number in a date
RelativeDate(start_date;num_days)	Returns a date relative to another date
ToDate(date_string;format)	Returns a character string formatted according to a date format
Week(date)	Returns the week number in the year
Year(date)	Returns the year in a date

Table 8.3 Date and Time Functions (Cont.)

8.2.4   Document Functions

Document functions provide the capability of identifying various attributes of a reporting document (see Table 8.4).

Function	Description
DocumentAuthor()	Returns the InfoView logon of the document creator
DocmentCreationDate()	Returns the date on which a document was created
DocumentCreationTime()	Returns the time when a document was created
DocumentDate()	Returns the date on which a document was last saved
DocumentName()	Returns the document name
DocumentPartiallyRefreshed()	Determines whether a document is partially refreshed
DocumentTime()	Returns the time when a document was last saved
DrillFilters(object|separator)	Returns the drill filters applied to a document or object in drill mode
PromptSummary()	Returns the prompt text and user response of all prompts in a document

Table 8.4 Document Functions

Function	Description
QuerySummary(query_name)	Returns information about the queries in a document
ReportFilter(object)	Returns the report filters applied to an object or report
ReportFilterSummary(report_name)	Returns a summary of the report filters in a document or report

Table 8.4 Document Functions (Cont.)

8.2.5 Data Provider Functions

Data Provider functions allow formulas to be created that retrieve various details about the query, retrieved result set, and universe used to build the query (see Table 8.5).

Function	Description
Connection([query_name])	Returns the parameters of the database connection used by a data provider
DataProvider(object)	Returns the name of the data provider containing a report object
DataProviderKeyDate([query_name])	Returns the keydate of a data provider
DataProviderKeyDateCaption([query_name])	Returns the keydate caption of a data provider
DataProviderSQL([query_name])	Returns the SQL generated by a data provider
DataProviderType([query_name])	Returns the type of a data provider
IsPromptAnswered([query_name];prompt_string)	Determines whether a prompt has been answered
LastExecutionDate([query_name])	Returns the date on which a data provider was last refreshed
LastExecutionDuration([query_name])	Returns the time in seconds taken by the last refresh of a data provider
LastExecutionTime([query_name])	Returns the time at which a data provider was last refreshed

Table 8.5 Data Provider Functions

Function	Description
`NumberOfDataProviders()`	Returns the number of data providers in a report
`NumberOfRows([query_name])`	Returns the number of rows in a data provider
`RefValueDate()`	Returns the date of the reference data used for data tracking
`RefValueUserResponse([query_ name];prompt_string;index)`	Returns the response to a prompt when the reference data was the current data
`UniverseName([query_name])`	Returns the name of the universe on which a data provider is based
`UserResponse([query_name];prompt_ string;index)`	Returns the response to a prompt

Table 8.5 Data Provider Functions (Cont.)

8.2.6 Misc. Functions

A wide variety of functions are included in the Misc. category that returns details about components and features of a report (see Table 8.6).

Function	Description
`BlockName()`	Returns the block name
`ColumnNumber()`	Returns the column number
`CurrentUser()`	Returns the InfoView login of the current user
`ForceMerge(measure)`	Includes synchronized dimensions in measure calculations when the dimensions aren't in the measure's calculation context
`GetContentLocale()`	Returns the locale of the data contained in the document (the Document Locale)
`GetDominantPreferredViewing Locale()`	Returns the dominant locale in the user's Preferred Viewing Locale group

Table 8.6 Misc. Functions

Function	Description
GetLocale()	Returns the user's locale used to format the Web Intelligence interface (the Product Locale)
GetLocalized(string;comment)	Returns a string localized according to the user's Preferred Viewing Locale
GetPreferredViewingLocale()	Returns the user's preferred locale for viewing document data (the Preferred Viewing Locale)
If...Then...Else: If bool_value Then true_value [Else false_value]	Returns a value based on whether an expression is true or false
If(boolean_value;true_value;false_value)	Returns a value based on whether an expression is true or false
LineNumber()	Returns the line number in a table
NameOf(object)	Returns the name of an object
NoFilter(object;all|drill)	Ignores filters when calculating a value
NumberOfPages()	Returns the number of pages in a report
Page()	Returns the current page number in a report
Previous(dimension|measure|Self;reset_dims;offset;NoNull)	Returns a previous value of an object
RefValue(object)	Returns the reference value of a report object when data tracking is activated
RelativeValue(measure|detail;slicing_dims;offset)	Returns previous or subsequent values of an object
ReportName()	Returns the name of a report
RowIndex()	Returns the number of a row
UniqueNameOf(object)	Returns the unique name of an object

Table 8.6 Misc. Functions (Cont.)

8.2.7 Logical Functions

Logical functions are used to determine whether an object is true or false by returning a 1 or 0 (see Table 8.7).

Function	Description
Even(number)	Determines whether a number is even
IsDate(object)	Determines whether a value is a date
IsError(object)	Determines whether an object returns an error
IsLogical(object)	Determines whether a value is Boolean
IsNull(object)	Determines whether a value is null
IsNumber(object)	Determines whether a value is a number
IsString(object)	Determines whether a value is a string
IsTime(object)	Determines whether a variable is a time variable
Odd(number)	Determines whether a number is odd

Table 8.7 Logical Functions

8.2.8 Numeric Functions

Numeric functions allow values to be manipulated and measured in a variety of ways (see Table 8.8).

Function	Description
Abs(number)	Returns the absolute value of a number
Ceil(number)	Returns a number rounded up to the nearest integer
Cos(angle)	Returns the cosine of an angle
EuroConvertFrom(euro_amount;curr_code;round_level)	Converts a euro amount to another currency
EuroConvertTo(noneuro_amount;curr_code;round_level)	Converts an amount to euros

Table 8.8 Numeric Functions

Function	Description
EuroFromRoundError(euro_ amount;curr_code;round_level)	Returns the rounding error in a conversion from euros
EuroToRoundError(noneuro_ amount;curr_code;round_level)	Returns the rounding error in a conversion to euros
Exp(power)	Returns an exponential (e raised to a power)
Fact(number)	Returns the factorial of a number
Floor(number)	Returns a number rounded down to the nearest integer
Ln(number)	Returns the natural logarithm of a number
Log(number;base)	Returns the logarithm of a number in a specified base
Log10(number)	Returns the base 10 logarithm of a number
Mod(dividend;divisor)	Returns the remainder from the division of two numbers
Power(number;power)	Returns a number raised to a power
Rank(measure;ranking_ dims;Top|Bottom;reset_dims)	Ranks a measure by dimensions
Round(number;round_level)	Rounds a number
Sign(number)	Returns the sign of a number
Sin(angle)	Returns the sine of an angle
Sqrt(number)	Returns the square root of a number
Tan(angle)	Returns the tangent of an angle
ToNumber(string)	Returns a string as a number
Truncate(number;truncate_level)	Truncates a number

Table 8.8 Numeric Functions (Cont.)

8.2.9 Operators

Operators are symbols used in formulas and variables to indicate the type of operation you want to perform. More than 35 operators are available for creating formulas in Web Intelligence reporting functions.

Formulas can contain several different combinations of operators, which are used to solve a variety of business problems.

Report operators are grouped into the following six categories.

- Mathematical
- Conditional
- Logical
- Function Specific
- Extended Syntax Operators
- Extended Syntax Keywords

The operators are broken into groups and described in Table 8.9 through Table 8.14.

Operator	Description
-	Subtraction
+	Addition
*	Multiplication
/	Division

Table 8.9 Mathematical Operators

Operator	Description
=	Equal to
>	Greater than
<	Less than
>=	Greater than or equal to
<=	Less than or equal to
<>	Not equal to

Table 8.10 Conditional Operators

Operator	Description
And	Links Boolean values, commonly used in IF statements
Or	Links Boolean values, commonly used in IF statements
Not	Returns the opposite of a Boolean value
Between	Determines if a value is between two values
InList	Determines if a value is within a list of values

Table 8.11 Logical Operators

Operator	Description
All	Used as an optional parameter in many functions to calculate All or Distinct values
Drill	Used with the NoFilter function to ignore report filters
Bottom	Ranks values in ascending order
Break	Forces the Percentage function to calculate within table breaks
Col	Optionally used to set the calculation direction in the following functions: Percentage, RunningAverage, RunningCount, RunningMax, RunningMin, RunningProduct, RunningSum
Distinct	Used as an optional parameter in many functions to calculate Distinct or All values
IncludeEmpty	Optionally used to tell an aggregate function to include empty values
Index	Used by the UserResponse and RefValueUserResponse functions to return the database primary key of a prompt response
Linear	Used by the Interpolation function to use linear regression
NoNull	Tells the Previous function to ignore null values
NotOnBreak	Optionally used by the Interpolation function to ignore section and block breaks
PointToPoint	Used by the Interpolation function to use point-to-point to account for missing values
Row	Optionally used to set the calculation direction in the following functions: Percentage, RunningAverage, RunningCount, RunningMax, RunningMin, RunningProduct, RunningSum

Table 8.12 Function Specific Operators

Operator	Description
Self	Refers the `Previous` function to the previous cell when it doesn't contain a report object
Top	Ranks values in descending order
Where	Restricts the data to calculate a measure

Table 8.12 Function Specific Operators (Cont.)

Operator	Description
In	Specifies an explicit list of dimensions to use in the context
ForAll	Removes dimensions from the default context
ForEach	Adds dimensions to the default

Table 8.13 Extended Syntax Operators

Operator	Description
Block	Refers to data within an entire block, ignores breaks, respects filters: `Sum([Revenue]) In Block`
Body	Displays the value of the data presented in a block and can be used in a footer, header, or body: `Sum([Revenue]) In Body`
Break	Calculates the total for the dimension used in a break: `Sum([Revenue] In Break`
Report	Displays all report data: `Sum([Revenue]) In Report`
Section	Calculates the section total of a measure when section has been set in a report: `Sum([Revenue]) in Section`

Table 8.14 Extended Syntax Keywords

8.3   Formula Syntax

The first step in writing formulas and creating variables in a report is to understand the Web Intelligence formula syntax. A few basic rules must be followed to create a valid formula. After you understand how to apply these basic rules, the task of writing a formula will no longer be an issue. You can then focus your efforts on writing formulas and building analytical Web Intelligence reports that provide the greatest value to the client.

8.3.1 Primary Formula Syntax Rules

The primary rules are listed here:

▸ Each formula must begin with the equals symbol (=).

▸ Data objects used in a formula must be encapsulated by brackets ([ ]).

▸ Use a semicolon to represent Else in an IF-THEN-ELSE statement: (;).

▸ Use a semicolon to represent Then in an IF-THEN-ELSE statement (;).

▸ Every statement with an open parenthesis must also include a closing parenthesis.

▸ Click the green checkmark button to validate the syntax of the formula or variable.

▸ Change the qualification type when creating a measure or detail variable.

▸ Assign a commonly used business term or phrase with the proper naming convention as the variable name.

8.3.2 If – Then – Else Syntax

Figure 8.10 shows a simple formula entered into the Variable Editor window. Several key areas of the formula are labeled in the screenshot. This includes three of the most important rules:

1. Begin a formula with the equals symbol.

2. Use a semicolon for THEN.

3. Use a semicolon for ELSE.

The formula in Figure 8.10 is listed as

```
=If([Service] InList ("Activities";"Bungalow";"Fast
Food";"Excursion";"Poolside Bar");[Revenue];"")
```

This statement is translated in English to the following:

If the Service data object contains values of Activities, Bungalow, Fast Food, Excursion, or Poolside Bar, then return the Revenue measure. If the Service data object has values other than the five items previously listed, then return nothing.

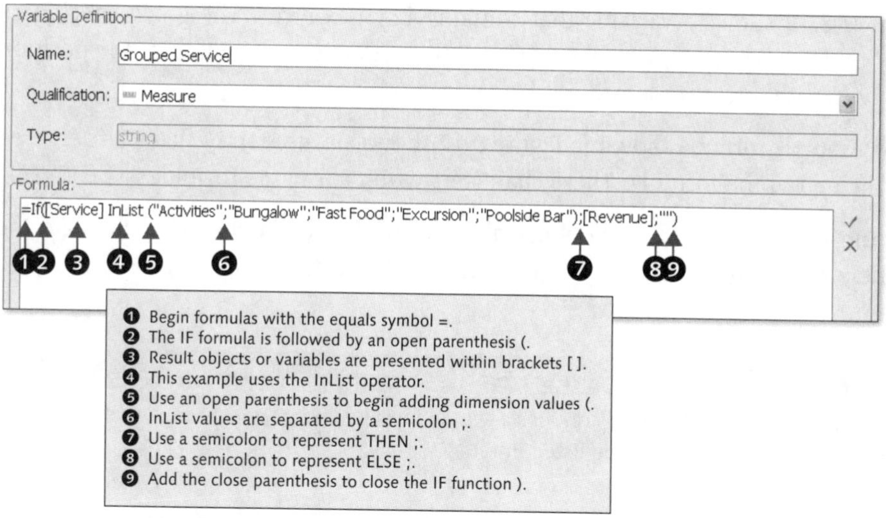

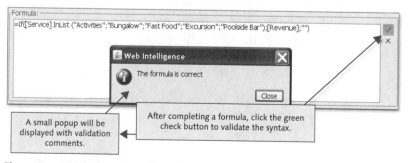

Figure 8.10   Variable Syntax

8.3.3   Saving a Variable

Before clicking OK in the Variable Editor and saving a formula, click the green checkmark button located to the right of the formula. This button validates the syntax in the formula.

If the syntax is valid, a small popup will appear that reads, "The formula is correct" as shown in Figure 8.11. In the figure, the green checkmark button is pressed, and the formula is validated. A small popup lets the developer know that the syntax is correct.

Click Close to close the validation message. Finish editing or creating the variable by clicking OK at the bottom of the Variable Editor.

Figure 8.11   Validating a Formula with the Correct Syntax

Figure 8.12 shows a variable that contains a syntax error. The green checkmark button becomes a very useful tool to help report developers pinpoint the position of syntactical errors in a formula.

The example formula shown in Figure 8.12 shows a couple stray characters entered at the end of the formula. These characters won't allow the formula to be saved.

In the screenshot, the green checkmark button has been clicked to validate the syntax of the formula. A message is displayed that identifies the position of the error.

> **Tip**
>
> If a formula is validated that contains a syntax error, the error will be highlighted in yellow, and the character will be listed in red.

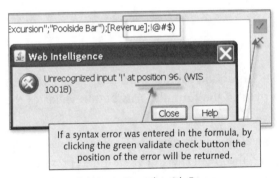

Figure 8.12 Validating a Formula with Errors

8.3.4 Modifying a Variable

When a variable is created in a Web Intelligence report, the new object will be added to the Data tab of the Report Manager. The variable will appear along with all of the existing result objects returned from the query. Figure 8.13 shows the Grouped Service variable created in the previous section.

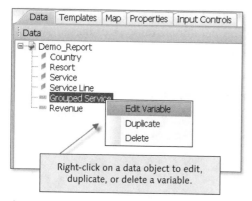

Figure 8.13 Right-Click on a Variable to Edit, Duplicate, or Delete

To modify a variable, right-click on the object, and select Edit Variable. This will relaunch the Variable Editor, allowing you to modify the formula, name, or qualification of the object.

> **Tip**
>
> If you need to create a new variable with a formula very similar to an existing one, right-click on the existing variable, and select Duplicate. This will create an exact copy of a variable and add (1) to the end of the name. Right-click on the newly created variable to edit the formula and variable name.

8.4   Summary

Functions and variables allow report developers to provide valuable analytical insight by using business data to create calculations. Data retrieved by a Web Intelligence query can be used in combination with over 140 functions and almost 40 operators to create complex and precise formulas.

Formulas can be converted into variables, used throughout an entire reporting document, and saved within a document to provide ongoing and maintenance-free analysis.

Use result objects returned by your queries to create functions that aggregate data, extract information from dates, or dissect string values by using character functions.

Formulas and variables can be created to calculate data at an even more detailed level of analysis by using a unique set of operators. Examples of these operators include filtering values with the `Where` operator, or aggregating values by block, section, or report.

Chapter 9 discusses the role of the scope of analysis feature in a Web Intelligence reporting document and provides details on performing drilling in a report.

Drill functionality puts the power of analysis into the end users' hands by enabling them to filter down on report tables and charts by simply clicking the mouse. New features allow not only drill down, but drill up, drill by, and drill upon bars and data points in a chart, making SAP BusinessObjects Web Intelligence XI 3.x a powerful end user reporting tool.

9 Scope of Analysis and Drilling Down

Drilling down on a report gives you the ability to see levels of data beyond your original query. For instance, you receive a monthly report summarizing Sales Revenue by State. Upon review of the report, you discover that sales revenue seems high for Massachusetts in the year 2006 (see Figure 9.1). To explore this anomaly further, it would normally require running numerous additional detailed reports or even requesting a customized query to get your desired result to determine the root cause of the anomaly.

	Sales Revenue by State					
	California	Colorado	DC	Florida	Illinois	Massachusetts
2004	$1,704,211	$448,302	$693,211	$405,985	$737,914	$238,819
2005	$2,782,680	$768,389	$1,215,158	$661,250	$1,150,659	$157,719
2006	$2,992,679	$843,584	$1,053,581	$811,924	$1,134,085	$887,169
Totals:	$7,479,569	$2,060,275	$2,961,950	$1,879,158	$3,022,658	$1,283,707

Figure 9.1 Sales Revenue for Massachusetts Is High for the Year 2006

This process means that a report request is made and another query generated producing another report showing sales revenue results at a monthly level by state. If this again did not answer your questions, then again another request would need to be made to produce another query to further drill down the data to a lower level of, perhaps, City or Week to pinpoint the reason for the poor revenue results. This process can become long and cumbersome.

A report developer can avoid these extra steps and put the ownership back into your hands as an end user by setting the scope of analysis and enabling drill on a report (see Figure 9.2).

	Sales Revenue by State					
	California	Colorado	DC	Florida	Illinois	Massachusetts
2004	$1,704,211	$448,302	$693,211	$405,985	$737,914	$238,819
2005	$2,782,680	$768,389	$1,215,158	$661,250	$1,150,659	$157,719
2006	$2,992,679	$843,584	$1,053,581	$811,924	$1,134,085	$887,169
Totals:	$7,479,569	$2,060,275	$2,961,950	$1,879,158	$3,022,658	$1,283,707

Figure 9.2 Enable Drill on the Table to Explore the Data Further

9.1 Setting the Scope of Analysis in the Query Panel

The first step to enabling drill is to set the *scope of analysis* in the Query Panel. This tells Web Intelligence to return additional data beyond the results specified in the Result Objects pane. The additional data returned doesn't appear in the initial report displayed upon execution of the query, but the objects returned can be seen in the Data pane of the report view (see Figure 9.3).

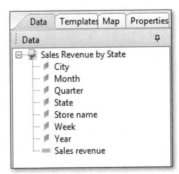

Figure 9.3 Data Tab in the Report Manager Shows Result Objects and Scope of Analysis Objects

Scope of analysis is the defined drill path for a data element in the universe and is only applicable for dimension objects. The default scope of analysis for a universe object is defined by the order of the objects within a class. For example, in the Store class, the objects are ordered from top to bottom as State, City, Store Name, so the hierarchy for the scope of analysis would be by State, City, and Store Name as shown in Figure 9.4. The universe designer can also overwrite these defaults and define custom hierarchies in the universe.

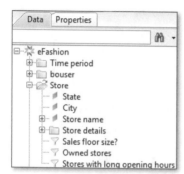

Figure 9.4 Default Object Hierarchy Defined by Order or Objects in the Universe

To view the defined hierarchies in the universe, go to the Query View in a Web Intelligence report. Select the Data tab, and then select the Display by Hierarchies radio button (see Figure 9.5).

From this view, the report developer can see the defined hierarchies in the universe.

To set the scope of analysis, you must first define the result objects for the query in the Edit Query View. After creating the initial query by adding result objects into the Result Object pane and adding any filters into the Query Filters pane, select the show/hide scope of analysis button on the query toolbar (see Figure 9.6). This will display the Scope of Analysis pane as shown in Figure 9.7.

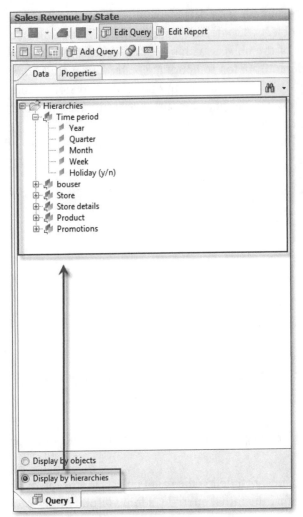

Figure 9.5 Display by Hierarchies Button in Edit Query View

Figure 9.6 Show/Hide Scope of Analysis Button on Edit Query View Menu Bar

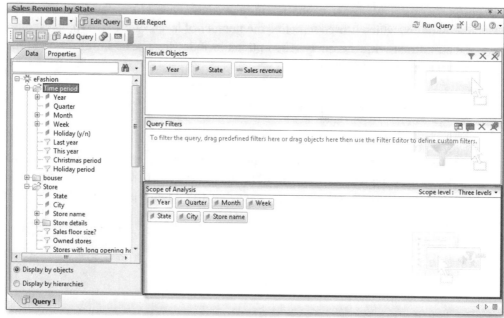

Figure 9.7 Scope of Analysis Pane

You'll notice that each of the dimension objects from your query appears in this pane. The additional objects shown after the result objects are the objects included in the hierarchy set up in the universe. Figure 9.7 shows a hierarchy for State that includes State, City, and Store Name. It also shows a hierarchy for Year that includes Year, Quarter, Month, and Week. These are the applicable levels of drill down that can be enabled for each dimension object included in the Result Objects pane shown in Figure 9.8.

Figure 9.8 Scope Level Options

In the top-right corner of the Scope of Analysis pane is a Scope level list drop-down box, which is used to define the number of levels of drill down that should be returned with the query. The options include None, One Level, Two Levels, Three Levels, and Custom.

9.1.1 Scope Level Options

The scope level options are described next:

▶ **None:** If None is selected, then only the result objects shown in the Result Objects pane will be returned in the query results. There will be no additional objects returned with the query to enable drill down (see Figure 9.9).

Figure 9.9 Scope Level: None

▶ **One Level:** If One Level is selected, then only one level of drill down will be enabled (see Figure 9.10). This will return the dimension object from the Result Objects pane as well as the next one dimension object listed in the scope of analysis. For the result object of State, the query would return State and City.

Figure 9.10 Scope Level: One Level

▶ **Two Levels:** If Two Levels is selected, then two levels of drill down will be enabled (see Figure 9.11). This will return the dimension object from the Result Objects pane as well as the next two dimension objects listed in the scope of analysis. For the result object of STATE, the query would return STATE, CITY, and STORE NAME.

Figure 9.11   Scope Level: Two Levels

▶ **Three Levels:** If Three Levels is selected, then three levels of drill down will be enabled (see Figure 9.12). This will return the dimension object from the Result Objects pane as well as the next three dimension objects listed in the scope of analysis. For the result object of YEAR, the query would return YEAR, QUARTER, MONTH, and WEEK.

For the STATE object, only two levels of hierarchy exist in the universe, therefore, only two will show in the Scope of Analysis pane.

Figure 9.12   Scope Level: Three Levels

▶ **Custom:** If Custom is selected, then all objects added manually into the Scope of Analysis pane as well as those objects in the Result Objects pane are returned.

This option is only available in the Java Report Panel and in Web Intelligence Rich Client.

In Figure 9.13, the custom scope of analysis is defined without Quarter. Therefore, when you drill down on the report, the Year objects will drill down directly to Month, skipping the Quarter level.

This is useful if certain levels of drill aren't applicable for reporting on certain business questions.

Figure 9.13 Scope Level: Custom

> **Note**
>
> It's important to remember when setting the scope of analysis that each new level of drill down increases the size of the microcube returned with the query results. The larger the microcube, the longer it will take to run the report and the larger the file size maintained in the repository.

While scope of analysis can add value to a report, it can also be a hindrance if end users must wait an unusual amount of time for their report data to populate. Report developers should gather appropriate reporting requirements to determine if drill-down capability would be a value addition for a report or whether this functionality should not be enabled. If end users will only be viewing one level of drill down, then it's important to explore the idea of creating two reports or two report tabs to achieve this result. The appropriate choice depends on each individual report based on factors such as end user requirements, data being returned, purpose of the report, and output medium.

9.2   Drill-Down Setup in the Report Panel

After the scope of analysis has been set up in the Edit Query View, the query results will return the additional data required to perform drill analysis. After the data is available at the report level, the user can drill within the report against the report's microcube. No further queries are necessary to be run against the database to gather more information as long as drill remains within the defined scope.

9.2.1   Enabling Drill

You can enable drill at the report level either as the report designer in the Web Intelligence Edit Report View or as the end user in the InfoView viewer toolbar.

As the Report Designer

The first step to enabling drill functionality in the Report Panel is to ensure you're in drill mode. In Web Intelligence, go to Edit Report View on the report that you want to drill on. Select the Drill button on the Web Intelligence toolbar as shown in Figure 9.14.

Figure 9.14   Drill Button on the Web Intelligence Toolbar

When you select the Drill button, a drill icon appears on the Report tab. If your Web Intelligence options have been set up in InfoView to open a new report for drilling, then a duplicate report will open in a new window. We'll discuss how to personalize your drill settings later in this chapter.

As the End User

If drill was not enabled by the report developer, the end user can enable drill down on a report in InfoView from the InfoView viewer toolbar. After you have selected to view a report in InfoView, the Drill button appears on the toolbar on the far right as shown in Figure 9.15. When the user selects to enable Drill, the user's Web Intelligence preferences specify whether the report will open in a new window or if drill will be enabled on the report in the current window.

Figure 9.15 Drill Button on InfoView Viewer Toolbar

9.2.2 Drill Toolbar

The drill toolbar is enabled at the top of our report to display the drill path (see Figure 9.16). Figure 9.17 shows the drill toolbar display when a user has drilled on Year and Lines on a table in the report. The drill toolbar shows what path has been taken. These dropdown boxes can also be used to drill back up in the hierarchy by selecting a different option from the list box.

The drill toolbar shows the filters applied to your report. You can also use the drill toolbar to filter additional data elements within your report by dragging the object from the Data tab to the drill toolbar. This functionality works like a report level filter and filters all elements in the report.

Figure 9.16 Show/Hide Drill Toolbar in InfoView

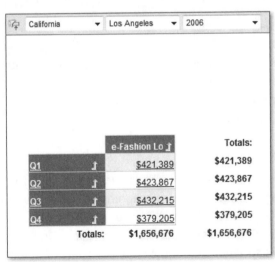

Figure 9.17 Drill Toolbar Showing State and Year Drill Filters

9.2.3   Drilling on Dimensions

When Web Intelligence projects the data elements of a query into the report, the measures are calculated based on the dimension objects placed in the same table or chart.

Figure 9.18 shows a table where Sales Revenue has been calculated by State and Store Name because the STATE and STORE NAME objects appear in the table with the measure. This concept is called *calculation context*. State and Store Name is the context for this calculation.

State	Store name	Sales revenue
California	e-Fashion Los Angeles	$4,220,929
California	e-Fashion San Francisco	$3,258,641
Colorado	e-Fashion Colorado Springs	$2,060,275
DC	e-Fashion Washington Tolbooth	$2,961,950
Florida	e-Fashion Miami Sundance	$1,879,159
Illinois	e-Fashion Chicago 33rd	$3,022,658
Massachusetts	e-Fashion Boston Newbury	$1,283,707
New York	e-Fashion New York 5th	$2,960,366
New York	e-Fashion New York Magnolia	$4,621,854
Texas	e-Fashion Austin	$2,699,673
Texas	e-Fashion Dallas	$1,970,034
Texas	e-Fashion Houston	$2,303,183
Texas	e-Fashion Houston Leighton	$3,144,774

Figure 9.18   Table with Sales Revenue Calculated by State and Store Name

Figure 9.19 shows what happens to the calculation of a measure object when the STORE NAME dimension object is removed from the table. Now the measure recalculates and is displayed for each State.

The measure recalculates automatically based on the dimension objects contained within the table with it.

State	Sales revenue
California	$7,479,569
Colorado	$2,060,275
DC	$2,961,950
Florida	$1,879,159
Illinois	$3,022,658
Massachusetts	$1,283,707
New York	$7,582,221
Texas	$10,117,664

Figure 9.19 Table Including State and Sales Revenue Objects

This same concept exists when performing a drill on a report table. As the user drills on a dimension object in a report table or chart, the measure or measures included in that table or chart are recalculated.

There are three forms of drill available on dimension objects, including drill down, drill up, and drill by. The concept of calculation context applies to each method.

Drill Down

After a report has been opened in drill mode, the objects in the tables appear with an underline. This shows you which objects are available for drill. To drill down on a dimension object, click on the object name in the table. You'll notice the drill toolbar appears showing the dimension object that has been filtered. You can continue to drill down to the lowest level of grain that was set up in your scope of analysis.

Drill down can be completed by selecting the underlined data element in the report as shown in Figure 9.20 or by right-clicking on the data element and selecting the Drill Down option from the menu as shown in Figure 9.21.

	Los Angeles	San Francisco
2004	$982,637	$721,574
2005	$1,581,616	$1,201,064
2006	$1,656,676	$1,336,003
Totals:	$4,220,929	$3,258,641

Select to drill down.
Drill down to Quarter

Figure 9.20 Select Underlined Data Element in Report to Drill-Down to Next Level in Hierarchy

Figure 9.21 Right-Click and Select Drill Down to Drill Down on a Data Element

To drill beyond the objects that were set up in the scope of analysis, the user must extend the scope of analysis. The right to extend a scope of analysis is set up by your SAP BusinessObjects administrator, so not all users will retain this right.

If you're enabled to extend the scope of analysis, then you'll be given the option to select filters when drilling outside of the scope of analysis.

If your Preferences have been set to prompt before extending the scope of analysis, then a dialog box will appear similar to that shown in Figure 9.22, allowing you to select what filters to apply to the next drill level.

In this example, the scope of analysis only included through Month, so Week is selected to include in further analysis. You can also checkmark the box to include Holiday at this point if you know that you'll want to include another level of drill as well.

Further discussion regarding setting your drill preferences is included in Section 9.5, User Settings for Drill Down, of this chapter.

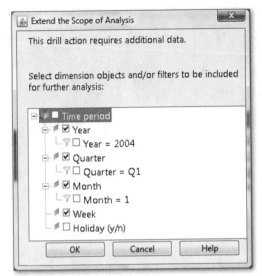

Figure 9.22 Dialog Box to Extend the Scope of Analysis

If you select to drill on Year for a scope of analysis of two levels, then you would have to extend the scope of analysis when you reach the dimension of Month.

The table results of using the extend scope of analysis option in this example are shown in Figure 9.23.

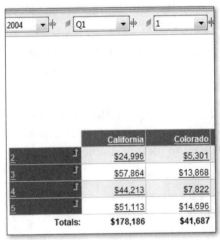

Figure 9.23 Table Results for Extended Scope of Analysis to Include Week

Drill Up

The Drill Up option enables the user to drill from a lower level of aggregation to a higher level of aggregation. After drilling down to a lower level, you may want to drill back up to a higher grain. You can right-click on the dimension and select Drill Up from the dropdown menu as shown in Figure 9.24. Another option is to click on the small arrow next to the name of the dimension that appears after you've drilled down at least one level as shown in Figure 9.25.

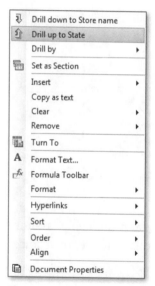

Figure 9.24 Dropdown List to Select the Drill Up Option

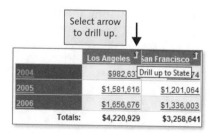

Figure 9.25 Select Arrow to Drill Up in Hierarchy

Drill By

Drill By is a new functionality available in Web Intelligence XI 3.x. The Drill By function is found on the right-click menu when the user selects a dimension object in a report block (see Figure 9.26).

If you go back to the report example shown earlier in Figure 9.18, you're viewing sales revenue by State and Store Name. Drill down and drill up functionality won't answer your business question if your desired result is to view sales revenue for this year by State. In this case, YEAR isn't an option in the drill path for either the STATE or STORE NAME objects.

By viewing the scope of analysis, the report developer can see that Year is a separate drill path. You can change from Store Name to Year by switching the drill path using the Drill By functionality.

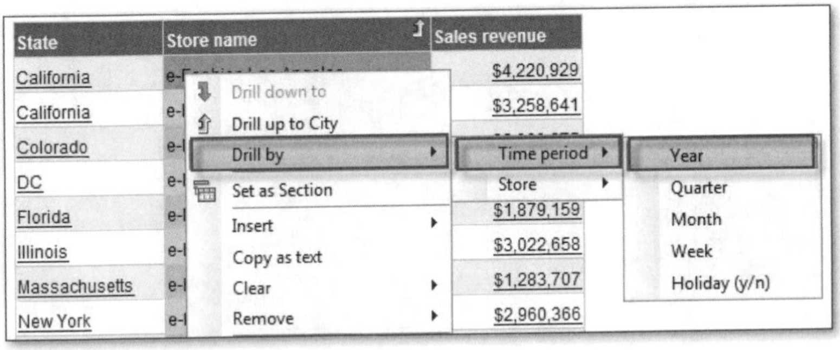

Figure 9.26 Right-Click Menu to Drill By a Dimension Object

By right-clicking on Store Name and selecting Drill By from the menu, another menu appears with the available choices to drill by. In this example, the choices are Time Period or Store.

Upon selecting Time Period, another menu appears showing the available objects in the Time Period hierarchy to Drill By. Upon selection of Year, the measure recalculates for the new dimension object of Year contained within the table (see Figure 9.27).

State	Year	Sales revenue
California	2004	$982,637
California	2005	$1,581,616
California	2006	$1,656,676

Figure 9.27 Table Recalculated for the Drill by Dimension of Year

9.2.4 Drilling on Measures

There is a slight difference seen when drilling on measures. When selecting a measure to drill down or drill up in the hierarchy, Web Intelligence automatically drills all dimensions contained in the table with the measure by one level. Then the measure recalculates for the new dimension objects in the table with it.

Figure 9.28 shows a table with Sales Revenue calculated by Year and State. When you select the measure object from the table to drill down, then both the State and Year objects are drilled down to the next level of hierarchy. Therefore, the new table appears as shown in Figure 9.29 with Sales Revenue calculated for City and Quarter.

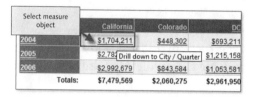

Figure 9.28 Drill Down on Measure Object

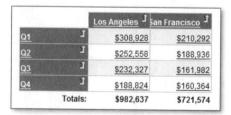

Figure 9.29 Table After Drill Down on Measure Object

9.2.5 Drilling on Charts

Users can drill on charts in the same ways that they can drill on tables: drill down, drill up, and drill by. There are exciting new chart drill features available in Web Intelligence XI 3.x that provide a more user-friendly experience to the report consumer.

Dimensions on Chart Axis

Drill functionality is available on dimensions included in the chart axis. Figure 9.30 shows a table and chart view of Sales Revenue by State and City. Cities can be seen along the X-axis, and dollars of sales revenue can be seen along the Y-axis. Each bar shows the amount of sales revenue for the respective city.

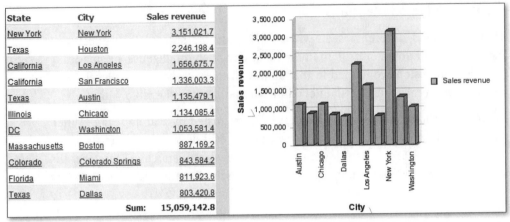

State	City	Sales revenue
New York	New York	3,151,021.7
Texas	Houston	2,246,198.4
California	Los Angeles	1,656,675.7
California	San Francisco	1,336,003.3
Texas	Austin	1,135,479.1
Illinois	Chicago	1,134,085.4
DC	Washington	1,053,581.4
Massachusetts	Boston	887,169.2
Colorado	Colorado Springs	843,584.2
Florida	Miami	811,923.6
Texas	Dallas	803,420.8
	Sum:	15,059,142.8

Figure 9.30 Table and Chart View of Sales Revenue by State and City

The user can click on one of the cities on the X-axis to drill down to the next level in the hierarchy. A pop-up box appears showing the next level of drill available as shown in Figure 9.31.

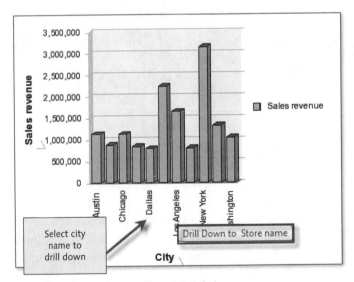

Figure 9.31 Drill Down on Chart Axis Label

Right-click on the dimension to drill up in order to drill back to the YEAR dimension or select the up arrow (see Figure 9.32).

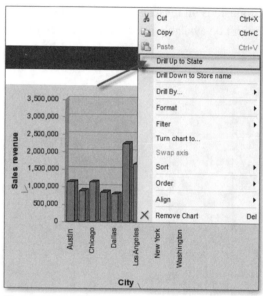

Figure 9.32 Drill Up on the Chart Axis Label

The user can also select to drill by an object by selecting the Drill By option from the right-click menu when selecting a dimension as shown in Figure 9.33. This functionality works the same as it does with a table.

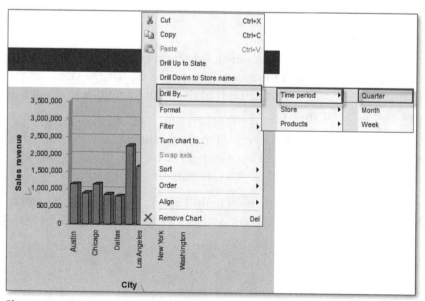

Figure 9.33 Drill By on the Chart Axis Label

In some cases, the chart has multiple dimensions on the axis as shown in Figure 9.34. In this case, the drill by functionality won't be available on the axis of the chart.

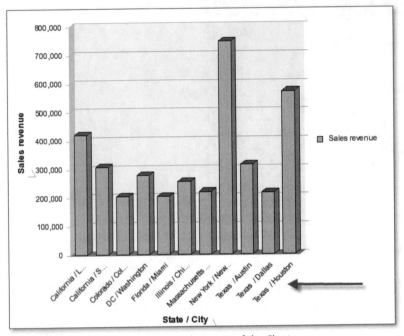

Figure 9.34 Multiple Dimensions on the X-axis of the Chart

Dimensions on Legends

Drill functionality is also available on dimensions included in the chart legend as long as the legend is viewable in the report. This can be especially helpful for pie charts because it can sometimes be difficult to determine which slice belongs to what data element as shown in Figure 9.35.

In this example, the user can click on one of the states listed in the legend to drill down to the next level in the hierarchy. A pop-up box appears showing the next level of drill available similar to Figure 9.31, shown earlier.

The user can right-click on the dimension to drill up in order to drill back to the State dimension as done with drill functionality on a chart axis.

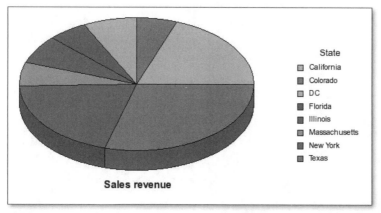

Figure 9.35 Pie Chart Showing Sales Revenue by State

The user can also select to drill by an object by selecting the Drill By option from the right-click menu when selecting a dimension as shown earlier in Figure 9.33. This functionality works the same as it does with a table.

In some cases, the chart has multiple dimensions on the axis as shown earlier in Figure 9.34. In this case, the drill by functionality won't be available on the legend of the chart.

Measures on Chart Bars and Markers

An exciting new feature in Web Intelligence XI 3.x is the ability to select the bar or marker in a chart to drill up or down. This functionality is available on bar charts, pie charts, line charts, and radar charts. For bar charts, users drill on the bars (see Figure 9.36). On pie charts, users drill on the pie slices. Drilling on line and radar charts is done by drilling on the line markers. The bars, slices, or markers of a chart consist of the measure data elements; therefore, the drill functionality would be the same as drilling on a measure in a table.

When drilling on a measure, all dimension objects placed with it are drilled down by one level, and the measure is recalculated to match the new data elements.

To drill down on the chart bars and markers, select the appropriate bar, and click to enable the drill down to the next level in the hierarchy.

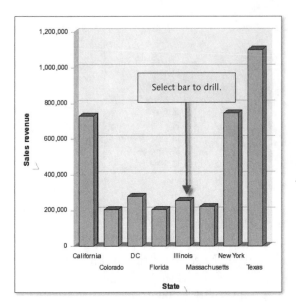

Figure 9.36 Drill on Bars of Chart

To drill up on the charts and markers, right-click on the bar or marker, and select Drill Up to reach the next highest level in the drill hierarchy (see Figure 9.37).

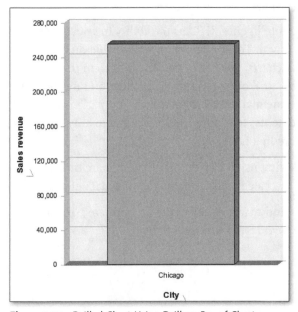

Figure 9.37 Drilled Chart Using Drill on Bar of Chart

There are some limitations to drilling on measures in chart bars and markers. Certain chart types don't drill down on all dimensions included in the chart when selecting the chart measure bars or markers. When drilling on these charts, only the dimension included in the chart legend is drilled upon, and therefore the measure object recalculates for this dimension change only.

These charts include the following:

▸ 2D area charts

▸ 3D area charts

▸ Stacked area charts

▸ Radar charts

▸ Scatter charts

Note

Measures can't be drilled upon in 3D surface charts.

9.3 Query Drill Option

Query drill gives the user the ability to drill upon a report without maintaining all of the data within the data provider. This minimizes the amount of space taken up by the report as well as minimizing the refresh time.

It's also essential when report measures must be calculated at the database level and can't be calculated properly through normal drill mode. Examples of these measure calculations would be ranks, percentages, distinct counts, standard deviations and variances, running aggregates, and lead and lag functions.

These measures would not recalculate correctly if recalculated at the report level during drill down. In this case, query drill would be beneficial to perform the calculation correctly at the database level. This can be especially useful for databases such as Oracle 9i OLAP, which contains aggregate functions that aren't supported at the report level in Web Intelligence XI 3.x.

To enable query drill, right-click on the report canvas and select Document Properties from the menu. Select the checkbox for Use Query Drill (see Figure 9.38).

Figure 9.38 Use Query Drill Option in the Document Properties Dialog Box

Query drill works differently from standard drill mode. When a user selects to drill down on YEAR and selects the year of 2001, Web Intelligence not only applies the drill filter to limit the results at the report level but also applies a query filter that limits the results at the query level.

This means that the user can no longer use the dropdown boxes in the drill toolbar to change the filter because only the year 2001 exists in the report.

Also, the new query filter will affect the entire report. The entire report is now filtered for only the year 2001.

> **Caution**
>
> Query drill applies the drill filter to the report query, so all Report tabs will be affected by the drill.
>
> If you drill from Year to Quarter in query drill mode, then the Year object will be removed from your query and replaced with the Quarter object. Therefore, the Year object will be removed from all Report tabs in your Web Intelligence report.

9.4 Taking a Snapshot

When performing report analysis using drill functionality, the user may need to refer to the current state of drill at a later date. Web Intelligence enables the user to take a snapshot of the current view of the report for future reference. On the report toolbar, there is a button that resembles a camera located next to the drill button. This is the snapshot button (see Figure 9.39). By selecting this button, a copy of the current report at the current state of drill down is opened in a new Report tab. This report snapshot can be saved and referenced later.

Figure 9.39 Snapshot Button

9.5 User Settings for Drill Down

The user can specify their specific settings for drill in their Preferences located on the InfoView toolbar (see Figure 9.40).

Figure 9.40 Preferences Button on InfoView Toolbar

On the Web Intelligence Preferences tab, there are Drill Options that can provide a more personalized drill experience based on the user's drill preferences (see Figure 9.41). The overall capability for each of these options is determined by the administrator in the Central Management Console (CMC), so not all options may be available to use based on these user rights.

Drill options:

☐ Prompt when drill requires additional data

☐ Synchronize drill on report blocks

☐ Hide Drill toolbar on startup

Start drill session:

○ On duplicate report

◉ On existing report

Figure 9.41 Drill Preferences

9.5.1 Prompt When Drill Requires Additional Data

When it's necessary to extend the scope of analysis to view a higher or lower level of drill than was set up in the report scope, then a query must be run to retrieve the additional data. If the Prompt When Drill Requires Additional Data option is selected, then users will be prompted to ensure that they desire to run a query before the query is run. If this option isn't selected, then a query will automatically be run if users select to extend the scope of analysis by drilling beyond the designated scope.

9.5.2 Synchronize Drill

The Synchronize Drill on Report Blocks option gives the user the ability to drill on all report blocks simultaneously. A report block can include tables or charts. If the Synchronized Drill on Report Block is enabled in the user's Web Intelligence preferences, then when a user selects to drill on an object that is contained in more than one report block, the object changes in all report blocks in which it's contained.

If the option isn't enabled, then when the user selects to drill on an object that is contained in more than one report block, the object changes only in the block in which he has selected to drill.

9.5.3 Hide Drill Toolbar

When drill is enabled on a report, a toolbar appears at the top of the screen that shows dropdown boxes with the selected drill filters. Users can change the filters by using these boxes. Users can also see which filters they have chosen in their drill path by referencing the boxes shown in the drill toolbar.

The drill toolbar can be hidden so it doesn't show when drill is enabled. To set this option, select the checkbox next to Hide Drill Toolbar on Startup in the Web Intelligence Preferences.

9.5.4 Start Drill Session

The Start Drill Session option sets whether drill is completed within the current report or whether a new report is opened in a new browser to complete drill mode. The two options are to Start Drill Session On Existing Report or to Start Drill Session On Duplicate Report.

9.6   Summary

Drill functionality is an important feature that puts the power of analysis in the end user's hands. It enables users to quickly and easily answer the important business questions by performing drill down, drill up, and drill by functions either by viewing a report in InfoView or editing a report in Web Intelligence. Reports can be set up by the Report Designer to provide drill objects within the report's data cube or enable query drill to perform live queries as drill analysis is completed by the end user.

Users can also create snapshots of their results for further analysis or distribution. It's important to know your audience and how the report will be used to set up the drill preferences appropriately for your audience.

Chapter 10 delves further into presenting data appropriate for your audience by discussing how to use charts and templates to present data in the most meaningful way to end users.

Graphically display business data in Web Intelligence reports with more than 30 different chart types available in 5 charting categories. Charts can be added to report sections to generate and display data in multiple chart instances.

10 Displaying Data with Charts

Charts provide a great way to graphically illustrate data and convey business information in Web Intelligence reports. Quickly make an impact with reports by using one or many of the 33 chart templates to visually display data in a report. Charts enhance and complement data displayed with tables and allow business users to discover data issues at a glance.

In addition to displaying data, charts serve as clickable and interactive objects. By enabling drilling, charts provide the functionality of changing dimensions when drilling up or drilling down the hierarchy of objects in a report.

This chapter introduces and explains the 5 chart categories and 33 types of charts available in the Web Intelligence report panel.

Figure 10.1 shows the five chart categories available in the Templates tab of the Report Manager when editing a Web Intelligence report.

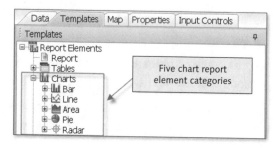

Figure 10.1 Five Categories of Chart Type Report Elements

Figure 10.2 shows the full list of chart types offered in Web Intelligence XI 3.1.

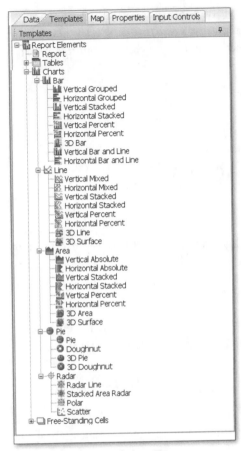

Figure 10.2 Full List of Chart Types

10.1 Chart Types

A single Web Intelligence report can contain any combination of report elements, and several different charts can appear on the same report.

Figure 10.3 shows a report that contains four different types of charts and a cross-tab data table. Charts provide a graphical alternative to data tables and can be customized to fit almost any color scheme.

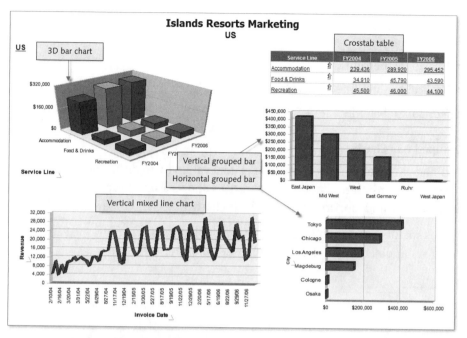

Figure 10.3 Four Charts and a Crosstab on a Single Report

In the next several pages, we'll discuss details for adding the different chart types to a report. Each chart type provides several different modifiable properties for adjusting the appearance, display, and axis settings of charts.

Sections and Charts

When sections are added to a report, charts containing the section object will break by the section and appear as multiple charts.

10.1.1   Bar Charts

Bar charts display data vertically or horizontally and are available in four different types: Grouped, Stacked, Percent, and Bar and Line. Following is the complete list of bar chart types available in Web Intelligence XI 3.1:

▸ Vertical grouped

▸ Horizontal grouped

▸ Vertical stacked

- ▶ Horizontal stacked
- ▶ Vertical percent
- ▶ Horizontal percent
- ▶ Vertical bar and line
- ▶ Horizontal bar and line

Grouped Bar Charts

Vertical bar charts compare dimensional item values by requiring at least one measure and dimension result object. Figure 10.4 shows a simple vertical grouped bar chart along with a horizontal grouped bar chart.

These charts are created by dragging and dropping the [Service Line] and [Revenue] result objects onto the chart while editing a report.

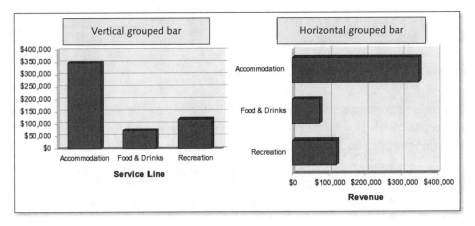

Figure 10.4 Vertical Grouped Bar Chart and Horizontal Grouped Bar Chart

Figure 10.5 shows the structure of the previous two charts. To populate a chart with data, drop result objects onto the appropriate section of a chart, and then click the View Results button to visualize the data. Figure 10.6 shows a vertical and horizontal grouped bar chart containing an optional dimension object.

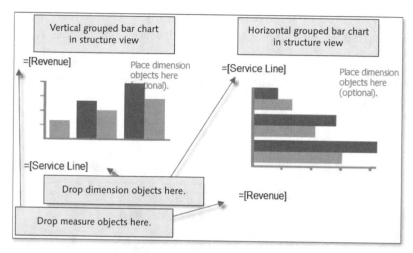

Figure 10.5 Vertical Bar Chart and Horizontal Bar Chart in Structure View

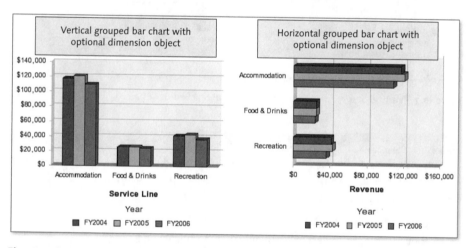

Figure 10.6 Vertical Bar and Horizontal Bar with Optional Dimension Object

Stacked Bar Charts

Stacked bar charts are used to display the relationship of parts to the whole. Each bar in a stacked chart represents the total value while the stacked items are the individual parts of each bar total.

Figure 10.7 shows a vertical stacked bar chart with yearly revenue values charted by service line and a horizontal stacked bar chart with service line revenue values charted by year.

One requirement of a stacked bar chart is to include at least two dimension objects and a measure. The charts in Figure 10.7 include the [Service Line], [Year], and [Revenue] result objects.

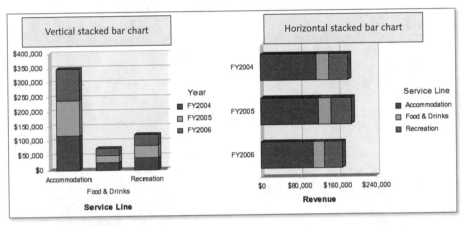

Figure 10.7   Vertical Stacked Bar Chart and Horizontal Stacked Bar Chart

Using Bar Charts

Bar charts are useful when comparing values of single dimensions or objects broken down into optional dimensional groups for a greater depth of analysis.

The following are a few key advantages of using bar charts to display data:

▸ Quickly identify the highest value by spotting the tallest bar

▸ Quickly identify the lowest value by spotting the smallest bar

▸ Easily compare the bar sizes

Percent Bar Charts

Figure 10.8 shows a vertical percent bar chart and horizontal percent bar chart with each chart containing two dimension objects and a single measure.

The vertical percent bar chart in Figure 10.8 was created by using the Island Resort Marketing universe to create the query and then adding the [Revenue] result object as the measure, the [Sales Person] result object as the dimension, and the [Service Line] result object as the optional dimension.

This example shows the revenue values by service line for each salesperson. But instead of charting the values, the percentage by service line is charted for each salesperson. This type of chart can be very helpful when analyzing business data and determining how money is spent in an organization.

The horizontal percent bar chart is very similar to the vertical percent bar chart, but the dimensions have changed position. The horizontal percent bar displays service line revenue by the percentage of each salesperson.

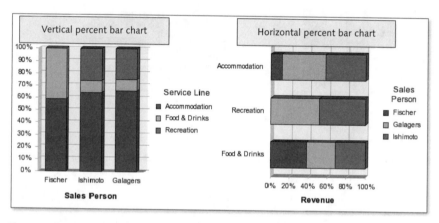

Figure 10.8 Vertical Percent Bar Chart and Horizontal Percent Bar Chart

Figure 10.9 shows the structure of the previously charted percent bar charts. As in other chart types, you'll need to add result objects to the charts while working in structure mode in a Web Intelligence XI 3.1 report.

Percent charts are used to show dimensional percentages of values within a single bar. Percent charts stack values with the total of each bar equaling 100%.

Percent Bar Charts – Edit Mode

When a report is being edited, percent charts are created the same way as other charts — by dragging and dropping the chart report element into the report panel and then clicking View Structure to visualize the structure of the chart.

Add result objects to the charts by dragging them from the Data tab in the Report Manager and then dropping them into the appropriate section of the chart.

Figure 10.9 shows a vertical percent chart and horizontal percent chart in structure mode with each chart containing two dimension objects and a single measure object.

To view the data in the chart, click the View Results button located in the reporting toolbar to toggle out of structure mode and back to the report.

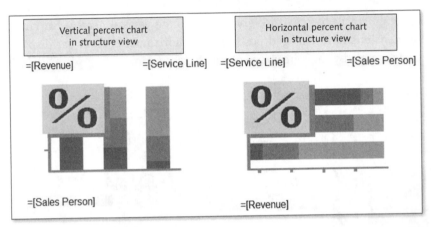

Figure 10.9 Vertical Percent Bar Chart and Horizontal Percent Bar Chart in Structure View

> **Note**
>
> When a report is being edited in the Java Report Panel, report data will be displayed, and the primary button on the reporting toolbar will read "View Structure."
>
> If View Structure is clicked, the structure of the report will be displayed, and the text of the button will change to "View Results." Complex reports can often be modified with more success in structure mode.

Bar and Line Charts

Often referred to as combination charts, bar and line charts are used to chart measures by charting values to be displayed along the Z-axis — (right side chart) and Y-axis — (left side of chart). Bar and line charts are available as either vertical bar and line or horizontal bar and line.

Figure 10.10 shows the [Revenue] object charted by bars with the values located on the left of the chart. The [Number of guests] values are charted with a line, and the values are displayed along the right side of the chart.

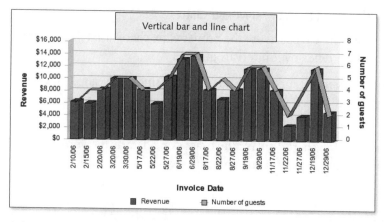

Figure 10.10   Vertical Bar and Line Chart

10.1.2   Line Charts

Line charts are primarily used to measure performance over time. When measuring values using line charts, it becomes possible to quickly identify upward and downward trends over time, reoccurring patterns, and spikes of proportionally high and low values.

Line charts are used to quickly identify significant trends and pinpoint patterns in the data that should be investigated. A variable that calculates the average of a measure can be easily added to illustrate the movement of data above or below the average.

Line Chart Types

Line charts are available in the eight different chart types listed here:

▶ Vertical mixed

▶ Horizontal mixed

▶ Vertical stacked

▶ Horizontal stacked

▶ Vertical percent

▶ Horizontal percent

▶ 3D line

▶ 3D surface

Vertical Mixed Charts and Horizontal Mixed Charts

Vertical and horizontal mixed charts are the primary line charts used by Web Intelligence to display data trends over intervals of time.

Figure 10.11 shows a vertical mixed line chart with a single measure, [Revenue], and a single dimension object, [Invoice Date]. The figure shows revenue values charted over time in horizontal and vertical mixed line charts.

The horizontal mixed line chart displays the exact same data as the vertical mixed line chart but the X- and Y values change places.

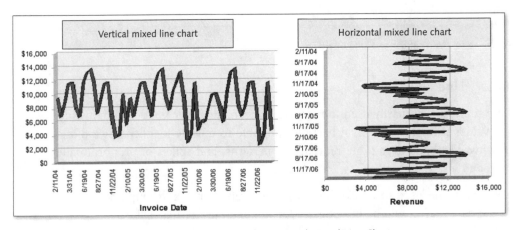

Figure 10.11   Vertical Mixed Line Chart and Horizontal Mixed Line Chart

Vertical Mixed Line Chart – Multiple Values

Mixed line charts provide the capability of charting multiple measure objects. Figure 10.12 shows a vertical mixed line chart with three measure objects.

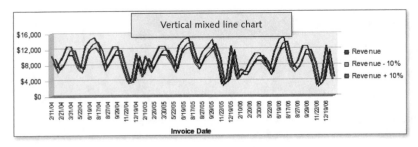

Figure 10.12   Vertical Mixed Line Chart with Multiple Measures

278

Stacked Line Charts

An example of a vertical stacked line chart is displayed in Figure 10.13. This example shows three measure objects charted over time with the values stacked. The property for the 3D look is set to yes in the screenshot.

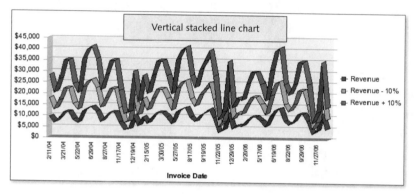

Figure 10.13   Vertical Stacked Line Chart with Three Measures Charted

Percent Line Charts

Line percent charts are used to display the relationship of individual objects to the column as a whole. Figure 10.14 shows a vertical percent chart with the 3D look setting set to off.

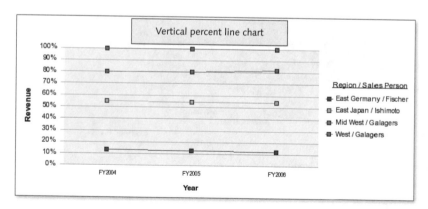

Figure 10.14   Vertical Percent Chart with 3D Disabled

Line charts are useful when comparing values of one or more measures across time intervals by connecting a series of data points with a straight line.

For additional trending analysis, Web Intelligence provides the option to add additional dimensions to a line chart to create grouped trends. Whenever possible, at least 20 data points should be charted to display a significant trend.

Key Applications of Line Charts

▶ Display data across time

▶ Analyze patterns in interval data

▶ Identify data shifts in trend data

▶ Recognize seasonal cycles

▶ Pinpoint high and low spikes in the data

3D Line and 3D Surface Charts

Three-dimensional line charts are used to display values from two or more dimension result objects with visual depth and dimension. Figure 10.15 shows a 3D line chart with two dimension objects and a single measure.

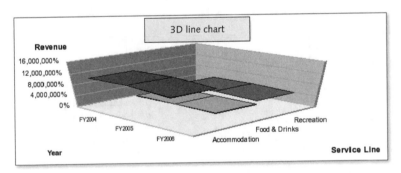

Figure 10.15 Three-Dimensional Line Chart

10.1.3 Area Charts

Area charts display a series of data points connected by a line with the area filled in below the line. Area charts and line charts are the only chart categories that are intended to display contiguous data.

Similar to grouped bar charts and mixed line charts, absolute area charts are the primary method of display data in an area chart. The eight area chart types available in Web Intelligence XI 3.1 are listed here:

- Vertical absolute
- Horizontal absolute
- Vertical stacked
- Horizontal stacked
- Vertical percent
- Horizontal percent
- 3D area
- 3D surface

Figure 10.16 shows the available area charts as they appear in the Templates tab of the Report Manager.

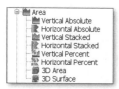

Figure 10.16 Area Chart Types

Vertical Absolute and Horizontal Absolute – Area Charts

Figure 10.17 shows a vertical absolute and horizontal absolute area chart with the 3D look display property checked. Both charts pictured contain two dimension objects and a single measure object.

Vertical Area and Horizontal Area Charts

Simple area charts are displayed with a single measure object and one dimension object in Figure 10.17. The vertical absolute area chart and horizontal absolute area chart in Figure 10.17 were created with the [Revenue] measure object and the [Invoice Date] dimension object.

As an additional layer of visual analysis, the year dimension has been added to the optional dimension area of the chart in structure mode. The addition of the optional dimension object allows the charted area to become grouped by year rather than appearing as one large area object.

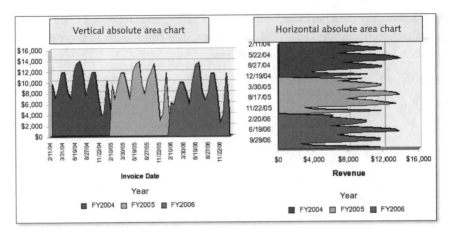

Figure 10.17   Vertical Absolute Area and Horizontal Absolute Area Charts

The horizontal absolute area chart contains the exact same result objects as in the vertical absolute area chart but the X-axis and Y-axis have been swapped.

Stacked Area Charts

Stacked area charts display data vertically and horizontally stacked. If only one series has been added to the chart, the data will be displayed in the stacked area charts identically to the absolute area charts.

Figure 10.18 shows a vertical stacked area chart and a horizontal stacked area chart that contains two measure objects and a single dimension result object.

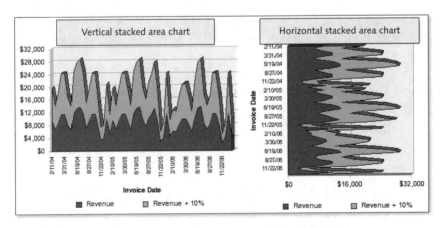

Figure 10.18   Vertical Stacked Area Chart and Horizontal Stacked Area Chart

Percent Charts

Percent stacked area charts provide multiple series values stacked vertically or horizontally as a percentage of the total stacked dimension object. These charts are best suited for displaying the relative contribution of data points.

Figure 10.19 shows a vertical percent chart when viewing the structure of the report. Drop result objects in the chart in structure mode to populate the chart.

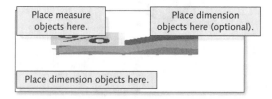

Figure 10.19 Vertical Percent Area Chart in Structure Mode

Figure 10.20 shows a vertical percent area chart and horizontal percent area chart created with two dimension objects and a single measure result object.

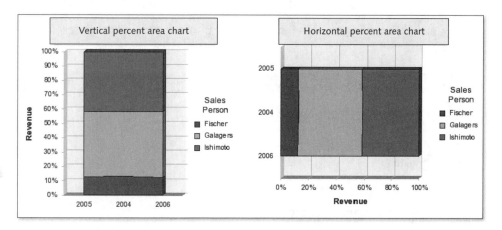

Figure 10.20 Vertical Percent Area and Horizontal Percent Area Charts

3D Area and 3D Surface Charts

3D area and 3D surface charts are used to add depth and a third dimension to area charts. Examples of these two chart types can be seen displaying data in Figure 10.21.

283

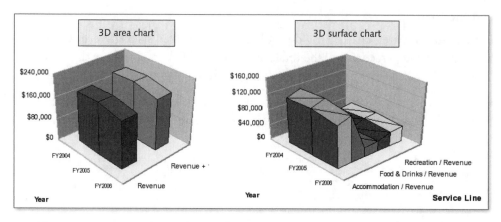

Figure 10.21 3D Area Chart and 3D Surface Chart

10.1.4 Pie Charts

Pie charts are used to show dimensional values as a proportion of the whole data set. The pie or doughnut represents the sum total of a measure while each slice represents the individual parts that are added together to become the whole.

Only one dimension can exist in a pie chart, and values can't represent over 100%.

The Four Pie Chart Types Available in Web Intelligence

▶ Pie
▶ Doughnut
▶ 3D Pie
▶ 3D Doughnut

2D Pie and 2D Doughnut Charts

Pie charts are ideal for displaying percentage values as proportions of the whole. Figure 10.22 shows a classic two-dimensional pie chart followed by a two-dimensional doughnut chart displaying the same information.

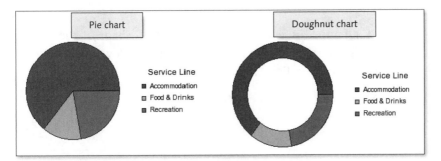

Figure 10.22 Two-Dimensional Pie Chart and Doughnut Chart

3D Pie and 3D Doughnut Charts

The charts pictured in Figure 10.23 display values three dimensionally as opposed to the two dimensional representations in Figure 10.22.

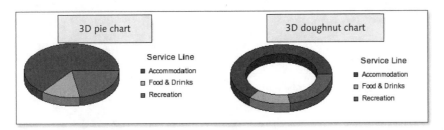

Figure 10.23 3D Pie and 3D Doughnut Charts

10.1.5 Radar Charts

Radar charts are used to quickly convey the "big picture" to the report consumer. The primary benefit of radar charts is to analyze several different factors related to a single item.

Following are the four types of charts available in the radar category:

▸ Radar line

▸ Stacked area radar

▸ Polar

▸ Scatter

Radar Chart Details

Outliers are easily identified when evaluating the overall shape of the charted values. The points closest to the center of the axis indicate a low value while the charted points near the edge indicate high values.

Figure 10.24 shows a stacked area radar chart and a radar line chart displaying revenue values by region.

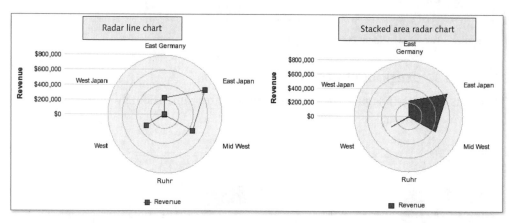

Figure 10.24 Radar Line Chart and Stacked Area Radar Charts

Scatter Charts

Scatter charts display the relationship of two variables that both relate to a specific event. Depending upon the direction of the plotted data points, a positive or negative correlation can be determined.

If the plotted points move from the upper left to the lower right, then the correlation is negative. If the plotted points move from the lower left to the upper right, the correlation is positive.

Polar Charts

Polar charts display a series of values grouped by a dimensional result object on a 360-degree circle. Values are measured by their lengths from the center of the chart. The farther the point is away from the center, the larger the value.

Figure 10.25 shows a polar chart and scatter chart. Both charts display the correlation of two measure objects by the [Region] dimension object.

Both examples show the relationship of [Revenue] to the [Number of guests] for the four selected regions.

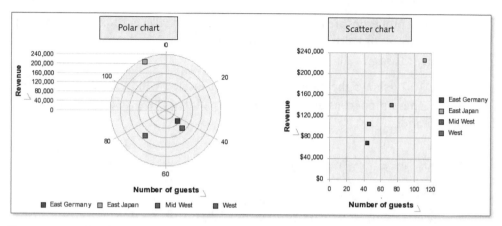

Figure 10.25 Polar Chart and Scatter Chart

10.2 Chart Properties

Chart properties are customized by selecting a chart and then clicking the Properties tab in the Report Manager. Every chart type contains an extensive set of chart-specific properties that can be edited.

Chart properties appear in five primary categories in the Properties tab of the Report Manager. These categories are displayed next and in Figure 10.26.

▸ General

▸ Display

▸ Appearance

▸ Page Layout

▸ Sorts

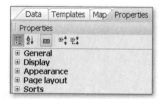

Figure 10.26 Five Chart Property Categories

Each category contains specific properties that can be modified or adjusted. To access these individual and category-specific properties, click the plus symbol to expand the primary property category.

Individual properties are modified by checking optional checkboxes, clicking ellipsis icons to set property definitions, or clicking into the editable portion of each property to assign values.

Figure 10.27 shows the individual properties located within the Appearance category. These properties are exposed by expanding the properties available for modification.

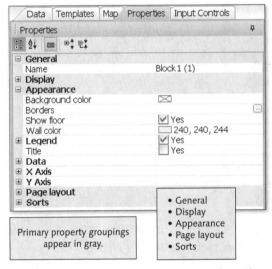

Figure 10.27 Properties of a Vertical Grouped Bar Chart

The Appearance properties for the vertical grouped bar chart are as follows:

▶ Background Color

▶ Borders

▶ Show Floor

▶ Wall Color

▶ Legend

▶ Title

▶ Data

▸ X Axis

▸ Y Axis

Figure 10.28 shows an expanded list of X-axis and Y-axis properties in a vertical grouped bar chart.

Axis properties of a vertical grouped bar chart

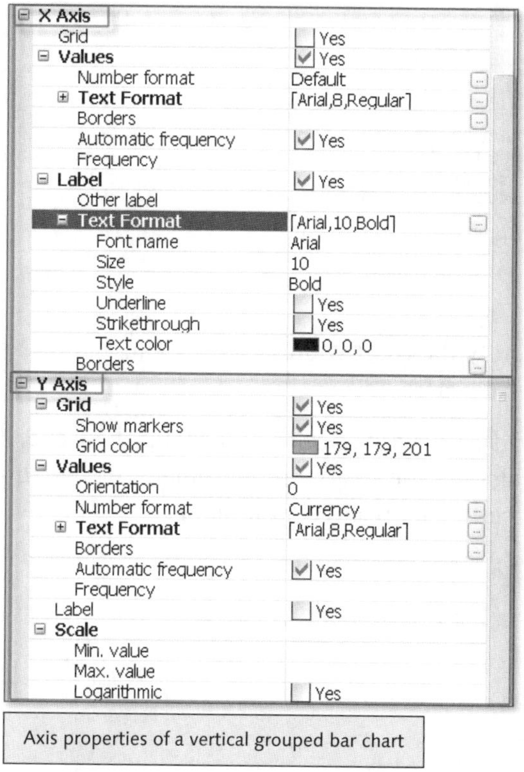

Figure 10.28 X-Axis and Y-Axis Properties Expanded

Note

Chart properties can be modified when viewing the structure or viewing results in a report.

The Data property is found in the Appearance category and allows for the color palette of the selected chart to be modified. It also contains the option to display charted values.

To display the values in a chart, check Yes in the Show Data property by expanding the Values property located within the Data category. The appearance of the displayed data values can also be modified.

Figure 10.29 shows the Data property expanded to display the Palette selection, Border Color, and Values property with the Show Data checkbox.

Figure 10.29   Data Properties Within the Appearance Property

Modify Chart Size and Display

Expand the Display property to modify the chart width, chart height, and three-dimensional appearance of the selected chart.

Figure 10.30 shows the General and Display properties of a chart. The General property allows you to revise the block name to a more meaningful name. This property becomes important when setting up relative positioning.

General	
Name	Block1 (1)
Display	
Avoid duplicate row aggregation	☐ Yes
Show rows with empty dimensio...	☐ Yes
Show when empty	☑ Yes
3D Look	☑ Yes
Width	341 px
Height	288 px

Figure 10.30   General and Display Properties

Figure 10.31 shows the Select Palette window launched when the ellipsis button is clicked beside the Palette property when modifying the appearance of a selected chart. The available predefined color palettes are displayed followed by the customized document palettes. To modify an existing palette, select a predefined palette, and then click Edit Palette to change selected colors.

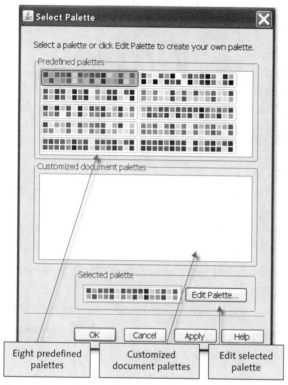

Figure 10.31 Select Palette Dialog Box

10.3 Convert a Chart with Turn To

Charts can be easily converted to data tables or other chart types by right-clicking on a chart object and selecting Turn To.

This method of converting an existing chart or table can be accomplished when viewing a report in InfoView, editing a Web Intelligence report, or creating a new reporting document.

10.3.1 Convert a Chart in Edit Mode

When a document is being edited or created, you can convert an existing chart to a data table or other chart type. Begin the process by right-clicking on the chart to be converted. Figure 10.32 shows a vertical mixed line chart selected and the right-click menu displayed. Click Turn To to change the chart type.

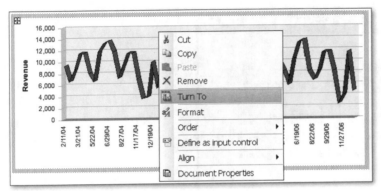

Figure 10.32 Converting an Existing Chart with Turn To

Other options are available when right clicking on an existing chart. Following is the full list of actions available when right-clicking on a chart:

- **Cut:** Removes a chart from a report; paste becomes enabled after Cut has been selected.

- **Copy:** Select Copy to begin the copy/paste process of duplicating a chart or data table. Copy must be used rather than the commonly used `Ctrl`+`C` command.

- **Remove:** Removes or deletes a chart from a report.

- **Format:** Highlights the Properties tab in the Report Manager when selected.

- **Order:** Layers objects, including Bring to Front, Send to Back, Bring Forward, and Send Backward.

- **Define as Input control:** Launches the Define Input Control window used to select a report object to filter (available only in SP2).

- **Align:** Select two or more objects to align the objects by Left, Center, Right, Top, Middle, and Bottom. Also available are the Relative Position, Show Grid, Snap to Grid, and Grid Settings options.

- **Document Properties:** Displays properties of the document, including document information, document options, data synchronization options, and the report order.

Figure 10.33 shows the Turn To chart selection window.

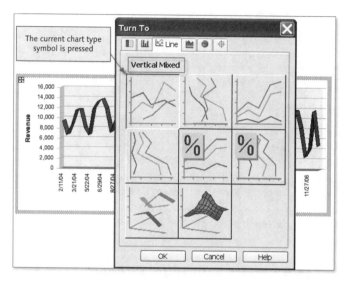

Figure 10.33 Turn To Menu for Selecting a Different Chart or Data Table

10.3.2 Convert a Chart While Viewing a Report

Charts can be converted to other chart types or data tables when viewing a report in InfoView. Begin the process by right-clicking on a chart and selecting Turn Chart To. The right-click menu contains slightly different choices when viewing a report compared to creating or editing a report.

Figure 10.34 shows the right-click menu when viewing a report. Select Turn Chart To to launch the Turn To dialog window.

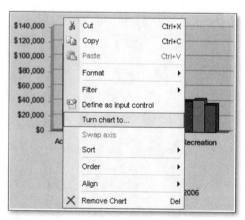

Figure 10.34 Right-Click Menu of a Chart – Viewing a Report

Figure 10.35 shows the chart and table types along with the available chart formats while viewing a report and selecting Turn Chart To.

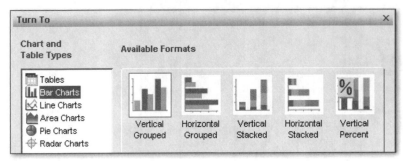

Figure 10.35   Turn To Menu – Viewing a Report

10.4   Adding Charts to a Report – Viewing a Report

Most of this chapter has discussed adding and revising chart objects while editing a report, but charts can also be added and modified while viewing reports. After a chart is added to a report, select result objects from the list of available objects to populate the chart.

Figure 10.36 shows the Format Chart window that will appear when a chart has been added to a report being viewed in InfoView.

The full list of available objects appears on the left side of the window, and the required areas of the chart are shown on the right side of the window. Items are added by completing the following steps:

1. Select an object from the Available Objects area.

2. Select the axis of choice: Y-Axis, Z-Axis, or X-Axis.

3. Click the > button to add the selected object.

Figure 10.36 Add Result Objects to a Chart – Viewing a Report

10.5 Summary

More than 30 different chart types are available in Web Intelligence to visually present data to users. The chart types include 9 bar charts, 8 line charts, 8 area charts, and 4 pie charts. In addition, 4 radar chart types are available for displaying data in a less traditional form with types such as a radar stacked area chart, polar chart, and scatter chart.

The modification of reporting data has never been easier for report consumers with the features available in Web Intelligence XI 3.1. Users can make changes and modifications to reports and then save the updated documents without ever entering edit mode.

It's also possible to format charts on the fly by right-clicking on a chart and then choosing an action from the menu options. In addition to formatting reports and reporting elements on the fly, you can add filters to individual charts or table objects, change the sort order, or turn the selected object into a different data table or chart with as few as three clicks.

Chapter 11 will introduce you to working with Web Intelligence documents in the InfoView portal.

The InfoView web portal used to access Web Intelligence documents provides a fully integrated interface for organizing, viewing, analyzing, and sharing business intelligence content. The added functionality and ease of use of the interface make InfoView a powerful tool for end users and report writers alike.

11 Working Within InfoView

Web Intelligence reports are accessed using the SAP BusinessObjects Enterprise web portal named InfoView. The InfoView portal allows you to access a variety of business content outside of Web Intelligence reports, including Crystal Reports, Desktop Intelligence reports, Voyager workspaces, Microsoft Office documents, and so on. This allows one secure location for business users to view business intelligence content. The ability to publish and distribute content to other users in Web Intelligence, Excel, PDF, and mHTML format is also available from within InfoView.

11.1 Accessing InfoView

Access to InfoView is restricted to users who have an SAP BusinessObjects Enterprise account. The SAP BusinessObjects administrator must set up a user account for you before you'll be granted access to InfoView. They will also set up your access level to which folders, universes, objects, and so on that you'll be granted access to. Section 11.4, Organizing in Folders Versus Categories, discusses the use of folders in detail.

A compatible browser is necessary to access the InfoView website. To access InfoView, one of the following browsers is required on your local machine:

- Internet Explorer
- Safari
- Firefox

After opening a new browser window, enter the URL given to you to access Info-View by your SAP BusinessObjects administrator. The following are the default URLs to access InfoView:

▶ For Java InfoView: *http://webserver:portnumber/InfoViewApp/*

▶ For .Net InfoView: *http://webserver/InfoViewApp/*

Replace "webserver" and "port number" in the default URL example with your environment-specific information.

After navigating to the appropriate InfoView URL, the InfoView log on screen will appear as shown in Figure 11.1. If your login screen has been customized, your view may vary from Figure 11.1. The system name auto-populates with the webservername:portnumber. No changes are necessary to the system information.

Different authentication types are available, including Enterprise, LDAP, Windows AD, and Windows NT. The appropriate type for your needs depends on your corporate environment. Ask your administrator if you're unsure of your user name, password, or authentication type. Enter your user name and password, and select the Logon button to enter InfoView. If your environment is set up to auto-authenticate, you won't be presented with the logon screen.

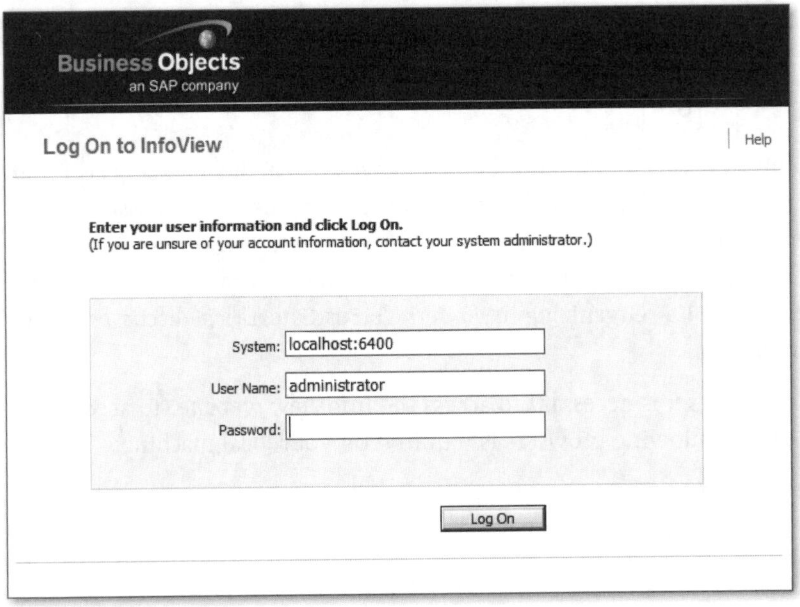

Figure 11.1 InfoView Log On Screen

11.2   Navigating in InfoView

Figure 11.2 shows the default view upon logging in to InfoView. The default home page can be customized in the General Preferences as discussed in Section 11.3, Setting InfoView Preferences. The initial view is divided into two sections: Header Panel and Workspace Panel. The Header Panel includes the InfoView toolbar with menu options applicable across InfoView. The Workspace Panel displays the objects, folders, and categories available to you based on your access level.

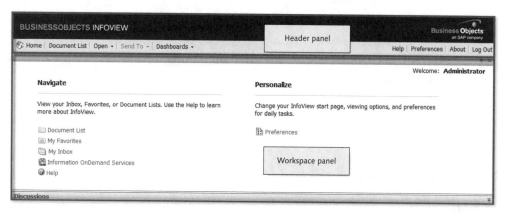

Figure 11.2   InfoView Default Home Page

11.2.1   Header Panel

The Header Panel view may vary depending on any customization that may have been applied to your environment. The default view is shown in Figure 11.3.

Figure 11.3   InfoView Header Panel

The Header Panel includes the customizable top header section with the SAP BusinessObjects logo and the InfoView toolbar. A number of menu options are available on the default InfoView toolbar. The availability of these options depends on your access rights.

InfoView Toolbar

The buttons on the InfoView toolbar are described in the following list:

▶ **Home:** Selecting the Home button brings you back to the initial view as shown earlier in Figure 11.2. Your Home view can be customized in your General Preferences as discussed in Section 11.3, Setting InfoView Preferences.

▶ **Document List:** Selecting the Document List option enables you to view the folders and categories organization structure as well as the documents available within these folders and categories.

▶ **Open:** Upon selecting Open from the InfoView toolbar, a drop-down list appears listing the available types that can be opened within InfoView as shown in Figure 11.4. These options will vary based on the settings in your environment as well as your user rights.

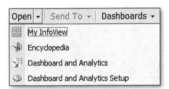

Figure 11.4 Open Menu on the InfoView Toolbar

▶ **Dashboards:** Upon selecting the Dashboards button, the drop-down list displays the available dashboards created within your organization. You also can create and organize corporate dashboards. The Dashboard option is part of another SAP BusinessObjects product, and the availability of this option will depend on whether your organization owns this product. Figure 11.5 shows the Dashboard button drop-down list options.

Figure 11.5 Dashboard Menu on InfoView toolbar

▶ **Help:** Selecting the Help button opens up a window with help resources.

▶ **Preferences:** Selecting the Preferences button opens up the personal preferences available to customize InfoView and Web Intelligence for your user ID.

Further discussion regarding setting preferences is contained within Section 11.3, Setting InfoView Preferences.

▶ **About:** Selecting About displays a box showing the specific information about your environment.

▶ **Log Out:** Selecting the Log Out button ends your current SAP BusinessObjects Enterprise session. It's important to log out of InfoView rather than closing the browser because your session will remain open until the default time-out period set up by your SAP BusinessObjects administrator. Depending on your company's licensing structure, numerous open sessions may restrict your access to InfoView. If you experience this problem, contact your SAP BusinessObjects administrator to re-enable your access.

11.2.2 Workspace Panel

The InfoView Workspace Panel contains objects such as folders, categories, Web Intelligence documents, and publications for your use in InfoView. By default, the Workspace Panel shows an initial view with shortcuts to the most popular areas for access in InfoView as shown in Figure 11.6.

Figure 11.6 InfoView Workspace Panel

Document List

Selecting Document List on the InfoView toolbar or from the shortcuts listed in the default InfoView Workspace Panel brings the view of the folders or categories set up within InfoView. Figure 11.7 shows a sample Document List structure. The Document List within each organization will be customized to their needs, so your Document List will be different from this view. Along with the document list in the Tree Panel of the Workspace Panel, you'll see the list of documents in the Details Panel as well as the workspace toolbar. Later in this chapter, Figure 11.13

shows a sample view of the Workspace Panel after selecting Document List from the InfoView toolbar.

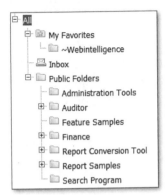

Figure 11.7 Document List Folder View

Workspace Toolbar

The workspace toolbar sits just below the InfoView toolbar and is viewable after selecting Document List from the InfoView toolbar. Figure 11.8 shows the options available on the workspace toolbar and the options are described in the list following.

Figure 11.8 Workspace Toolbar

- ▶ **Folder icon:** Selecting the folder icon changes your tree view to display the folder hierarchy. Further discussion regarding Folders is included in Section 11.4, Organizing in Folders Versus Categories.

- ▶ **Category icon:** Selecting the category icon changes your tree view to display the hierarchy by category. Further discussion regarding categories is included in Section 11.4, Setting InfoView Preferences.

- ▶ **Refresh icon:** Selecting the Refresh icon refreshes the Tree and Workspace Panels. This can be helpful when a new report is added to InfoView or after creating a new folder or category.

- ▶ **New:** Upon selecting the New button from the InfoView workspace toolbar, a drop-down list displays the available options as shown in Figure 11.9. The available options depend on your environment and user settings.

Figure 11.9   New Menu on the Workspace Toolbar

▶ **Add:** Upon selecting the Add button, the drop-down list displays your available options. These options depend on your environment and user settings. The Add button only becomes enabled when selecting a folder that allows you to add content. Figure 11.10 shows the Add menu options.

Figure 11.10   Add Menu on the Workspace Toolbar

▶ **Organize:** The Organize menu contains options that are standard in a number of programs, including Cut, Copy, Copy Shortcut, Paste, and Delete as shown in Figure 11.11. The Organize button only becomes enabled when selecting a folder where your rights allow you to perform this action.

Figure 11.11   Organize Menu on the Workspace Toolbar

▶ **Actions:** The Action menu displays only after selecting an object from the Workspace Panel. This menu contains a number of options available to perform upon a Web Intelligence document from within InfoView (see Figure 11.12)

▸ **Properties:** Displays the object properties, including name, description, keywords, and categories.

▸ **Categories:** Allows you to select which categories within which an object should display.

▸ **View:** Allows you to view the object within InfoView.

▸ **View Latest Instance:** Allows you to view the latest instance of an object in InfoView. Refer to Chapter 16, Sharing a Web Intelligence Report, for more information on instances and scheduling.

▸ **Modify:** Allows you to modify the object. For a Web Intelligence report, selecting the Modify option opens the report in Web Intelligence to make any necessary changes.

▸ **Schedule:** Allows you to schedule upon a designated distribution. Refer to Chapter 16 for detailed information on scheduling reports.

▸ **History:** Displays the schedule history. Refer to Chapter 16 for detailed information on scheduling reports.

Figure 11.12 Actions Menu on the Workspace toolbar

▸ **Search:** The Search box allows you to search with a variety of options to find objects in the InfoView environment. The search results will only display objects that you're authorized to view according to your user rights. More about search capabilities in InfoView is covered in Section 11.8, Search Within InfoView.

▸ **Page navigation:** The page navigation includes the current page number of the Details Panel and arrows allowing you to quickly navigate between pages. The default number of items displayed per page is set in the General Preferences discussed in Section 11.3, Setting InfoView Preferences.

11.3 Setting InfoView Preferences

The majority of user settings are set by the SAP BusinessObjects administrator in the Central Management Console (CMC). Additional preferences are available to be set by the user. These include preferences for InfoView and Web Intelligence and may also include other settings dependent on your environment such as Crystal Reports or Voyager preferences. Web Intelligence preferences are discussed in detail in Chapter 1, SAP BusinessObjects Web Intelligence XI 3.1. Settings that are specific to the InfoView environment are defined within the General Preferences.

11.3.1 General Preferences

The General Preferences include settings for your InfoView environment. The General Preferences are shown in Figure 11.14. The first setting allows you to define the InfoView Start Page.

The InfoView Start Page options are described in the following list:

- **Home:** The Home option is the default setting as shown earlier in Figure 11.2.
- **My InfoView:** The My InfoView page is a customized page set up by the user to create a specialized view of objects, categories, and folders or internal and external websites.
- **Favorites:** The Favorites option opens InfoView with the tree view selected on your Favorites folder and the Workspace Detail Panel showing the contents of your Favorites folder.
- **Inbox:** The Inbox option opens InfoView with the tree view selected on your BusinessObjects inbox and the Workspace Detail Panel showing the contents of your inbox.
- **Folder:** The Folder option shows the tree view set to the folder you specify in the Browse folder box and the Workspace Detail Panel showing the contents of the selected folder.
- **Category:** The Category option shows the tree view set to the category you specify in the Browse category box and the Workspace Detail Panel showing the contents of the selected category.

▶ **Dashboard:** The Dashboard option shows the tree view set to the dashboard you specify in the Browse dashboard box and the Workspace Detail Panel showing the dashboard specified.

▶ **InfoView Page Layout:** The InfoView Page Layout option lets you select a previously created custom page layout. InfoView page layouts are created by selecting InfoView Page Layout from the New menu on the InfoView toolbar.

The Document Navigation view preference allows you to select the default view of either folder or categories that will display in the Tree Panel of your workspace. The differences between folders and categories are discussed in further detail in the next section.

The next option allows you to set the maximum number of objects to show at one time per page in the Workspace Details Panel of InfoView. The default setting is set to 10 objects per page. Increasing the number of objects shown per page can have an impact on performance, so exercise caution when changing these settings.

The Document List Display options allow you to select which properties will be displayed by default when viewing the document list in the Workspace Details Panel. These are displayed as columns at the top of the Details Panel. Select the checkbox to display the property according to your preference. Options include Description, Owner, Date, and Instance Count. Figure 11.13 shows this view in more detail.

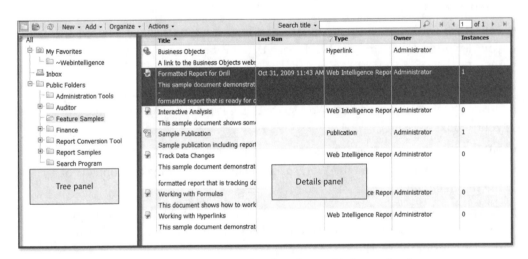

Figure 11.13   Tree Panel and Details Panel in the InfoView Workspace Panel

The Document Viewing properties specify how you'll view documents upon selection of View from the Actions menu on the InfoView workspace toolbar.

The available options include the following:

▶ In the InfoView Portal

▶ In a Single Fullscreen Browser Window, One Document at a Time

▶ In Multiple Fullscreen Browser Windows, One Window for Each Document

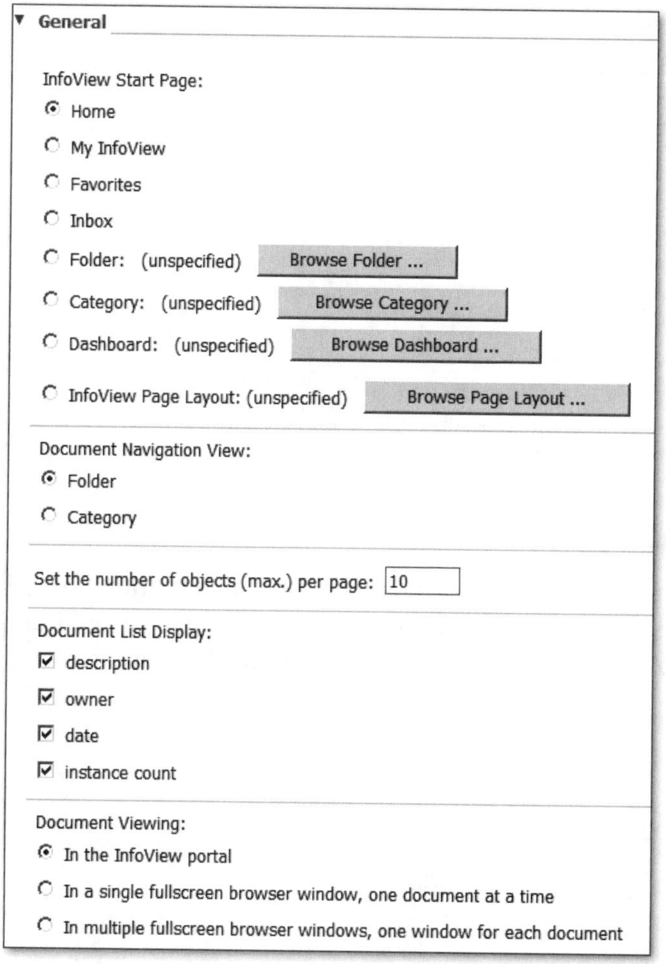

Figure 11.14 General Preferences

Additional properties specific to your locale are shown in Figure 11.15. Locale-specific properties are usually defined in the CMC by your SAP BusinessObjects administrator. If you prefer to use customized personal properties, then the option is available in the General Preferences.

These properties include the following:

▶ **Product Locale:** The default setting uses the locale of your browser.

▶ **Current Time Zone:** The default setting uses the time zone of the web server used by SAP BusinessObjects.

▶ **Preferred Viewing Locale:** The default setting uses the locale of your browser.

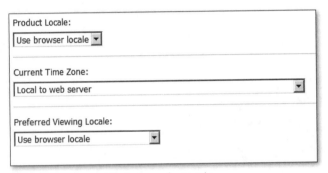

Figure 11.15 General Preferences for Locale

11.3.2 Changing Your Password

The ability to change your password depends on your authentication type. If you're set to Enterprise authentication, then you can change your password if the administrator has enabled this right. The Change Password Preference is shown in Figure 11.16.

▶ **Change Password**	
User Name:	Administrator
Old Password:	
New Password:	
Confirm New Password:	

Figure 11.16 Change Password Preferences

> **Note**
>
> The options that are available to you in the Preferences may be different depending on the settings in the CMC set by your SAP BusinessObjects administrator as well as your specific SAP BusinessObjects deployment.

11.4 Organizing in Folders Versus Categories

There are two ways to organize your documents within InfoView: folders and categories. The key difference between folders and categories is that every document must belong to a folder, but a document doesn't have to belong to a category. Categories are a way to organize your documents into logical groupings without having to create copies or shortcuts of your documents. The documents contained within categories aren't duplicates, but the same original document organized in a different way.

For example, your Public folders may be organized by region so that each region is restricted to see its folder alone. The category structure could be organized by logical groupings of time when reports are normally viewed or run: Yearly, Monthly, Weekly, or Daily. This helps users quickly see which reports to view using categories but also allows them to navigate based on their company structure using folders.

11.4.1 Folders

There are two types of folders: public and personal. Public folders are usually set up by the SAP BusinessObjects administrator and restricted on who can set up new public folders. They also can be restricted on who can publish documents to the public folders to maintain a system of testing and quality assurance before reports are published for public consumption. Personal folders contain those documents that can only be viewed by yourself or users with administrative access. Each user has his own personal folders to organize documents for his personal use. These documents aren't available for public consumption.

Personal folders include the My Favorites documents and the user's SAP BusinessObjects Inbox. Users across an organization can share documents by sending them to each other's inboxes. More detail on sharing documents is discussed in Chapter 16, Sharing a Web Intelligence Report. The My Favorites folder consists of personal documents for the user's own consumption. You can create additional personal folders within your Favorites to further organize your documents provided you have been given the appropriate rights. Figure 11.17 shows a sample folder structure in InfoView.

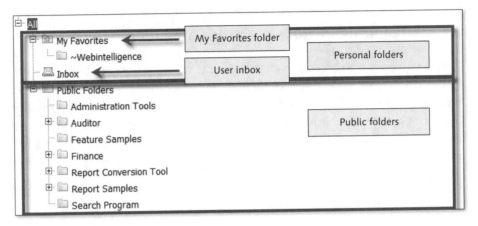

Figure 11.17 Sample Folder View

11.4.2 Categories

Categories are created to help organize documents in a way that is different from the folder view. A report can belong to only one folder, but it can belong to numerous categories. Categories, similar to folders, include both personal and corporate. Corporate categories are available across an organization while personal categories are only available to the specific user. Figure 11.18 shows a sample category view in InfoView.

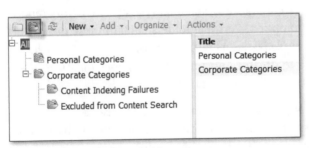

Figure 11.18 Sample Category View

11.4.3 Organizing Objects

Objects such as Web Intelligence documents, are organized in InfoView using folders and categories. Depending on your user rights, you can create new folders and categories, move and copy existing folders and categories, sort objects within folders and categories, delete unneeded folders and categories, and set folder and category preferences.

Creating New Folders and Categories

To create a new folder, it's necessary to be in the folder view. Ensure your Info-View workspace toolbar is highlighted on the folder icon. Select New from the InfoView workspace toolbar, and choose Folder from the drop-down list.

To create a new category, it's necessary to be in the category view. Ensure your InfoView workspace toolbar is highlighted on the category icon. Select New from the InfoView Workspace toolbar, and choose Category from the drop-down list.

Moving Objects in Folders and Categories

To move an object in a folder or category, you use the Cut option from the Organize menu. First select the object to be moved. Then select the Organize button from the InfoView workspace toolbar, and choose Cut. This removes the object from its current location and allows you to paste to the new location. Navigate to the new folder or category location, and select Paste from the Organize menu.

> **Note**
>
> Any shortcuts applied to an object will be maintained when copying and pasting objects to a new location.

Copying Objects in Folders and Categories

To copy an object in a folder or category to another location, highlight the object to be copied, and select Copy from the Organize menu on the InfoView workspace toolbar. Then navigate to the new folder or category to add the object to the new location, and select Paste from the Organize menu. This will create another instance of this object in the new location. If changes are made to one object, they will also need to be made to the other object to maintain consistency. If you desire to have the second instance reflect any changes to the original object, then you should use the shortcut function discussed in Section 11.6, Creating Shortcuts and Hyperlinks in InfoView.

Sorting Objects in Folders and Categories

Objects can be sorted from within folders and categories by selecting the heading of the column of the Workspace Panel. This will resort in ascending or descending order. The default setting is to sort objects from A to Z by title.

Deleting Objects in Folders and Categories

To delete an object in a folder or category, select the object and choose the X button in the workspace toolbar. Whether you're authorized to delete objects depends on your user rights. Usually users are authorized to delete objects only in their personal folders or categories unless they have administrative-level access.

Setting Object Properties

To set object properties, highlight the object in the Workspace Panel, and select Properties from the Actions menu. The properties box allows you to define categories for the object as well as the object title, description, and keywords.

11.5 Viewing, Printing, and Saving Objects in InfoView

Web Intelligence documents can be viewed, printed, and saved within InfoView without having to edit in Web Intelligence. From within the Details Panel, select the Web Intelligence document that you want to view within InfoView. Select View from the Actions menu on the InfoView workspace toolbar. How the document opens within InfoView depends on your General Preferences as discussed in Section 11.3.1, General Preferences. When viewing a Web Intelligence document within InfoView, the InfoView viewer toolbar will appear with the options available to you. Figure 11.19 shows the InfoView viewer toolbar.

Figure 11.19 InfoView Viewer Toolbar

11.5.1   Document Options

The first button on the InfoView viewer toolbar is the Document menu. From the Document menu, you can choose to Close, Edit, Save, or Export the Web Intelligence report.

Following are the Document menu options as shown in Figure 11.20:

- ▶ **Close:** Closes the Web Intelligence report and returns your view to the Document List.

- ▶ **Edit:** Opens the report in Web Intelligence to perform modifications.

- ▶ **Save:** Saves any changes made to the report.

- ▶ **Save As:** Saves any changes made to the report as a new name and/or to a new location.

- ▶ **Save to My Computer As/Save Report to My Computer As:** Saves the Web Intelligence report in PDF, Excel, or CSV format. See Chapter 16, Sharing a Web Intelligence Report, for further details on these options.

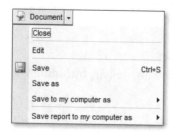

Figure 11.20   Document Menu on the InfoView Viewer Toolbar

11.5.2   Viewing Options

The options available in the View menu define how you'll view your report in InfoView. Available options include Quick Display Mode, Page Mode, Draft Mode, and PDF Mode. The View menu also allows you to toggle on or off your display of the Left Panel and Status Bar.

View options as displayed in Figure 11.21 are listed here:

- ▶ **Quick Display Mode:** Default viewing format.

- ▶ **Page Mode:** Displays using a paginated view.

- ▶ **Draft Mode:** Displays using a nonpaginated view.

▶ **PDF Mode:** Displays in PDF format, which is useful for seeing how a document will print prior to printing.

Figure 11.21 View Menu on the InfoView Viewer Toolbar

11.5.3 Printing Options

The export to PDF button on the InfoView viewer toolbar shows a picture resembling a printer with an arrow. Web Intelligence documents must first be exported to PDF before they can be printed. Upon selecting the export to PDF button, you'll be prompted to open the PDF or save it. To create a printed copy, it's not necessary to save the PDF, although you may want to save the PDF for further reference.

11.5.4 Additional Options

Additional buttons are available on the InfoView Viewer toolbar, including the following:

▶ **Save icon:** The save icon resembles a computer disk. It allows you to save the Web Intelligence document with any changes made.

▶ **Find icon:** The find icon resembles binoculars. You can search for specific text within a document using the find functionality.

▶ **Undo/Redo icons:** Undo and Redo icons will be active only after making a change to a document. These allow you to undo or redo an action previously performed.

▶ **Zoom:** The zoom box allows you to define the amount of zoom percentage to perform on the document to view at a higher or lower percentage.

▶ **Navigation:** The navigation arrows and page number box allows you to quickly page through a document.

▶ **Edit:** The Edit button opens the document in Web Intelligence to make any desired changes, similar to the Edit option on the Document menu.

▶ **Refresh Data:** The Refresh Data button runs the report query or queries against the database and returns the new query results into the report.

▶ **Track:** The Track button allows you to turn on data tracking and view related results. More information on tracking data changes is discussed in Section 11.7, Tracking Data Changes.

▶ **Start/end drill mode:** The start/end drill mode button resembles a magnifying glass. This button enables you to begin or end a drill session on a document. Drill functionality is discussed in further detail in Chapter 9, Scope of Analysis and Drilling Down.

▶ **Snapshot:** The snapshot button resembles a camera. The snapshot enables you to take a snapshot of data while in drill mode for further analysis. Further details regarding drill mode and taking snapshots are discussed in Chapter 9. This button will only be enabled while in drill mode.

11.6 Creating Shortcuts and Hyperlinks in InfoView

Another method of sharing content within InfoView is to create a hyperlink or a shortcut to another location or document. This enables quick collaboration and ease of updating a report without having to update numerous copies of the same report.

11.6.1 Shortcuts

You create shortcuts by selecting the report and then selecting Copy Shortcut from the Organize menu on the InfoView toolbar as shown in Figure 11.22. You'll be prompted to specify where you want the shortcut of the report to reside. Creating a shortcut can help in the organization of documents that are viewed by different security profiles without having to maintain numerous copies of the same report.

Figure 11.22 Copy Shortcut from the Organize Menu

11.6.2 Hyperlinks

Hyperlinks can be created within InfoView to reference other important web pages or information resources. To create a hyperlink, select the New button on the InfoView toolbar, and choose the Hyperlink option from the drop-down menu as shown in Figure 11.23.

Figure 11.23   Hyperlink from New Menu on the InfoView Toolbar

A box will appear to enter the properties, URL address, and categories for the hyperlink as shown in Figure 11.24. The hyperlink will appear as an object in the designated folder and/or categories. Hyperlinks can be helpful in sharing online help resources or internal help resources for quick reference.

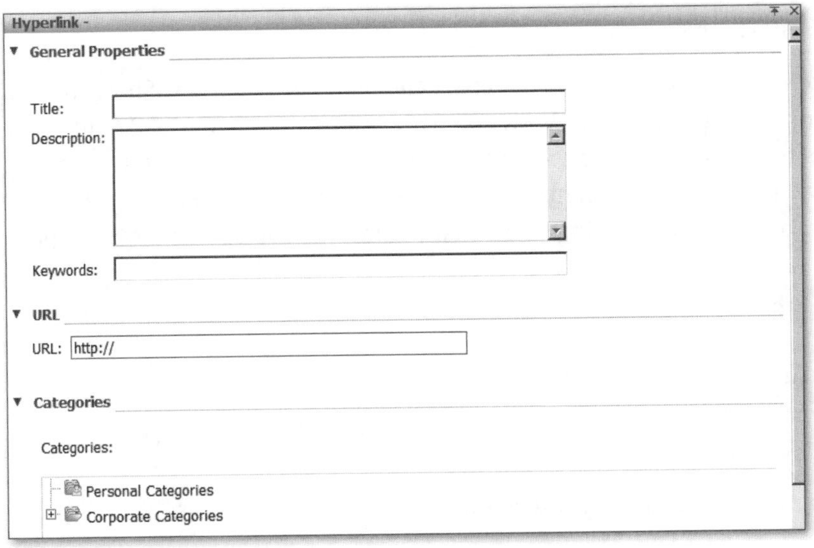

Figure 11.24   Hyperlink Options

11.7   Tracking Data Changes

The ability to track data changes is an exciting new feature available in Web Intelligence XI 3.x. This functionality enables you to easily pinpoint changes to data to make informed decisions in a timely manner. Reference data is chosen upon setup and used to base the changes. Changes are highlighted in your reports based on your selections. You can also use formulas and functions within Web Intelligence and build custom alerters to highlight changed data. The following data changes can be tracked within a Web Intelligence report as shown in Figure 11.25:

▸ Added data

▸ Removed data

▸ Modified data

▸ Increased data

▸ Decreased data

The setup of the reference data and display of the changes is completed from within Web Intelligence.

	Q1	Q2	Q3	Q4	Sum
Sweat-T-Shirts	1,967,328.20	2,121,860.20	1,506,478.90	1,863,826.20	7,459,493.50
Accessories	357,834.80	526,371.10	645,054.70	370,144.10	1,899,404.70
Sweaters	337,200.70	426,442.70	525,878.30	370,518.60	1,660,040.30
Shirt Waist	495,577.90	377,973.70	391,807.80	388,999.10	1,654,358.50
Dresses	295,717.80	355,629.50	564,570.30	192,677.30	1,408,594.90
Jackets	109,943.30	51,513.60	70,667.70	72,555.80	304,680.40
Trousers	60,114.60	87,518.50	71,101.20	53,702.00	272,436.30
City Skirts	19,634.30	55,353.90	103,390.20	17,906.60	196,285.00
Overcoats	40,269.40	518.20	22,308.70	7,915.60	71,011.90

Increased
Decreased
Changed
Inserted
~~Removed~~

Product Line Sales for 2006

Figure 11.25 Sample Report with Data Tracking

11.7.1 Setting Reference Data

When you enable tracking of data changes, you select a particular data refresh as your reference point. This data is known as your reference data. If you make changes to your data provider, the reference data is lost, and data tracking won't be available. These actions cause changes that cause the current version of the document to be incompatible with the reference data, making data tracking misleading.

The following actions are incompatible with data tracking:

▶ Drill out of scope

▶ Query drill

▶ Deleting a query

▶ Any changes to the SQL generated by the data provider

▶ Modifications to security rights, which will affect the SQL generated

▶ Purging the document data

▶ Refresh on open (prior data is purged when document is refreshed on open)

Reference data is set from within Web Intelligence. To set reference data, select Data Tracking Option on the main toolbar or select Auto-update/Fixed Data hyperlink in the status bar to display the data tracking options dialog box. Select the Reference Data tab. There are two options available for the selection of reference data:

▶ **Auto-Update the Reference Data with Each Data Refresh:** The data existing before the refresh data button is selected becomes the reference data, and the new data after the refresh is tracked against this prior refresh.

▶ **Use Fixed Reference Data From:** The data selected becomes the reference data and remains the reference data after each refresh regardless of the number of times the data is refreshed. The newly refreshed data is tracked against the fixed reference data.

11.7.2 Manual Versus Automatic Tracking

Select the Track button on the InfoView Viewer toolbar to activate data tracking from within InfoView. From within Web Intelligence, select the Track button on the main toolbar from the Edit Report view. This opens the Activate Data Tracking dialog box with options to either track automatically or manually. Automatic tracking uses the current refresh against the prior refresh each time, while manual tracking allows you to define specific reference data to track against.

The Data Tracking options are as follows:

▶ **Auto-Update the Reference Data with Each Data Refresh:** The data existing before the refresh data button is selected becomes the reference data, and the new data after the refresh is tracked against this prior refresh.

▶ **Use the Current Data as Reference Data:** The current data becomes the reference data and remains the reference data after each refresh regardless of the number of times the data is refreshed. The newly refreshed data is tracked against the fixed reference data.

11.7.3 Formatting Changed Data

The default setting for formatting changed data is defined by the SAP BusinessObjects administrator in the CMC. You can overwrite these defaults by setting your formatting within the Data Tracking Options dialog box. Select the Format tab to specify your formatting dependent on the type of changed data. Figure 11.26 shows the options available in the Data Tracking Options dialog box.

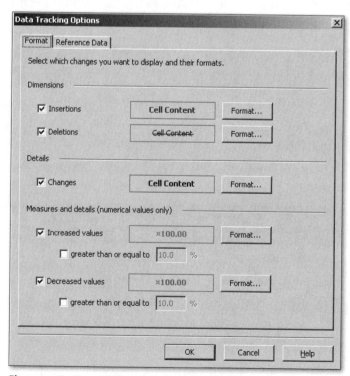

Figure 11.26 Format Tab in Data Tracking dialog box

The following changes are available for configuring formatting:

- ▸ Inserted dimension and detail values
- ▸ Deleted dimension and detail values
- ▸ Changed dimension and detail values
- ▸ Increased measure values
- ▸ Decreased measure values

Changed data is displayed differently in blocks, sections, breaks, charts, and reports with merged dimensions.

Displayed Data in Blocks

If data is removed from a row in a block, deleted data formatting is applied to all cells as defined in the Data Tracking properties. If a measure increases for a row, increased data formatting is applied to the measure cell. If a measure has decreased, decreased data formatting is applied to the measure cell. New data appearing in a block shows inserted data formatting on all cells. The following example details how these formatting changes will appear given a block of sample data.

Example Reference Data		
Year	State	Sales Revenue
2008	Arizona	$1,100,000
2009	Arizona	$1,200,000
2007	California	$1,100,000
2007	New York	$1,150,000

Example Changed Data		
Year	State	Sales Revenue
2009	Arizona	$1,300,000
2008	California	$1,900,000
2007	New York	$1,000,000
2009	Washington	$1,700,000

Example with Data Tracking activated and results displayed			
Year	**State**	**Sales Revenue**	**Formatting**
2008	Arizona	$1,100,000	[deleted data formatting on all cells]
2009	Arizona	$1,300,000	[increased data formatting on Revenue cell]
2007	California	$1,300,000	[deleted data formatting on all cells]
2008	California	$1,900,000	[inserted data formatting on all cells]
2007	New York	$1,150,000	[decreased data formatting on Revenue cell]
2009	Washington	$1,700,000	[inserted data formatting on all cells]

Displayed Data in Sections

The data in the section header can be displayed in one of two ways depending on whether the entire section data changed or just some of the rows in the section changed:

▸ If all rows in the section have changed in the same way, the section header format will be the same as all the rows.

▸ If only some rows in a section have changed or the rows have changed in different ways, the section header will stay in its default format.

Displayed Data in Breaks

If the Center Value Across Break option is applied to the break in the properties, the same formatting rules apply as with sections:

▸ If all rows in the break for the centered value have changed in the same way, the centered break value format will be the same as all the rows.

▸ If only some rows in a centered break section have changed or the rows have changed in different ways, the centered break value will stay in its default format.

Displayed Data in Charts

Tracked data isn't displayed within a chart. When data tracking is applied to a chart, an icon will appear above the chart. Select the icon to display the tracked data changes. The chart will be converted to a table to allow you to see the details of the tracked data changes.

Displayed Data in Reports with Merged Dimensions

When using merged dimensions, Web Intelligence does not display that a new data element was added to a block unless the data element has been added to all dimensions participating in the merge.

11.7.4 Displaying Tracked Data

Select the hide changes/show changes button to the right of the Track button on the toolbar in Edit Report view or the InfoView viewer toolbar to display tracked data.

11.7.5 Advanced Tracking Techniques

There are formulas available for use within Web Intelligence to perform advanced techniques with the data tracking functionality (see Table 11.1).

`RefValue`	`RefValue` returns the value of the reference data.
`RefValueDate`	`RefValueDate` returns the date of the reference data.

Table 11.1 Web Intelligence Functions for Data Tracking

These functions can be used in a formula to find the difference between changed data and reference data. For example:

```
=[Sales Revenue] - RefValue([Sales Revenue])
```

If the current refresh returned sales revenue equal to $2.5 million, and the reference data showed sales revenue equal to $1.5 million, then the difference formula shown here would return a result of $1 million.

11.8 Searching within InfoView

There are enhanced search capabilities available in SAP BusinessObjects Enterprise XI 3.x. New functionality is available within Advanced Search and Content Search that provide easy access to objects within InfoView. Search is divided into three types: simple, advanced, and content search. Upon completion of a search, your search results are saved into the Search folder in the public folders for future access during your InfoView session.

11.8.1 Simple Search

Simple search is the most basic form of search and is most useful when you have a good idea of the report information that you're looking for and don't need any more advanced help in finding the document. Simple search allows you to search either public or personal folders and categories, but you aren't able to search both public and personal at the same time. To have this functionality, you need to use advanced search.

11.8.2 Advanced Search

Advanced search provides additional capabilities to search with more defined parameters. Advanced searches can be performed against the following fields: keywords, title, descriptions, owner type, or last modification time. You can also use any combination of these fields in an advanced search.

To perform an advanced search, select Advanced Search in the drop-down next to the Search box on the workspace toolbar. You'll be prompted to select the location to be searched. You can select from Public Folders, Private Folders, Inbox, Personal Categories, and Corporate Categories. You can also select more than one location to perform your search. After selecting the search location, you define the search parameters based on your field choices. After all parameters are entered, select the Search button to view the list of objects meeting your qualifications.

11.8.3 Content Search

The content search allows you to search within the content of objects contained within InfoView. For Web Intelligence documents, content search allows you to search on the following content within the Web Intelligence report:

▶ Report title
▶ Report description (as defined in report properties)
▶ Universe filter names
▶ Universe object names
▶ Data contained in the report
▶ Static text contained within the report

Web Intelligence documents, Desktop Intelligence documents, Crystal Reports, Microsoft Excel, Microsoft Word, RTF, PDF, and text files are all searchable using content search if contained within the InfoView environment. The files that you can search will depend on your access rights. The data regarded by a content search is different for each document type. Other document types are also searchable, but they will be searched similar to an advanced search rather than searching the additional content viewed in a content search.

11.9   Summary

The InfoView portal provides a multifunctional interface for the casual user to organize, view, print, and share Web Intelligence documents. Additional features such as tracking data changes and robust search capabilities make the SAP Business-Objects Enterprise interface a powerful tool for collaboration across the business.

Chapter 12 discusses the use of multiple data providers within your Web Intelligence queries. The feature enables you to merge dimensions from different sources to provide further business intelligence for your organization.

Integrate data from multiple sources into a single Web Intelligence document to produce powerful and analytical reports. Merge compatible dimension objects from disparate sources to join unrelated results.

12 Using Multiple Data Sources

SAP BusinessObjects Web Intelligence XI 3.1 provides the capability of combining result data retrieved from separate queries into a single reporting document. Several different queries can be added to a single document by querying the same universe, querying different universes, or accessing other data sources such as text files, Microsoft Excel files, or Web Services.

Chapter 3, Creating a Web Intelligence XI 3.x Query, briefly discussed the use of multiple data sources in a single report. This chapter will take you deeper into the processes of merging dimensions, synchronizing data, and using local data providers to bring data into a document with Web Intelligence in InfoView or Rich Client.

The concept of merging dimensions and synchronizing data was first introduced to Web Intelligence with XI R2. Before XI R2, the only way to include data from multiple sources in a single report was to use the full-client tool currently known as Desktop Intelligence. With Desktop Intelligence, multiple new data providers were (and still are) added to a single document. Comparable dimensions are then linked in the Data Manager.

The process of merging dimensions in Web Intelligence is much different from its Desktop Intelligence predecessor. The first section in this chapter describes the process of retrieving data from multiple sources and is followed by an explanation of merging and synchronizing dimension objects.

12.1 Accessing Multiple Data Sources

Multiple data sources in a single document allow developers to produce powerful reports by combining the features in the Web Intelligence Report Panel with data retrieved from different queries, universes, or local sources.

12.1.1 Accessing Multiple Data Sources from InfoView

Follow these steps to include the results from a different query in an existing document.

1. Create or edit an existing document.

2. Click Edit Query to access the Query Panel.

3. Click Add Query to launch the Universe selection window.

Figure 12.1 shows the Query Panel of a Web Intelligence document in InfoView. The Add Query button is used to include a new query in the existing document.

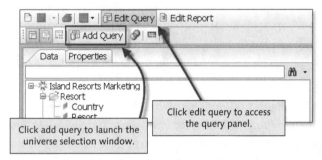

Figure 12.1 Add New Queries to Existing Documents from the Query Panel

After clicking Add Query, you'll be prompted to select a universe as the source for your query.

Note

The option to add a nonuniverse access type as the data source is only available when using Web Intelligence Rich Client.

The Universe selection window provides you with a list of universes being used in the current document and a list of all available universes. The Available Universes section lists all universes that you have the rights to access.

If you're looking for a particular universe that isn't listed in the Available Universes section, contact your system administrator or business intelligence contact to have the proper permissions granted.

Figure 12.2 shows the Universe selection window after clicking Add Query.

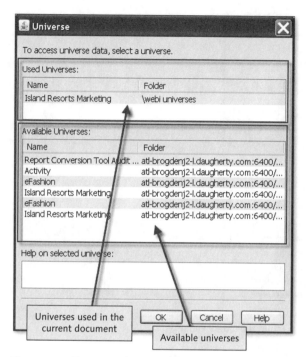

Figure 12.2 Universe Selection Window When Adding a Query

After selecting a universe, the new query will be added as a tab in the Query Panel. Right-click on any tab in the Query Panel to rename or delete a query.

The following list includes all of the actions that can be performed when right-clicking on a Query tab. Figure 12.3 shows the menu for right-clicking on a Query tab.

- **Rename Query:** Change the query name from the default Query 1 standard.
- **Move Query:** Move left or move right depending on the tab location.
- **Run Query:** Execute the selected query.
- **Add Query:** Add an additional query to the document.
- **Duplicate Query:** Create a duplicate copy of the selected tab.
- **Delete Query:** Remove the query of the selected tab.

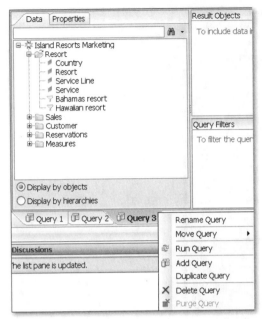

Figure 12.3 Right-clicking on a Query Tab in the Query Panel

12.1.2 Accessing Multiple Data Sources in Web Intelligence Rich Client

You'll be prompted to select a Data Access Type when adding queries to existing documents in Web Intelligence Rich Client.

Figure 12.4 shows the two selection types when adding a query using Rich Client; Universe is selected by default. Click Next to launch the Universe selection window previously shown in Figure 12.2.

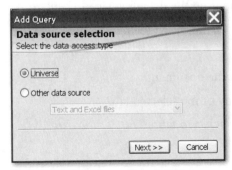

Figure 12.4 Data Access Type Selection

Select Other Data Source to enable the drop-down box shown in Figure 12.4 and give you a choice of two other data source selections:

- Text and Excel Files
- Web Services

Text and Excel Files

If Text and Excel Files is chosen, click Next to launch the PDP window. PDP stands for Personal Data Provider. This window allows you to browse to a personal or local data source to import into your document.

PDPs allow you to create Web Intelligence reports from Microsoft Excel worksheets, .txt files, or three other file types.

Reports can be published to the SAP BusinessObjects server and distributed to users across the enterprise through the InfoView portal.

Following is a list of file types that can be used as a PDP source.

- *.TXT
- *.CSV
- *.PRN
- *.ASC
- *.XLS

Figure 12.5 shows the PDP window for browsing to local data documents.

Figure 12.5 PDP (Personal Data Providers) Access Screen

If an XLS file is selected as the data source type, the PDP window shown in Figure 12.5 expands to include a Worksheet/Workbook File section. This section requires that you select the Sheet Name that you want to import.

After selecting the Sheet Name, you can choose one of two Field Selection options:

▶ All Fields

▶ Range Definition

Field Selections

Select the All Fields option to use all of the fields in the selected sheet that contain values. Select the Range Definition option to define a specific cell range to use as the field selection.

You'll have the opportunity to include the first row of fields selected to serve as column names by checking the First Row Contains Column Names checkbox box at the bottom of the expanded PDP window (this is checked by default.

Figure 12.6 shows the expanded PDP window that is displayed when Excel is selected as the other data source access type.

Figure 12.6   Expanded PDP Window - Using an Excel File as a Data Source

> **Note**
>
> XLSX files can't be included as a selectable data source. Be sure to save all Excel 2007 files as Excel 97-2003 Workbook type objects before selecting.
>
> Figure 12.7 shows the error message that is displayed if you attempt to select an XLSX file as the data source.

Figure 12.7   Error Received When Selecting an XLSX File as Other Data Source

Web Services

You'll be prompted to enter and submit a source URL if Web Services is selected as the Other Data Source access type.

The Custom Data Provider – Web Services window is used to connect to data by typing or pasting a Web Services URL.

Integrate data from Query as a Web Service (QaaWS) into a Web Intelligence Rich Client report by using this feature.

Figure 12.8 shows the details for connecting to a WSDL or Web Service as the Other Data Source – Data Access Type.

After submitting the URL, you'll be prompted for three selections in the Service Details section of the Web Service Details window. Drop-downs are provided for all three detail categories, and a selectable value is associated to your URL.

The example in Figure 12.8 shows WS_1 as the Service Name of the Web Service URL that was entered.

To receive data from the Web Service data source, you must complete the following service detail requirements:

▶ Service Name

▶ Port Name

▶ Operation Name

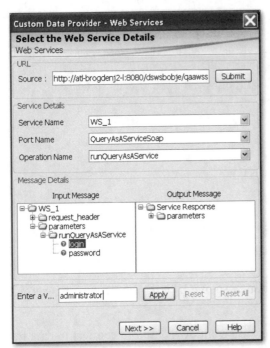

Figure 12.8 Custom Data Provider – Web Services: Details

The Message Details section consists of the following two sections:

▶ Input Message

▶ Output Message

A login and password must be entered and applied in the `runQueryAsAService` parameter for the selected Web Service(s). Follow these steps:

1. Click Login after expanding `runQueryAsAService`.

2. Type the user name with proper credentials into the available text box.

3. Click Apply.

4. Repeat the process for the password.

Be sure to select an Output Message to retrieve data from the Web Service data source.

Chapter 17, Web Intelligence Rich Client, provides you with many more details on working with Web Intelligence Rich Client.

> **Note**
>
> Unlike Web Intelligence in InfoView, Web Intelligence Rich Client is a downloadable software tool that must be installed on your PC. To download and install Web Intelligence Rich Client, follow these steps:
>
> ▶ Click Preferences in the upper-right corner of Web Intelligence.
>
> ▶ Expand the Web Intelligence Properties.
>
> ▶ Click Install Now beside Desktop (Web Intelligence Rich Client).

12.2   Merging Dimensions

After you've added a new query and the data is returned to the Report Panel, you can begin using the result objects available in the Data tab to create reports. But, there is a catch.

Until the data providers have been synchronized through one or more merged dimensions, the results from separate data sources must appear in separate blocks.

Figure 12.9 shows an attempt to insert a result object from a second data source into a data block from an existing data set without merging dimensions. The result is a message that states, "Can't drop here. Incompatible object."

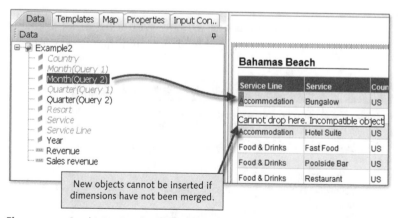

Figure 12.9 Combining Result Objects Without Merging Dimensions

To synchronize the data returned by the separate queries, you need to verify that both queries contain at least one compatible dimension object. After this has been confirmed, you can merge the compatible dimensions.

There are two requirements for merging dimensions:

▶ The result objects to be merged must have the same data type.

▶ The result objects to be merged must contain compatible and related data.

12.2.1 Manually Merging Dimensions

As stated in the previous section, the process of merging dimensions begins by including compatible dimension objects in every data source to be merged.

Continue building out the queries in your document, and then refresh the queries to access the data. Now that you have result objects in the Data tab, click the merge dimensions icon located on the reporting toolbar shown in Figure 12.10.

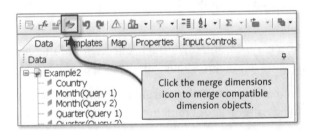

Figure 12.10 Merge Dimensions Icon on the Reporting Toolbar

Figure 12.11 shows the Merge Dimensions window with a list of all available dimensions to be merged. Select the compatible objects, and then click Merge.

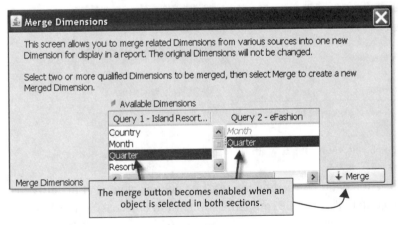

Figure 12.11 Merge Dimensions

After selecting a dimension in the first section, only objects with the same data type will be enabled in the list of dimensions in the other data sources.

Figure 12.12 shows the Merge Dimensions window with the Quarter object selected in the first list of available dimensions. Quarter is the only field in the second list with the same data type.

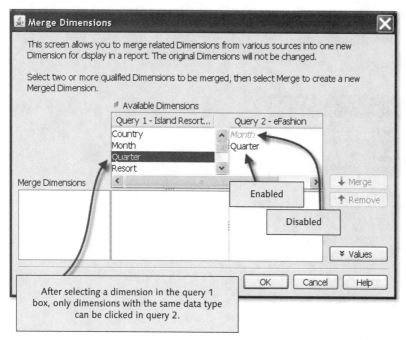

Figure 12.12 Merge Dimensions

Follow the next set of steps to complete the dimension merging process:

1. Select the compatible object in both data source boxes.

2. Click the Values button to view a sample of the data from each object selected. Verify that the data is compatible.

3. Click Merge.

4. Verify or update the new Merged Dimension Name. Click OK.

12.2.2 Edit Merged Dimension Names Before Merging

When dimensions are selected from two or more data sources in the Merge Dimensions window and Merge is clicked, the Edit Merged Dimension box opens.

Figure 12.13 shows the Edit Merged Dimension dialog box displayed before merging the source dimensions into a new dimension.

The following sections are modifiable in the Edit Merged Dimension window:

▶ Merged Dimensions Name

▶ Description

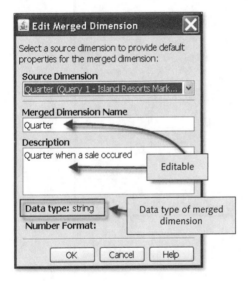

Figure 12.13 Edit Merged Dimension Window

Click OK to accept changes and return to the Merge Dimension window.

Figure 12.14 shows that the Quarter dimension was merged. This process has removed both Quarter objects from the Available Dimensions boxes and placed them down one level into the Merge Dimensions boxes.

After two or more dimensions have been merged, the Remove and Values buttons become enabled. This gives you the opportunity to remove a merged dimension or view the values.

In Figure 12.14, the Values button has been clicked to display the values of the selected dimension objects in the third row of boxes. Click OK to accept merge.

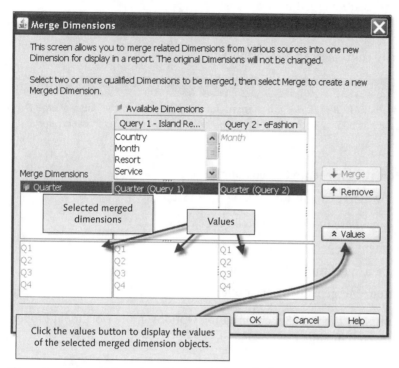

Figure 12.14 Merge Dimensions Displaying Values of Selected Objects

12.3   Data Synchronization

Data synchronization refers to the process of synching related dimension objects from two or more data providers. This process is very important for ensuring that your reports display the correct results. Working with unsynchronized data will be discussed in Section 12.4, Working with Unsynchronized Data.

The primary purpose of using multiple data sources in a single document is to produce reports that combine the results obtained from disparate sources or results retrieved from similar sources but using different query filters and result objects to provide more meaningful and analytical reporting documents.

The extent of your ability to use data from multiple sources depends on the capability to include and merge related dimension objects from all data sources.

Dimension objects are merged in two ways:

► Manually (previously described in Section 12.2, Merging Dimensions)
► Automatically (auto-merged dimensions)

The Result of Auto-Merged Dimensions

Dimensions from multiple queries are merged automatically when the Auto-Merge Dimension setting has been selected and the same object name appears in each query.

Steps to Automatically Merge Dimensions

To automatically merge dimensions, follow these steps:

1. Right-click anywhere in the Web Intelligence report.
2. Select Document Properties from the menu.
3. Locate the Data Synchronization Options.
4. Check the Auto-Merge Dimensions option.

Figure 12.15 displays the Data Synchronization Options in the Document Properties section of a Web Intelligence document.

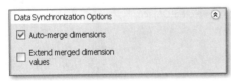

Figure 12.15 Data Synchronization Options

In the event that two objects from different data sources have the same name but do not represent compatible data, uncheck the Auto-Merge Dimensions setting in the Data Synchronization Options box prior to adding the data.

Note

After removing the default setting to Auto-Merge Dimensions, the change takes effect when any subsequent queries are added.

Extend Merged Dimension Values

The Extend Merged Dimension Values setting in the Data Synchronization Options section is used to perform a full outer join of merged dimension objects. This setting allows for all of the values from both data sources to be merged into the newly created merged dimension object.

Things to Remember About Merging Dimensions

Keep the following in mind about merging dimensions:

▸ Multiple queries from the same universe can be added to a single document to include results with different result objects and query filters.

▸ Multiple queries can be inserted using different universes.

▸ Dimensions to be merged must have the same data type.

▸ When manually merging dimensions, only the data type of the selected objects is required to create the merged dimension. Both objects should, however, contain compatible data. The object has no bearing.

▸ An unlimited number of data sources can exist within a single document.

▸ An unlimited number of data source dimensions can be merged.

When dimensions are merged, the new objects are available in the Data tab of the Report Manager in the Report Panel.

Figure 12.16 shows the Merged Dimensions folder with the Quarter object in the Data tab of the Report Manager.

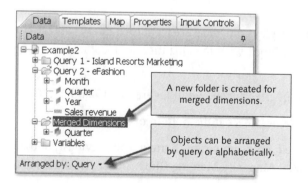

Figure 12.16 Data Tab with Merged Dimensions Folder

Arrange the Available Objects and Variables in One of Two Ways

You can arrange the objects and variables by query or alphabetically.

After adding additional queries to your report, both queries can be refreshed by clicking Refresh All in the primary toolbar, or an individual query can be refreshed. Figure 12.17 show the refreshing options.

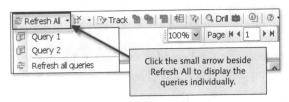

Figure 12.17 Refresh Multiple Queries

12.4   Working with Unsynchronized Data

When multiple data providers are used in a single document and at least one dimension has not been merged, the data is considered to be unsynchronized. The results from both data sources can be used separately in the reporting document, but measures can't appear within the same block. If measures from unsynchronized sources appear in the same block, at least one measure will display inaccurate results.

Figure 12.18 shows an example created by using the [Sales revenue] and [Quantity sold] measure objects, each coming from different queries generated from the eFashion universe.

In the example, a vertical table displays one measure from each query source. The result is an unsynchronized data block with the Quantity Sold column showing inaccurate values.

The result objects used in both queries are shown in Figures 12.19 and 12.20.

Figure 12.21 shows the Store Name object at the bottom of a hierarchy.

To synchronize the data, click the merge dimension shortcut icon previously shown in Figure 12.10 in Section 12.2.1, Manually Merging Dimensions. The dimension merged in this example is the Store Name object.

City	Sales revenue	Quantity sold
Austin	$2,699,673	223,229
Boston	$1,283,707	223,229
Chicago	$3,022,658	223,229
Colorado Springs	$2,060,275	223,229
Dallas	$1,970,034	223,229
Houston	$5,447,957	223,229
Los Angeles	$4,220,929	223,229
Miami	$1,879,159	223,229
New York	$7,582,221	223,229
San Francisco	$3,258,641	223,229
Washington	$2,961,950	223,229
Sum:	$36,387,203	223,229

Unsynchronized data

Figure 12.18 Unsynchronized Data Example

Result Objects

State | City | Store name | Sales revenue

Figure 12.19 First Query in the Example – Three Dimension Objects

Result Objects

Store name | Quantity sold

Figure 12.20 Second Query in the Example – One Dimension Object

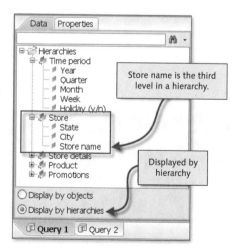

Data | Properties

Hierarchies
  Time period
      Year
      Quarter   Store name is the third
      Month   level in a hierarchy.
      Week
      Holiday (y/n)
  Store
      State
      City
      Store name
  Store details
  Product   Displayed by
  Promotions   hierarchy

○ Display by objects
◉ Display by hierarchies

Query 1 | Query 2

Figure 12.21 Data Objects in the Query Panel – Displayed by Hierarchy

341

After merging the [Store name] dimension in both queries, the data block appears exactly as it did in Figure 12.18 because the dimension in the table is the City object.

Use the `forceMerge()` formula to provide synchronization to data providers with different aggregation levels. This allows both measures to display accurate results when using any of the following objects: State, City, or Store Name.

The forceMerge() Formula

The `forceMerge()` formula works when the dimensions merged have objects above it in the hierarchy. Figure 12.21, shown earlier, displays the Store Name object and its location in the hierarchy.

Figure 12.22 shows the same vertical table as in Figure 12.18, but the [Quantity sold] measure has been encapsulated in the `ForceMerge()` formula.

City	Sales revenue	Quantity sold
Austin	$2,699,673	17,078
Boston	$1,283,707	7,676
Chicago	$3,022,658	17,976
Colorado Springs	$2,060,275	12,787
Dallas	$1,970,034	12,365
Houston	$5,447,957	18,988
Los Angeles	$4,220,929	26,244
Miami	$1,879,159	11,267
New York	$7,582,221	28,264
San Francisco	$3,258,641	19,830
Washington	$2,961,950	18,744
Sum:	$36,387,203	223,229

formula bar: `fx` `=ForceMerge([Quantity sold])`

Figure 12.22 Quantity Sold with the ForceMerge() Formula

Note

► Filtering in reports can't be applied to merged dimension objects. The pre-merged dimension objects must be used when adding report filters.

► When a filter is added to a report that was used to create a merged dimension, the filter is applied to all synchronized data providers.

12.5   Summary

Use multiple data sources in a single document to expand the capabilities of your reports by combining data from a variety of sources.

Report writers and developers can include the results from multiple queries sourced from the same universe, different universes, and other data sources such as Excel files, TXT files, CSV files, or Web Services.

Data synchronization is the key to combining the results from multiple data sources. This is achieved by auto-merging dimensions or manually merging dimension objects through the Merge Dimensions Editor.

Use the `forceMerge()` function to synchronize data providers with different aggregate levels if the dimensions objects have other dimensions above it in the hierarchy.

Chapter 13 builds on the information discussed in Chapter 3, Creating a Web Intelligence XI 3.x Query, to provide you with advanced techniques for creating powerful queries in the Query Panel.

Apply complex filtering strategies when retrieving data to create reports with highly customized and refined data sets. Use advanced querying techniques to produce highly focused reporting documents.

13 Extending Query Panel Functionality

All reporting requirements begin with a business question and end with a refined set of data displayed in a report that delivers a clear business answer. Reporting objectives are achieved and better decisions are made when data is transformed into actionable information. SAP BusinessObjects Web Intelligence XI 3.1 allows report viewers and report writers to achieve these goals by providing a variety of different query filtering options for producing highly constrained data sets.

Many advanced techniques can be used in the Query Panel to retrieve data and create powerful and interactive reports. These techniques include modifying the generated SQL with freehand SQL, creating complex and nested filters, and prompting the user for input with optional filters.

When queries are refreshed and data is returned, each Web Intelligence document stores the data in its own microcube. After data is in the microcube, reports can be created by adding result objects to a variety of available components. Chapters 4 through 7 provide very detailed information for creating and filtering reports.

Visually tracking data changes in a report is discussed later in this chapter. Data tracking is used to assist users with identifying revised or updated data from the most recent refresh compared to the previously refreshed instance.

13.1 Complex Filtering Options

Several techniques can be employed in the Query Panel to filter data retrieved by a query. Chapter 3, Creating a Web Intelligence XI 3.1 Query, discussed the use of combined queries and subqueries in the Query Panel.

This chapter covers additional methods of filtering queries to produce reports that contain the data needed for solving specific business problems.

13.1.1   Filtering with Wildcards

Wildcards are used to assist with filtering an object when the entire value isn't known. This type of filter is commonly used to create a filter when only the first letter in the value is known. Wildcards are also used when the exact spelling of the intended filter value isn't known.

Wildcards are used with the Matches Pattern operator. Matches Pattern is converted to LIKE when the SQL is generated.

Figure 13.1 shows the [Country] object using the Matches Pattern operator to return all countries beginning with U. Figure 13.2 shows the SQL translation.

Two Wildcard Characters

The wildcard characters are described here:

▶ **%:** Used to represent any number of characters.

▶ **_:** Used to represent a single character.

Figure 13.1   Query Filter with Matches Pattern Operator and % Wildcard

Figure 13.2   Matches Pattern Converted to LIKE in Generated SQL

Use the underscore character for each character to be represented in a filtered value. For example, if you want to filter an object to return both FRENCH and FRANCE, use both wildcards in combination with the known characters. This is achieved by using the characters featured in Figure 13.3 to show both wildcards used to filter the [Country] object.

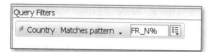

Figure 13.3 Custom Filter Containing Two Wildcards

SQL Generated by Filter with the Matches Pattern Operator

Figure 13.4 shows the SQL generated by the Matches Pattern operator.

Figure 13.4 SQL Generated by the Matches Pattern Operator

13.1.2 Nested Query Filters

Nested query filters are used for grouping a series of carefully targeted constraints that return a precisely targeted data set.

By nesting filters, dimensions and measures can be grouped into several combinations with the AND or OR operator. Nested filters can be applied to many layers of grouped objects with the AND or OR operator. This complex method of filtering is very easy to set up.

Adding and Nesting Query Filters

To add and nest query filters, follow these steps:

1. Drag and drop predefined filters, prompted objects, or standard results objects into the Query Panel.
2. Drop the filter directly on top of an existing filter object to nest the filter.
3. Drop the filter immediately beneath an existing filter to apply filtering outside of a nested relationship.
4. Double-click the AND and OR operator located immediately to the left of the nested group to toggle the operator type.

Figure 13.5 shows several query filters included at the same level in a Web Intelligence document grouped by default with the AND operator. If a query containing the filters in the screenshot were executed, the result would not return any rows because [Region] can't be equal to Bavaria and East Germany at the same time.

But if the filters were defined with the In List operator or were created in nested groups, the SQL statement would be generated differently and results would be returned to the document microcube.

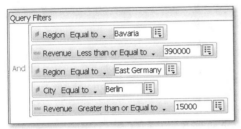

Figure 13.5 Query Filters Without Nesting

Nesting Filters

Figure 13.6 shows the exact same filters listed in the previous screenshot plus two additional filters. This SQL statement generated with this set of query filters successfully returns rows of data to the microcube because of the nesting operators used when grouping the filters.

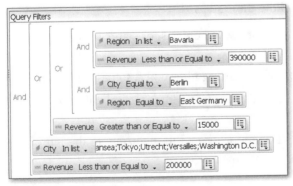

Figure 13.6 Nested Query Filters

Query filters can be added to a nested group with objects that have already been added to the Query Filters pane or by dragging and dropping new custom or pre-defined filter objects into the Query Filters pane.

Creating a Nested Group

To create a nested group, drop an object on top of an existing filter in the Query pane. A pair of thin horizontal rectangles will be displayed on top of the object to symbolize that a nested group will be created when the object is dropped.

This can also be achieved with existing filters by dragging and dropping an object on top of the filter object to be grouped with. Figure 13.7 shows the existing [Resort] object being dragged from an existing nested group and dropped onto another object to create a new nested group layer.

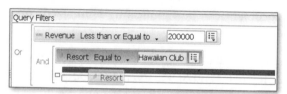

Figure 13.7   Creating a New Nested Group with Existing Query Filters

Creating Nested Groups with Existing Filter Objects

Each time a new nested group is created, the filter objects are nested together with the AND operator. A thin vertical line located to the left of the nested objects is used to visually denote the objects within the nested group.

Double-click AND to the left of the thin vertical line to switch the nested group to the OR operator.

Un-Nest Query Filters

To remove a query filter from a nested group, drag and drop it to a different location. This can mean moving it to a different nested group or moving it completely out of all nested groups.

Figure 13.8 shows the [City] object being moved dragged from a nested group and dropped to the bottom of the query filters.

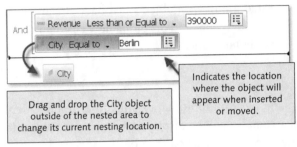

Figure 13.8 Removing a Query Filter from a Nested Group

13.1.3 Database Ranking

Database ranking is used in a reporting document to return only the rows specific in the ranking criteria. By pushing ranking onto the database, the amount of data retrieved in a Web Intelligence document can be significantly minimized compared to performing ranking locally.

Database ranking can only be used if your database supports it. Databases that support ranking include Oracle, DB2, Teradata, and SQL Server. The add a database ranking shortcut icon will be disabled if your database doesn't support ranking.

Adding Database Ranking

You can add database ranking to a document by clicking the add a database ranking button located in the upper-right corner of the Query Filters pane (see Figure 13.9). Click this icon to launch the Database Ranking Parameters filter object.

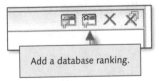

Figure 13.9 Adding Database Ranking in the Query Panel

The Database Ranking Parameters filter will be added to the Query Filters pane when add a database ranking is clicked. Figure 13.10 shows the database ranking parameter filter object.

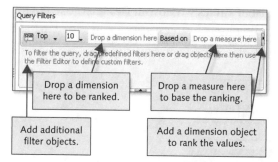

Figure 13.10 Database Ranking Parameters

The primary parameters in database ranking are listed here:

▶ Direction of ranked values

▶ Number of records to rank

▶ Dimension object that provides the context for ranking

▶ The measure to base the ranking on

Steps for Completing the Parameters for Database Ranking

To complete the parameters for database ranking, follow these steps:

1. Select a ranking direction – Top or Bottom.

2. Enter the number of records to be ranked, or click the small down arrow beside the value box to select Prompt. The default value is Constant.

3. Drop a dimension object for the context of the ranking.

4. Drop measure object to be ranked in the Based On box.

5. (Optionally) Specify additional calculation context by clicking the small arrow to the right of the Based On measure to expand the ranking parameters box and display a For Each (dimension) option.

13.2   Cascading and Optional Prompts

Cascading prompts are used to assist users with selecting values in prompted Web Intelligence reports.

Use the Designer tool to create and modify cascading prompts for dimension objects by creating a Cascading List of Values (LOVs). Figure 13.11 shows the steps for opening the Create a Cascading List of Values window in Designer. Use the following path to begin setting up cascading lists of values: Tools • Lists of Values • Create cascading Lists of Values.

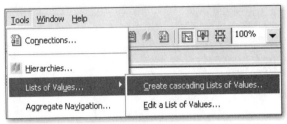

Figure 13.11 Create a Cascading Lists of Values in Designer

13.2.1 Defining a Cascading Lists of Values in Designer

The selection launches the Create Cascading List of Values window displayed in Figure 13.12. Select dimensions from the list of available objects, and click the > icon to add them to the list. LOVs should be created hierarchically.

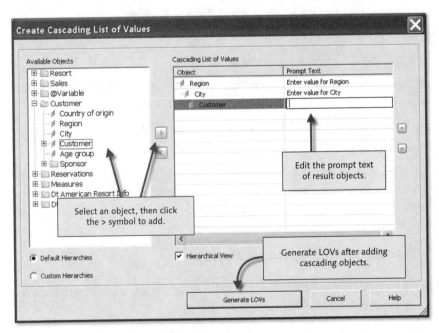

Figure 13.12 Cascading Lists of Values Dialog Window

To creating a cascading LOV, follow these steps:

1. Select objects to generate a cascading list of values.

2. Click the > symbol to add objects to the Cascading List of Values section.

3. (Optionally) Revise the Prompt Text of each object.

4. Click Generate LOVs to accept the selections and create the cascading list.

Note

Be sure to save and export your universe to the repository after creating the LOV.

13.2.2 Using a Cascading List of Values Object as a Prompted Filter in a Report

After creating cascading LOVs in the universe, any object in the list of values can be used as a prompted filter by following these steps:

1. Drop the object onto the Query Filters pane.

2. Select Prompt as the filter type (see Figure 13.13).

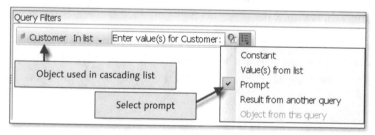

Figure 13.13   Using a Cascading Objects as a Prompted Filter

3. After selecting the Prompt filter type, click the Settings button to view the Prompt settings.

4. Be sure to check the Prompt with List of Values checkbox as shown in Figure 13.14.

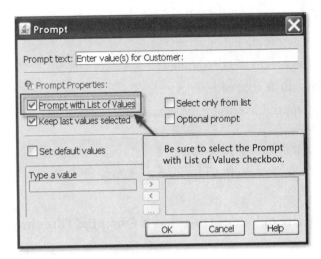

Figure 13.14 Prompt Properties

13.2.3 Refreshing a Report with a Prompted LOV Object Filter

Cascading prompt filters become useful when refreshing reports. All objects in the cascading list will appear in the prompted values list in tree form. Navigate into the tree to select the values you want.

As an example, Figure 13.15 shows the order of the cascading list of objects. Notice that the [Customer] object is at the bottom of the hierarchy, the [City] object is one level up, and the [Region] object is at the top of the hierarchy.

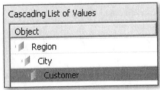

Figure 13.15 Hierarchy of Cascading List of Values

Prompt Filter with Cascading List of Values

When the [Customer] object is added as a prompted filter and the report is refreshed, you'll be prompted to select a value from the list of available customer objects.

When the object being filtered is at the bottom of the hierarchy in a cascading LOV, you'll need to expand the object values above it in the hierarchy until you get down to the level of the object.

In this example, the [Country] object prompts the user to expand a [Region] value, followed by expanding a [City] within the region selected, and finally selecting the [Customer] value (see Figure 13.16). Click the > symbol to add the value to the list, and then click Run Query.

The Run Query button becomes enabled when at least one value is added.

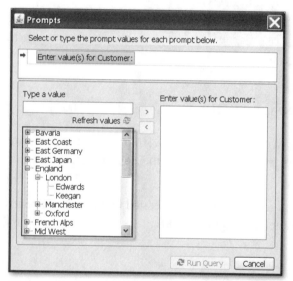

Figure 13.16   Prompted Filter of Cascading List of Values Object

13.2.4   Optional Prompts

Check the Optional Prompt checkbox to make a prompted filter object optional when answering prompts rather than requiring the user to select or enter a value.

To access this setting, set the filter type to Prompt, and then launch the Prompt properties dialog box. Figure 13.17 shows the Optional Prompt selection in the Prompt properties window.

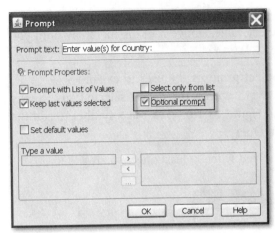

Figure 13.17 Making a Prompt Filter Optional

13.3 Using Custom Freehand SQL

Freehand SQL can be used in a Web Intelligence XI 3.1 report to enable report developers to rewrite, revise, or completely replace the SQL generated by the Query Panel.

Edit a Web Intelligence document to view the SQL generated by the result objects and query filters in the Query Panel (see Figure 13.18).

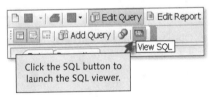

Figure 13.18 View SQL Button in the Query Toolbar

Viewing Generated SQL

The SQL Viewer is used to display the SQL generated by the objects in your query. The SQL is displayed in light gray lettering until the Use Custom SQL option button is selected.

Figure 13.19 shows the SQL Viewer with the generated SQL displayed. The Undo and Validate buttons are disabled unless using custom SQL.

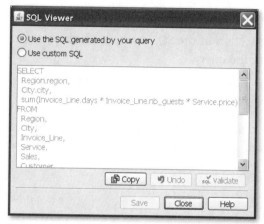

Figure 13.19 SQL Viewer Displaying Generated SQL

Use Custom SQL

Click the Use Custom SQL button to enable the text area displaying the generated SQL. The code is then displayed in black lettering and is editable.

Figure 13.20 shows the SQL Viewer with customizable SQL. Modify or replace the existing SQL, and click Validate to test the syntax of your changes.

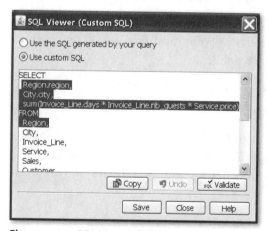

Figure 13.20 SQL Viewer with Custom SQL

If no errors were found after validating the SQL, click Save to overwrite the SQL generated by the result objects in the Query Panel.

The two requirements for editing the generated SQL are listed here:

▸ The number of items in the Select section of the SQL must match the number of result objects originally placed in the query.

▸ The data type of the objects in the Custom SQL Viewer must match the data type of the result objects originally placed in the query

Figure 13.21 shows an error message that you'll receive if you attempt to add two additional Select objects in the Custom SQL Viewer when only three objects are in the Result Objects pane.

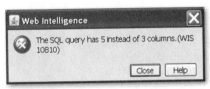

Figure 13.21 Error When Modifying Generated SQL

13.4   Visually Tracking Data Changes in the Report Panel

Tracking data changes allows you to visually identify data changes at a glance when a query is refreshed. Many viewing options can be modified to customize the appearance of data values that have changed when a report is refreshed.

To compare the changes in data, a reference point must first be set. Two options are available when setting the reference point:

▸ Auto-update the reference data with each data refresh (default).

▸ Use the current data as reference data.

Data tracking is toggled off or on by clicking the Track button in the default toolbar located in the upper-right corner of the Report Panel. Two new shortcut icons are displayed immediately to the right of the Track button when tracking is enabled as shown in Figure 13.22:

▸ Hide changes/show changes

▸ Data tracking options

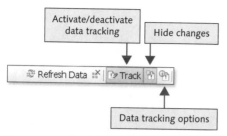

Figure 13.22 Track Data Changes Button

13.4.1 Showing and Hiding Data Changes

The button located immediately to the right of the Track button is used to toggle back and forth to show or hide data changes in a report. Figure 13.23 shows the default data tracking formatting for when values from the reference are different from the values in the latest refresh.

The screenshot shows the report when data changes are set to be shown.

East Japan

Region	City	Revenue
East Japan	Tokyo	652,919
East Japan	Yokohama	359,808
	ast Japan (Subtotal):	1,012,727

Mid West

Region	City	Revenue
Mid West	Chicago	441,594
	Mid West (Subtotal):	441,594

Figure 13.23 Visible Changes When Tracking Data Changes

13.4.2 Data Tracking Options

The Data Tracking Options dialog box is launched by clicking the button to the right of the hide/show changes tracking button on the default toolbar in the Report Panel.

Formatting can be applied to modify a variety of font- and background-related attributes. Figure 13.24 shows the options to visually display data changes.

Changes can be displayed for five categories:

► Insertions

► Deletions

► Changes

► Increased Values

► Decreased Values

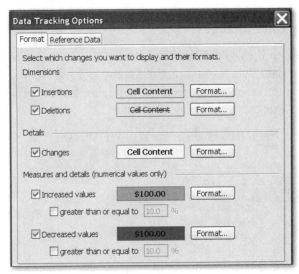

Figure 13.24 Data Tracking Options

13.4.3 Purging Data

The option to purge data is commonly used before publishing Web Intelligence reports to the server that potentially contain restricted information.

The option to purge data is available in the Query Panel and Report Panel. Figure 13.25 shows the purge data shortcut icon located on the default toolbar in the Report Panel.

Figure 13.25 Purge Data

13.4.4 Identify and Modify Partial Results

If a query refreshes successfully but returns partial results, the bottom-right corner of the report will display the phrase "Partial results" beside a yellow icon containing an exclamation point.

Figure 13.26 shows the bottom right of a Web Intelligence report that was returned with partial results.

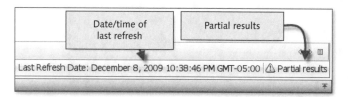

Figure 13.26 Indicates Partial Results

Resolving Partial Results

Partial results leave reporting documents incomplete and should be resolved before publishing, printing, or exporting a report locally or to the CMS.

There are two primary areas to examine and potentially modify your query returns partials results:

▸ Max Rows Retrieved setting in the Limits category in the Properties tab of the Data Manager in the Query Panel as shown in Figure 13.27

▸ Controls tab in the Universe Parameters dialog box shown in Figure 13.28

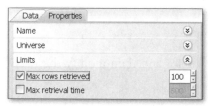

Figure 13.27 Max Rows Retrieved Setting in the Properties Tab of the Data Manager

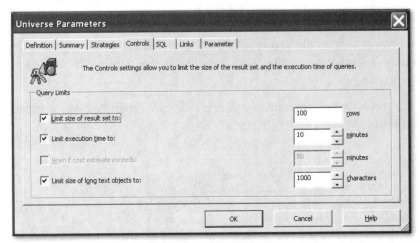

Figure 13.28 Controls Tab in the Universe Parameters

Take the following steps to modify the maximum number of rows retrieved in the query:

1. Click Edit Query to enter the Query Panel.

2. Click the Properties tab of the Data Manager.

3. Check or uncheck the Max Rows Retrieved setting.

4. If checked, modify the number of rows.

Use the following steps to modify the maximum number of retrievable rows from a universe:

1. Launch Designer.

2. Open the Universe Parameters dialog box.

3. Click the Controls tab.

4. Check or uncheck the Limit Size of Result Set To, and then modify the maximum number of rows to be retrieved.

13.4.5 User Settings

User settings are setup when editing a Web Intelligence document by clicking the Show User Settings button located in the upper-right corner of the report. Figure 13.29 shows the icon that launches the User Settings window.

Figure 13.29   Showing User Settings

User settings are setup in the Query Panel but enhance the report design capabilities in the Report Panel.

Function of User Settings

The user settings provide two primary functions in the Report Panel, and they both involve the use of a design grid (see Figure 13.30):

▶ Show Grid

▶ Snap to Grid

A grid can be displayed in the Report Panel to assist report writers with placing report elements in a clean and aligned format. A grid can be measured in pixels, inches, or centimeters, and the grid spacing can be manually adjusted.

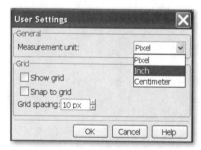

Figure 13.30   User Settings

13.5   Summary

Get the most out of your queries by including complex nested filters, prompted filters with cascading lists of values, database ranking, and custom SQL in a Web Intelligence report. Then produce the most accurate, valuable, and actionable reports possible for your clients by using the extensive features available in the Query Panel.

Use a variety of data tracking features in a report to allow business users to easily identify changes in company data compared to values from a specified reference point.

Chapter 14 explains several advanced universe design techniques that also extend the functionality of Web Intelligence reports.

Extend the capabilities of Web Intelligence by including interactive objects created in the universe. Use advanced design techniques to improve the query performance in reporting documents and provide added functionality and flexibility to report consumers.

14   Advanced Universe Design Topics

Increase the flexibility of your Web Intelligence reporting documents by extending the functionality of your universes. Many advanced universe design options can be added to existing universes that improve report building and query filtering capabilities.

After mastering the topics of universe design discussed in Chapter 2, The SAP BusinessObjects Universe, use this chapter to learn several techniques for extending universe capabilities.

This chapter introduces the following topics for extending the functionality of universes by working with the Designer tool:

- Creating interactive dimension objects with `@Functions`
- Linking universes to share commonly used objects
- Creating derived virtual tables in a universe
- Working with Lists of Values (LOVs)

The first section discusses the `@Functions` that can be used to create objects in the universe to prompt Web Intelligence report viewers for input and reuse the definitions of existing objects.

14.1   @Functions

Five different universe-level functions are available in the SAP BusinessObjects XI 3.1 Designer tool to create interactive objects to be used in Web Intelligence reports. These functions are known as `@Functions`.

Six @Functions are available in the Edit Properties dialog box when defining a Select statement or Where clause of an object in the Designer client tool.

Only five of the functions available should be used for building objects in Web Intelligence reporting documents. These @Functions are listed here:

- @Aggregate_Aware
- @Prompt
- @Select
- @Variable
- @Where

Figure 14.1 shows the @Functions available in the property editor window.

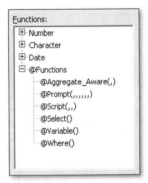

Figure 14.1 @Functions in the Property Editor in Designer

The @Script function shown in Figure 14.1 is used only in a Desktop Intelligence .REP file and returns the result of a VBA macro included in a Desktop Intelligence/BusinessObjects document.

This function is included in the Where clause of an object used for running processes in Desktop Intelligence.

The @Script function can't be used in a Web Intelligence document.

14.1.1 Creating an Object with an @Function

Objects with @Functions are created by editing the definition of a new or existing object in a universe. Click the buttons to the right of the Select or Where section in the object properties window to create the statements by using the columns and functions available.

Figure 14.2 shows the Definition tab in the properties window of a new object.

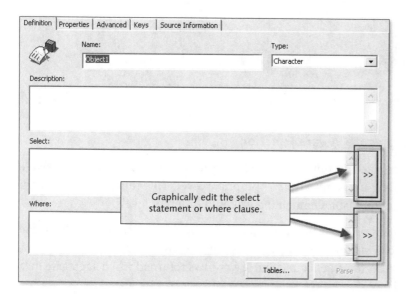

Figure 14.2 Definition Tab of the Edit Properties Window

After clicking the >> button to the right of the Select or Where section on the Definition tab, the Edit Select Statement or Edit Where Clause editor is launched to assist you with building queries.

Both editors provide objects in four categories:

▶ Tables and Columns

▶ Classes and Objects

▶ Operators

▶ Functions

Figure 14.3 shows the categories available in the Select statement and Where clause editors. Expand the @Functions grouping in the Functions section to display the @Functions available.

A description of the selected function will be displayed with a sample of the syntax structure to be used when creating a Select statement or Where clause containing the selected function.

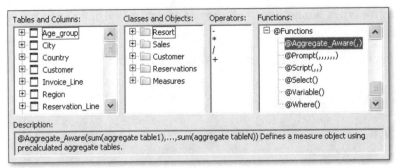

Figure 14.3   Categories of Objects Available for Defining Universe Objects

14.1.2   @Aggregate_Aware Function

The `@Aggregate_Aware()` function is used to create an object with aggregate awareness by providing measures at the appropriate level. This function accepts arguments from multiple tables containing values at different levels.

An example of an object using the `@Aggregate_Aware()` function contains aggregate measure objects for country, region, state, and city. This function allows for more efficient SQL to be generated and fewer rows returned when aggregate measures are available.

Setting up aggregate awareness is accomplished in four steps:

1. Build objects.
2. Specify incompatible objects.
3. Define all necessary contexts.
4. Test results.

Build Objects

To build objects, follow these steps:

1. Identify all possible columns to be aggregated.
2. Place the objects in order by level of aggregation.
3. Create the `@Aggregate_Aware` function to accept the aggregated columns as arguments. The column with the highest level of aggregation is listed first.

Identify Incompatible Objects

To identify incompatible objects, follow these steps:

1. Launch the Aggregate Navigation window by clicking Tools from the menu across the top of the screen in the Designer, and then selecting Aggregate Navigation as shown in Figure 14.4.

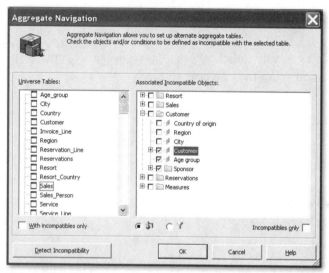

Figure 14.4 Aggregate Navigation Tools Option

2. Select an aggregate universe table on the left side of the Aggregate Navigation window, and check the associated incompatible objects on the right.

3. Repeat the two previous steps for each aggregate universe table included.

Figure 14.5 shows the Aggregate Navigation window for incompatible objects.

Figure 14.5 Aggregate Navigation

Define Any Necessary Contexts

You should create one context per aggregation.

Test the Results

To test the results:

▶ Run several queries.

▶ Validate the results.

Figure 14.6 shows the syntax of a hypothetical `@Aggregate_Aware ()` function in the `Select` statement of an object in the universe.

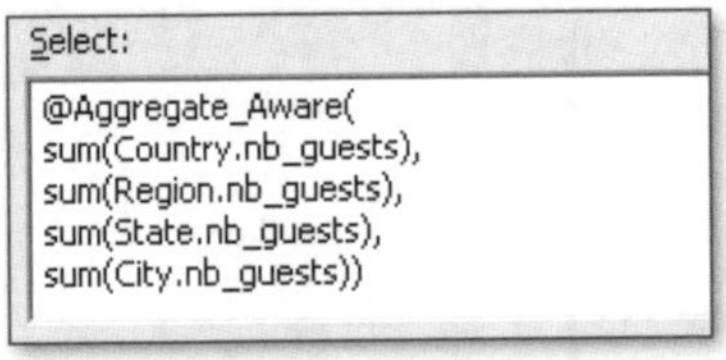

```
Select:
@Aggregate_Aware(
sum(Country.nb_guests),
sum(Region.nb_guests),
sum(State.nb_guests),
sum(City.nb_guests))
```

Figure 14.6 Aggregate_Aware Syntax

14.1.3 @Prompt Function

The `@Prompt` function is the most commonly used `@Function` and is used for creating interactive objects that prompt report viewers for input.

With the `@Prompt` function, universe designers can create objects that force users to enter one or more values that are passed to query filters when the object defined by using the `@Prompt` function is included in the Result Objects section of a Web Intelligence report. The `@Prompt` function provides a very flexible method of restricting data from being returned when a query is refreshed.

> **Note**
>
> The first two parameters, `Prompt Message` and `Data Type`, are the only two parameters required to create an object using the `@Prompt` function. Three trailing commas are also required if only the first two parameters are included.

@Prompt Parameters

`@Prompt` functions are created by assigning values for up to seven different parameters. Each parameter is separated by commas, and the first three parameters must be within single quotes. The parameters are described here:

▶ `Prompt Message:` Text message or question displayed to report users in the dialog box when a report is refreshed. Can be modified and must be contained within single quotes.

▶ `Data Type:` Specifies the data type being returned. The choices are: `'A'` for alphanumeric, `'D'` date, and `'N'` for number.

▶ `LOV` **pointer or hard-coded Lists of Values:** Points to a list of values defined in an existing object and referenced by the universe class followed by a backslash and then the object name in single quotes, for example, `'Sales\Year'`. Hard-coded values are values separated by commas and stored within brackets, for example, {`'London'`,`'Atlanta'`,`'Paris'`}.

▶ `Mono` **or** `Multi:` `Mono` accepts a single value; `multi` accepts one or many.

▶ `Free, Constrained,` **or** `Primary Key:` Selection availability.

▶ `Persistent` **or** `Not Persistent:` Retain or remove the last values used

▶ `Default Value` **or** `Key Value:` Allows a default value or key to be assigned.

An example of the simplest form of the `@Prompt` function is shown in Figure 14.7. This function prompts the user to enter a value then assigns it to the `Region.region` object.

`Region.region` is also assigned to the Select section of the object.

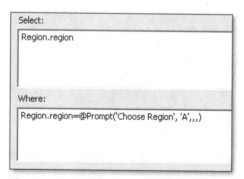

Figure 14.7 Simplest Use of the @Prompt Function

Figure 14.8 shows the prompt as it will appear when using the object in a Web Intelligence report and refreshing the query. Enter a value, and click Run Query.

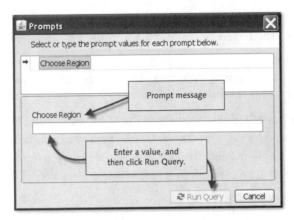

Figure 14.8 Prompt in Web Intelligence Reports

To prompt a user to select a single value from a list of objects, use the syntax shown in Figure 14.9 in the Where section of the object. In the screenshot, `Customer\Region` is displayed in the third position of the formula. The first word represents the universe class, and the second represents the object name.

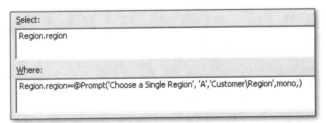

Figure 14.9 Prompt Definition to Select a Single Value from a LOV

Figure 14.10 shows the prompt that will appear to a Web Intelligence user. Select or type a value, click the > symbol, and then click Run Query.

To allow report consumers to select multiple values when prompted, include the word Multi in the fourth position. Figure 14.11 illustrates this point. Be sure to change the equal symbol to IN to allow the Query Panel to generate the correct SQL syntax.

Figure 14.12 shows the prompt when a report is refreshed in InfoView. Type or select one or more values, and then click Run Query.

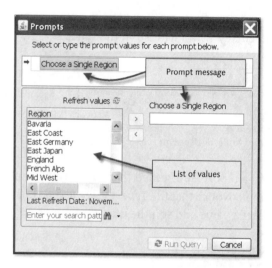

Figure 14.10   Prompt Filter - Refreshing a Report in InfoView

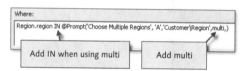

Figure 14.11   Prompt Object Setup to Accept Multiple Values

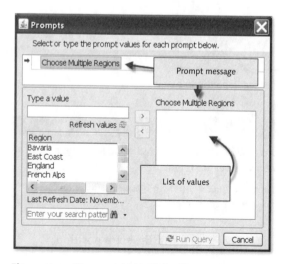

Figure 14.12   Type or Add Multiple Objects to a Prompted Object

Remove the ability to type a value by adding the constrained keyword to the syntax. Figure 14.13 shows the constrained keyword included in the syntax.

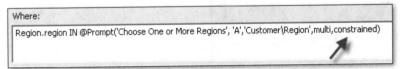

Where:

Region.region IN @Prompt('Choose One or More Regions', 'A','Customer\Region',multi,constrained)

Figure 14.13 Include the Constrained Keyword to Block User Entry

Figure 14.14 shows the prompt when a report is refreshed that contains the constrained keyword in the object definition. Notice that the Type a Value text box has been removed. The user can only select a value and run the query.

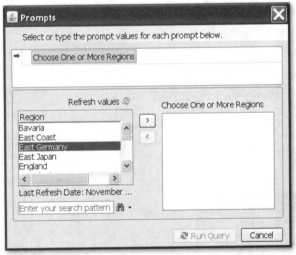

Figure 14.14 Constrained Prompt of Refreshing Report in InfoView

> **Note**
>
> Include the `not_persistent` keyword to clear the last selected value from the previous refresh. This setting is very important in very secure reports.
>
> Without including `not_persistent` in the object definition, the last value selected during the previous refresh is visible to the report consumer.

Figure 14.15 shows the syntax with `not_persistent` in the sixth position.

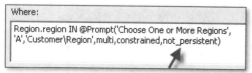

Figure 14.15 Use Not_Persistent to Clear Previous Selections

Prompting for Lower Level Objects

One very valuable application of the @Prompt function can be used to prompt a user to select values that will be assigned to an object that are different from the object being selected.

Figure 14.16 shows the @Prompt function used to prompt a user to select one or more regions while returning values for the city dimension. This allows a universe designer to force report consumers to choose a region to display the cities within the selected region. This method becomes very useful when you don't know the cities required for the report but you do know the region.

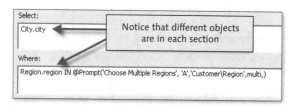

Figure 14.16 Prompting at Different Hierarchy Levels

14.1.4 @Select Function

The @Select function is used to reference the Select section of another object within the same universe. This feature can be very useful when reusing existing objects that contain complex Select definitions.

An example of a situation when the @Select function becomes useful is when a new object needs to be created to duplicate the Select definition of an existing object but include different code in the Where section of the object.

Figure 14.17 shows the @Select function being used in the Select and Where sections of a new object named "US Service Lines." The object created in Figure 14.17 returns Service Line values when the Country is 'US'.

The syntax of the @Select function is @Select(Class_Name\Object_Name).

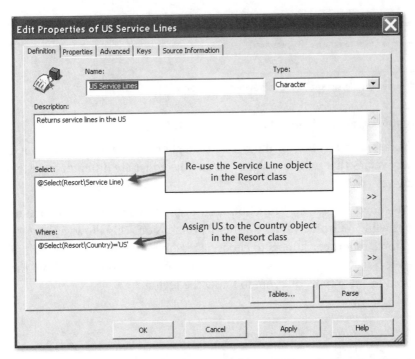

Figure 14.17 @Select Function Applied to the Select and Where Section of an Object

The @Select function provides a pointer to an existing object and minimizes the need to maintain multiple objects containing the same Select definition. This reduces the potential for mistakes when new objects are created.

As your database evolves and universe object definitions change, only the referenced objects will need to be updated. Objects created with the @Select function will be valid as long as the referenced object is up to date.

14.1.5 @Variable Function

The @Variable function is the least commonly used @Function in a Web Intelligence report because this function is used to access information relevant to the current document.

The @Variable function can be used in the Select or Where section in the definition of an object. Following is the syntax for the variables that can be used with the @Variable function followed by a brief description:

- @Variable('BOUSER'): User login.

- @Variable('DBUSER'): Database username.

- @Variable('DBPASS'): Database user password.

- @Variable('DOCNAME'): Document name.

- @Variable('DPNAME'): Data provider name.

- @Variable('DPTYPE'): The data provider type.

- @Variable('UNVNAME'): Universe name.

- @Variable('UNVID'): Universe ID.

14.1.6   @Where Function

The @Where function is very similar to the @Select function but is used to reference the Where section of an existing object rather than the Select section.

The potential for errors are minimized by pointing to the Where section of an existing object rather than rewriting the code in additional objects. The syntax is also very similar to the @Select function. Following is the syntax that should be used when adding an @Where function to an object.

```
@Where(Class_Name\Object_Name)
```

14.2   Linked Universes

Universes can be linked in Designer to share classes, objects, and joins of separate universes within a single universe. Linked universes are created as a method for centralizing commonly used classes and objects rather than recreating them multiple times in several different universes.

This minimizes the amount of support required to maintain object definitions of commonly used dimensions or measures. If the same objects are created in several different universes, and the object definition changes, updates will need to be made in every universe.

Alternatively, if a single linked universe contains many commonly used objects, updates will only need to be made in one place, thus reducing the amount of time required for maintenance and support.

There are many requirements and limitations to using linked universes that should be understood before linking is performed in a production environment. The next section provides a list of requirements for linking universes.

14.2.1 Universe Linking Requirements

The requirements for linking universes are described here:

▶ The linked universes must connect to the same data source and use the same connection.

▶ Both the core and derived universes used in linking need to exist on the same repository.

▶ The core universe must have been exported to the repository and imported.

14.2.2 Universe Linking Restrictions and Limitations

The restrictions and limitations when linking universes include the following:

▶ You can't link to a universe containing a stored procedure.

▶ You can only use one level of linking. A derived universe can't be created from another derived universe.

▶ All classes and objects must be unique in both the core and derived universes.

▶ Contexts must be redetected in derived universes.

▶ Lists of values in a core universe aren't saved when exporting a linked universe containing a derived universe.

14.2.3 Link Universes

To set up linking between universes, begin by launching Designer and opening the universe that will become the derived universe. The linked universe will become the core universe. The core universe must exist on the repository and must also be stored locally. Follow these steps for linking two universes:

1. Launch the universe parameters by clicking File and then selecting Parameters in Designer.

2. Click the Links tab in the Universe Parameters dialog box (see Figure 14.18).

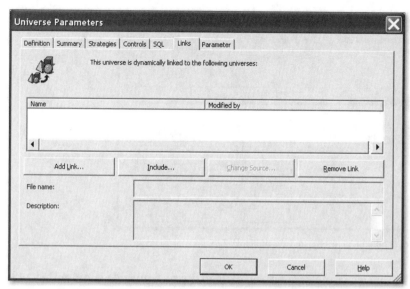

Figure 14.18　Links Tab in the Universe Parameters Dialog Window

3. Click the Add Link button to launch the Universe to Link window and select the core universe that must be saved locally (see Figure 14.19).

4. Select the locally saved .UNV universe file, and click Open.

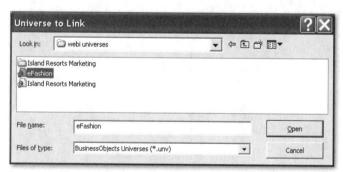

Figure 14.19　Select the Core Universe to Link To

Selecting the Core Universe

5. After clicking Open, the linked universe will appear on the Links tab in the Universe Parameters dialog box. (see Figure 14.20)

6. Click OK, and the core universe will be added to the derived universe.

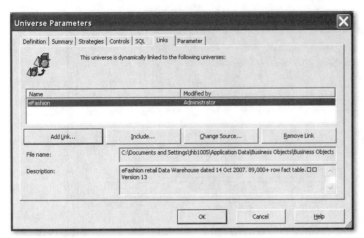

Figure 14.20   Linked Universe Listed on the Links Tab

The tables or views in the core universe are easily recognizable because they will be faintly displayed compared to the tables and views in the derived universe.

Figure 14.21 will shows an eFashion universe linked to the Island Resorts Marketing universe.

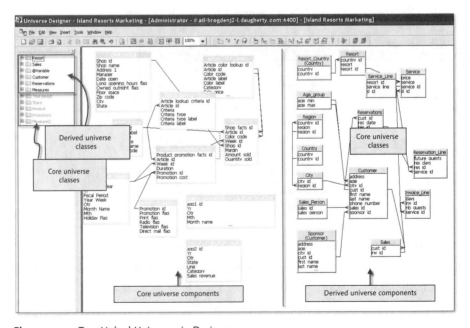

Figure 14.21   Two Linked Universes in Designer

14.3   Derived Tables

Derived tables are created in Designer by developers to include virtual objects in a universe with a SQL query statement. Derived tables are similar to views but with more flexibility. Complex SQL statements can be written to return a highly filtered result set that functions as a logical table.

Derived tables provide a very beneficial method of including dimensions and measures when the tables used in the derived table can't be included in the universe directly.

Nested derived tables can be added to a universe by writing a SQL expression that uses an existing derived table as the From object in the SQL query. The `@DerivedTable(DT_Existing_Derived_Table)` function is used to accept the existing derived table as the argument.

14.3.1   Create a Derived Table

Follow these steps to create a derived table in a universe:

1. Launch Designer.
2. Open or import the universe to add the derived table.
3. Click Insert from the menu across the top, and select Derived Tables to launch the Derived Tables dialog box.
4. Enter a SQL expression.
5. Modify the Derived Table name.
6. Click Check Syntax to validate the SQL expression entered.
7. If the syntax parsing completes successfully, click OK to add the new derived table to the universe.

> **Note**
>
> A common practice in creating derived tables is to use a naming convention that clearly labels derived tables. Rename the derived table to begin with DT followed by a brief description of the objects in the table.

Figure 14.22 shows the Derived Tables window that allows you to enter a SQL expression to create a new derived table. Click the SQL Expression Editor to expand the text area.

The Check Syntax button becomes enabled when an expression is entered in the text area. This step is important to ensure that proper syntax was added.

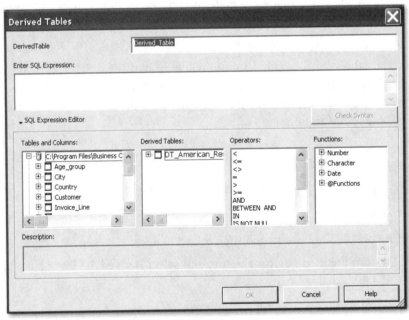

Figure 14.22 Derived Tables Dialog Window

14.3.2 Create a Nested Derived Table

Nested derived tables provide the capability of using existing derived tables to create new derived tables. This method of table creation can be used to create an unlimited number of tables created with complex calculations and formulas.

> **Note**
>
> Use the @DerivedTable() function to write nested derived SQL expressions.

After a derived table has been added to a universe, the table will be listed in the Derived Tables box in the Derived Tables window. The @DerivedTable() function will also be added to the @Functions list.

Figure 14.23 shows the creation of a nested derived table. Use the objects in the four category boxes to help you with writing the SQL expression. If you double-click the derived table, @DerivedTable(DT_Table_Name) will be added to the SQL expression.

Expand the @Functions category to display the @DerivedTable function. This function is only present when a derived table exists in the universe.

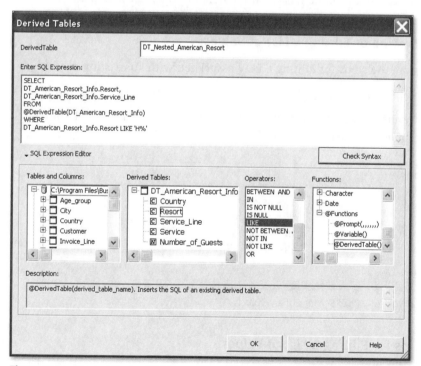

Figure 14.23 Nested Derived Table

After creating a derived table in a universe, add the recently created objects to a universe class to be used in Web Intelligence reporting documents.

Save the universe, and then export it to the repository to begin using the objects in reports.

14.4   Lists of Values

Lists of values (LOVs), are used to assist the report consumer when refreshing a prompted report. LOVs display the values for a prompted filter by running a `Select Distinct` command for the object being filtered.

By default, all dimension and detail objects created in a universe have LOVs attached to them. It's important to disable LOVs if the full list of values can't be displayed within three seconds. Slow-loading LOVs will have a negative impact on the user audience, and the overall acceptance of the report will be affected.

Custom lists of values can be created if the default LOV is slow to load.

14.4.1   Viewing or Editing a List of Values

Following are the steps for editing a LOV associated with an existing object:

1. Double-click an object in a universe to launch the Edit Properties window.

2. Click the Properties tab to view the LOV properties. Figure 14.24 shows the LOV settings for a selected object.

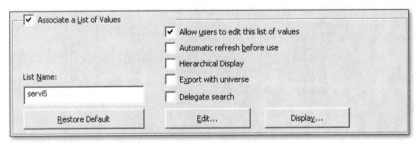

Figure 14.24   List of Values Settings of an Object

14.4.2   Tips for Editing a List of Values

Use these tips when editing LOVs:

▶ Uncheck the *Associate a List of Values* checkbox to disable the LOV of the selected object. This should be done when a LOV takes more than a couple seconds to load when the object is used in a prompt filter.

▶ Click Display to show the actual list of values of the selected object. This button can be used as a performance test for loading the values.

▶ Click Edit to launch the Query Panel to modify the `Select Distinct` statement created by default. Apply filters or modify the result objects of the LOV to improve the LOV performance.

14.4.3 Additional List of Values Settings

The following settings are enabled or disabled by checking or unchecking the associated checkbox:

▶ Allow Users to Edit This List of Values

▶ Automatic Refresh Before Use

▶ Hierarchical Display

▶ Export with Universe

▶ Delegate Search

14.5 Summary

Many advanced techniques can be used in a universe by the Designer tool to enhance the reporting experience for business users. Whether creating, editing, viewing, or refreshing reports, many modifications can be applied to increase reporting functionality.

The `@Functions` provide the capability to interact with objects by prompting users for input and then passing the entered parameters to the Query Filters pane. These special functions allow universe designers to set restrictions on specific objects anytime they are used in a Web Intelligence reporting document.

Another valuable feature in Designer is the capability of linking universes. This feature can save time and maintenance by integrating the classes, objects, and joins of two or more universes into a single universe file. Save countless hours of updating object definitions in multiple universes if frequent changes occur in the data source. Linked universes let you make the changes in one place rather than multiple times in many different universes.

One more valuable feature in Designer is the capability of adding objects generated by a SQL statement. This feature is known as adding a derived table to a universe. Nested derived tables can also be added to a universe to further restrict the data of a set of objects.

The next chapter describes the process of adding hyperlinks to Web Intelligence reports and passing values from one report to another.

*Embed hyperlinks into Web Intelligence reports to connect to multiple
document types, including Xcelsius dashboards, and other Web Intelligence
reports with a single click. Use hyperlinks to pass variables to prompted
reports, refresh queries, and open reports — all with a single hyperlink
using the openDocument() function and accompanying syntax.*

15 Linking in Web Intelligence Reports

Hyperlinks enable report developers to produce reports that connect to other SAP
BusinessObjects documents. This feature can be used to furnish business users
with single-click navigation for guided data analysis by using hyperlinks.

Strategically insert links into Web Intelligence reports to expand on the data being
viewed by opening, refreshing, and passing parameters to other reporting documents. Hyperlinks allow reports to be opened for a variety of purposes. Launch
reports that open in a printer-friendly PDF format, connect to Xcelsius presentations for next generation data visualizations, or provide additional information
associated with a parameter passed to a report.

One of the most significant and exciting benefits of hyperlinking is opening and
refreshing reports that pass parameters to prompted Web Intelligence reports. This
feature gives business users access to live reports that are refreshed at the moment
the link is clicked.

Links can also go outside of the published content of the SAP BusinessObjects
Enterprise system. Add links to reports that open websites in the InfoView
portal.

15.1 Adding Hyperlinks While Viewing Reports

Hyperlinks can be added to new or existing Web Intelligence reports while viewing or editing reports in the Java Report Panel, or while working within Web Intelligence Rich Client.

The next several pages introduce the steps for adding hyperlinks to reports and show ways to customize and add additional parameters to hyperlinks.

15.1.1 Add Hyperlinks to Published Documents

Follow these steps to add a hyperlink to a document published to the SAP Business-Objects Enterprise file repository.

Figure 15.1 shows the menu that appears when you right-click on a table column. The same hyperlink option appears when right-clicking on a free-standing cell.

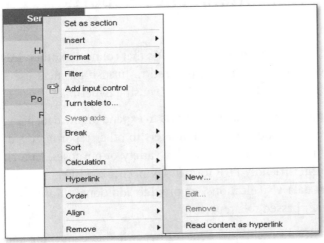

Figure 15.1 Adding a Hyperlink While Viewing a Report

Mouse over the hyperlink menu item to choose from four hyperlink options. If you've right-clicked on a cell or column that doesn't contain a hyperlink, the Edit and Remove selections will be disabled.

Alternately, if a cell or column contains a hyperlink, the *New* selection will be disabled while the Edit and Remove selections will be enabled. The *Read Contents as Hyperlink* selection will also be checked.

The New option launches the Create Hyperlink window. The Read Contents as Hyperlink option is checked or unchecked depending on the presence of a hyperlink.

Figure 15.2 shows the *Create Hyperlink* window opened when *New* is selected. Two buttons are located on the left side of the screenshot to provide the basic hyperlink functionality:

► Link to Document

► Link to Web Page

The default selection of Link to Document is selected when the Create Hyperlink window is launched. Click Browse to choose a document published to the CMS.

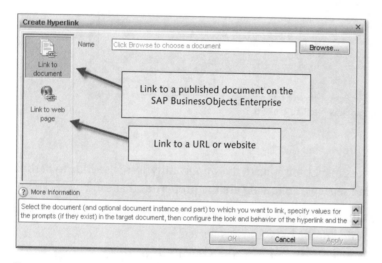

Figure 15.2   Create a Hyperlink

Browsing for Documents

Clicking Browse launches the *Choose a Document* window where you'll see a full list of reporting documents that you have the rights to access.

Figure 15.3 shows the window opened when browsing for a document. Follow these steps to select a document to link to while viewing a report:

1. Expand or collapse the folders on the left side of the window to view the published documents belonging to the selected folder on the right side.

2. Select the document to link to, and then click OK to confirm.

3. Click the Categories tab to view the published documents by category rather than folders.

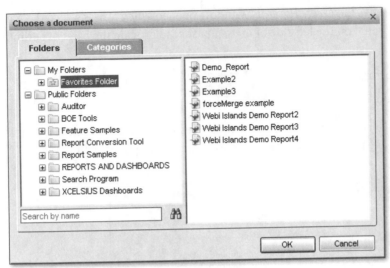

Figure 15.3 Choosing a Document to Link To

Setting Hyperlink Properties

After selecting a document, you'll have the opportunity to revise four hyperlink properties and three settings. Following are the properties that can be checked:

- **Use Complete URL Path to Complete Hyperlink:** Web server name and port number are included in the hyperlink if selected.

- **Refresh on Open:** Set the linked report to refresh on open.

- **Link to Document Instance:** Link to a specific instance of a report.

- **Target Area Within the Document:** Link to a specific report tab if multiple reports exist in the linked document, or link to a report part.

Target Area Within the Document

The option to select a *Target Area Within a Document* allows you to create a hyperlink to a *report name* or *report part*. If the Report Part option is selected, click Select to choose the report tab of the linked report, and then right-click on the desired part.

An additional option is provided to *Display Report Part Only* in the linked document or *Position at Report Part (Full Document Available)*. Figure 15.4 shows the options for targeting an area within a document.

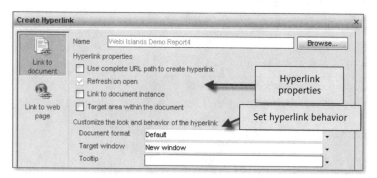

Figure 15.4 Target a Report Part

Customizing Link Behavior

Three properties shown in Figure 15.5 display the look and behavior of hyperlink settings.

▶ **Document Format:** Choose from Default, HTML, PDF, Excel, and Word.

▶ **Target Window:** Open documents in the Current Window or a New Window.

▶ **Tooltip:** Type a message, Select Object, or Build Formula

Figure 15.5 Hyperlink Property Modification

Note

After checking property boxes and making selections from the behavior drop-downs, click Apply and then OK to accept the changes and set the hyperlink.

When a hyperlink has been applied to a column, the values will be displayed by default with a blue text color and underlined.

15.1.2 Editing Existing Links While Viewing a Report

After a link has been created, right-click on the column or cell containing the link, and then choose either Edit or Remove to modify the link.

Figure 15.6 shows the hyperlink options available when right-clicking on an existing hyperlink. Notice that *Read Content as Hyperlink* has been checked.

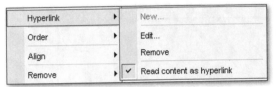

Figure 15.6 Mouse Over Existing Hyperlinks to Edit or Remove Link

15.1.3 Insert a Hyperlink to a Web Page

The second type of linking that can be added to a Web Intelligence report is to web pages on the Internet. This setting allows you to create and embed hyperlinks to your company websites, blog sites, or other types of web pages.

Figure 15.7 shows the Link to Web Page selection in the Create Hyperlink window to insert a link to a web page.

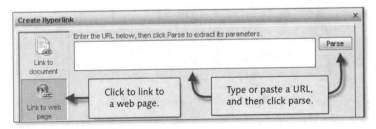

Figure 15.7 Create Hyperlinks to Web Pages

Type or paste a URL in the text box, and then click Parse to display for more options.

Link to Web Page

After a URL has been entered, click Parse to display additional link settings. Figure 15.8 shows the expanded Create Hyperlink window that enables you to modify two default link behavior settings:

▶ **Target Window:** Documents are opened in New Window or Current Window.

▶ **Tooltip:** Enter a tooltip to be displayed on mouseover of a hyperlink. Two dropdown choices can be used to assign a formula or object as the tooltip.

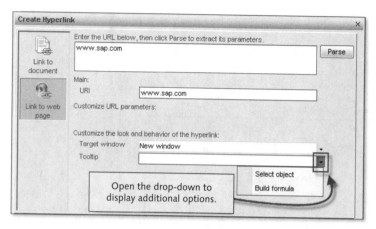

Figure 15.8 Modify Hyperlink Property Settings

15.1.4 Adding Hyperlinks to Prompted Reports

When a *prompted* Web Intelligence report is selected in the *Choose a Document* window, an additional set of options is displayed for *Document Prompts*. This section allows you to pass values to a prompted filter in the linked report.

The Document Prompts section displays a list of all prompted filters listed by the prompt text of each filter in the linked document.

A drop-down list is provided to give you five different ways of dynamically passing values to a prompted filter in the linked document. These five value selection types are displayed in Figure 15.9 and listed here:

▸ **Select Object:** Choose to select an object or variable from the current document.

▸ **Build Formula:** Opens the Formula Editor for custom formula creation.

▸ **Enter a Constant:** Choose this selection to manually enter a value.

▸ **Prompt User at Runtime:** Prompts the user at runtime.

▸ **Use Document Default:** Uses the default prompt value selection type.

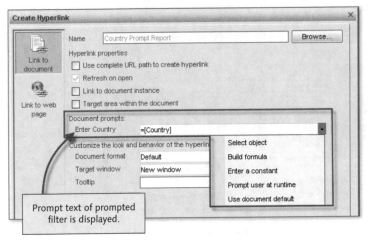

Figure 15.9 Creating a Hyperlink to a Prompted Web Intelligence Report

Figure 15.10 shows the Select Prompts window when a new hyperlink has been created based on the [Country] result object in a table and linked to a report that contains two prompted filters. Choose the filter to pass the values to.

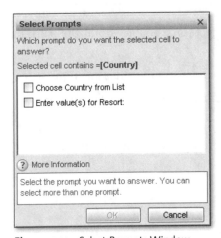

Figure 15.10 Select Prompts Window

Passing a Selected Object to a Prompted Report

An excellent way of linking Web Intelligence reports is to create a hyperlink based on the value of a selected object. This type of linking works best when the linked report contains a single prompted filter that contains compatible values. This is most commonly used when creating a hyperlink on a dimension object when the same object serves as the prompt filter in another report.

An example of this type of linking is shown in Figure 15.11 when right-clicking on a column in a vertical table that contains the [Country] object to create a new hyperlink.

Click New to launch the Create Hyperlink window. Select a report that contains a prompt filter for the [Country] object.

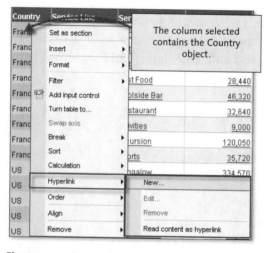

Figure 15.11   Create a Hyperlink Based on the Country Object

Figure 15.12 shows the [Country] object being passed to a prompted filter.

> **Note**
>
> The result of setting up a hyperlink containing this parameter-passing feature is that any [Country] value in the hyperlink is dynamically passed to the linked report when the value is selected.

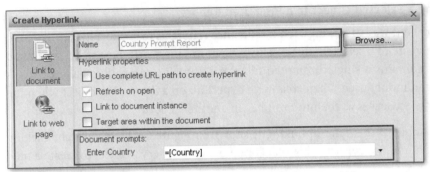

Figure 15.12 Link to a Prompted Report and Pass the Selected Country Value

15.2 Adding Hyperlinks While Creating or Editing Reports

Hyperlinks can also be added to reports while creating or editing existing reports. The right-click menu is slightly different, and the overall look and feel of creating a hyperlink while editing a report is also different. Figure 15.13 shows the right-click menu while editing an existing report.

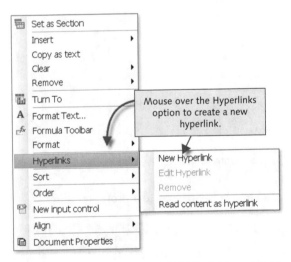

Figure 15.13 Add a New Hyperlink While Editing a Report

The biggest difference between adding hyperlinks when editing a report versus when viewing a report is that the Browse button doesn't exist when adding a hyperlink to a report in edit mode.

The absence of the Browse button in edit mode makes creating hyperlinks much more of a manual process when editing or creating a report as compared to viewing a report.

Figure 15.14 shows the Hyperlinks window when adding a new hyperlink in edit mode. Use this window to paste or type a URL, and then click the Parse button.

Click Parse to list and edit the dynamic elements of the URL entered in the provided text box.

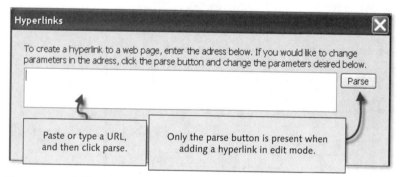

Figure 15.14 Adding a New Hyperlink in Edit Mode

Hyperlinks can be added in edit mode that link to published documents or to external web pages. Both link types contain a pair of visual and interactive properties that can be modified:

▶ **Tooltip:** Manually enter a constant, select an object, or build a formula.

▶ **Target Window:** Open the target window in the current window or open the linked document in a new window.

To link to external web pages, use the standard URL structure:

www.sap.com

▶ To link to published documents on the CMS, use the OpenDocument syntax:

http://<servername>:<port>/OpenDocument/opendoc/<platformspecific>

The exact OpenDocument syntax is dependent upon your implementation:

▶ If your implementation is for .NET, use `openDocument.aspx` in place of the `<platformspecific>` parameter.

▶ If your implementation is for Java, use `openDocument.jsp` in place of the `<plat-formspecific>` parameter.

Paste a manually created URL using OpenDocument syntax into the text area, and then click Parse. Figure 15.15 shows the dynamic URL elements after parsing a manually created URL using the OpenDocument syntax.

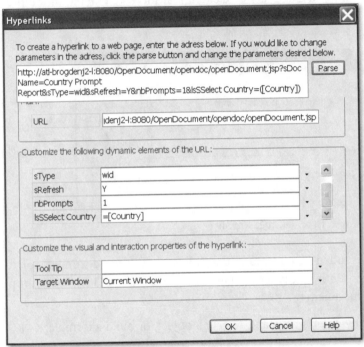

Figure 15.15 Hyperlink Created with OpenDocument URL in Edit Mode

15.2.1 Manually Created OpenDocument URL Details

The following is a closer look at the URL used in Figure 15.16.

▶ **Full OpenDocument URL:**

```
http://atl-brogdenj2-1:8080/OpenDocument/opendoc/openDocument.jsp?
sDocName=Country Prompt Report&sType=wid&sRefresh=Y&mode=full
&nbPrompts=1&lsSSelect Country=([Country])
```

▶ **Main URL:**

`http://atl-brogdenj2-1:8080/OpenDocument/opendoc/openDocument.jsp?`

The `openDocument.jsp` is used for Java implementations.

▶ **Document Name:**

`sDocName=Country Prompt Report`

> ▶ Be sure to leave spaces between the words in the report name.

> ▶ Don't include the plus symbol between words in the report name.

▶ **Document Type:**

`sType=wid`

> ▶ `wid` is used for Web Intelligence documents.

▶ **Refresh:**

`sRefresh=Y`

> ▶ Include a `Y` to tell the document to refresh when opened.

▶ **Number of Prompts:**

`nbPrompts=1`

▶ **Prompt Name:**

`lsSSelect Country=([Country])`

> ▶ Always include lsS before the prompt text of the filter.

> ▶ Select the [Country] object from the drop-down in the Dynamic Elements section.

> ▶ By selecting the object, parentheses are added to the URL when parsed, and the equal symbol is added in front of the object in the `lsS` selection.

15.2.2 Using OpenDocument Syntax While Viewing a Report

The same hyperlink using the OpenDocument URL can be added while viewing a Web Intelligence report in InfoView. But instead of clicking Link to Document, click Link to Web Page, paste or type the full URL in the text area, and click Parse. The URL parameters will be categorized for verification and modification. Figure 15.16 shows an OpenDocument URL pasted into the text area and parsed.

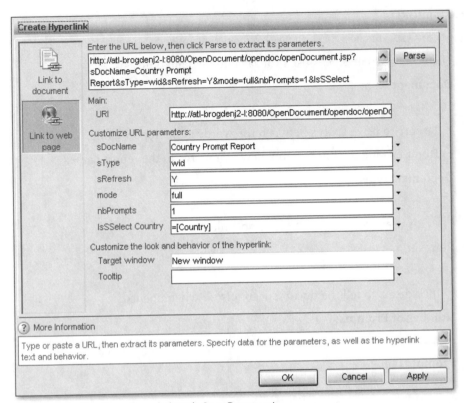

Figure 15.16 Creating a Hyperlink with OpenDocument

Note

Be sure to select the object for the 1sS parameter from the drop-down by using the Select Object or Build Formula options.

15.2.3 Add a Hyperlink to an External Site

Links can also be created to external websites by typing or pasting a URL in the provided text area and clicking Parse (see Figure 15.17).

After parsing the URL, three new sections are revealed in the hyperlinks window to display the following categorized sections:

▸ **Main:** Displays the full URL.

▸ **Dynamic Elements:** Dynamic elements used to pass variables.

▶ **Interaction Properties:** Add tooltips and target window assignment.

  ▶ Tooltips: Manually enter a constant, select an object, or build a formula.

  ▶ Target Window: Open the linked target in the current or new window.

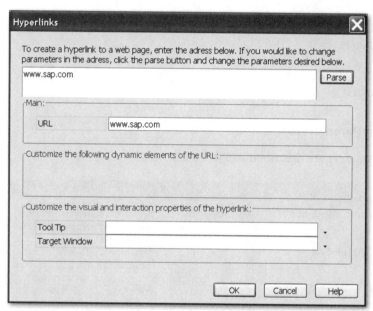

Figure 15.17 Hyperlink Added to External Web Page in Edit Mode

15.2.4 Create a Hyperlink to an Xcelsius Presentation

Hyperlinks to Xcelsius presentations can be created by adding two parameters to the end of the main URL:

▶ sDocName

▶ sType

Following is the URL to an Xcelsius document exported to the SAP BusinessObjects platform:

▶ *http://atl-brogdenj2-l:8080/OpenDocument/opendoc/openDocument.jsp? sDocName=testLink&sType=flash*

15.3   OpenDocument Syntax

The OpenDocument syntax can be used to pass a wide variety of parameters to the document being opened with the OpenDocument URL hyperlink.

Parameters are grouped into three different categories:

▶ Platform parameters

▶ Input parameters

▶ Output parameters

15.3.1   Platform Parameters

The platform parameters are described in Table 15.1.

Parameter	Description	Mandatory	Additional Information
iDocID	Document identifier	Yes*	Document ID located in document properties
sDocName	Document name	Yes*	Use spaces between words
sIDType	CMS Object ID type	Yes*	Values: CUID, GUID, RUID, ParentID
sKind	Used for DeskI document	Yes*	Values: FullClient
sPath	Folder name of document	Yes*	
sType	File type of target document	Yes	Values: wid, rpt, car, flash
token	Valid logon token	No	Logon token of CMS session

Table 15.1 Platform Parameters

▶ *iDocID is required if the sDocName parameter isn't used.

▶ *sDocName is required if the iDocID parameter isn't used.

▶ *sIDType is required if linking to a Crystal Report.

▶ *sKind is required when linking to a Desktop Intelligence document.

▶ *sPath is required if sDocName is used and the document name isn't unique.

15.3.2 Input Parameters

The input parameters are described in Table 15.2.

Parameter	Description	Additional Information
lsC[Name]	Specifies a contextual prompt if there is an ambiguity during SQL generation (SAP BusinessObjects and Web Intelligence documents only).	Resolves ambiguity of generated SQL by providing a prompt value.
lsM[Name]	Specifies multiple values for a prompt. [NAME] is the text of the prompt.	Allows multiple prompt values to be passed to a prompt filter. Values are separated by commas.
lsR[Name]	Specifies a range of values for a prompt. [NAME] is the text of the prompt.	A range of values are passed to the prompt, separated by a double period (..). Use no_value to ignore an optional prompt.
lsS[Name]	Specifies a value for a single prompt. [NAME] is the text of the prompt.	Pass single values using the lsS parameter, multiple values using lsM.
sInstance	Indicates a specific instance of the target report to be opened. Open the latest instance owned by the current user, latest instance of the report, or latest instance of report with matching parameter values.	User (Link to latest instance owned by current user). Last (Link to latest instance for report). Param (Link to latest instance of report with matching parameter values).
sPartContext	Used when linking to a Crystal Report.	Data context of report part.
sRefresh	Indicates whether a refresh should be forced when the target document is opened.	Use Y to force the document to refresh on open.
sReportMode	For Crystal targets only, indicates whether the link should open the full target report or just the report part specified in sReportPart.	Use Full or Part as the report mode.

Table 15.2 Input Parameters

Parameter	Description	Additional Information
sReportName	Identifies the report to open if the target document contains multiple reports.	Use the report name in a Web Intelligence document.
sReportPart	Indicates which specific part of the target report to open.	Name of the report part. Easily selected when creating a hyperlink and selecting a report part while viewing a report in InfoView.

Table 15.2 Input Parameters (Cont.)

The only required input parameter is for sPartContext when an sReportPart has been included in a URL.

15.3.3 Output Parameters

The output parameters are described in Table 15.3.

Parameter	Description	Additional Information
NAII	Forces the display of the prompt selection page. Web Intelligence only.	Document ID located in document properties
sOutputFormat	Defines the format of target document.	H (HTML), P (PDF), E (Excel), W (Word)
sViewer	Indicates the viewer used in target document.	Values: html For Crystal Reports only: part, actx, java
sWindow	Window of target report	Same (current window), New (new window)

Table 15.3 Output Parameters

15.4 Summary

Hyperlinks are useful additions to Web Intelligence reports. They allow report developers or consumers to graphically embed links to other reporting documents. Links can be adding to documents while viewing reports in InfoView, editing a document in the Java Report Panel, or working with the Web Intelligence Rich Client.

Guided analysis to deeper information can be easily added to reports by strategically inserting hyperlinks that contain related data at different hierarchy levels or featuring different dimension objects.

One of the greatest benefits of inserting hyperlinks in reports is the capability of passing dynamic values to prompted filters. This feature allows entire columns to serve as hyperlinks that pass only the selected value to a prompted filter in a report. Reports can also be refreshed and opened to display up-to-the-minute data — all with a single hyperlink.

An extensive list of input, output, and platform parameters are available for dynamically passing values to linked reports published to the SAP BusinessObjects platform. These parameters are appended to URLs created with the `OpenDocument` syntax structure.

Chapter 16 will discuss sharing, scheduling, and exporting documents to other business users.

The core functionality of Web Intelligence involves querying, reporting, analyzing, and sharing information across the enterprise. The ability to share information quickly and easily is vital to successful business intelligence reporting. SAP BusinessObjects Web Intelligence XI 3.x provides enhanced sharing capabilities to schedule, publish, and burst your information to your internal and external audience.

16 Sharing a Web Intelligence Report

So you learned how to create a Web Intelligence report, how to use advanced query techniques and multiple data providers, how to create unique charts, and how to format your report to create the most meaningful output for your audience. Now that your report design is complete, it's time to share your results with others.

SAP BusinessObjects Web Intelligence XI 3.x provides a variety of ways to distribute and share your reports across the organization, including many new features to enhance the publishing capabilities previously available. From the simple ability to copy and paste data from within a Web Intelligence report to the new capability to create publications and burst them out for end-user consumption, you have a wide variety of options for sharing reports from within Web Intelligence or InfoView.

16.1 Copying and Pasting to Another Application

The most basic way to share a Web Intelligence report is a method used often in numerous tools: copy and paste. Although copy and paste is a commonly used functionality, it can be a powerful tool for sharing reports and enabling the end user to bring report parts into other applications.

Report parts can be pasted into spreadsheets, presentations, and word processing documents to integrate with additional business content. There are a couple different ways to copy and paste within Web Intelligence.

From within the Edit Report view on a Web Intelligence document, right-click on the report part that should be copied to display the menu options as shown in Figure 16.1. Select to either Copy or Copy as Text.

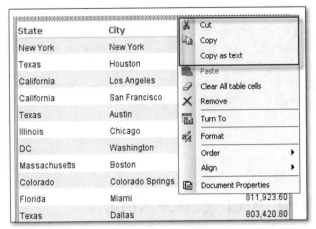

Figure 16.1 Copy Options in Web Intelligence

Copy copies the data contained within the report block in the format as it appears on your screen. This is useful to copy the report part into a Word document or within a PowerPoint presentation because it will maintain its formatting.

The Copy as Text option converts all elements to a text format. A report block copied using the Copy function to Excel will appear in Excel as a picture of the report part. Copy as Text is needed to copy the data itself into the columns in the spreadsheet to perform further manipulation of the data within Excel. Figure 16.2 displays the copy options in Microsoft Excel.

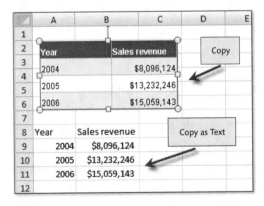

Figure 16.2 Copy Options to Excel

16.2 Using the Send Feature in InfoView

You can easily share reports from within the InfoView portal provided that you have been given the rights by the SAP BusinessObjects administrator.

> **Note**
>
> Chapter 11, Working Within InfoView, discusses how to view a Web Intelligence report in InfoView and discusses other InfoView features.

Another option available in InfoView is the ability to send Web Intelligence reports.

To activate the Send To option on the InfoView toolbar, you must first select the report to be sent so that it's highlighted in the Workspace Panel. The Send To button will become active.

Select the Send To button to display the drop-down list options shown in Figure 16.3: Business Objects Inbox, Email, FTP Location, and File Location.

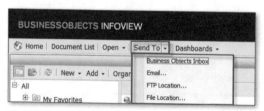

Figure 16.3 InfoView Toolbar Send To Menu

16.2.1 Business Objects Inbox

You can send a Web Intelligence document to another SAP BusinessObjects Enterprise user's Inbox. The report will be displayed in the user's Personal Folders in the Inbox as shown in Figure 16.4.

Upon first selecting the option to Send a report to a Business Objects Inbox, the Use Default Settings checkbox is marked. To select personalized settings for the report destination, you must first uncheck this box.

Figure 16.5 shows the selection of users and Send To Inbox settings.

Figure 16.4 SAP BusinessObjects Inbox

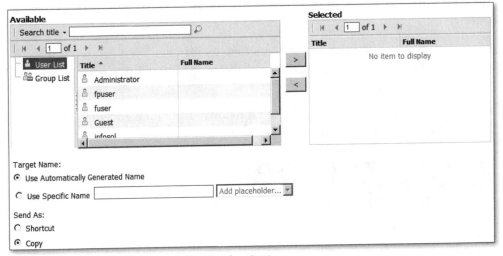

Figure 16.5 Send To Business Objects Inbox Settings

You'll be prompted to select the destination Business Objects Inbox from the User List or from the Group List.

Selecting from the Group List will enable you to select all members of a group to receive the same report in their Business Objects Inbox. A Search box is also available to aid in finding the appropriate name from the user or group list. Select the arrows to move the names into the Selected box.

The next option is to designate a Target Name by selecting one of these options:

▸ **Use Automatically Generated Name:** This option uses the current name of the document selected as the name of the report as it appears in the recipient's Inbox.

▶ **Use Specific Name:** This option enables you to generate a unique name to use for the report name as it will appear in the Inbox. There is also a drop-down list to add the following placeholder values:

  ▶ Title: Inserts the title as it exists when the report is sent.

  ▶ ID: Inserts the unique identifier number for the report as it exists in the system at the time the report is sent.

  ▶ Owner: Inserts the name of the Owner of the document as it appears in the properties.

  ▶ DateTime: Inserts the current date and time when the report is sent.

  ▶ Email Address: Inserts the email address the report is being sent to.

  ▶ User Full Name: Inserts the user's full name.

  ▶ Document Name: Inserts the document name as it exists when the document is sent.

  ▶ File Extension: Inserts the file extension of the document type.

The final option, Send As, enables you to select whether the recipient will receive a shortcut or copy of the report. After these options have been marked, select Submit to send your document to the recipient's BusinessObjects Inbox.

> **Note**
>
> Use caution when sending a shortcut. If the recipients don't have rights to view reports in the folder where the original report resides, then they will be unable to view the report.
>
> For example, if you send a report that resides in your Personal Folders (i.e., Favorites or Inbox) to another user, the recipient won't have rights to view these reports unless he has administrative level access.

16.2.2 Email

A Web Intelligence report can be sent to an email address for the user to view outside of InfoView. If Web Intelligence format is sent by email, the user must have an Enterprise account to view the Web Intelligence report because he will need to enter his credentials to log on to the SAP BusinessObjects Enterprise.

There is an additional placeholder in the list for the message body from those mentioned in Section 16.2.1. The placeholder of Viewer Hyperlink allows you to insert a hyperlink to the report within the InfoView environment. The user selects the hyperlink and logs in to the SAP BusinessObjects Enterprise environment to view the report. Figure 16.6 provides a view of the Send To email options.

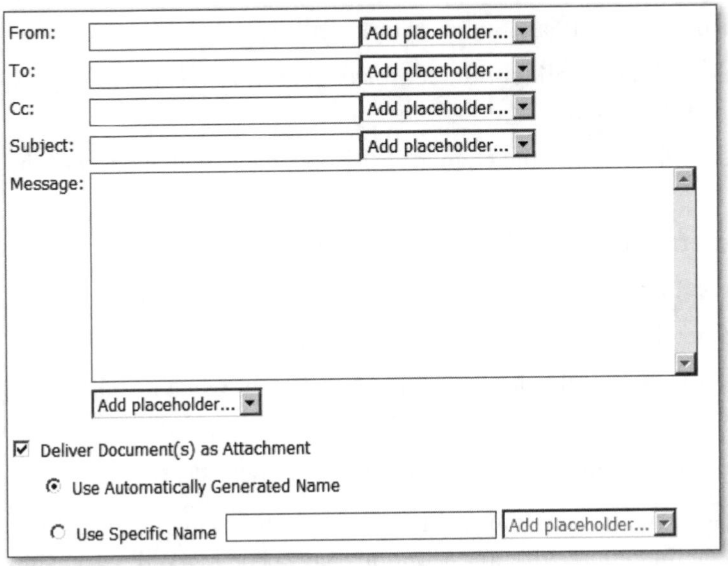

Figure 16.6 Send To Email options

16.2.3 FTP Location

Send To FTP Location enables the user to send the Web Intelligence document to a File Transfer Protocol (FTP) location. A FTP location is a standard network protocol location used to exchange files over a network.

Specific information regarding the FTP location must be specified in the options box including host, port, user name, password, account, and directory. This information is specific to the FTP location the document is being sent to.

After the FTP-specific properties are set, the file name properties are specified such as whether the report is automatically generated or uses a specific name with placeholder options. Figure 16.7 shows the options for sending documents to FTP locations.

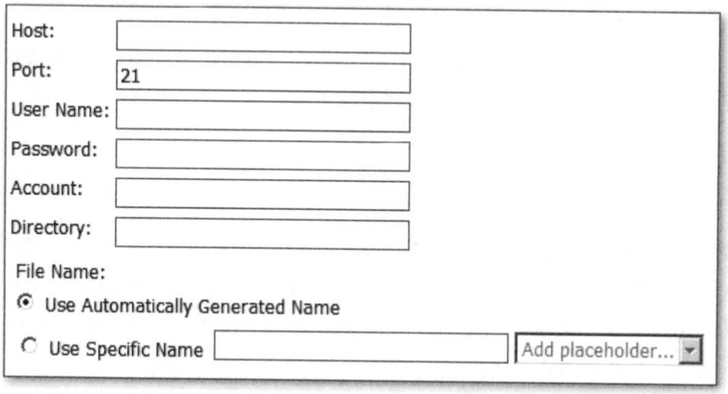

Figure 16.7 Send to FTP Location Options

16.2.4 File Location

The final sent to location available is a file location. This can be useful to send Web Intelligence documents to a location on a shared drive that can be viewed by numerous users for collaborative purposes and ease of access.

When specifying a file location, the directory path must be specified as well as a user name and password for that directory if applicable. Then the file name property can be set to use an automatically generated name or a specific name with placeholder options. Figure 16.8 shows the file location options when scheduling a report.

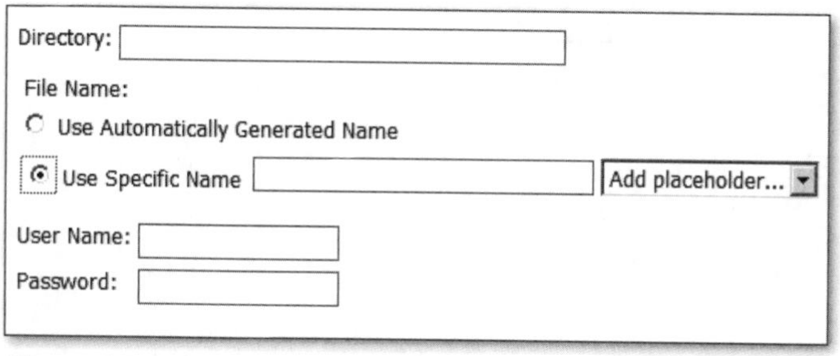

Figure 16.8 File Location Options

16.3 Exporting a Web Intelligence Report

Business users are very commonly faced with the requirement of analyzing company data in Excel for even more detailed analysis or distributing reports in the PDF format.

Web Intelligence provides report consumers with the capability of exporting report data retrieved from the universe and database into one of the following four file formats: Microsoft Excel, PDF, CSV, or CSV (with options).

16.3.1 Export Options in InfoView

The export options available to you within InfoView depend on your user settings created by the SAP BusinessObjects Administrator. There are two drop-down menu options in the Document Menu in the InfoView Viewer toolbar when viewing a Web Intelligence report in InfoView.

The Save to My Computer As menu, as shown in Figure 16.9, includes the export options of Excel, PDF, CSV, and CSV (With Options). The Save Report to My Computer As menu, as shown in Figure 16.10, includes the options of Excel and PDF only.

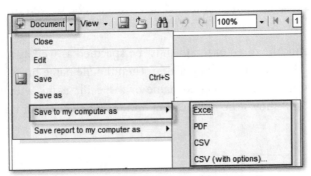

Figure 16.9 Export Options on InfoView Viewer Toolbar

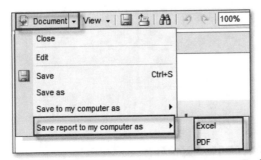

Figure 16.10 Export Options in InfoView Viewer Toolbar

Excel

Selecting to save in Excel format converts the Web Intelligence report into Excel format and allows you to open or save the report.

The data in the tables of the Web Intelligence document will drop into the columns and rows of the Excel spreadsheet as seen when selecting the Copy As Text option in Web Intelligence. Further manipulation of the data is then available in this format.

PDF

Selecting to save in Adobe Acrobat PDF format will convert the Web Intelligence report into PDF format and allow you to open or save the report. The report will appear similar to a picture, so further manipulation of the data won't be available. This is a preferable format to use when you want to maintain the report formatting and ensure the data can't be manually changed.

CSV

The CSV export option saves the Web Intelligence report in comma-separated value format. This enables you to import the report into a number of different programs outside of Excel.

CSV (With Options)

The CSV with Options selection gives you additional options for customizing the format of your comma-separated value output file. This enables you to designate the specific format to make the CSV file compatible with the end program where you may be importing your data.

16.3.2 Export Options in Web Intelligence

The same options for export are also available within Web Intelligence. From the Edit Report view, select the arrow next to the disk icon on the report toolbar. Upon selecting the Save to My Computer As option, a menu will display the options of Excel, PDF, CSV, or CSV (With Options) as your file output format for export as shown in Figure 16.11.

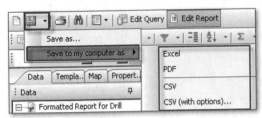

Figure 16.11 Export Options in Web Intelligence Edit Report Toolbar

16.4 Scheduling a Web Intelligence Report

The processes discussed so far have all been manually generated methods of sharing Web Intelligence reports. A document can also be scheduled to be distributed out to recipients in a variety of formats and methods. This scheduling ability is available within InfoView.

From within InfoView, you can schedule a report, view the latest instance of a scheduled report, and view the scheduling history of the report.

16.4.1 Scheduling in InfoView

After selecting the report to be scheduled in the Workspace Panel, navigate to the Actions menu on the InfoView toolbar as shown in Figure 16.12. Select the Schedule option to set the scheduling properties.

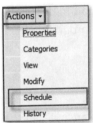

Figure 16.12 Select Schedule from the Actions Menu on the InfoView Toolbar

You'll be prompted to complete the items described in the following sections.

Instance Title

Type in the title for this instance of the report, or use the default title already entered.

Recurrence

Numerous options are available in the drop-down menu for selection dependent upon your report distribution requirements.

The Run Object menu options are listed here:

▶ **Now:** Runs your report schedule immediately upon completion of your scheduling properties and selecting the Submit button.

▶ **Once:** Runs your report schedule once during the timeframe specified in the Recurrence properties box as shown in Figure 16.13.

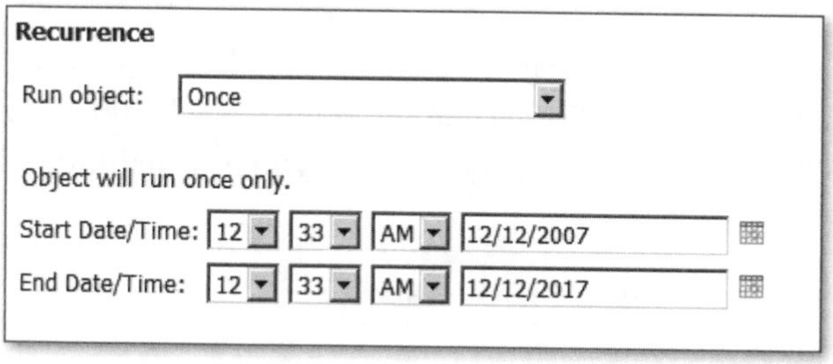

Figure 16.13 Once View

▶ **Hourly:** Runs the report at the hourly increments specified in the hours and minutes boxes in the Recurrence properties. The Start and End Date/Time are also specified. Figure 16.14 shows the Hourly settings.

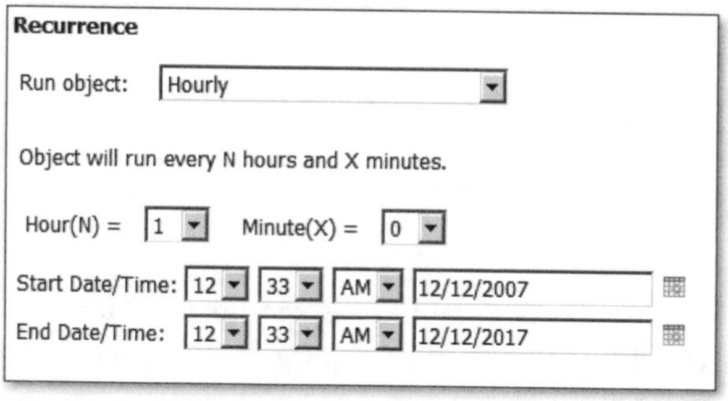

Figure 16.14 Hourly View

▶ **Daily:** Runs the report daily for N number of days as specified in the Recurrence properties. The Start and End Date/Time are also specified. Figure 16.15 shows the Daily settings.

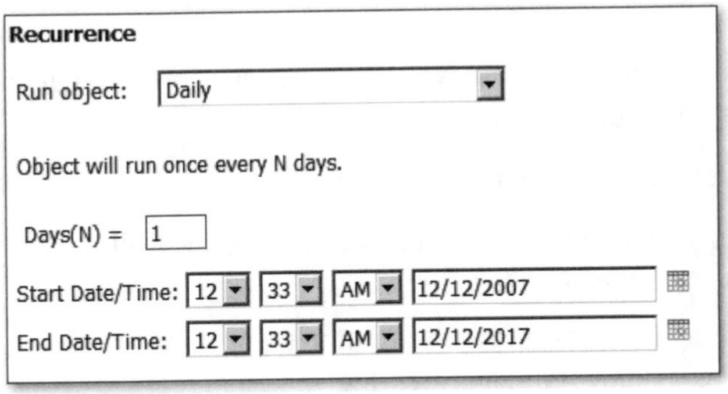

Figure 16.15 Daily View

▶ **Weekly:** Runs the report weekly on the day or days specified by the check boxes. You also specify the Start and End Date/Time for when the schedule will start and end. Figure 16.16 shows the Weekly settings when scheduling a report.

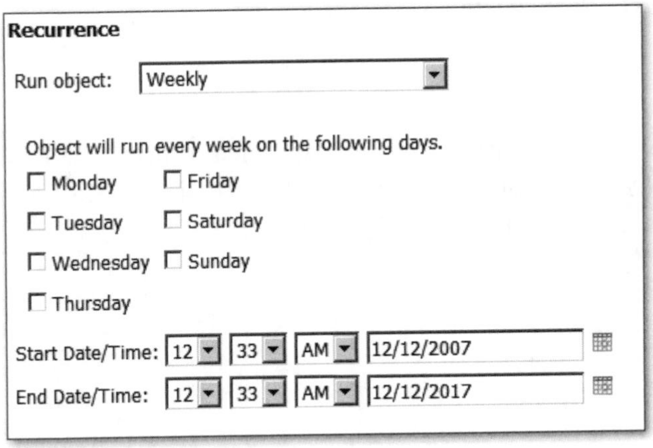

Figure 16.16 Weekly View

▶ **Monthly:** Runs the report monthly every N months as specified. A Start and End Date/Time are also specified for this schedule. Figure 16.17 displays the Monthly settings.

▶ **Nth of Month:** Allows you to specify the exact day of the month to run the schedule. This can be especially useful for financial reports run for month-end reporting. A Start and End Date/Time is also specified for the schedule. This is displayed in Figure 16.18.

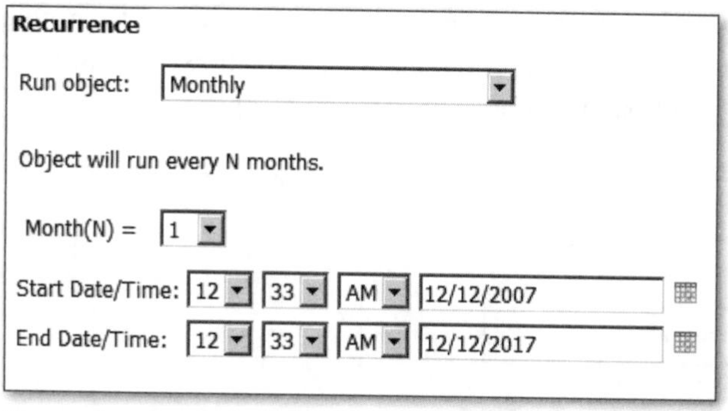

Figure 16.17 Monthly View

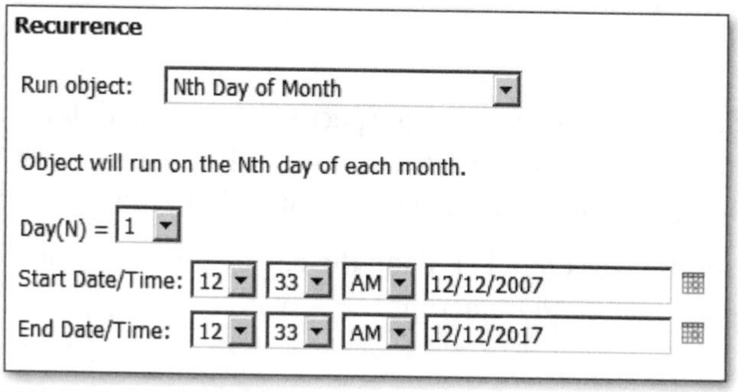

Figure 16.18 Nth of Month View

▸ **1st Monday of Month:** Allows you to run the report on the first Monday of every month. This can be useful for monthly reports to maintain consistency in the run date. You'll also specify the schedule Start and End Date/Time. This can be seen in Figure 16.19.

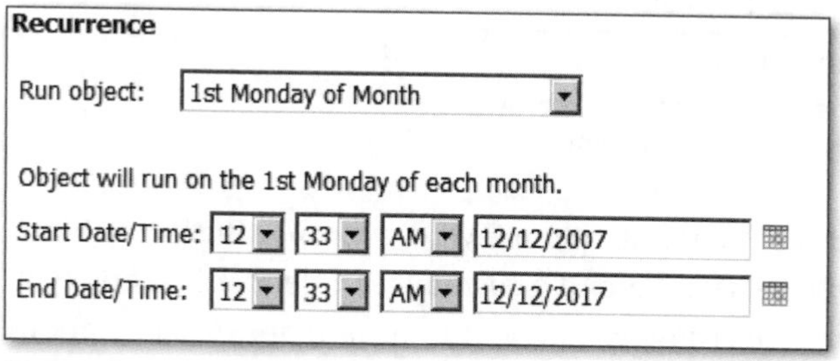

Figure 16.19 1st Monday of Month View

▸ **Last Day of Month:** Runs the report on the final day of each month. You'll specify the schedule Start and End Date/Time. Figure 16.20 shows the options available when selecting the Last Day of Month recurrence option.

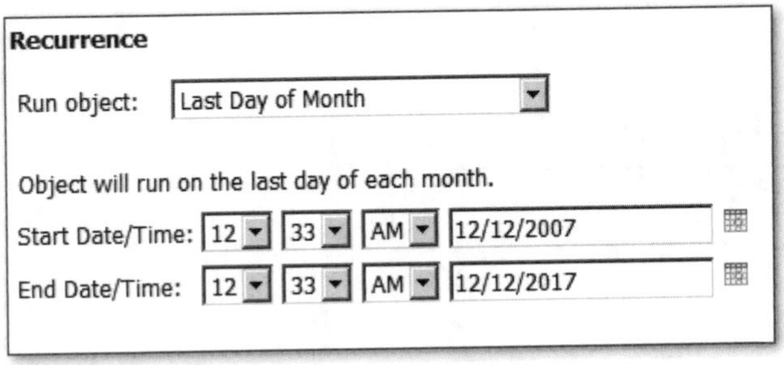

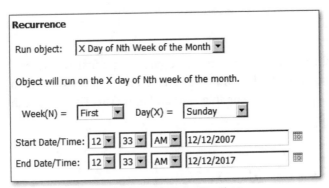

Figure 16.20 Last Day of Month View

▸ **X Day of Nth Week of the Month:** Enables you to specify the week and day of each month that the schedule should be run (see Figure 16.21). For example, you can specify to run the report on the third Thursday of each month.

In this case, you would specify week number 3 and the day of Thursday. You'll also specify the schedule Start and End Date/Time.

Figure 16.21 X Day of Nth Week of the Month View

▸ **Calendar:** Calendars need to be set up in the CMC by the SAP BusinessObjects administrator for them to be seen here. If a customized calendar is set up, you can specify to use them here. These enable you to have more specific options on dates to run the report.

Formats and Destinations

Output formats include Web Intelligence, Microsoft Excel, and Adobe Acrobat. Available destinations include Inbox, File Locations, FTP Server, and Email Recipients.

Destination Options and Settings change dependent on the Output Format Details selected in the Output Format and Destination section. These settings are the same as discussed in Section 16.2, Using the Send Feature in InfoView.

When checking the box for Cleanup Instance After Scheduling, the instance will be removed from the history after it has been sent out to the selected recipients. This removes unnecessary extra copies of the report to maximize disk space.

Caching

Select the formats to preload the cache with when scheduling (only applicable if scheduling in Web Intelligence format). Available formats to cache include Excel, standard HTML, and Adobe Acrobat. Select the formatting locales to preload the cache with when scheduling. The available locales appear in the left box. You must select the arrow to move to the Selected locales box to specify your selection.

Events

Events are set up by your SAP BusinessObjects administrator in the CMC. Available events are listed in the box on the left. Select the arrows to move your selections to the Events to Wait For box. You may also select the event in the Available Schedule Events box to move to the Events to Trigger on completion. This will specify which events must occur for the job to be triggered. This can be useful to ensure that a nightly data load job has completed loading the new data before the report is run.

Scheduling Server Group

The Scheduling Server Group option enables you to specify a specific server group to use when scheduling your document. The usual setting is to use the first available server. Be aware that if a specified server is busy, your job will likely fail. The Scheduling Server Group options are detailed in Figure 16.22.

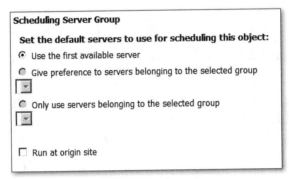

Figure 16.22 Scheduling Server Group Box

16.4.2 Viewing Latest Instance

After scheduling a report, you can view the latest instance of the report. After selecting the report name in the Workspace Panel, select the Actions menu on the InfoView toolbar to view the drop-down list options. Figure 16.23 displays the Actions available when viewing a report.

If a report has been scheduled previously, then the View Latest Instance option will appear in the menu. The latest instance shows you the last scheduled version of the report as distributed to your selected recipients.

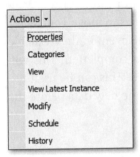

Figure 16.23 Action Menu Options

16.4.3 Viewing History

You're also able to see the history of all instances scheduled for a report by selecting History from the Actions drop-down list. The History view shows a listing of all scheduled reports, including the date/time of the instance, title, run by, parameters (if applicable), format, and status.

In Figure 16.24, the instance in the History view is showing a status of Running. This indicates that the report schedule is currently running and not yet complete to view. There are additional radio buttons and checkboxes at the top of the History view to aid you in filtering a longer list of instances to customize your view.

These options include Show All, Show Completed, Show Only Instances Owned by Me, and Filter Instances by Type.

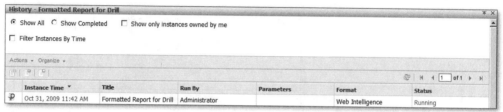

Figure 16.24 History View

16.5   Creating Publications

Enhancements made to the SAP BusinessObjects Enterprise environment of InfoView provide new publishing features that include new capabilities for processing, formats (including enhanced PDF), destinations, processing extensions, dynamic recipients, and delivery rules.

A *publication* is a collection of reports that are distributed for mass consumption to an internal or external audience. Publications can be set up within InfoView or by the SAP BusinessObjects administrator in the CMC. Your ability to create publications and subscriptions depends on the rights set up by your SAP BusinessObjects administrator.

Publications can be created by selecting the Publication option from the New menu on the main toolbar in InfoView as shown in Figure 16.25.

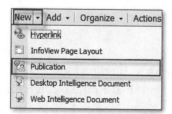

Figure 16.25 Select Publication from the New Shortcut Icon in InfoView

16.5.1 General Properties

When you choose to create a new publication, the General Properties box appears to set the Title, Description, and searchable Keywords as shown in Figure 16.26.

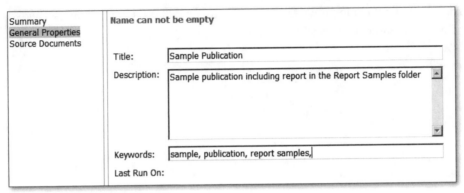

Figure 16.26 General Properties Box

16.5.2 Source Documents

Source documents can include Web Intelligence, Desktop Intelligence, and Crystal Reports documents, or a combination of these document formats. Select the documents from the list that you want to include in your publication as shown in Figure 16.27.

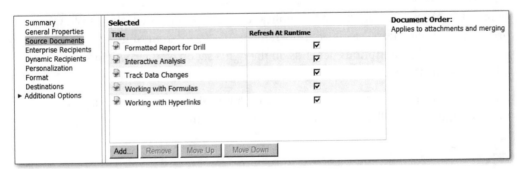

Figure 16.27 Select Source Documents Box

You may also indicate whether the report should refresh at runtime by selecting the checkbox to the right of the report name in the refresh at runtime column.

Figure 16.28 shows the Source Documents properties box options. After selecting the source documents to include in the publication, you can proceed to select your publication recipients.

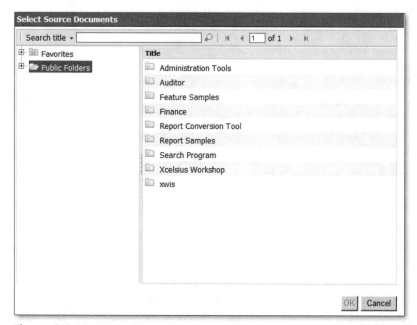

Figure 16.28   Source Documents Box

16.5.3   Recipients

After defining the source documents to be sent in the distribution, you'll need to determine the recipients. There are two possibilities for recipients: Enterprise and dynamic.

Enterprise

Enterprise recipients are those users who have access to your SAP BusinessObjects Enterprise environment. These include the users and groups shown in the Enterprise properties as listed in Figure 16.29. For these recipients, you can select the user sand group to include or exclude from the distribution. Users selected to receive the publication can unsubscribe themselves at any time as discussed in Section 16.5.8, Subscriptions.

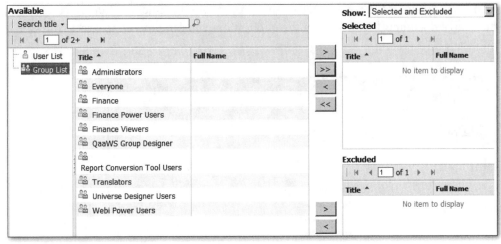

Figure 16.29 Enterprise Recipients Box

Dynamic

The ability to select dynamic recipients enables you to use a list of recipients generated by the query output of a Web Intelligence, Desktop Intelligence, or Crystal Report to determine the recipients for the distribution. You can select the option to use the query output or use the output from the report. The source report that contains the recipient information must be created prior to setting up your publication. The information needed in your report is contingent upon the distribution type. For example, if your publication is distributed via email, then the email addresses needs to be contained within your dynamic distribution source report. Figure 16.30 shows the properties for selecting dynamic recipients. Select the document type from the drop-down list, and then select the source document containing the dynamic list. Further properties are contingent upon the type of distribution being sent.

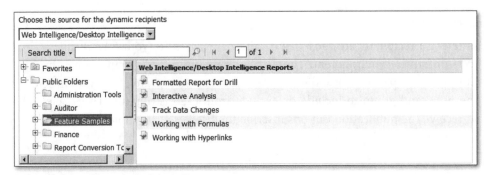

Figure 16.30 Dynamic Recipients Box

16.5.4 Personalization

Personalization enables you to customize the content of the publication reports to only include information that is relevant to the recipient. Profiles are set up by the SAP BusinessObjects administrator in the CMC. These profiles are mapped to sources and targets for each user. A target can be a variable in a report such as a department. The source for a specific user can be the department they belong to, such as the finance department. When personalization is applied, the user receives the report filtered for only the finance department. You can also filter all documents that a user receives by applying a global target. A global profile target applies the filter to all reports using a specified universe based on a specified universe object. Figure 16.31 shows the options available in the personalization options properties.

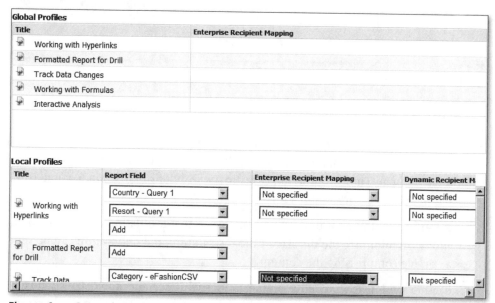

Figure 16.31 Personalization Options

16.5.5 Formats

Each report selected can be published in a different format. Each recipient will receive the reports in the same format as selected. You can also select for the report to be published in more than one format, including breaking up the report into separate report tabs and publishing each tab in a different or multiple formats as shown in Figure 16.32.

The available formats for Web Intelligence reports are listed here:

- ▶ **mHTML (.html):** Publishes the report in mHTML format. The mHTML can also be embedded in an email.

- ▶ **PDF (.pdf):** Publishes the report in Adobe Acrobat PDF format.

- ▶ **Excel (.xls):** Publishes the report in Microsoft Excel (.xls) format.

- ▶ **Web Intelligence (.wid):** Publishes the Web Intelligence report in its source format.

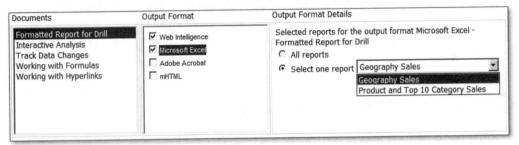

Figure 16.32 Format Options

16.5.6 Destinations

The destination properties enable you to select where the publication will be distributed: Default Enterprise Location, Business Objects Inbox, Email, FTP Server, and File System. These are the same destination options defined in Section 16.2, Using the Send Feature in InfoView.

There are two additional properties available in the destination options for publications. To minimize the file size of the distribution, the publication can be sent as a .zip file compressing the content.

The other option is the Deliver Objects to Each User checkbox. If this box is checked, a separate publication is generated for each user. This may be necessary if personalization is applied, and each user is receiving a customized view of the reports. Clearing this box can decrease the overall processing time because the publication is generated as only one instance and distributed out to the recipients.

16.5.7 Additional Options

The additional options for creating publications are listed here:

▶ **Prompts:** These properties allow you to specify the default prompts to use when each report is run in your publication.

▶ **Recurrence:** Numerous options are available in the drop-down menu for selection depending on your report distribution requirements. See Section 16.4.1, Scheduling in InfoView, for a review of these options.

▶ **Events:** Events are set up by your SAP BusinessObjects administrator in the CMC. Available events are listed in the box on the left. Select the arrows to move your selections to the Events to Wait For box. You may also select the event in the Available Schedule Events box to move to the Events to Trigger on completion. This specifies which events must occur for the job to be triggered, which can be useful to ensure a nightly data load job has completed loading the new data before the report is run.

▶ **Scheduling Server Group:** This option enables you to specify a specific server group to use when scheduling your document. The usual setting is to use the first available server. If you specify a server to use as default that is busy, your job may fail.

▶ **Advanced:** The Advanced properties aid in optimizing the overall processing time of the publication. See Figure 16.33 for specific properties available for selection in the advanced publication properties.

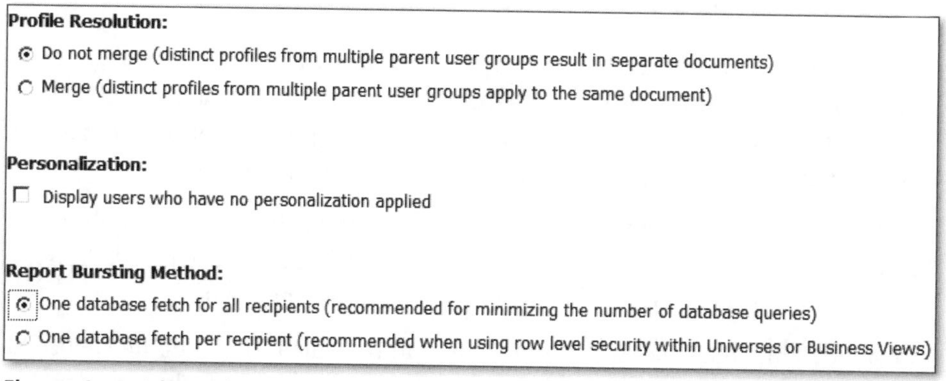

Profile Resolution:

⦿ Do not merge (distinct profiles from multiple parent user groups result in separate documents)

○ Merge (distinct profiles from multiple parent user groups apply to the same document)

Personalization:

☐ Display users who have no personalization applied

Report Bursting Method:

⦿ One database fetch for all recipients (recommended for minimizing the number of database queries)

○ One database fetch per recipient (recommended when using row level security within Universes or Business Views)

Figure 16.33 Advanced Options

16.5.8 Subscriptions

Subscriptions enable users who weren't included in the recipient list when the publication was originally created to receive a copy of the publication on future runs. Users can also unsubscribe to a publication if they no longer want to be included on the distribution list.

The Subscribe and Unsubscribe options are included in the Action menu on the InfoView toolbar (see Figure 16.34). These options only appear after you select the publication in the Workspace Panel.

Another option available in the Action menu for a publication is Test Mode. This option enables you send a test publication to yourself to ensure you have applied the appropriate properties prior to the start of the publication's schedule.

Figure 16.34 Action Menu Options for Publications

16.6 Summary

The collaboration features available in SAP BusinessObjects Web Intelligence XI 3.x make it a powerful business intelligence reporting tool. The manual sharing capabilities of copy and paste or sending to a user or group enable quick and easy collaboration. Scheduling enables the user to automate the process.

The powerful new features available for creating and subscribing to publications has added a plethora of new possibilities for the Web Intelligence report designer and report consumer to share reports with ease across the organization.

Chapter 17 discusses another exciting new feature available in Web Intelligence XI 3.x. Rich Client is a locally installed version of Web Intelligence that enables you to work with documents stored locally or in the CMC. It brings the power of Web Intelligence to your local machine, opening the door to additional data providers and options not available in the traditional Web Intelligence Java Report Panel.

Web Intelligence Rich Client puts the power of Web Intelligence reporting on the user's local machine. Rich Client provides all of the same capabilities while working in offline or standalone mode — no Central Management Server required.

17 Web Intelligence Rich Client

Prior to the release of SAP BusinessObjects Web Intelligence 3.x, Web Intelligence reporting existed over the web only. Users were required to log in to the web portal of InfoView to view, create, modify, and share Web Intelligence report content. With the introduction of this thin client version, Web Intelligence 3.x provides us with the ability to use all of the functionality of Web Intelligence from our local personal computer completely unconnected from the CMS. Web Intelligence documents can be stored locally, providing us with another means for backing up our reports. Local data providers can be used to create reports with Rich Client.

There are two ways to install Web Intelligence Rich Client. The SAP BusinessObjects Enterprise CD can be used to install Rich Client as part of a client installation. You can also easily install Rich Client from InfoView by selecting Install Now in the Web Intelligence Preferences. The installation of Rich Client is discussed further in Chapter 12, Using Multiple Data Sources.

17.1 How Rich Client Is Different

Rich Client enables you to access Web Intelligence from a Windows-based application installed on your local computer. The familiar interface of Rich Client makes it a favorite destination for report writers as shown in Figure 17.1. Access to the Central Management Console (CMC) isn't required. Documents can be saved to your local computer, and you can use local data providers when building queries. Timeouts or web-based issues won't create interruptions to your Web Intelligence report writing and viewing. These features provide exciting new capabilities for the Web Intelligence report consumer.

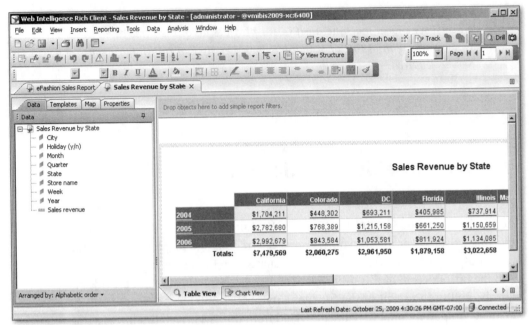

Figure 17.1 Rich Client Interface

Reasons users turn to Web Intelligence Rich Client for their reporting needs include the following:

▶ When unable to connect to the CMS, Rich Client can work offline without a connection to the CMS.

▶ When it's beneficial to perform calculations locally for improved performance, Rich Client performs calculations locally rather than on the server.

▶ When there is no CMS or application server installed, Rich Client can be used in standalone mode.

▶ When the data source is contained in Excel, CSV, or as a Web Service, Rich Client can be used for a local data source.

All of the features of Web Intelligence via InfoView are available in Rich Client. There are additional features available as discussed prior and in further detail in this chapter. For the purposes of this chapter, we won't duplicate our discussions in other chapters on the core functionality of Web Intelligence. Instead, we'll discuss only the differences found when using Rich Client for your Web Intelligence reporting needs.

There are three modes applicable in Web Intelligence Rich Client: offline, connected, and standalone.

There are two ways to access Rich Client: locally or through InfoView. After Rich Client is installed in your local machine, you can select Web Intelligence Rich Client from START • PROGRAMS • BUSINESSOBJECTS 3.1 • BUSINESSOBJECTS ENTERPRISE • WEB INTELLIGENCE RICH CLIENT as shown in Figure 17.2. When opening Rich Client, you are presented with the login screen. To launch Rich Client from InfoView, set your Web Intelligence preferences to use Desktop as your default creation/editing tool.

Figure 17.2 Rich Client Program Path

17.1.1 Working in Offline Mode

The first new option available is the Use in Offline Mode checkbox shown in Figure 17.3. Offline mode uses the security of the CMS stored on your local machine. The first time you log in to Rich Client, you have to log in using connected mode for the CMS security information to be downloaded to your local machine. Every document and universe stored locally on your machine carries an access control list that stores the groups and users that have access rights to the object. Therefore, when working in offline mode, you aren't connected to the CMS, but CMS security is applied. You can work with secured or unsecured local documents and universes. When creating or refreshing documents, you need a local universe and local connection server.

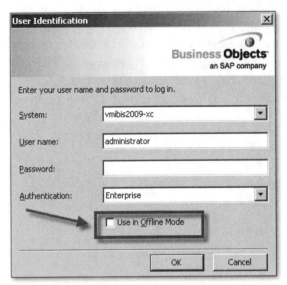

Figure 17.3 Offline Mode

17.1.2 Working in Connected Mode

Working in connected mode enables you to import documents and universes from the CMS as well as export Web Intelligence documents back to the CMS. This capability isn't available in offline or standalone modes. There are two options to log in to connected mode. From within InfoView, set your Web Intelligence preferences to use Desktop as your default creation/editing tool. When you choose to edit an existing Web Intelligence document from or create a new Web Intelligence document form InfoView, Rich Client is launched on your local computer. When using this method, Web Intelligence connects to the CMS in client-server mode, and database middleware is needed on your local machine.

Another method involves logging in to Rich Client by launching Web Intelligence Rich Client from your Programs on your local machine. When presented with the login dialog box, select the CMS, and then select the same authentication type used when logging into InfoView.

17.1.3 Working in Standalone Mode

To log in using standalone mode, select Standalone from the list of authentication types when entering your login credentials as shown in Figure 17.4. Standalone mode doesn't connect to the CMS, and there isn't enforced security as in offline mode. While in connected and offline mode, you can work with secured or unsecured documents and universes. In standalone mode, however, you can work with secured documents and universes only. This requires the appropriate database connection middleware to enable you to create and refresh documents with local universes.

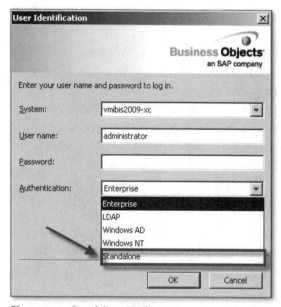

Figure 17.4 Standalone Mode

17.2 Data Provider Options

Chapter 12, Using Multiple Data Sources, discusses accessing multiple data sources in Web Intelligence Rich Client in Section 12.1.2, Accessing Multiple Data Sources in Web Intelligence Rich Client. There are two types of data sources available in Rich Client: Universe and Other Data Source.

The Universe data source includes all universes stored within the CMC as discussed in previous chapters. The Other Data Source includes Text and Excel or

Web Services. When selecting the Text and Excel sources, the Personal Data Providers dialog box opens. Personal data providers include the following file types:

- ▶ *.TXT
- ▶ *.CSV
- ▶ *.PRN
- ▶ *.ASC
- ▶ *.XLS

After selecting the file type, you'll are prompted to define further options for selection of your data source. Refer to Chapter 12, Section 12.1.2, for further details on creating a personal data provider.

Another data source available is the use of a Web Service. When selecting these options from the other data sources menu, you'll are prompted to enter your source URL as well as additional pertinent information about your Web Service. This functionality can be used to bring in real-time information to your Web Intelligence document. Data from Query as a Web Service can be integrated into your Web Intelligence Rich Client document. Refer to Chapter 12, Section 12.1.2, for further details on using a Web Service as your custom data provider.

17.2.1 Import a universe from the CMS

When creating a new Web Intelligence report in Rich Client, you'll are prompted to select your data source. When selecting a universe as a data source, you can select a local universe or a universe saved in the CMS.

> **Note**
> You can only use a universe in the CMS if you're working in connected mode.

If you want to store additional universes locally for use in unconnected sessions, you can use the TOOLS • UNIVERSES menu to import universes from the CMS. When you select Universes from the Tools menu, a list of available universes appears as shown in Figure 17.5. Select the universe to be imported locally, and choose the Import button. The universe is now available locally.

> **Note**
> Universes showing a green checkmark have already been imported locally.

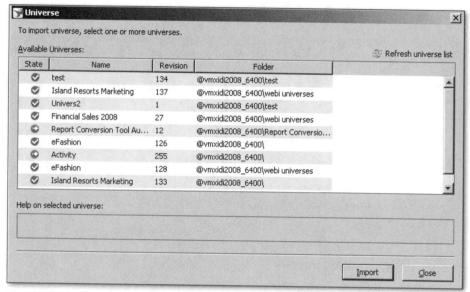

Figure 17.5   Import Universe Dialog Box

17.2.2   Query Panel in Rich Client

Within Rich Client, select DATA • EDIT QUERY to view the Query Panel. This is a change from web-based Web Intelligence where you select the Edit Query button on the toolbar. When you choose Edit Query, the Edit Query dialog box appears. You can make any appropriate changes to the query from this panel and then click Run Query to see your changes reflected in your report. This functionality works the same as within web-based Web Intelligence.

17.3   Working with Web Intelligence Reports

When working in Rich Client, you use the same menu you use when working with Web Intelligence reports over the web, but additional Windows-based menus exist at the top of the screen. This provides a familiar source of organization for the options available for use when designing Web Intelligence reports. Figure 17.6 shows the menu options in Web Intelligence Rich Client.

Figure 17.6   Rich Client Menu

The Rich Client menu options are listed in Table 17.1.

Menu	Options
File	▶ New
	▶ Open
	▶ Save
	▶ Save As
	▶ Close
	▶ Import from CMS
	▶ Export to CMS
	▶ Send by Email Attachment
	▶ Print
	▶ Properties
	▶ Recent Documents
	▶ Recent Data Sources
	▶ Exit
Edit	▶ Undo
	▶ Redo
	▶ Cut
	▶ Copy
	▶ Paste
	▶ Clear
	▶ Delete
	▶ Find
	▶ Find Next
	▶ Find Previous
View	▶ Quick Display Mode
	▶ Page Mode
	▶ Results Mode
	▶ Structure Mode
	▶ Data
	▶ Data/Properties

Table 17.1 Rich Client Menu Bar Options

Menu	Options
View	▸ Data/Properties on right
	▸ Collapsed Data/Properties
	▸ Toolbars
	▸ Reset to default
Insert	▸ Row
	▸ Column
	▸ Filters
	▸ Breaks
	▸ Sorts
	▸ Calculations
Reporting	▸ Merge/Split cells
	▸ Set as Section
	▸ Turn to
	▸ Ranking
	▸ Alerters
Tools	▸ Universes
	▸ Login As
	▸ Change Password
	▸ Options
Data	▸ Edit query
	▸ Variables
	▸ Merge dimensions
	▸ Tracking changes
Analysis	▸ Drill
	▸ Drill snapshot
Window	▸ [shows name of each open Web Intelligence report]
Help	▸ Welcome
	▸ Web Intelligence Help
	▸ Online Guides
	▸ About

Table 17.1 Rich Client Menu Bar Options (Cont.)

17.3.1 Importing Reports from CMS

To import a report from the CMS, you first must be in connected mode. Select FILE • IMPORT FROM CMS. The Import Documents dialog box appears as shown in Figure 17.7. Select the name of the document from either the Folders or Categories view of the document list. You may also search for the document by using the search box at the top of the dialog box. These search options are similar to that seen within InfoView. You can select one or many documents to be installed on your local machine. After selecting a document, click the Add button to move the document to your list of documents to be imported locally. When complete, select the Import button at the bottom of the dialog box.

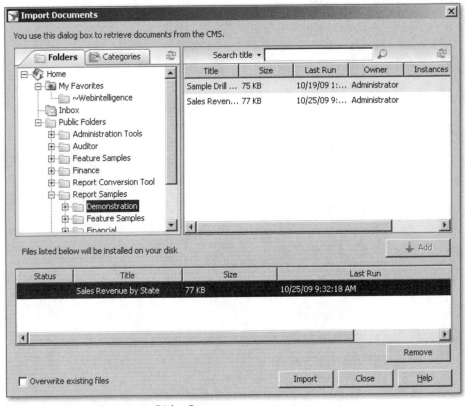

Figure 17.7 Import Documents Dialog Box

A message appears as shown in Figure 17.8 indicating the import was successful. You must select the "Click to Continue" message to return to the Import documents dialog box. You can now select to import additional documents, open all documents in your list, or close the dialog box.

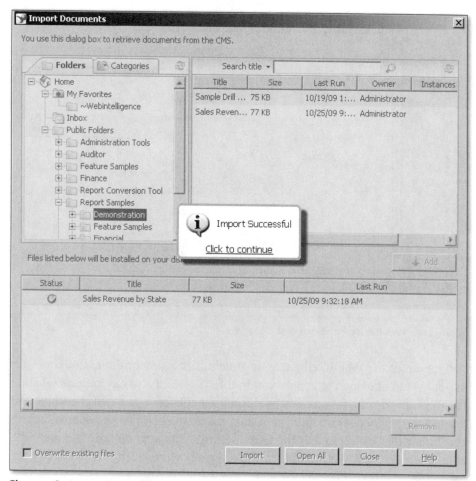

Figure 17.8 Import Successful Message

17.3.2 Saving Reports Locally

To save a Web Intelligence Rich Client document locally, you can select Save or Save As from the File menu. Save will save the document as its original name to its original location. Save As has a number of options, including Web Intelligence Document, Excel, PDF, or CSV (Data Only). These documents won't be viewable in InfoView.

The Save as a Web Intelligence document option opens another dialog box as shown in Figure 17.9.

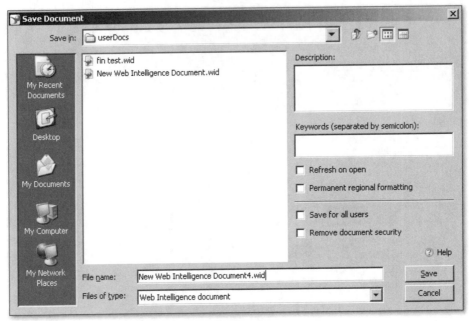

Figure 17.9 Web Intelligence Document Dialog Box

You can enter the Web Intelligence document name, descriptions, and keywords as you would like them to appear within InfoView. You also can indicate whether to refresh the document on open by selecting the Refresh on Open checkbox. The Permanent Regional Formatting checkbox maintains permanent regional formatting rather than adjusting per the user's settings. The new options that are available when saving a Web Intelligence document within Rich Client include the following:

▶ **Save for All Users:** Saves the document for all users to view and enables the Web Intelligence report to be moved between environments.

▶ **Remove Document Security:** Saves the document as unsecured so it can be viewed in standalone or offline mode.

After selecting available options and indicating the report name, description, and keywords, you can select a location to save the document outside of the SAP BusinessObjects Enterprise environment. The default location is to save to your user-Docs folder. The path for this folder is defined within your Rich Client Options as discussed in Section 17.4, Setting Preferences in Rich Client.

The Save as Excel option opens another dialog box as shown in Figure 17.10. When saving a Web Intelligence document as an Excel file, you can convert all report tabs to Excel or select only certain report tabs for export. You can also select the Prioritize the format of reports in the Excel document. The default setting for these preferences are defined in the Rich Client Options in the Tools menu. Further information on these options is discussed in Chapter 11, Working Within InfoView.

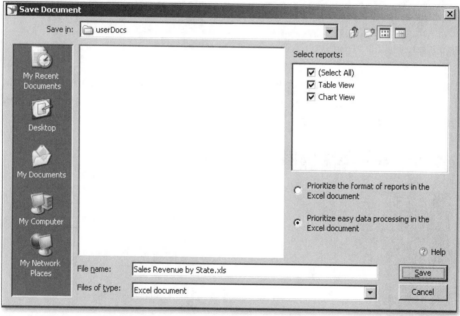

Figure 17.10 Save as Excel Dialog Box

The Save as PDF option opens another dialog box as shown in Figure 17.11. When saving as a PDF, you're given the option to define which reports and pages to include in your PDF.

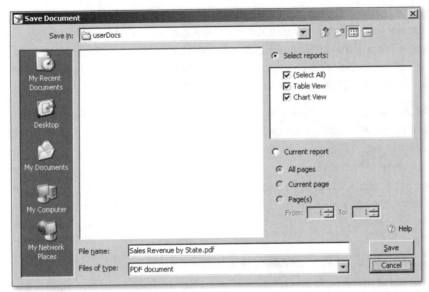

Figure 17.11 Save as PDF dialog box

The Save as CSV (Data Only) option opens another dialog box as shown in Figure 17.12. You're given the option to define the text qualifier, column delimiter, and character set for the CSV file.

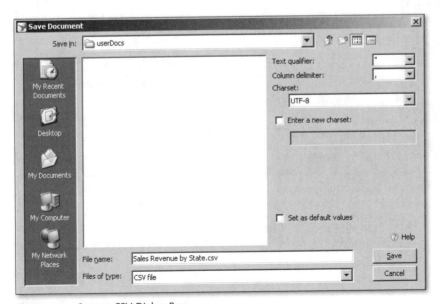

Figure 17.12 Save as CSV Dialog Box

17.3.3 Exporting Reports to CMS

To view these documents within InfoView and share with other users in the web portal, you have to export your report to the CMS. To export your document to the CMS, you must first be in connected mode. Then select FILE • EXPORT TO CMS. Select the folder and categories to export your document for viewing within Info-View, and then select the Export button as shown in Figure 17.13. A message will appear at the bottom of the dialog when complete that reads "Export successful." You can choose additional locations to export your document or select the Close button to close the export dialog box.

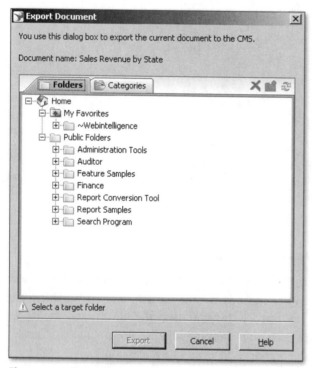

Figure 17.13 Export Document Dialog Box

17.3.4 Printing from Rich Client

To print from Rich Client, select FILE • PRINT. You are presented with print options as shown in Figure 17.14. The document will be sent to the printer without having to open it within PDF format first.

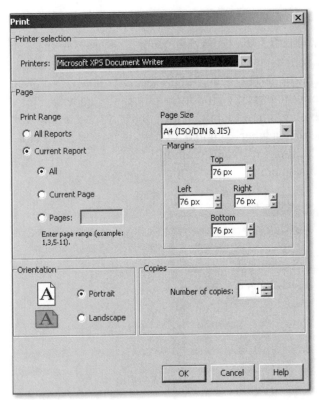

Figure 17.14 Print Dialog Box

17.3.5 Sending Reports as Email Attachments

Another option is available in Rich Client that isn't available in web-based Web Intelligence. The ability to send a report as an email attachment is available from the File menu. Select FILE • SEND BY EMAIL ATTACHMENT. You can send the document in a number of formats, including Web Intelligence document, as an unsecured Web Intelligence document, Excel, PDF, and CSV (data only).

17.4 Setting Preferences in Rich Client

Preferences are available in Rich Client as shown in the Web Intelligence Preferences in InfoView. These options are available by choosing TOOLS • OPTIONS. Preferences can be defined for drilling, locales, viewing, and general preferences.

These are defined separately in Rich Client from what is defined for Web Intelligence documents viewed in InfoView.

17.5 Summary

Web Intelligence Rich Client brings the features of web-based Web Intelligence onto your desktop, opening up new features that are instrumental to the report writer. Former SAP BusinessObjects Desktop Intelligence users will appreciate the new thin client capabilities of Web Intelligence provided within Web Intelligence XI 3.x. The ability to work whether connected or disconnected from the CMS, easily print reports, save universes and documents locally, use local data providers, and send Web Intelligence documents as email attachments provides additional capabilities to aid the report designer in the report creation, consumption, and sharing processes.

Chapter 18 discusses the ability to bring Web Intelligence report content into Microsoft Office documents using another tool called SAP BusinessObjects Live Office. This provides another familiar interface for report writers and consumers alike to work with data within the easy-to-use environment of programs such as Microsoft Excel.

SAP BusinessObjects Live Office XI 3.x is a powerful tool to enable the use of business intelligence content within Microsoft Office documents. Live Office enables a larger audience to consume, query, analyze, and visualize Web Intelligence content in a familiar interface.

18 Connecting SAP BusinessObjects Live Office to Web Intelligence XI 3.x

SAP BusinessObjects Live Office enables you to work with your business intelligence content within Microsoft Office applications such as Word, Excel, PowerPoint, and Outlook. This functionality enables you to quickly and easily collaborate with other users across your organization. It also enables users of different skill sets or comfort levels to manipulate their Web Intelligence query results within other mediums. Live Office XI 3.x is compatible with Office 2007 and Office 2003.

18.1 About Live Office

Live Office is an Excel plug-in that is installed on a client machine. After Live Office has been installed on your machine, a new Live Office menu will appear on your toolbar when you're in the Microsoft Office applications of Word, Excel, PowerPoint or Outlook as shown in Figure 18.1. Live Office allows you to bring report data from Web Intelligence reports, Crystal Reports, and universe queries to do further manipulation within the Microsoft Office application. Excel is a frequently used application with Live Office because it provides the ability to perform further analysis of the data in a familiar place. Users in finance departments are often very familiar with Excel, and Live Office provides them with a tool that works within their comfort zone and requires little additional training.

Figure 18.1 Live Office Menu

18.1.1 Integration with Web Intelligence Reports

Live Office enables you to insert Web Intelligence report content into your Microsoft Office document. Web Intelligence content is inserted in table format into your destination. If using PowerPoint, make sure you have adequate space available for your table to display.

> **Tip**
>
> When using Live Office with Microsoft PowerPoint, start with a blank slide. This ensures you have adequate space to insert your Web Intelligence content and that appropriate formatting remains intact.

Excel is the most commonly used destination for Web Intelligence content because it already uses a tabular interface and enables further manipulation of the data. A user who isn't fully trained in how to use Web Intelligence, can easily create a report using Web Intelligence content from within Live Office.

Web Intelligence content involves report objects, report instances, and reports parts. *Report objects* are the actual Web Intelligence reports that are contained within the SAP BusinessObjects Enterprise. *Report instances* are the versions of reports created when a report is scheduled. A report instance will contain data from a specified report refresh with the prompt values used at the time of that refresh. *Report parts* are the different elements of the report such as the tables and charts contained within the report. It's important to understand the differentiation of each of these elements when using the Live Office Wizard for specification of the Web Intelligence content to integrate in your Office document.

18.1.2 Live Office Toolbar

The Live Office toolbar is available from within your Word, Excel, PowerPoint, or Outlook document. It enables quick access to the most commonly used functions available within Live Office. Refer to Figure 18.1, shown earlier, to see the buttons on the Live Office toolbar.

The following options are available on the Live Office toolbar:

▸ **Insert Crystal Reports :** This option opens the Live Office Wizard to define the options available for inserting content from a Crystal Report.

▸ **Insert Web Intelligence :** This option opens the Live Office Wizard to define the options available for inserting content from a Web Intelligence report.

▸ **Insert Universe Query:** This option opens the Live Office Wizard to define the options available for creating a universe query to insert results into your destination Office document.

▸ **Go To Object:** This option enables you to go to a specific object in your Live Office document.

▸ **Modify Object:** This option enables you to modify the properties for a specific object. More detail on this functionality is discussed in Section 18.2, Creating Live Office Documents with Web Intelligence Content.

▸ **Refresh Object:** This option enables you to refresh a specific object only.

▸ **Refresh All Objects:** This option enables you to refresh all objects contained in your Live Office document.

▸ **Create Snapshot:** This option enables you to create a snapshot of the document in the current state to save for further reference. More information on snapshots is discussed in Chapter 9, Scope of Analysis and Drilling Down.

▸ **Save to BOE:** This option saves the Live Office document to the SAP BusinessObjects Enterprise to share and collaborate with others in your organization.

▸ **Save as New to BOE:** This option allows you to save as a different name or to a different location for a Live Office document existing in the SAP BusinessObjects Enterprise.

▸ **Open from BOE:** This option allows you to open a Live Office document saved to the SAP BusinessObjects Enterprise.

▸ **Object Properties:** This option allows you to define object-specific properties. More details on setting object properties are contained in Section 18.3, Setting Preferences.

▸ **Refresh Options:** This option allows you to define refresh options for the Live Office document. More details on defining refresh options are contained in Section 18.3, Setting Preferences.

▸ **Application Options:** This option allows you to define Live Office application options. More details on these options are contained in Section 18.3, Setting Preferences.

▸ **View Object in Browser:** This option opens the object in a browser window.

▸ **Help:** This option opens the Live Office Help dialog box.

▸ **About Live Office:** This option shows the version information for your current Live Office installation.

18.2 Creating Live Office Documents with Web Intelligence Content

The integration of Web Intelligence content within Live Office provides a powerful tool for the end user and report writer alike. To integrate Web Intelligence content, a Web Intelligence report must already exist in the SAP BusinessObjects Enterprise for access within Live Office. This report content can be brought into Word, Excel, PowerPoint, or Outlook. For the purpose of this section, we'll assume that we're using Excel to integrate our Web Intelligence content.

18.2.1 Accessing the Live Office Wizard

Navigate to the appropriate cell where you want the content to be dropped in your Excel worksheet. From the Live Office toolbar, select the Insert Web Intelligence content button. If you haven't already logged in or selected auto-authentication, then the log on dialog box will appear. After authentication, the Live Office Wizard will appear.

18.2.2 Selecting the Web Intelligence document

The first option in the Live Office Wizard is to select the Web Intelligence document to use for content in your Excel document. Figure 18.2 shows the Choose Document screen in the Live Office Wizard.

The screen displays the Web Intelligence documents available for integration within the SAP BusinessObjects Enterprise. This view resembles the Document List in InfoView. You can navigate by folders or categories by selecting the icons at the left. You can also search by Title, Keyword, Content, or All Fields to find a document. You can select Web Intelligence objects, instances, or publications to include Web Intelligence content. Highlight the name of your chosen document, and select Next.

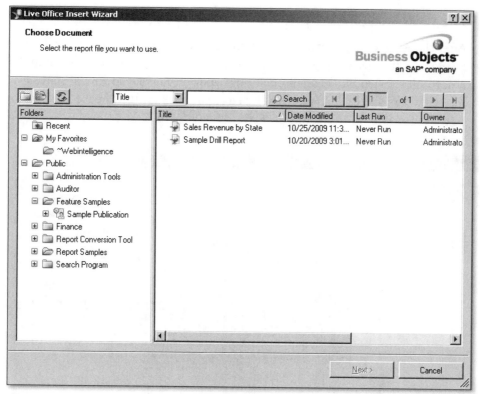

Figure 18.2 Choose a Document in the Live Office Wizard

18.2.3 Setting Context

If more than one context exists for the Web Intelligence report, then you're prompted to set context as part of the Live Office Wizard. After choosing the appropriate context, select Next.

18.2.4 Configuring Prompt Values

The option to configure prompt values only appears if prompts are set up on the Web Intelligence report. If no prompts exist, then this option won't appear. The prompt properties allow you to select the prompt value from a list or select to be prompted to enter the prompt value each time the data is refreshed. After specifying prompt values, select Next.

18.2.5 Selecting Report Content

After choosing the Web Intelligence document, you select the report content to be included in the Live Office document. Select each report block to include it in the report. All selected blocks are brought into your Live Office document starting at the cell where you placed your cursor. See Figure 18.3 for the Choose Data dialog box. After making all selections of relevant report parts, select Next.

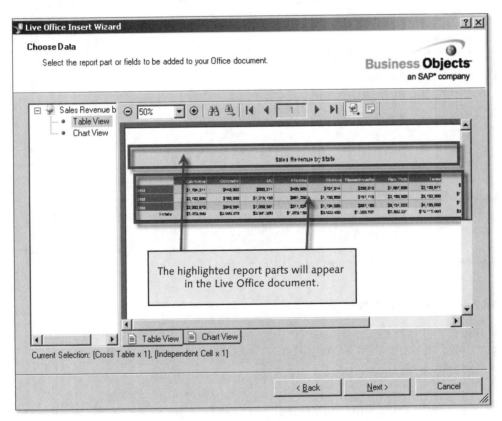

Figure 18.3 Choose Data in the Live Office Wizard

18.2.6 Creating the Summary

When you select the report parts to be included in your Live Office document, you are shown the Summary, which enables you to give a name to your particular Live Office content before selecting Finish. Figure 18.4 shows Web Intelligence report content in an Excel document using Live Office.

	A	B	C	D	E	F	G	H	I	J
1	s Revenue by State									
2										
3		California	Colorado	DC	Florida	Illinois	Massachusetts	New York	Texas	Totals:
4	2004	1704210.8	448301.5	693210.5	405985.1	737914.2	238818.7	1667695.8	2199677.4	8095814
5	2005	2782679.5	768389.5	1215158	661249.8	1150658.8	157718.7	2763503.1	3732888.6	13232246
6	2006	2992679	843584.2	1053581.4	811923.6	1134085.4	887169.2	3151021.7	4185098.3	15059142.8
7	Totals:	7479569.3	2060275.2	2961949.9	1879158.5	3022658.4	1283706.6	7582220.6	10117664.3	36387202.8
8										

Figure 18.4 Web Intelligence Live Office Content in Excel

18.2.7 Adding More Content

After your selected report content is displayed within Excel, you may want to add in more report blocks from the same report. To add additional content, right-click on the report content within Excel to display the right-click menu. Select the Live Office option to view the available options as shown in Figure 18.5.

Options are available to insert or remove rows and columns within your Live Office object. Using these menu items ensures that you don't use your object mapping. You have the option to refresh or set options from the right-click menu as well. To add more content from the same report, select the option for New Object From Same Report. The Live Office Wizard appears to select the relevant options using the same Web Intelligence document.

To insert new content from a new Web Intelligence document, select the Insert Web Intelligence button from the Live Office toolbar and select the appropriate new report in the Live Office Wizard.

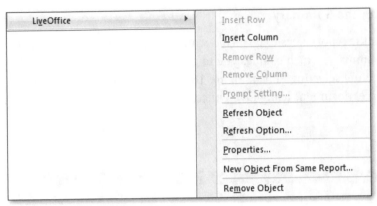

Figure 18.5 Live Office Menu Options

18.3 Setting Preferences

There are a number of preferences within Live Office to customize your session. Preferences apply to application options, refresh options, object properties, and prompt binding options.

18.3.1 Application Options

The application options enable you to define default settings for all your Live Office documents within the application. To define application options, select Application Options from the Live Office toolbar. There are three types of application options defined by the dialog box tabs: General, View, and Enterprise.

General

General properties will vary dependent on the Office application. In the General options tab from Excel as show in Figure 18.6, you can define the shortcut menu options. In addition, options for the treatment of Live Office cells and refresh options are available. If the option to Prompt Before Overwriting Live Office Cells is selected, you'll be prompted before you can type over content that is being fed by your business intelligence content. If the option to Refresh Live Office Object When Binding Cell Changes is selected, the content will refresh when you bind your business intelligence content to cells in your Excel spreadsheet. If you select to Refresh Live Office Object on Document Open, then Live Office will go to the SAP BusinessObjects repository and return the most recent results for your specified content. The Copy and Paste with Live Office Connectivity option enables you to move bound ranges without losing the connectivity to Live Office. If this is disabled, then only the results will move, and the copied content won't be refreshed when the Live Office content is refreshed.

Figure 18.6 General Application Options

View

The View options apply to how the data will be displayed in your Live Office document. The Appearance options are set to determine if the formatting from the original report should be maintained. The Appearance options also allow you to set whether to show filters as comments in the Live Office document and to alert you when a time-consuming operation occurs that will affect a defined number of cells.

The View options also define how cells will display for default cell values of no data, data error, and concealed data. You can also define column headings to be set to the field name, field description, or both by default. View Options are shown in Figure 18.7.

Figure 18.7 View Application Options

Enterprise

The Enterprise options allow you to define your login criteria as show in Figure 18.8. The appropriate criteria should be given by your SAP BusinessObjects administrator. The User Name and Password will be your SAP BusinessObjects Enterprise user name and password. The Authentication and System will be the same as used for your enterprise logon. The Web Services URL is defined as *http://webserver:portnumber/dswsbobje/services/session*. Web server and port number should be replaced with the appropriate information for your SAP BusinessObjects deployment. The next setting allows you to define the open document URL for viewing content in a web browser.

Figure 18.8 Enterprise Application Options

18.3.2 Data Refresh Options

The data in a report can be set to refresh based on the original report, an instance, or on demand. The available options for refresh include the following (see Figure 18.9):

▶ **Latest Instance From the Latest Instance Scheduled By:** This option refreshes data based on the latest instance of a scheduled report. Therefore, the Live Office data refreshes as the scheduled report data refreshes. The Live Office object uses the latest instance of the report for its data.

▶ **On Demand From the Database:** This option enables you to manually refresh the Live Office document when you want updated data. The source of the update comes from the database rather than the original Web Intelligence report or instance.

▶ **Use Report Saved Data From Saved Data Report:** This option refreshes the Live Office objects with the data saved in the original Web Intelligence report contained in the SAP BusinessObjects Enterprise environment.

▶ **Specific Instance From a Specific Instance off the Report:** This option enables you to use one of the scheduled instances of a Web Intelligence report as the source data for the Live Office report.

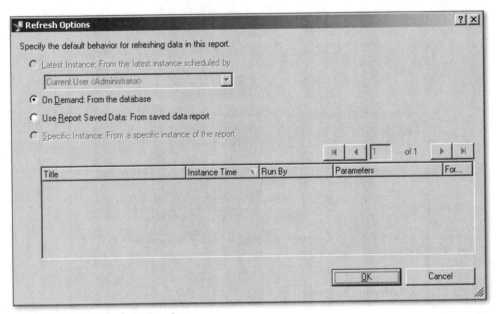

Figure 18.9 Refresh Options Box

18.3.3 Object Properties

The Live Office Object Properties box shown in Figure 18.10 allows you to specify properties that are specific to an object contained in your Live Office document. An object is defined as one of the report parts from the Web Intelligence report.

In the sample report, there are two report objects as shown in the Objects of the Report box. When you select each object, detailed information about the object is shown on the right of the box. Specific details on the Web Intelligence report used in the Live Office document are also contained within the Objects/Reports box at the top. By selecting each of these objects, you can see the properties display to the right.

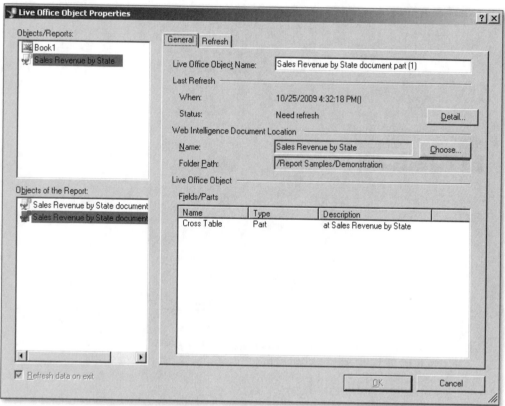

Figure 18.10 General Object Properties box

To set refresh properties for the object, select the object from the Objects of the Report box on the bottom left, and then select the appropriate properties in the Refresh tab. Available properties include whether to Apply Report Format When Refreshing, Conceal Data on Saving, and Refresh Setting (see Figure 18.11). Conceal Data on Saving enables you to secure the data so that a refresh must be made before a user can view the data. This ensures that they are seeing only the data that they are allowed to access given their security settings.

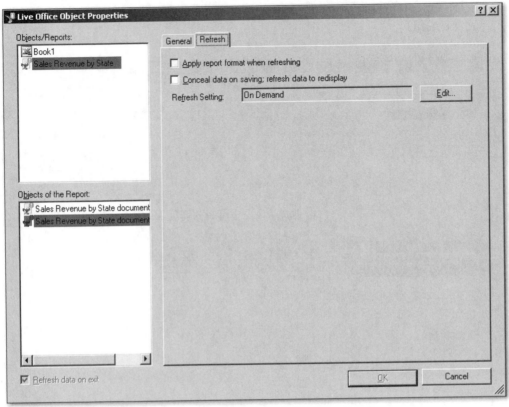

Figure 18.11 Refresh Object Properties box

18.4 Summary

Live Office is a powerful tool enabling the consumption of Web Intelligence report content within Microsoft Office documents. This combines the power of business intelligence queries in a comfortable, familiar setting for end users and report writers alike.

The next chapter discusses another powerful tool to customize your Web Intelligence reporting experience. The Web Intelligence SDK enables you to build customized applications for your organization, which is one more step toward a completely integrated business intelligence reporting environment.

Whether you're using Java or .NET as a development environment, the Web Intelligence SDK provides a huge range of possibilities. You can create custom solutions, automate reporting activities, embed reports into your applications, use custom single sign-on (SSO), and much more.

19 Introducing the Web Intelligence SDK

Web Intelligence provides its users with a very powerful user interface with extensive query capabilities and satisfies a large percentage of potential requirements. However, what happens when you want to do something not available "out of the box"? This is the time to look into the different Software Development Kits (SDKs) that are available and try to understand if they can deliver the necessary functionality.

SAP BusinessObjects offers a wide assortment of SDKs for both the Java and .NET environments. Before embarking on a development project, it's important to understand what each SDK can offer and the SAP BusinessObjects product it addresses.

This chapter looks at samples of what kind of applications the SDKs can help you deliver, followed by details of what SDKs are out there, giving a description of the functionality of each one and noting where its use is most applicable. Then, the chapter covers the details of how to set up the SDK development environment with an overview of the core coding needed to get started.

> **Note**
>
> For many SDKs, both the environment and aspects of the functionality may vary from one version to another of SAP BusinessObjects. In this overview, we'll look at the SDKs as they are defined as of SAP BusinessObjects Web Intelligence XI 3.1 and later.

19.1 What Can I Achieve with the SDK?

There is such a wide range of possibilities of what you can do with the various SDKs that we believe the best means of identifying the possibilities is to highlight major application areas and then allow you to delve into the details of how to address your own specific requirements. Don't think of this list as exhaustive by any means because new and innovative customization projects are the norm not the exception.

19.1.1 System Administration

The SAP BusinessObjects SDKs allow you to manage servers, clusters, users, groups, and all system objects from an external system. A common application is to automatically create users when they are entered into another system.

Security and authentication is another classic function. A typical example is the integration of a custom or nonstandard single sign-on (SSO) process.

19.1.2 Automation of Reporting

Scheduling and publishing documents may be automated and distributed based on business logic. An example is slicing report data for individual customers on a weekly basis, and then shipping the output via email or FTP in the format that each individual customer requires, such as PDF, HTML, or CSV.

19.1.3 Interfacing with Other Internal or External Systems

The synchronization and transfer of information between systems can also be automated. This may involve large data transfers or simple updates to an external database.

19.1.4 Creation of Custom Solutions

In many cases, you may not want to supply your users with a full reporting system such as InfoView. Often, all that is required is to open a basic list of reports on a click, especially for external or nonexpert users. You may also want to deliver an application that has your own corporate look and feel and branding. Full customization and delivery features are available in the various SDKs that allow to you create your own application, including just about any functionality that is available in InfoView.

19.1.5 Distribution of Applications

If you need to distribute your application via an intranet, an extranet, or Web Services, the SDKs offer all of these capabilities.

19.1.6 Embed Reporting into Applications

If you simply need to include reporting in your existing applications, there are quite a number of potential solutions, whether the requirement is solely to view the report or to be able to create new reports and edit existing ones.

Don't Customize InfoView

After you've got the feel of the SDK, you may be tempted to hack InfoView code to change its functionality. Apart from dealing with very complex code structures, this will almost certainly result in hours, if not days, of unexpected maintenance, especially when you come to upgrading the system. SAP BusinessObjects recently released the Extension Points SDK, which offers many different customization options for InfoView. We'll look at the Extension Points SDK in Chapter 20, Customizing Web Intelligence using Web Intelligence Extensions Points.

19.2 Getting Started with the SDK

Let's now go through each of the major SDKs and try to understand where each fits in based on the SAP BusinessObjects products you'll use and what your customization project hopes to achieve. Also remember, delivering a customized Web Intelligence application may involve the use of more than one SDK. Many of the kits available are created to be complementary; for example, the solution may use the SAP BusinessObjects Enterprise SDK as a basis for SSO connectivity and the Report Engine SDK as the means of providing users with reports that can be edited at runtime.

A summary of the main SDKs is shown in Table 19.1.

SDK	Technology	Products	Usage
SAP BusinessObjects Enterprise (BOE)	Java, .NET	SAP BusinessObjects Enterprise (BOE), Crystal Reports Server (CRS)	All BI platform services, including authentication, security, and system management
Java Server Faces (JSF)	Java	BOE, CRS	Authentication, view and list documents, navigate content
ReportEngine (RE)	Java, .NET	BOE	Create, modify, export, and present Web Intelligence documents
Web Services (WS)	Java, .NET	BOE, CRS	Create distributed Web Services applications

Table 19.1 A Summary of the Main SDKs

19.2.1 The SAP BusinessObjects Enterprise SDK (.NET and Java)

The SAP BusinessObjects Enterprise SDK (BOE SDK) allows you to build applications that talk directly to the Enterprise system and is available on both the Java and .NET platforms. The BOE SDK allows you to access and control programmatically all features of the Enterprise platform. To give you some idea of the power of this SDK, both InfoView and the Central Management Console (CMC) were developed using the BOE SDK. When used in conjunction with other SDKs, such as the Report Engine SDK, you can achieve full InfoView type functionality. The most common uses of this SDK are to provide connectivity for the user, provide access objects such as folders and documents from the CMC, set security options, and schedule content. However, this is a large SDK with a large range of capabilities. Some of the main areas of capability include the following:

▶ **SAP BusinessObjects Enterprise authentication:** Basic logon and logoff functionality, including standard, LDAP, AD, and NT connections. You can also create custom SSO and trusted authentication applications.

▶ **User and group security:** Access rights for objects, servers, and applications can be defined both prior to application startup and at runtime.

▶ **Web Intelligence object management:** You can create, delete, and manage the status of reports, documents, folders, categories, and other objects in much the same way you would undertake these tasks in the CMC.

▶ **Server administration:** The server admin tasks that are available in the CMC are available as programmable options. You can start, stop, clone, or group any server. You can manage and configure server services and server service containers. Additionally, server auditing can be controlled programmatically.

▶ **Scheduling:** You can schedule reports, documents, programs, packages, and most objects. Type of output, timing, frequency, and destination of the schedule can all be defined. Equally, it's possible to pump variable values into the schedule. An example of this may be the distribution of report documents to a user base, setting a report parameter so that the scheduler delivers a filtered report containing only data pertinent to each of the recipients.

▶ **Publications:** A publication is a set of objects that can be scheduled and distributed to multiple recipients on a regular basis. Recipients can be either SAP BusinessObjects Enterprise users or external users. Publications can be delivered via email, the Inbox, or other electronic means. Using the BOE SDK, you can create the publication, add documents, and define the output type and destinations in addition to customizing individual documents.

▶ **Custom, schedule, and file events:** The SAP BusinessObjects infrastructure allows you to create events programmatically that trigger predefined activities.

As you can probably see from its core functionality, the BOE SDK will be a fundamental building block in any Enterprise-type application whether you're using .NET or Java as the underlying technology.

19.2.2 The Report Engine SDK (.NET and Java)

The Report Engine SDK (RE SDK) is available for both .NET (RENET) and Java (REBEAN). Its primary purpose is to view Web Intelligence and Desktop Intelligence documents. Generally, you use this SDK in conjunction with the BOE SDK, which manages authentication and document access. After you retrieve a document, you then employ either REBEAN or RENET depending on the technology platform to deal with the document.

However, it's possible to do much more than merely view reports with this SDK. You can print, drill down, export, and interact with report documents. You can manipulate the source data drivers, modify the documents, and update the look and feel of individual reports.

Looking through the main features of this SDK, remember that not all features are supported by RENET:

▶ **Document management:** You can open, refresh, save, and schedule documents; change parent folders and categories; send the document to a user Inbox; and change user rights. A very powerful option lets you access the report parts of the document. With report parts, you can retrieve specific parts or multiple parts of a report and thus display a hierarchical view of the document, for example, presenting the document structure in tree format. A basic document view sample is shown in Figure 19.1.

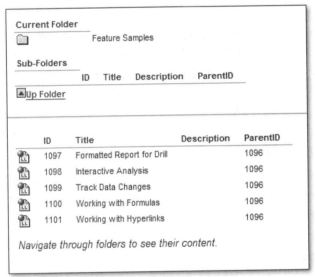

Figure 19.1 Using the Report Engine SDK to View Documents by Folder

▶ **Viewing and exporting reports:** You can display documents and individual reports in both web and interactive mode. Additional output options for reports include Excel, PDF, CSV, and XML. Note that CSV and XML output options aren't available for the whole document, only reports. To export the whole document, you need to use the data provider. To display the report hierarchy, retrieve the report map, and use that to access report sections.

▶ **Create new reports (REBEAN only):** By accessing the cadenza thin Java applet, you can create new Web Intelligence reports.

▶ **Handle prompts:** The `Prompt` classes allow you to control single, multiple, and nested report prompts. The `List of Values` (LOV) class gives access to valid prompt values where they have been defined for the report.

▶ **Drilling in reports:** Drilling in Web Intelligence reports allows a user to view more or less detailed (depending on the drill direction) information about report data based on hierarchical dimensions created in the universe. The RE SDK provides access to these hierarchies so that you can manage them programmatically and display the resulting data using formatted html.

▶ **Formatting reports (REBEAN only):** The RESDK provides classes that allow you to format the report itself. Options include the creation and editing of new document structures, sections, cells, and page decoration. You can also control page layout managing break behavior, repeating blocks, and calculations, as well as setting the visibility of report elements.

▶ **Managing data providers:** A data provider is an object that holds information about a query that populates a report. The RE SDK exposes the data sources of the data providers giving direct access to the universe. Using this feature or by calling the Web Intelligence Java Report Panel, you can create new data providers and edit existing queries. After a query has been accessed, you can run this query and, if necessary, pump in any required prompts.

▶ **Dealing with recordsets:** Using the recordset data structure, you can retrieve the results stored in a data provider. If you're familiar with SQL result set programming, the `Recordset` classes work in a very similar manner. The data are stored in matrix form. You access each column of the matrix either by its name or index number. You can scroll through the matrix retrieving each row of data sequentially or jump directly to a specified row.

The RE SDK helps you to manipulate documents and reports as well as the underlying data that drives the reports.

19.2.3 The Java Server Faces SDK

Java Server Faces is a standard framework of components for building rich user interfaces for Java applications. The JSF SDK uses this framework to supply both visual and nonvisual controls that help you deliver common Web Intelligence functionality in your custom applications.

As you can imagine from the name, this SDK is only available for the Java platform and runs on Crystal Reports Server as well as SAP BusinessObjects Enterprise.

There are two core types of object found in the JSF SDK. They are the UI components and Managed Java Beans. The UI components are typically used in a JSP tag library and help simplify the fairly complex coding that is sometimes needed to interact with the underlying BOE SDK. Some of the more commonly used UI components include the following:

▶ **Logon:** A customizable logon form that allows you to define the type of input items that are needed to connect to the SAP BusinessObjects system, including user id, password, authentication type, and the system server. Figure 19.2 shows a logon web page with basic background and image styling.

Figure 19.2 A Basic Custom Logon Page Generated Using the JSF Logon Component

▶ **Path:** This component shows the representation of a selected object such as a folder to its root item.

▶ **Items Grid and Items Columns:** These components help you build a table that presents an object or objects such as a Web Intelligence document. You can set the properties of the components to select which details of the object are displayed. You can also allow a user to select, sort, and page through the displayed items.

▶ **Schedule and Destination:** These two components help in the creation of forms that enable a user to define document scheduling criteria and the output destination of that document.

▸ **ReportPageViewer:** A component that displays reports with a toolbar in a web page. It also provides options for the user to export the report in various formats. Note that this functionality is only available for Crystal Reports.

The Managed Java Beans store information about reports, folders, and connections on the server. The server keeps these beans live for the duration of the session or until they are cleared and can therefore be used repeatedly. There are three Managed Java Beans available:

▸ **Enterprise Item:** This is the source for a single SAP BusinessObjects Enterprise object such as a report or a folder. Retrieving objects from the CMC is greatly simplified because information is retrieved by setting properties rather than making specific calls to the CMC.

▸ **Enterprise Items:** This bean stores a collection of Enterprise Item Beans.

▸ **Identity:** This bean contains the authentication credentials to log on and off SAP BusinessObjects Enterprise.

19.2.4 The Web Services Consumer SDK (.NET and Java)

If you're looking to distribute your Web Intelligence applications via a Web Service, the Web Services Consumer SDK is available for both .NET and Java. The versions for both technologies are virtually identical because they are generated from the same Web Service Definition Language (WSDL) files. The only real difference between the two, as you would expect, is in the naming convention of the classes and methods. Both provide full access to all Enterprise plug-ins such as Publishing and Scheduling.

There are quite a number of benefits to be gained when deploying applications with this SDK:

▸ **View reports:** The Web Service Consumers permits viewing of all report types. Report views are available as HTML, PDF, Excel, RTF, and XML.

▸ **Access to the repository:** The retrieval of objects from the SAP BusinessObjects Enterprise repository is greatly simplified using a URI-based query.

▸ **Server management:** Servers can be started, stopped, and restarted.

▸ **User and group management:** You can create, update, and delete users and groups. User and group rights for objects such as folders and documents can be created and amended.

▸ **Folder and category management:** Folders and categories can be created, amended, and deleted.

▸ **Schedule documents:** Using the relevant plug-in, you can send all types of SAP BusinessObjects documents to the scheduler.

Figure 19.3 provides a high-level overview of how web services are used by BusinessObjects to communicate with client browsers.

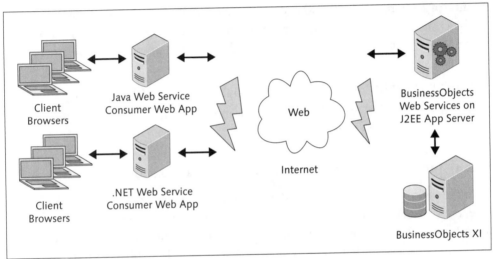

Figure 19.3   NET and Java Web Service Consumers with a J2EE Producer

You should consider using the Web Services SDK if the purpose of your application is to share BI services between companies and departments; if you have firewall problems and you need a means of circumventing that infrastructure; and when you need to create smart client applications that connect to Enterprise data.

There are, of course, some downsides to deploying a Web Service. Performance in a Web Service deployment is affected by increased communication flows between the producer and consumer. If you need very high performance, you should probably think about using the SAP BusinessObjects Enterprise bus.

19.2.5   Other SDKs

A number of other SDKs are available that address reporting with Crystal Reports, including the Report Application Server (RAS), Crystal Reports .NET, and Crystal Reports for Eclipse.

The Data Access Driver SDK (Java only) provides the basis for supplying the SAP BusinessObjects Connection Server with data access for data sources where no drivers are currently available. Driver types may be open, which work in the same way as a standard driver or based on a Java Bean.

Additionally, many COM SDKS are available that provide capability for report viewing and universe design. As Microsoft is running down support levels, the COM SDKs are gradually being deprecated.

19.3　The Java Program Object

The Java Program Object is potentially one of the most powerful customization components available to an SDK developer. It's based on the `IProgramBase` interface in the BOE SDK. While not an SDK in itself, it's worth spending some time to understand what a Program Object can do.

By creating classes that implement this interface, you can create Java applications that can make use of all of the SDK functionality in addition to any other external Java applications you may want to include. Sample applications include updating user details, updating external databases, scheduling and distributing reports, and just about any InfoView activity.

Once created, Java programs are installed directly into the repository from the CMC and can be run at will or scheduled from within InfoView as shown in Figure 19.4. No system connection or authorization code needs to be written as the SAP BusinessObjects system passes both a live `IEnterpriseSession` and an instantiated `IInfoStore` directly to the Program Object at runtime. The Program Object uses either the security credentials of the user that created it or a user account that has been specified by the system administrator. The Java Policy File sets generic security for all Program Objects.

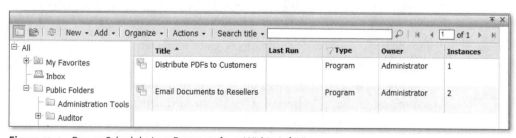

Figure 19.4　Run or Schedule Java Programs from Within InfoView

The signature of the interface is

```
void run(IEnterpriseSession enterpriseSession,
         IInfoStore infoStore, java.lang.String[] args)
```

The `args` parameter can be used to pass any number of variables into the Program Objects. These may include, for example, logging levels, customer details, and document names.

There is a drawback to using Program Objects. If you want to communicate directly with the application server that contains InfoView, for example, to retrieve a database connection from a connection pool, this isn't possible.

19.4 Selecting the Right SDKs

After you've decided that you need a customized application to enhance Web Intelligence and have defined your customization requirements, it's good practice to ask a number of questions about the application that you're going to develop. This should help identify which SDKs are needed and which can be discarded.

The first and most obvious question focuses on what platform is to be used. Although hybrid developments combining .NET and Java are increasingly common, in general, this is a quick decision. In-house teams tend to have specialized skills in one of the two areas. However, it may prove to be a little more complex than this, as capabilities aren't always 100% compatible between the two platforms. For example, formatting reports in the REP SDK is only available in Java. So if the ability to format reports is a prerequisite, and you want to use the REP SDK, then you'll probably have to go down the Java route.

The next question is to ask what you want your project to deliver. If the only requirement is to provide basic reporting, then resorting to writing code may not be necessary. The URL reporting `openDocument` capability addresses many of the basic reporting features. See Chapter 15, Linking in Web Intelligence Reports, for more information on `openDocument`.

Subsequently, ask if your application needs authentication services, interacts with the repository, or will be distributed outside the immediate vicinity. Equally, will you need to scale the application or navigate an infrastructure marshaled by firewalls? If so, this will involve using either the BOE or the Web Services SDK. If you select the BOE SDK and are using a Java platform, you have the option of ready-made components in the JSF SDK to help simplify the creation of functions such as logging on to the CMC. As mentioned earlier, choosing between systems based on an Enterprise and based on Web Services depends on criteria such as performance and integration requirements. It may also depend on corporate IT strategies.

If you need to do more than simply view Web Intelligence or Desktop Intelligence reports, then the REP SDK is probably a must. Similarly, if what interests you is working with the data contained within a report and not the report itself, then use the data provider and recordset capabilities of the RE SDK. As for the BOE SDK, if you're using Java, you can include the JSF SDK to help out with standard functionality such as the presentation of a table of documents.

Another point to consider is whether or not your data sources have the necessary drivers available. If not, you'll have to consider writing custom drivers using the Data Access Driver SDK.

Figure 19.5 presents a quick overview of how you may combine individual SDKs to create a reporting application.

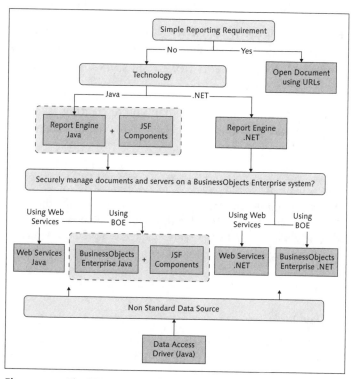

Figure 19.5 The SDK Hierarchy for a Reporting Application

19.5 Setting Up the Development Environment

Given the range of SDKs, assembling the correct libraries for development is one of the first obstacles to overcome. To help you shortcut this process, this section provides a quick overview of what you need to get your development process started.

19.5.1 Java SDK Setup

Most Java implementations involve working with an application server such as Tomcat, so you should be familiar with the basics of developing and deploying Java Platform Enterprise Edition (Java EE) web components.

To run a SAP BusinessObjects Enterprise web application, all of your client and server components must be running: your web server, application server, and your Central Management Server (CMS).

For the necessary web application JAR files, see the following sections for a listing of the files you'll need for each SDK you're going to use and where you can locate them. Then copy those files into the WEB-INF/LIB directory of the web application.

You'll also require a WEB.XML file for the WEB-INF directory. You can check out the online documentation on setting up the XML file, or you can take one from one of the .war files found in the <BUSINESS OBJECTS HOME>\\BUSINESSOBJECTS ENTERPRISE 12.0\JAVA\APPLICATIONS DIRECTORY.

The only exception to using the J2EE standard is when you're creating Java Program Objects. The Program Object is a standalone class that is deployed directly into the CMC.

> **Tip**
>
> To test Java Program Objects during development, write an application class that includes a main method that connects to the CMC using the BOE SDK. Run as a Java application, the Program Object works in exactly the same manner as it would when run from InfoView. In this way, you can use your standard procedures for testing output and debugging the code.

Setup for the BOE SDK (Java)

To develop applications in Java using the BOE SDK, you'll need the relevant JAR files in an accessible location either for your web application or development project (see Table 19.2). The core JAR files can be found within your SAP BusinessObjects installation in the <Business Objects Home>\common\4.0\java\ lib directory. So in a typical installation, this would be C:\Program Files\Business Objects\common\4.0\java\lib. The dependent JAR files are found in the /external subdirectory.

Core JAR Files	Dependent JAR Files	Additional Languages**
biarengine.jar	asn1.jar*	ceresprops_xx.jar
biplugins.jar	backport-util-concurrent-2.2.jar	cecore_xx.jar
cecore.jar		celib_xx.jar
celib.jar	certj.jar*	
ceplugins_client.jar	commons-logging.jar	
ceplugins_core.jar	derby.jar	
ceplugins_cr.jar	freessl201.jar*	
cereports.jar	jsafe.jar*	
cesession.jar	log4j.jar	
ceutils.jar	sslj.jar*	
corbaidl.jar		
ebus405.jar		
flash.jar		
logging.jar		
pluginhelper.jar		
SL_plugins.jar		
xcelsius.jar		
* Only needed for SSL.		
** Replace xx with relevant language.		

Table 19.2 The BOE SDK JAR Files

Files Required for the Report Engine Java SDK

The core JAR files (see Table 19.3) can be found within your SAP BusinessObjects installation in <Business Objects Home>\common\4.0\java\lib. So in a typical installation, this would be C:\Program Files\Business Objects\common\4.0\java\ lib. All but one of the dependent JAR files are found in the /external subdirectory. The exception is cdzlet.jar. You can extract this file from the <Business Objects Home>\\BusinessObjects Enterprise 12.0\java\applications\AnalyticalReporting.war file using the JAR utility or WinZip.

477

Core JAR Files	Dependent JAR Files	Additional Languages*
boconfig.jar	cdzlet.jar	rebean.wi_xx.jar
jtools.jar	xalan.jar	
rebean.common.jar	xercesImpl.jar	
rebean.fc.jar	xml-apis.jar	
rebean.wi.jar	xpp3.jar	
rebean.jar		
wilog.jar		
* Replace xx with relevant language.		

Table 19.3 The Report Engine SDK JAR Files

Files Required for the JSF SDK

See the files defined in the "Files Required for the BOE SDK (Java)" section, and copy those files to your web application or development project. Then locate the JSFPLATFORM.WAR file in the <BUSINESS OBJECTS HOME>/BUSINESSOBJECTS ENTERPRISE 12.0\JAVA\APPLICATIONS directory. Use the JAR utility or a program such as WinZip to extract the contained files. Add the JAR files in the table. The core JAR files are shown in Table 19.4.

Core JAR Files	Additional Languages*
bobj_platform_jsf.jar	reporttemplate_xx.jar
bobj_platform_jsfcommon.jar	
clientlogic.jar	
commons-beanutils.jar	
commons-collections.jar	
commons-digester.jar	
jsf-api.jar	
jsf-impl.jar	
jsfsamples.jar	
jstl.jar	
MetafileRenderer.jar	
reportsourcebridge.jar	
serialization.jar	
URIUtil.jar	
* Replace xx with relevant language.	

Table 19.4 The Java Server Faces SDK JAR Files

Files Required for the Web Services Consumer Java SDK

The core JAR files (see Table 19.5) can be found within your SAP BusinessObjects installation in <BUSINESS OBJECTS HOME>\ BUSINESS OBJECTS\BUSINESSOBJECTS ENTERPRISE 12.0\WEB SERVICES\EN\DSWS_CONSUMER\DATA\DSWSJAVAAPI. So in a typical installation, this would be C:\PROGRAM FILES\BUSINESS OBJECTS\BUSINESS-OBJECTS ENTERPRISE 12.0\WEB SERVICES\EN\DSWS_CONSUMER\DATA\DSWSJAVAAPI.

Core JAR Files	Dependent JAR Files
dsws-bicatalog.jar	activation-1.1.jar
dsws-biplatform.jar	axiom-api-1.2.5.jar
dsws-common.jar	axiom-impl-1.2.5.jar
dsws-publish.jar	axis2-kernel-1.3.jar
dsws-queryservice.jar	axis2-saaj-1.3.jar
dsws-reportengine.jar	axis2-xmlbeans-1.3.jar
dsws-saveservice.jar	backport-util-concurrent-2.2.jar
dsws-session.jar	commons-codec-1.3.jar
wilog.jar	commons-httpclient-3.0.1.jar
	commons-logging-1.1.jar
	log4j-1.2.14.jar
	mail.jar
	stax-api-1.0.1.jar
	struts.jar
	wsdl4j-1.6.2.jar
	wstx-asl-3.2.1.jar
	xbean-2.2.0.jar
	XmlSchema-1.3.2.jar

Table 19.5 The Web Services Consumer Java SDK JAR Files

19.5.2 Setup for .NET

To use BOE SDKs with .NET and assuming you're using Visual Studio .NET, make sure that you install Visual Studio on your machine before you install SAP BusinessObjects Enterprise for .NET. This will also mean that the Microsoft .NET framework has been installed on your machine. To run a SAP BusinessObjects Enterprise .NET application, all of your client and server components should be running, including your web server and your SAP BusinessObjects Enterprise server components.

After ensuring that the necessary items have been installed, on opening Visual Studio, all of the assembly references you need should be available.

Setup for SAP BusinessObjects Enterprise .NET and Report Engine .NET

The SAP BusinessObjects assemblies you need for Enterprise application development begin with either `BusinessObjects.Enterprise` or `CrystalDecisions.Enterprise`.

Web Services Consumer Setup for .NET

Once in Visual Studio, add the following assembly references for the Web Services SDK:

▶ `BusinessObjects.DSWS.BIPlatform.dll`

▶ `BusinessObjects.DSWS.BICatalog.dll`

▶ `BusinessObjects.DSWS.dll`

▶ `BusinessObjects.DSWS.ReportEngine.dll`

▶ `BusinessObjects.DSWS.Session.dll`

▶ `BusinessObjects.DSWS.Publish.dll`

▶ `BusinessObjects.DSWS.QueryService.dll`

▶ `BusinessObjects.DSWS.SaveService.dll`

19.6   Building Applications

Now that you have an idea of what the various SDKs can do, let's first take a look at some of the more important objects that you'll need to get started writing the application code. Because the names and functionality of the objects for both .NET and Java are very similar, examples for each will be given in the same section.

We'll also look at the SAP BusinessObjects Query Language that is used to manage interactions with all items that are stored in the repository.

19.6.1   Authentication Objects

There are two main objects that you must tackle when connecting to the CMC: the Session Manager, which controls the authentication process, and the Enterprise Session, which is created when a user logs on. The Enterprise Session provides access to user information, client-side security objects, and access to CMC services.

To connect, you'll need the user name, the password, the connection server name, and the authentication type. There are four main authentication type options:

▶ **secEnterprise:** Using a native Enterprise account.

▶ **secLDAP:** Using users and groups from an LDAP server.

▶ **secWinNT:** Using users and groups from an NT server (.NET only).

▶ **secWinAD:** Using users and groups from an Active Directory Server.

Connecting Using Java

The session manager interface, `ISessionMgr`, is retrieved using the static method `getSessionMgr` in the `CrystalEnterprise` class.

An `IEnterpriseSession` interface is retrieved through the `ISessionMgr.logon` method with the authentication variables passed as parameters.

```
try{
    ISessionMgr sm = CrystalEnterprise.getSessionMgr();
    IEnterpriseSession enterpriseSession =
      sm.logon("fred", "password", "cms", "secEnterprise");
}
Catch(SDKException sdkEx){ .....
```

Connecting Using .NET

The session manager is created by instantiating the `SessionMgr` class. The `Logon` method of that class is used to create an `EnterpriseSession` connection object with the authentication variables passed as parameters.

```
SessionMgr sessionMgr = new SessionMgr();
EnterpriseSession enterpriseSession;
enterpriseSession = sessionMgr.Logon("fred", "password",
                       "cms", "secEnterprise");
```

19.6.2 The InfoStore Class

The `InfoStore` class acts as a controller or gateway to the CMS repository (which is a database), where all instances of `InfoObject` are stored. The `InfoStore` class is used to instantiate, retrieve, and commit all `InfoObject` class instances that are stored in the CMS repository.

You can retrieve an instantiated `InfoStore` class by calling the relevant method on the `EnterpriseSession`.

If you're using a Java Program Object, the `InfoStore` is passed as a parameter.

Retrieving an InfoStore Object in Java

For Java applications, the `IInfoStore` interface represents the SAP BusinessObjects Enterprise `InfoStore` service.

Assuming you have a successfully connected the `EnterpriseSession` object called `entSession`, you can access an `InfoStore` using the `getService` method of the session:

```
IInfoStore infoStore =
        (IInfoStore)entSession.getService("InfoStore");
```

Retrieving an InfoStore Object in .NET

In .NET, assuming you have a successfully connected `EnterpriseSession` object called `enterpriseSession`, use the `GetService` method of the `EnterpriseSession` object to create an `EnterpriseService`, and then cast that object to `InfoStore`.

```
EnterpriseSession enterpriseSession;
InfoStore infoStore;
EnterpriseService enterpriseService;

enterpriseService = enterpriseSession.GetService("InfoStore");
infoStore = new InfoStore(enterpriseService);
infoStore = (InfoStore)enterpriseService;
```

19.6.3 The SAP BusinessObjects Query Language

Before moving on to look at other important SDK classes, it's a worthwhile exercise to get an understanding of how the SDK interacts with the repository. You don't directly instantiate the classes that represent the objects in the repository; you must first make use of the SAP BusinessObjects Query Language to retrieve them. Using the `InfoStore` object, you can run queries that have a very similar syntax to SQL. These SQL-like statements are used to access, create, update, and delete all items that are stored in the repository.

You access the repository entities generally from two tables. CI_INFOOBJECTS contains objects used to build the desktop, such as folders and reports. CI_SYSTE-

MOBJECTS contains objects that are often used to build the admin desktop and internal system objects, such as servers, connections, users, and user groups.

▸ To access objects, standard SQL type clauses are used. `SELECT`, `FROM`, `WHERE`, and `ORDER BY` are all valid.

▸ The operators are also familiar: `=` `!=`, `>`, `<`, `>=`, `<=`, `LIKE`, `IN`, `NOT IN`, and `BETWEEN`.

▸ The columns of the select clauses and the conditions of the where clause are generally properties of the object stored in the repository. Commonly used properties are `SI_ID`, `SI_NAME`, `SI_INSTANCE`, `SI_PROGID`, `SI_KIND`, and `SI_DESCRIPTION`.

▸ Two functions are available: `Top`, which limits the number of items selected, and `Count`, which counts the distinct values of a property.

For example, to retrieve the name, id, and object type for an object named `'testReport'`, you could use the following statement:

```
SELECT SI_NAME, SI_ID, SI_KIND FROM CI_INFOOBJECTS WHERE SI_NAME =
'testReport'
```

To retrieve three objects where you already know the value of their ids:

```
SELECT SI_ID, SI_NAME FROM CI_INFOOBJECTS WHERE SI_ID IN (103,105,106)
```

> **Tip**
>
> To test the validity of your SDK query language calls, use the SAP BusinessObjects Query Builder tool. Manually type in and run the query to verify the results. You can also use the Query Builder to view what properties are available for a specific object type (see Figure 19.6).

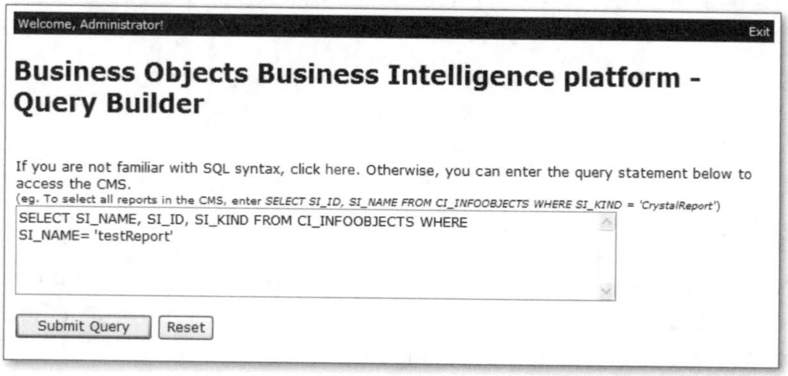

Figure 19.6 Use the Query Builder to Test Repository Object Retrieval

19.6.4 The InfoObjects and InfoObject Classes

The InfoObject class acts as the superclass for all Enterprise information entities. These entities may be reports, folders, users, groups, servers, calendars, sessions, or any object that is stored in the CMC.

InfoObjects is a collection class that contains instances of InfoObject that have been retrieved from the repository. InfoObjects provide a snapshot of an InfoStore query. The contents will not change even if other applications update the InfoStore.

Neither the InfoObjects nor the InfoStore classes are directly instantiated; they are created by querying the CMC using the SAP BusinessObjects Query Language.

Populating an InfoObject in Java

In Java, InfoObject and InfoObjects are represented respectively by the interfaces, IInfoObject and IInfoObjects. To access either, you'll need a valid InfoStore object that can be used to interact with the CMC. You'll also have to cast the value returned.

```
IInfoObject webiReport;
IInfoObjects webiReports = infoStore.query("select SI_ID, SI_NAME from
CI_INFOOBJECTS where SI_PROGID='CrystalEnterprise.Webi'");
if (webiReports.size() > 0)
    webiReport = (IInfoObject) webiReports.get(0);
```

Populating an InfoObject in .NET

In .NET, the InfoObjects and InfoObject classes represent the objects of the same name. As for Java, you'll need a valid InfoStore object, and you'll have to cast the results of the objects that the InfoStore returns.

```
IInfoObjects webiReports = infoStore.query("select SI_ID, SI_NAME from
CI_INFOOBJECTS where SI_PROGID='CrystalEnterprise.Webi'");
IInfoObject webiReport = (IInfoObject) webiReports[1];
```

19.6.5 Plug-ins

Plug-ins are objects that allow you to create and modify InfoObjects. You can access plug-ins via a factory type Plugin Manager. Use the getPluginInfo method in the Plugin Manager to get the required plug-in.

To store, update, or delete the `InfoObject`, you'll still need a valid `InfoStore`. The `InfoStore` allows you to create an `InfoObjects` collection, which you'll use to update the repository.

Plug-ins Using Java

`IPluginMgr` is the Java interface that represents the Plugin Manager, and `IPlugin-Info` is the interface representing the descriptive information about the plug-in. As for other repository interactions, you'll need a valid `InfoStore` object.

```
IPluginMgr pluginMgr = infoStore.getPluginMgr();
IPluginInfo userGroupPlugin = pluginMgr.getPluginInfo("CrystalEnterprise.
UserGroup");
```

The value used as a parameter in the `getPluginInfo` method is the equivalent of the `SI_PROGID` value in the repository. You can retrieve a convenient list of constant string values of these IDs from the interface, `com.crystaldecisions.sdk.plugin.CeProgID`.

Plug-ins Using .NET

In .NET, the `PluginManager` and the `PluginInfo` classes represent the objects of the same name. Note that, again, you require a valid `InfoStore` object.

```
PluginManager pluginManager = infoStore.PluginManager;
PluginInfo pluginInfo = pluginManager.GetPluginInfo("CrystalEnterprise.
UserGroup");
```

The value used as a parameter in the `GetPluginInfo` method is the equivalent of the `SI_PROGID` value in the repository. You can retrieve a convenient list of constant string values of these IDs from the structure, `CrystalDecisions.Enterprise.CeKind`.

Additionally, you can use the `InfoStore` to delete an existing object collection in both Java and .NET:

```
infoStore.delete (newInfoObjects);
```

19.7 Summary

The array of SDKs supplied by SAP BusinessObjects Web Intelligence offers a very broad choice of customization capability whether your preferred platform is Java or .NET. The possibilities vary from supplying the users with a basic reporting system to very complex system integrations.

The initial issues for those wanting to create customized solutions will be selecting the right SDKs and setting up a development environment to create and test the solution.

To help with your development process, the SDKs are delivered with API documentation, developer guides, and tutorials. Another good place to look for help is *www.sdn.sap.com/irj/boc/sdklibrary*.

However, the SDKs don't afford you much help when you need to deliver customized workflows or a new look and feel to the Web Intelligence user interface. A new SDK, Web Intelligence Extension Points, has been released to make our life a lot easier in this regard. In the next chapter, we'll take a look in some detail at this new kit.

Changing the look and feel or the functionality of the user interface will rank very highly among the requests you receive from Web Intelligence users. This is now possible and relatively simple in some cases. Web Intelligence Extension Points allow you to customize, embed, and configure the DHTML client, the Java Report Panel, the Java Clients, and the Desktop Rich Client.

20 Customizing Web Intelligence Using Web Intelligence Extensions Points

Web Intelligence Extension Points (EP) graduated from Business Objects Labs in 2007 and offered a breakthrough in the ability to customize Web Intelligence. Before the release of this set of tools, changing the user interface (UI) or adding workflows basically meant hacking some very complex code. Add to this, that every time Business Objects released some form of upgrade, whether bug fix or an enhancement, that code was likely to change. This meant, of course, that you would have to re-write any customization work that had been undertaken. You can clearly see why Business Objects would discourage its users from this approach.

Using SAP BusinessObjects Web Intelligence Extension Points (EP), you now have access to a very powerful range of customization capabilities. You can change the look and feel of applications, change the splash screen, add new workflows, and make external calls to Web Intelligence functions. Although primarily aimed at partners and developers, some aspects of customization are fairly straightforward, involving only the editing of property files, and could be undertaken by a power user.

SAP BusinessObjects has been consistently enhancing the core features, so it's worthwhile to check the SAP website to see what's new. Another important point to note, unlike hacking the various Java Server Pages (JSPs) that make up Web Intelligence, Extension Points customization is supported by SAP BusinessObjects.

This chapter looks at what Extension Points are and how they differ from the standard Web Intelligence SDKs. Then we'll take a look at what you can achieve with

Extension Points, providing examples of how they can be used. Finally, we'll walk through setting up a development environment and how to get started with the Extension Points customization.

> **Note**
>
> To use the EP APIs, you'll need at least SAP BusinessObjects Web Intelligence XI 3.1. For the more recent enhancements, particularly when working with the DHTML client, you'll need SAP BusinessObjects Web Intelligence XI 3.1 SP2.

20.1 What Are Web Intelligence Extensions Points?

Simply put, Web Intelligence Extension Points (EP) provides a supported means of customizing Web Intelligence that permits changes to the Java Report Panel, the DHTML client, and the Rich Client. If you're not familiar with the Web Intelligence Rich Client, it's a relatively new feature that runs as a desktop application. It allows you to view, modify, and create Web Intelligence documents.

By writing Java and JavaScript code or by defining values in property files, you can provide customized applications to your users or clients. Developer or OEM suppliers can deliver applications, based on Web Intelligence, that they themselves are able to support. SAP BusinessObjects, in turn, provides the support for EP. This helps to make any custom code upgradeable.

While you'll need to write Java applications for some of the more sophisticated enhancements for the Java Report Panel and Rich Client, you're certainly not limited to a Java environment. Many aspects of EP can be applied to a .NET setup. For example, you can write JavaScript or edit property files to create much of the customization for the DHTML client.

The main EP APIs are listed here:

- **EP for the Web Intelligence Java Client, the online Java Report Panel, and the desktop Rich Client:** As an example, Figure 20.1 shows the Query Panel section of the Java Client with a new panel and options both created using Java-based code.

- **EP for Web Intelligence Interactive Viewing (also known as the DHTML Client):** In addition, the Integration Points API allows you to integrate the viewer into an application.

▶ **EP for the Creation of Customized Functions:** With this API, you use C++ to create custom functions that are added to the existing list of Web Intelligence reporting functions.

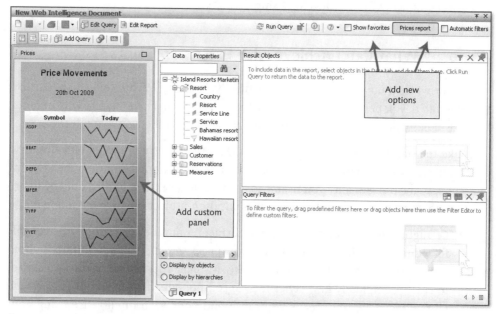

Figure 20.1 How Do Extension Points Differ from the Standard Web Intelligence SDKs?

The standard SDKs address a wide set of capabilities, including connecting to Enterprise systems, single sign-on (SSO), and report data manipulation. They work with all of the functionality of InfoView. When used to customize Web Intelligence, they are intrusive and nonsupported. If, for example, you want to create a mini Web Intelligence type application that lists documents, gives users the capability to view and schedule those documents in addition to the security issues it involves, this is a fairly major development task. Depending on the size of the application, it will mean development, integration, maintenance, and support costs.

EP, on the other hand, is nonintrusive and supported. It's specifically designed for manipulating Web Intelligence. Third-party application builders can build their own applications with their own look and feel, as well as their own functionality, and then distribute them to their own customers. An example of this may be a report contained within an existing application where unnecessary toolbar and menu items are removed to restrict what a user can do with the application. EP also offers the option of customization with no coding work at all. Many features are available that let you amend the UI and workflow by simply editing a property file.

A quick distinction of the difference between the standard SDKs and EP is that you configure using EP and develop using the SDKs.

20.2   What Can I Achieve with Extension Points?

EP provides a means to supply customized versions of Web Intelligence. This is a boon to developers, consultants, partners, OEM suppliers, or anyone with an interest in embedding Web Intelligence functionality into their own applications.

Like the standard Web Intelligence SDKs, EP offers a very powerful range of capabilities. As for the standard SDKs; you have access to external libraries when writing code, so the functionality you're able to create is, to an extent, limited only by imagination. Some of the most common customization projects include the following:

▸ **Configure the look and feel of the interface:** A number of options are available for editing the UI. You can define the splash screen, the logo, and the about screen. You can also make use of JIDE (*www.jidesoft.com*) compliant Java classes to create completely new styles for the components used in any of the Java clients. Effectively, this means you can brand your Web Intelligence using your own in-house styles.

▸ **Hide, show or disable menus, frames, buttons and other options on the client interfaces:** By editing a properties file, you're able to control in fine detail what features are available to a user or to a user group. For example, in the Java Reporting Client, you can restrict the ability to run new queries to a subset of users belonging to a specific group. Figure 20.2 shows a DHTML client with all nonreport items removed from the viewer.

Home Document List Open ▾ Send To ▾ Dashboards ▾				
Web Intelligence - Track Data Changes				
Inserted ~~Removed~~		Product Line Sales for 2006		
	Q1	Q2	Q3	Q4	Sum
Sweat-T-Shirts	1,967,328.20	2,121,860.20	1,506,478.90	1,863,826.20	7,459,493.50
Accessories	357,834.80	526,371.10	645,054.70	370,144.10	1,899,404.70
Sweaters	337,200.70	426,442.70	525,878.30	370,518.60	1,660,040.30

Figure 20.2   The Web Intelligence DHTML Client with All Editing Features Removed

▶ **Add new toolbars and frames; add new buttons and menu options:** Each new option you include can be deployed to offer new functionality to one of the Web Intelligence clients and can be defined to call a JavaScript, Java, or JSP routine. You may, for instance, want to add a menu item in the DHTML client that emails the user's current document to all members of a user group.

▶ **Workflow simplification:** Where users repeatedly perform some activity, EP can be employed to automate the process. This may include activities such as placing commonly used objects in a custom panel or pre-setting the header and footer designs when creating new reports.

▶ **Enhance, change, or simplify workflows:** By working with custom event handlers, using the Java Swing or other libraries, you can redefine the UI functionality. This capability opens up the potential for a very wide range of new features whether it involves queries, analysis, or reporting.

▶ **Create seamless navigation:** Call Web Intelligence functions from external applications and vice-versa. For example, you can use the Java applet as a back-end service manager while using your own client interface.

▶ **Add new Web Intelligence reporting functions:** Use C++ with the Calculation EP to create custom functions adding to those already available. This API allows you to implement some very interesting ideas; you may want to provide a function that uses a web feed to do real-time currency conversion or that updates a database every time it's used.

20.3 Building Applications with Extension Points

In this section, we'll look at what you need to develop, create, and deploy applications created by each of the EP APIs. The core components required to make use of EP are all available within the standard BOXI deployment. However, you can download samples and documentation from the SAP Community Network at *www.sdn.sap.com/irj/scn*. Check the readme.txt file delivered with each sample for further details on how to set up the individual sample. If you intend to build commercial applications, make sure to check the terms and conditions of the software license.

The selection of the relevant EP API is fairly straightforward (see Figure 20.3). To customize one of the Java Panels or the Web Intelligence Rich Client, use the Web Intelligence Customization Extension Points API. To customize the DHTML client, use the Interactive Viewing Extension and Integration Points API, and to add new functions, use the Calculation Extension Points API.

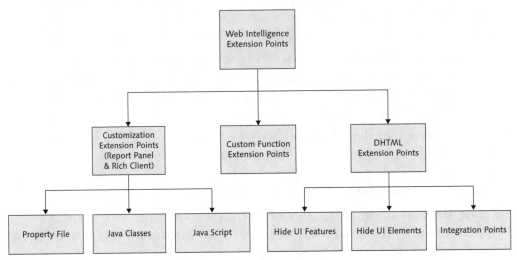

Figure 20.3 The Extension Points API Structure

20.3.1 Web Intelligence Customization Extension Points

As previously stated, this API focuses on delivering customization for the Java Report Panel and the Rich Client. For all customizations, whether simple UI amendments or more complex efforts using JavaScript or Java classes, you'll have to define aspects of your work in the webi_plugin.properties file.

webi_plugin.properties

The webi_plugin.properties file contains key/value pairs that you edit to set the visibility of UI options, to manage threading, or to tell the application where to look for items such as JAR files and Java classes. Locate a copy of the file in the directory structure of your application server. By default, you'll find it in <XIR31INSTALLPATH>/BUSINESSOBJECTS/YOURAPPLICATIONSERVERNAME/WEBAPPS/ANALYTICALREPORTING/WEBIAPPLET/.

On a standard win32 deployment using Tomcat, this is typically C:\PROGRAM FILES\BUSINESS OBJECTS\TOMCAT55\WEBAPPS\ANALYTICALREPORTING\WEBIAPPLET.

If you're customizing the standalone Rich Client, you'll have to place a copy of the properties file in the main SAP BusinessObjects installation: <XIR31INSTALLPATH>/ BUSINESSOBJECTS ENTERPRISE 12.0/CLASSES.

Restart the Web Application Server Context

After changing the webi_plugin.properties file, you should not have to restart the application context for the changes to become apparent; you don't even need to log off. All that is required is to close the Java Report Panel and open it up again.

However, when using the Rich Client, you have to exit and startup the application again to see the effects of any changes in the properties file.

Let's now take a look at some of the basic keys that are used to hide or disable aspects of the UI. Unless stated otherwise, these options are available for both the Java Report Panel and the Rich Client.

▶ `JavaReportPanel.reporting.toolbar.main`: Activates or hides the main toolbar, which contains the New, Open, and Save options among others. Valid options are `hidden` or `enable`.

▶ `JavaReportPanel.query.panel`: Activates, hides, or disables the query button on the main toolbar. If the main toolbar has already been hidden, then this button won't be visible, however, this value is set. Valid options are `hidden`, `disable`, or `enable`.

▶ `JavaReportPanel.reporting.actions`: Activates or hides actions that can be undertaken in the report. Valid options are `hidden` or `enable`.

▶ `JavaReportPanel.reporting.frame.reportmap`: Activates or hides the Map tab that displays the report map. Valid options are `hidden` or `enable`.

There are a number of keys that are used for thread management allowing you to set specific threads to be synchronous or asynchronous.

▶ `WebI.extpoint.start.threaded`: Valid values are `true` and `false`. If `false` is selected, the client object is run in synchronous mode, and the `start` method of the `IWebiRichClientPlugin` must complete before any other activity takes place.

In Listing 20.1, we can see a webi_plugin.properties file with all of the Report Panel header toolbars enabled (remember lines beginning with # are ignored and used as comments); the result can be seen in Figure 20.4. However, in Listing 20.2, all of the main options with the exception of the main toolbar are hidden. Figure

20.5 shows the panel header with no query button and no reporting, formatting, or navigation toolbars.

```
# Determines visibility of "Edit Query Panel" button
JavaReportPanel.query.panel=enable
# Reporting toolbars
JavaReportPanel.reporting.toolbar.main=enable
JavaReportPanel.reporting.toolbar.reporting=enable
JavaReportPanel.reporting.toolbar.formatting=enable
JavaReportPanel.reporting.toolbar.navigation=enable
```

Listing 20.1 The webi_plugin.properties File with No Restriction

Figure 20.4 A Java Report Panel Header with No Restriction

```
# Determines visibility of Edit Query Panel button
JavaReportPanel.query.panel=hidden
# Reporting toolbars
JavaReportPanel.reporting.toolbar.main=enable
JavaReportPanel.reporting.toolbar.reporting=hidden
JavaReportPanel.reporting.toolbar.formatting=hidden
JavaReportPanel.reporting.toolbar.navigation=hidden
```

Listing 20.2 The webi_plugin.properties File with Hidden Elements

Figure 20.5 A Java Report Panel with Hidden Elements

Customization Using Java Classes - Preparation

You can use Java to enhance both the Java Report Panel and the Rich Client. The core classes used for customization are located in the com.businessobjects.jrp. plugin package and subpackages. They are stored in the ThinCadenza.jar file. Additional classes used for the Rich Client are located in the com.businessobjects. offline.plugin package and stored in the cdz_ui.jar file.

You'll find a copy of the ThinCadenza.jar in <XIR31INSTALLPATH>/BUSINESSOBJECTS/ YOURAPPLICATIONSERVERNAME/WEBAPPS/ANALYTICALREPORTING/WEBIAPPLET/. A copy of cdz_ui.jar can be found in <XIR31INSTALLPATH>/ BUSINESSOBJECTS ENTERPRISE 12.0/CLASSES.

To load and run any customized Java applications, you must add keys to the webi_plugin.properties file, defining the location of the main plug-in application class and a class path descriptor.

For the Java Report Panel, the plug-in class must implement the `IJavaReportPanelPlugin` interface. In the properties file, set the `JavaReportPanel.plugin` key to the class name, including any package information. Use indexes for multiple plug-ins:

```
JavaReportPanel.plugin=myclass.app.ExPoint.class
JavaReportPanel.plugin.2=myclass.app.ExPoint2.class
```

For the Rich Client, the plug-in class must implement the `IWebIRichClientPlugin` interface, and the key name is `WebIRichClient.plugin`. For example:

```
WebIRichClient.plugin=myclient.app.RichClientPlugin.class
```

The `WebI.classpath` key defines the path to any JAR files that are used in the applications. Note that to work with the Java Report Panel, you must place the JAR files in the following path: <XIR31INSTALLPATH>/BUSINESSOBJECTS/ YOURAPPLICATIONSERVERNAME/WEBAPPS/ANALYTICALREPORTING/WEBIAPPLET/.

You can place Rich Client JAR files on any part of the system that is accessible by the application:

```
WebI.classpath=C:\temp\myclasses.jar;C:\temp\myclasses2.jar
```

Report Panel Java Classes

For customizing the Java Report Panel, you'll find options available to add or edit individual sections or items in the report. You also have various means of adding custom classes as event listeners that you can deploy to change the behavior of the panel.

Report Panel customization should begin with a class that implements the `IJavaReportPanelPlugin` interface. This interface contains only two method signatures:

```
public void start(IJavaReportPanel jrp)
```

The method `start` is called at initialization and provides you a copy of the `IJava-ReportPanel` via a parameter.

```
public void stop()
```

The method `stop` is called when the Report Panel stops execution.

After you've retrieved an instantiated copy of the `IJavaReportPanel`, you have access to methods that give you information about the document. You can also add a drag-and-drop listener.

One of the most common uses of the `IJavaReportPanel` is to supply the Report and Query Panels. Use the following methods to do that:

```
public IReportingPanel getReportingPanel()
public IQueryPanel getQueryPanel()
```

An `IReportingPanel` object offers a very complete range of options for managing the Report Panel, permitting you to do the following:

▸ Refresh the data providers.

▸ Access the structure and items within the document.

▸ Add and edit toolbar components.

▸ Add and edit panel frames.

▸ Add custom report listeners.

▸ Set the layout.

The code snippet in Listing 20.3 shows a basic start method implementation, the retrieval of the Report Panel, and the addition of an anonymous class as a report event listener.

```
public void start(IJavaReportPanel jrp) {
    IReportingPanel _irp = jrp.getReportingPanel();
    // Register this class to the reporting event mechanism
    _irp.addReportingListener(new IReportingListener(){
    public void reportChanged(ReportEvent e) {
    }
    public void reportSelectionChanged(final ReportSelectionEvent e) {
    }
    public void reportActionPerformed(ReportActionEvent e) { }
    private void applyTemplate(ReportEvent e){
    }
```

```
      private String getFullPath(String resource){
      }
    });
}
```

Listing 20.3 Implementation of the Start Method in IJavaReportPanelPlugin

Table 20.1 and Table 20.2 show a full list of the available Java Report Panel classes for the `com.businessobjects.jrp.plugin` and `com.businessobjects.jrp.plugin.reporting` packages, respectively. Don't forget to check the online documentation as new classes and features will become available.

Class Name	Usage
IJavaReportPanelPlugin	The core interface for Report Panel applications. Implement this as the base application entry class.
IReportingPanel	Defines actions on toolbars and manages the Report Panel.
IJavaReportPanel	Provides information about the Java Report Panel in use.

Table 20.1 The com.businessobjects.jrp.plugin Interfaces

Class Name	Usage
ICell	Allows text management in a cell element
IDataSummaryPanel	Provides action on the Data Summary Panel
IDecoration	Provides information to decorate a report element
IFreeCell	Provides free cell information such as size and change position
IPageHeaderFooter	Creates element in the header or the footer of the page
IReport	Retrieves the structure of the current report: body, page header, and footer
IReportBody	Manages elements in the report body
IReportElement	Provides information on a report element
IReportElementContainer	Superclass of all report containers

Table 20.2 The com.businessobjects.jrp.plugin.reporting Classes and Interfaces

Class Name	Usage
IReportFilter	Exposes features to define report filter
IReportFilterNode	Superclass of objects that allow filter management to be exposed as a tree
IReportFilterOperator	Represents a filter container that contains at least two IReportFilter interfaces
IReportFilterPanel	Provides the information used in the Report Filter Panel
IReportingListener	Defines a listener that retrieves change on the current report
IReportPanel	Provides information on the Report Panel
ISectionContainer	Creates elements in a section
ITable	Represents a table in the report (vertical, horizontal, or cross table)
ReportActionEvent	Provides information on an action (other than a selection) done on the current report
ReportElementSelection	Provides information on a detected selection done on the current report
ReportEvent	Provides information on the Report Panel that has been changed
ReportSelectionEvent	Provides information on the selection done on the current report

Table 20.2 The com.businessobjects.jrp.plugin.reporting Classes and Interfaces (Cont.)

Query Panel Classes

To customize the Query Panel in the Java Report Panel, you'll need access to an IQueryPanel object. You can retrieve this object in the same way that you would retrieve the IReportingPanel.

```
public void start(IJavaReportPanel jrp) {

    IQueryPanel _iqp = jrp.getQueryPanel();
```

An IQueryPanel object provides the following:

- Access to the data providers
- Ability to run the query
- Add and edit query toolbar components
- Add and edit Query Panel frames
- Creates a listener to retrieve information on the query
- Sets the layout

Listing 20.4 shows the retrieval of the IQueryPanel object, which, in turn, is used to retrieve the Query Panel. Once obtained, a Java Swing checkbox component with an event listener is added to the query toolbar. You can make use of the listener to drive custom activities such as the population of a frame with external content.

```
public void start(IJavaReportPanel jrp){
    final IQueryPanel queryPanel=jrp.getQueryPanel();
    final JCheckBox chk = new JCheckBox("Automatic filters");
    chk.setOpaque(false);
    chk.addActionListener(new ActionListener(){
        public void actionPerformed(ActionEvent e){
        bFilter=chk.isSelected();
        }
    });
    queryPanel.addQueryToolbarComponent(IQueryPanel.MAIN_TOOLBAR, chk);
```

Listing 20.4 Add a Checkbox Component to the Query Toolbar

Table 20.3 lists the Query Panel customization classes and interfaces available in the com.businessobjects.jrp.plugin.query package.

Class Name	Usage
IDataProviderPanel	Provides information on the Data Provider used to query data
IFilterPanel	Exposes features to create a filter to the current Data Provider
IQueryListener	Defines a listener that retrieves change on a query
IQueryPanel	Defines actions on the Query Panel

Table 20.3 The com.businessobjects.jrp.plugin.query Classes and Interfaces

Class Name	Usage
IResultObject	Retrieves the result object name and the associated report expression
IResultObjectPanel	Adds, removes, and manages result objects in the Query Panel
ITreePanel	Manages the tree card panel added to the universe panel
IUniversePanel	Allows card panel creation and management in the universe panel
QueryEvent	Provides information on query change
SimpleFilter	Provides simple filter characteristics

Table 20.3 The com.businessobjects.jrp.plugin.query Classes and Interfaces (Cont.)

Web Intelligence Rich Client Classes

Like the Report and Query Panels, you must implement an interface to customize the Rich Client. This interface is `IWebIRichClientPlugin`, and the method signatures are almost exactly the same as for `IJavaReportPanelPlugin`.

```
public void start(IWebIRichClient wrc)
public void stop()
```

The only difference between the two interfaces is that an `IWebIRichClient` object is passed as a parameter. Use the `IWebIRichClient` object to log on to SAP BusinessObjects either in online or offline mode. A successful logon returns an `IWebIRichClientInstance`.

After you have access to an `IWebIRichClientInstance` object, you can do the following:

▶ Load documents.

▶ Create a new document.

▶ Retrieve the underlying Report Panel and customize it as shown in the previous sections.

▶ Mail the document to other users.

Listing 20.5 shows an example of obtaining an `IWebIRichClientInstance` object, logging onto SAP BusinessObjects using an online connection, and then loading a document.

```
IWebIRichClientInstance _wrcInstance;
public void start(IWebIRichClient wrc) {
    try {
      boolean offline_mode = false;
      String document_to_be_loaded = "customization/Companies.wid";
      _wrcInstance = wrc.login("myserver", "user", "pwd",
"secEnterprise", offline_mode);
      _wrcInstance.loadDocument(document_to_be_loaded);
    }catch(Exception e) {
      e.printStackTrace();
    }
}
```

Listing 20.5 Using the IWebiRichClientInstance

Table 20.4 lists the Rich Client customization classes and interfaces available in the `com.businessobjects.offline.plugin` package.

Class Name	Usage
IFramework	Manages the desktop environment of the Web Intelligence Rich Client
IWebIRichClient	Defines features of the Web Intelligence Rich Client
IWebIRichClientInstance	Manages Web Intelligence Rich Client documents such as creation, loading, saving
IWebIRichClientListener	Defines a listener that retrieves change on Web Intelligence Rich Client state
IWebIRichClientPlugin	Defines the beginning and the end of the instruction execution on the Web Intelligence Rich Client plug-in
WebIRichClientEvent	Provides information on the Web Intelligence Rich Client state change

Table 20.4 The com.businessobjects.offline.plugin Classes and Interfaces

Customization with JavaScript

The release of Java 6 included a scripting engine for JavaScript. You can make use of this facility to write your Java Report Panel and Rich Client customizations in JavaScript. The structure of the code, the objects you'll use, and the means of deployment are very similar to what you do with standard Java classes. For example, you define the JavaScript plug-in file in the webi_plugin.properties file.

```
WebIRichClient.plugin=/richclient_plugin.js
```

Import the same packages you would in Java:

```
importPackage(com.businessobjects.offline.plugin);
importPackage(com.businessobjects.jrp.plugin.reporting);
```

Implement the required methods:

```
function start(wrc)
function stop()
```

After setup, you can write JavaScript with much the same functionality as in Java. Listing 20.6 shows a code snippet that retrieves a Report Panel and then adds a listener that will use the output method (not shown) to inform the user that the report has changed.

```
javaReportPanel = wrcInstance.getJavaReportPanel(0);
reportingPanel = javaReportPanel.getReportingPanel();
// How to register a listener ...
var reportingListenerImpl = {
    reportActionPerformed: function(event){
        //some code
    },
    reportChanged: function(event){
        output("reportChanged:"+event);
    },
    reportSelectionChanged: function(event){
        //and more
    }
};
```

Listing 20.6 Implementing a Report Listener in JavaScript

20.3.2 Interactive Viewing Customization Using Extension and Integration Points

To customize the Web Intelligence Interactive Viewing client (DHTML client), use the Interactive Viewing Extension and Integration Points API. This API has three main subareas of interest:

- The UI Customization API, which allows you to hide elements in the viewer.

- The Extension Point API, which allows you to add new components to parts of the viewer, for example, new menu items. These options can be combined with a URL call to external objects such as a JSP file to provide additional functionality.

- The Integration Points API helps you integrate the DHTML viewer into an application.

Control Files

Two files control the functionality of this API: webiviewer.properties and user.js. Find them in the following locations:

- <XIR31INSTALLPATH>/BUSINESSOBJECTS/YOURAPPLICATIONSERVERNAME/ WEBAPPS/ANALYTICALREPORTING/WEB-INF/CLASSES/WEBIVIEWER.PROPERTIES

- <XIR31INSTALLPATH>/BUSINESSOBJECTS/YOURAPPLICATIONSERVERNAME/ WEBAPPS/ANALYTICALREPORTING/VIEWERS/CDZ_ADV/CUSTOMIZE/USER.JS

For DHTML viewer customization to become active, you must set the ALLOW_ CUSTOMIZATION variable to 'yes' in the webiviewer.properties file.

```
#Allow customization [yes/no]
ALLOW_CUSTOMIZATION=yes
```

You declare and trigger EP by writing JavaScript code in the user.js file.

> **Refreshing the user.js File**
>
> Although you don't need to restart the application server context when you edit user.js, you may find that the changes you make aren't reflected in what you see in the browser. If so, this is most likely because the browser has cached a copy of user.js. To fix this, use the options within the browser to delete temporary Internet files.

The UI Customization API

To hide UI elements and features, you define methods in the user.js file adding a method call for each element or feature you want to hide. You also have the option to restrict visibility for all users or only members of a specific user group as defined in the CMC application. See the EP documentation for a full listing of all of the element and feature options that are available.

You add a call to the hide_ui_element method for each element you want to suppress.

```
hide_ui_element(property, groupname)
```

For example, `hide_ui_element("MENUBAR", "hrgroup");` will remove the menu bar for all users in the user group, 'hrgroup'.

When you want to hide a feature, such as a toolbar button, use the `hide_feature` method. Again, you have the ability to select for group membership if required.

```
hide_feature(property, groupname)
```

The edited user.js file shown in Listing 20.7 will remove two elements, the left panel and the status bar. It will also remove the capability from all users (as no group name is specified) to drill or export the document to Excel or CSV.

```
// --------<UI Elements>
hide_ui_element("LEFTPANEL");
hide_ui_element("STATUSBAR");
// ------<Features>
hide_feature("EXPORT_TO_EXCEL");
hide_feature("EXPORT_TO_CSV");
hide_feature("DRILL");
```

Listing 20.7 The user.js File Hiding UI Elements and Features

Extension Points API

If you want to add (rather than hide) functionality, use the EP API, which allows you to add new components to the interactive viewer. Like the UI Customization API, extensions are created by defining calls to a method, `user_extension`, in the user.js file. The parameters you insert when setting up the method calls will define visible text and icons as well as the URL call the new object will make when clicked. The method signature is

```
user_extension (property, paramObject, groupName)
```

The `property` parameter represents a section of the DHTML client where you'll add a new object or details about a new viewer. Valid options are listed here:

► `LEFTPANEL`: Adds a button or icon to the left panel control bar.

► `MENUBAR`: Adds a button or icon to the menu bar.

► `DOCUMENT_MENU`: Adds a menu item to the document menu.

► `VIEW_MENU`: Adds a menu item to the view menu.

▶ REPORTPART: Allows a user to click on the cell and chart to access data and is only available when displaying report parts.

▶ CUSTOM_VIEW_MODE: Allows you to create your own viewer.

The paramObject parameter is potentially fairly complex and contains a range of arguments passed as a single object. Each argument is in the form 'name : value' and separated by a comma. Finally, to complete the parameter, you must contain it within braces. For each property, different arguments are valid, so check the API documentation for more details. The most common arguments are listed here:

▶ title: The text or tooltip for the object.

▶ iconURL: The URL of the 16x16 GIF image that you use for the object.

▶ align: Use left or right to align the object.

▶ targetPage: The URL of the target page that you want to show when the object is clicked.

▶ appendViewerContextParameters: Set this to true if you want a list of all of the required DHTML viewer parameters added to the target page URL.

▶ targetWindow: The window where the target page will be displayed.

If you want to restrict the amendments to a group of users, set the groupName parameter to the name of that group.

Listing 20.8 shows an example implementation of the user_extension method. We add a new option called "Run New Application," give it the icon CSV.gif,, and align it toward the bottom of its available space. We then tell it to run the newApp. jsp file, add a list of the viewer parameters, and open the output from that JSP file in the report window. You can see a sample of the new document menu in Figure 20.6.

```
user_extension ("DOCUMENT_MENU",
    {
        title: "Run New Application",
        iconURL: "customize/images/CSV.gif",
        valign: "bottom",
        targetPage: "customize/custom/newApp.jsp",
        appendViewerContextParameters: true,
        targetWindow: "inPlace"
    });
```

Listing 20.8 Add a New Item to the DHTML Client Document Menu

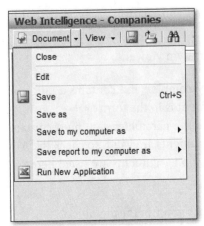

Figure 20.6 The DHTML Client Document Menu with a New Item

The Integration Points API

In conjunction with the `CUSTOM_VIEW_MODE` setting in the EP API, you can use the Integration Points API to integrate the Web Intelligence DHTML client into an application. To do this, you make use of five different objects that are defined in the webiIntegration.js JavaScript file. All of these objects inherit from a parent object called `commonObject`.

You can find a copy of the webiIntegration.js at <XIR31INSTALLPATH>/BUSINESSOB-JECTS/YOURAPPLICATIONSERVERNAME/WEBAPPS/ANALYTICALREPORTING/VIEWERS/CDZ_ADV/CUSTOMIZE/.

The objects contained within webiIntegration.js each refer to a different application area:

▶ `webiViewerIntegration`: Works with the main part of the viewer.

▶ `leftPanelIntegration`: Works with the left panel.

▶ `dialogIntegration`: Works with a custom view in a dialog box.

▶ `popupIntegration`: Works with a custom view in a popup window.

▶ `toolbarIntegration`: Works with the toolbar of the custom view.

When using Integration Points, include the webiIntegration.js file in other files, for example, a JSP, to access the application objects.

<SCRIPT TYPE="TEXT/JAVASCRIPT" SRC="../WEBIINTEGRATION.JS"></SCRIPT>

After you have one of the common objects available, you can manipulate its child objects, set the values of its properties, and add event listeners. Listing 20.9 shows an example of an event listener that runs when a `dialogIntegration` object loads. The event listener calls a method that sets its title, sets its size, hides the OK button, and shows the Cancel button.

```
Var dlg = dialogIntegration;

// Dialog load event listener
dlg.addListener(dialogIntegration.ONLOAD_EVENT,loadDialgCB);
// Dialog button event listeners
dlg.addListener(dialogIntegration.CANCEL_EVENT,cancelCB);
function loadDialgCB ()
{
    dlg.setTitle("Sample Dialog Window");
    dlg.resize(400,170);
    dlg.setBtnDisplayed(dialogIntegration.OK_BTN,false);
    dlg.setBtnDisplayed(dialogIntegration.CANCEL_BTN,true);

}
```

Listing 20.9 Setting Values and a Listener to a dialogIntegration Object

20.3.3 Calculation Extension Points API

The Calculation EP allows you to create custom functions that are added to the existing set of functions that comes standard with Web Intelligence. Just like the existing functions, these external functions are visible and useable from the Formula Editor.

Unlike other EP APIs, custom functions are written in C++. One major advantage of using C++ is that it opens up resources that are available on the operating system as well as over the network and Internet. It also provides you with access to all available C++ libraries.

The process to deploy a custom function within Web Intelligence isn't complex. You'll need to define some XML options and compile the C++ library to a `dll` for win32 or to an `SO` for UNIX. An overview of the procedure is as follows:

1. Create an XML function declaration.

2. Create an XML catalog declaration.

3. Implement the library using the external function API.

4. Compile the source to a dll or SO.

5. Copy the XML and library to the WebiCalcPlugin folder.

6. Restart the Web Intelligence server.

The WebiCalcPlugin folder is located at [INSTALLATION DIRECTORY]\ [BusinessObjectsVersion]\[OS]_[PLATFORM]\WebiCalcPlugin.

So on a typical win32 system, this would be C:\Program Files\Business Objects\ BusinessObjects Enterprise 12.0\Win32_x86\WebiCalcPlugin.

The XML Function Declaration

For the XML function declaration, you define a GUID, the function name, the arguments, the category, and a hint. Listing 20.10 shows a sample.

```
<CATALOG>
   <LIBRARY file="SimplePower">
      <FUNCTION guid="CC3E9742-67A7-4844-9DBF-2CCD4F6ECABE"
name="MySquareFct">
         <ARGLIST>
         <ARG type="Numeric" name="input_number"/>
         </ARGLIST>
         <RETURN type="Numeric"/>
         <CATEGORY type="Num"/>
         <HINT value="My square function."/>
      </FUNCTION>
   </LIBRARY>
</CATALOG>
```

Listing 20.10 The XML Function Declaration

The C++ Library Implementation

To implement the C++ file, you must add the ibovariant.h header. Find a copy of this file at <XIR31InstallPath>/BusinessObjects/BusinessObjects Enterprise 12.0/userlibs/WebI/API.

For each method you add, you must start the declaration with the BO_DECLARE_ USER_FCT macro.

If the function is successful, it returns BONOERROR; otherwise, the #EXTERNAL error message is sent to the report. Listing 20.11 presents a code listing of a basic function that calculates the square of a numeric value and returns it.

```
#include <ibovariant.h>
using namespace BOExtFunct;
BO_DECLARE_USER_FCT ( MySquareFct,
// Name of function as it was defined in the XML.          retVal,

// Name of the return value object.
            parameters
               // Name of the parameters object.
                  )
{
   try   {
      // Get the first parameter.
      const iBOValue&param0 = parameters[0];
      // Transform the parameter to the correct type.
      double valPar0(param0);
      // Assign value to the return value.
      retVal = valPar0 * valPar0;
   }
   catch(...)
   {
      return BOERROR; // Unknown exception so notify WebI
   }
   return BONOERROR; // OK
}
```

Listing 20.11 A Simple Function That Returns the Square of a Number

To complete the process, copy the XML files and the compiled C++ library to the WEBICALCPLUGIN section of the bin folder, and restart the Web Intelligence server.

20.3.4 Custom Data Provider Plug-in

Where the Data Access Driver Development Kit (DDK) provides the capability to integrate custom data sources to the universe semantic layer, the Custom Data Provider plug-in offers similar capability for the Web Intelligence Rich Client. Example custom data sources include local files, URI locations, and in-memory data structures.

The plug-in contains two frameworks: a UI framework, which addresses client-side issues, and a DataProviderSource, which addresses the server side. To allow your Rich Client users to create a new Web Intelligence document with a custom data source, you'll need to create the data source plug-in, and then configure and deploy it on the SAP BusinessObjects installation.

To begin development, you'll have to implement two Java interfaces for the UI and two interfaces for the data source. SAP BusinessObjects has simplified the process somewhat by providing abstract classes that you can extend rather than fully implementing these objects.

All of these classes are available in a single binary called cdsuiframework.jar. You can find this file in the <BOBJ ENTERPRISE DIRECTORY>CLASSES subdirectory.

Table 20.5 lists the interfaces and abstract classes used to create the Custom Data Provider UI.

Class Name	Usage
CustomDSExtension	Java Interface: UI plug-in entry point
CustomDSComponent	Java Interface: UI component plug-in
AbstractCustomDSExtension	An abstract implementation of CustomDSExtension
AbstractCustomDSComponent	An abstract implementation of CustomDSComponent

Table 20.5 User Interface Interfaces and Abstract Classes

Table 20.6 lists the interfaces and abstract classes used to create the Data Provider source.

Class Name	Usage
CustomDataSource	Java Interface: The Data Provider source entry point
CustomDataProvider	Java Interface: The Data Provider application.
AbstractCustomDataSource	An abstract implementation of CustomDataSource
AbstractCustomDataProvider	An abstract implementation of CustomDataProvider

Table 20.6 The Data Provider Interfaces and Abstract Classes

After development of the plug-in is complete, you'll need to create (or edit) the webi_customds_extension.xml file, which acts as a repository of Custom Data Providers. This file must be placed in the <BOBJ ENTERPRISE DIRECTORY>/OS_XXX/ CONFIG subdirectory (where OS_XXX is the operating system shorthand, e.g., win32_x86).

To get sample code and deployment files, look in the <BOBJ ENTERPRISE DIRECTORY>/SAMPLES/CUSTOMDS subdirectory. You can also check the SAP Community Network at *www.sdn.sap.com/irj/scn* for more examples.

20.4 Summary

The Web Intelligence Extension Points kit offers a great way to add customization to the various clients that are available to an end user without the need to delve into and modify its intricate code structures. As Extension Points APIs are available for the Java Report Panel, the Query Panel, the Web Intelligence Rich Client, and the DHTML Client, you should be able to develop custom applications for just about any UI. You also can create new functions to further enhance the user experience.

In addition, SAP BusinessObjects provides support for the Extension Points APIs, removing an element of risk and making it more likely that you can upgrade your applications as SAP BusinessObjects releases new upgrades. Chapter 21 will describe the process of creating Web Intelligence SDK applications.

After you have an idea of what can be achieved with the Web Intelligence SDK and Extension Points, you'll probably want to try to put together a sample application. Here, we set out a basic example that should help to give you a feel for how to build a customized application.

21 Web Intelligence SDK Sample Applications

In this chapter, we'll put together a working client-side application using the SDKs and APIs you learned about in Chapters 19 and 20. The application will provide samples in both a Java and .NET environment. As you'll see, the code structure for both environments is very similar, so we'll list the samples together. The application will show samples of connecting to the SAP BusinessObjects Central Management Server (CMS) and retrieving a valid connection object. Once connected, the application will present the user with a list of documents with hyperlinks. A click on any of the document hyperlinks will open the document in a viewer. Using the Extension Points API, we'll simplify the document viewer, removing unnecessary options.

Remember that this is purely a sample application and not something to be deployed in a live user environment. We have not placed much emphasis on custom styling, security, or effective error handling. The primary purpose here is to offer example usage of some of the important aspects of the Web Intelligence SDKs.

To set up the development environment for the Web Intelligence SDKs, locate the required libraries and external definition files. Refer to chapter 19 in section 19.5 titled Setting Up the Development Environment for more details. If you're using the Java example, this sample uses the BOE SDK.

Let's start by connecting to the SAP BusinessObjects CMS.

21.1 Connecting to the Central Management Server

For the connection example, we'll assume that the values needed to log on are posted directly to an ASP or JSP object from an HTML form. The form can be created using whatever tools you prefer as long as four values are passed to the server object (see Figure 21.1). These values are listed here:

- The user id
- A password
- The server name
- The authorization type; one of `secEnterprise`, `secLDAP`, or `secWinAD`

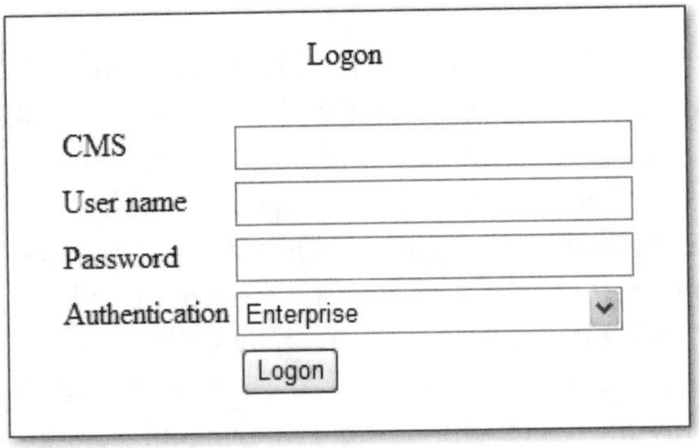

Figure 21.1 An HTML Logon Form

To work with a SAP BusinessObjects server, you need access to an Enterprise session object. To create a valid Enterprise session object, first retrieve a Session Manager, and then pass the four values obtained from the logon form to the logon method of that Session Manager.

On retrieving the Enterprise session, you're in a position to get the `InfoStore` service. Remember that the `InfoStore` is the key to all object access from the CMS.

Then place a reference to it onto the HTTP session so that it's available every time you make a new URL call. That way, the next time you make a call to the server, you avoid the overhead of logging on again; just bring down the `InfoStore` object from the HTTP session.

You employ the Logon Token Manager in combination with the Enterprise session to get a copy of the logon token. The logon token is a convenient way of rapidly retrieving the current user connection. You then place a reference to the token on the HTTP session as this will be used in a later process.

Another option you may want to think about when creating connection services is to use the Java Server Faces SDK Logon component.

21.1.1 Connecting in Java

Let's look at some of the methods you'll use to manage connectivity in Java.

Listing 21.1 shows `handleLogin` as a declared method in a JSP file. The method requires the HTTP session as a parameter, which is easily obtained from the main JSP file as an implicit object, `request`. You also pass the values needed to log on. The assumption is that you only call this method when you have no valid existing connection.

To get an `ISessionMgr`, use the static `CrystalEnterprise.getSessionMgr` method call. Then use the `ISessionMgr` to log on. The next step is to retrieve an `IInfoStore` object with the `enterpriseSession.getService("InfoStore")` call, and place a reference onto the HTTP session.

Finally, also place the logon token on the HTTP session after retrieving it with `enterpriseSession.getLogonTokenMgr().getDefaultToken()`.

```
<%!
private IInfoStore handleLogin(HttpSession session,
  String userName, String userPass, String sCMS, String sAuth)
        throws SDKException {
  IEnterpriseSession enterpriseSession = null;
  ISessionMgr sessionMgr =
CrystalEnterprise.getSessionMgr();
  enterpriseSession = sessionMgr.logon(userName,
userPass , sCMS, sAuth);
  IInfoStore infoStore = (IInfoStore)
    enterpriseSession.getService("InfoStore");
  session.setAttribute("SESSION_INFOSTORE", infoStore);
  session.setAttribute("token",
      enterpriseSession.getLogonTokenMgr().
getDefaultToken() );
  return infoStore;
}
%>
```

Listing 21.1 handleLogin Method Declaration

In the opening section of the JSP, we first test to see if the application has already placed a valid IInfoStore object on the session. If there is no IInfoStore, we retrieve the values required to log on from the HTTP request object and then attempt to obtain the IInfoStore using the handleLogin method (see Listing 21.2).

```
<%
IInfoStore infoStore = (IInfoStore)session.getAttribute("SESSION_
INFOSTORE");
if( infoStore == null){
    String sUser = request.getParameter("user");
    String sPass = request.getParameter("pass");
    String sCMS = request.getParameter("cms");
    String sAuth = request.getParameter("auth");
    try{
        infoStore = handleLogin(session, sUser,
                sPass, sCMS, sAuth);
    }
    catch(SDKException sdkEX){
        //handle the exception
    }
}
%>
```

Listing 21.2 Initializing the Connection Process

21.1.2 Connecting in .NET

For .NET, we can assume that the logon form is created using an ASPX form, which calls the loginButton_Click method shown in Listing 21.3. We can also assume that the values needed to log on are posted via various text fields and a combo box in the case of the authentication type.

Create a SessionMgr object with an instantiation, sessionMgr = new SessionMgr(). After you have a Session Manager, use its Logon method to create an EnterpriseSession object. To retrieve the all-important InfoStore object, you first need the EnterpriseService, enterpriseSession.GetService("InfoStore"), from which you can generate the InfoStore. Place a reference to the InfoStore on the HTTP session.

Finally, use the LogonTokenMgr to obtain the logon token and also store a reference to this token on the HTTP session.

```
protected void loginButton_Click(object sender, EventArgs e)
    {
        SessionMgr sessionMgr = new SessionMgr();
        EnterpriseSession enterpriseSession;
        InfoStore infoStore;
        EnterpriseService enterpriseService;
        try
        {
            enterpriseSession =
        sessionMgr.Logon(txtUsername.Text,
                txtPassword.Text,
                txtHost.Text,
                lsAuthType.SelectedItem.Value);
        }
        catch (Exception ex)
        {
        //handle error
    }
enterpriseService =
    enterpriseSession.GetService("InfoStore");
infoStore = new InfoStore(enterpriseService);
Session["InfoStore"] = infoStore;
Session["Token"] =
            enterpriseSession.LogonTokenMgr.DefaultToken;
```

Listing 21.3 The Logon Method Called on Clicking the Logon Button

Now that you have a connection and the necessary objects stored on the HTTP session, we can move on to presenting a list of documents that a user can select for viewing.

21.2   Displaying a Document List

Once connected, the application displays a list of reports that a user can select to view. You use the InfoStore object that was obtained on logon to query the CMS repository for documents that begin with a certain text value. In this example, you're going to look for all documents whose title begins with "Average." However, it would be a very simple addition to add a dropdown or free text entry to allow a user to vary the text value that you'll use in the query. Of course, you could also make a search for any matching text by adding a "%" character at the beginning of the text value as well as the end. A sample of the document list output is shown in Figure 21.1.

A successful query will return a list of objects of type `InfoObject`, each one representing a document. From each of these objects, you'll extract information such as its ID, textual name, and description. You'll also retrieve the `Properties` object associated with each `InfoObject` to get the name of the document owner. As the information you require from each `InfoObject` is generic, you won't need to cast it to another type. On many occasions, this won't be the case, and some form of casting will be necessary to get the information you need.

The application then uses the information about each document to create a hyperlink that makes an `OpenDocument` URL call. `OpenDocument` calls were covered in Chapter 15, Linking in Web Intelligence Reports, but it may be worthwhile to review what the application is doing.

21.2.1   The OpenDocument Call

To open a document in a viewer with `OpenDocument`, you need at least a unique document id and a logon token. After the repository query has run, you'll have both of these items. One of the query items is the object id, in this case, a Cluster Unique Identifier (CUID). If you recall, in the logon section, you stored the logon token on the HTTP session for later use.

So to build the `OpenDocument` URL, you only need to add a parameter that defines the id type. As the type is a CUID, add an HTTP parameter: `sIDType=CUID`. You'll then have a URL that looks something like the following:

```
http://myserver:8080/OpenDocument/opendoc/openDocument.jsp?sIDType=CUID
&iDocID=AXUVnCxjXIhFo7qYMK3xV7A&token=myserver:6400@5620JhpXz5wyYi4h3ho
N5619JrTYoK4iWR8T7sJU
```

One other point when building `OpenDocument` URL calls is to note whether or not the call you make is from within the application server context. If it's from outside, you'll need to create a full rather than relative URL string.

Figure 21.2 shows a list of documents generated from a repository query.

```
//the opendoc url when called from within the same context
private String opendocCall =
    "/OpenDocument/opendoc/openDocument.jsp?";
```

```
//the opendoc url when called from outside the context
//private String opendocCall =
   "http://myserver/OpenDocument/opendoc/openDocument.jsp?";
```

Click Document Name to View

Document	Description	Owner
Average Number of Users Logged In	How many users are on my system?	Administrator
Average Refresh Time	What is the average time for documents to refresh?	Administrator
Average Session Duration	What is the average session duration?	Administrator
Average Session Duration per Cluster	What is the average session duration per cluster?	Administrator
Average Session Duration per User	What is the average session duration per user?	Administrator

Figure 21.2 A List of Documents Generated from a Repository Query

21.2.2 Displaying a Document List Using Java

Putting together the document list is a little more complicated than simply getting a connection and needs a few more methods to accomplish the task.

The `getDocumentDetails` method returns an `ArrayList` object, which, in turn, contains a `String` array in each of its elements. The `infoStore` parameter is a reference to the `IInfoStore` object that was created on connecting to the CMS. Use `infoStore` to run a query against the CMS, which requests the document id, name, description, and owner for all objects that have a name beginning with the `wildCard` parameter. Setting `SI_KIND` to 'webi' will ensure the query will retrieve only Web Intelligence documents.

Loop through each of the returned documents to extract the document information. You do this with a call to the `getDocumentDetails` method. GETDOCUMENTDE-TAILS uses generic method calls to get details such as the id and the `IProperties` object. Place them into a `String` array, and return the array so that it can be added to the `ArrayList`.

Listing 21.4 shows the `getDocumentDetail` and `getDocumentDetails` defined in a JSP declaration.

```
<%!
private ArrayList<String[]>getDocumentDetails(
   IInfoStore infoStore, String wildCard)
            throws SDKException{
  ArrayList<String[]>docList = new ArrayList<String[]>();
  //create the selection string using the wild card
  String sQuery = "SELECT SI_CUID,SI_NAME,SI_DESCRIPTION," +
      "SI_OWNER FROM CI_INFOOBJECTS WHERE SI_KIND='webi'" +
      "AND SI_NAME LIKE '"
       + wildCard
       + "%' ORDER BY SI_NAME";

  IInfoObjects docs = infoStore.query(sQuery);
  if (!docs.isEmpty()) {
     for (int i = 0; i < docs.size(); i++) {
    IInfoObject doc =  (IInfoObject) docs.get(i);
    //get the document info and place in the array
    docList.add( getDocumentDetails(doc)  );
  }
  }
  return docList;
}
%>
<%!
protected String[] getDocumentDetails(IInfoObject doc) throws
SDKException {
   //initialize the string array
   String[] details = new String[4];
   details[0] = String.valueOf( doc.getCUID() );
   details[1] = doc.getTitle();
   details[2] = doc.getDescription();
   // now try to get the owner info from the properties
   IProperties props = doc.properties();
   details[3] = (String)
      props.getProperty("SI_OWNER").getValue();

   return details;
}
%>
```

Listing 21.4 Java Document Management Methods

The `createOpendocCall` is another declared method. It's used as a utility that creates an `OpenDocument` URL based on the CUID, logon token, and document name that are all passed in as parameters.

The `String` variable `opendocCall` is a class variable used as a base from which to build the `OpenDocument` call.

```
private String opendocCall =
        "/OpenDocument/opendoc/openDocument.jsp?sIDType=CUID&";
<%!
private String createOpendocCall(String cuid, String token,
String docName) {
return "<a href=" + opendocCall + "iDocID=" + cuid +
    "&token=" + token + ">" + docName + "</a>";
}
%>
```

You have now completed most of the document listing work. All you need to do now is declare the `docListDetails` array and populate it with the `getDocumentDetails` method you have already defined.

Then retrieve the token you stored on the HTTP session earlier and generate an HTML table creating the `OpenDocument` call with the `createOpendocCall` method. Pump this data into a `StringBuffer` before sending it to the output stream.

```
<%
    private ArrayList<String[]>docListDetails;
    try{
        docListDetails = getDocumentDetails(
                infoStore, "Average" );
    }
    catch(SDKException sdkEX){
    //handle exception
    }
    StringBuffer sbText = new StringBuffer();
    String token = (String)session.getAttribute("token");

    for( int i=0; i<docListDetails.size(); i++){
     String[] details = docListDetails.get(i);

     sbText.append("<tr><td>").append(
            createOpendocCall(
                    details[0], token, details[1]))
                    .append("</td>");
```

```
    sbText.append("<td>").
                append( details[2]).append("</td>");
    sbText.append("<td>").append(
                details[3]).append("</td></tr>");
    }
    out.print(sbText.toString() );
%>
```

Listing 21.5 Generating the Document Table List in the JSP

21.2.3 Displaying a Document List Using .NET

To create an HTML document list in .NET, you'll use four methods.

The GETDOCUMENTDETAILS method (see Listing 21.6) returns a 2D String array that contains another String array in each of its elements. The infoStore parameter is a reference to the InfoStore object that was created on connecting to the CMS. Use infoStore to run a query against the CMS, which requests the document id, name, description, and owner for all objects that have a name beginning with the wildCard parameter. Setting SI_KIND to 'webi' will ensure the query will retrieve only Web Intelligence documents.

Then loop through each of the returned documents to extract the document information. You do this with generic method calls to get details such as the id and the Properties object.

```
protected String[,] GetDocumentDetails(InfoStore infoStore,
String wildCard)
  {
    String[,] docList = null;
  //create the selection string using the wild card
  String sQuery = "SELECT SI_CUID,SI_NAME, " +
                    "SI_DESCRIPTION, SI_OWNER" +
                   "FROM CI_INFOOBJECTS " +
                    "WHERE SI_KIND='webi' AND " +
                    "SI_NAME LIKE '" +
                 wildCard +
                 "%' ORDER BY SI_NAME";

    InfoObjects docs = infoStore.Query(sQuery);
    int iLoc = 0;
    if (docs.Count > 0)
    {
```

```
        docList = new String[docs.Count, 4];
        foreach (InfoObject doc in docs)
        {
            docList[iLoc,0] = doc.CUID;
            docList[iLoc, 1] = doc.Title;
            docList[iLoc, 2] = doc.Description;

            Properties props = doc.Properties;
            Property siOwner = props["SI_OWNER"];
            if (siOwner != null)
            {
                docList[iLoc, 3] =
            (String)siOwner.Value;
            }
            iLoc++;
        }
    }
  return docList;
}
```

Listing 21.6 The Main .NET Data Retrieval Method

The AddDocTableRows method (see Listing 21.7) takes the 2D String array created in the GetDocumentDetails method and converts it into an HTML table containing the detailed information for documents in the docList parameter. AddDocTable-Rows also retrieves the logon token created on connection to the CMS and passes it to the CreateOpendocCall method, where it's used to generate the OpenDocument URL.

```
private void AddDocTableRows(String[,] docList)
    {
        String token = (String)Session["Token"];
        for (int i = 0; i < docList.GetUpperBound(0); i++)
        {
            TableRow row = new TableRow();
            //build the link cell
            TableCell linkCell = new TableCell();
            linkCell.Text = CreateOpendocCall(
                docList[i, 0], token, docList[i, 1]);
            row.Cells.Add(linkCell);

            for (int j = 2; j < 4; j++)
            {
```

```
            TableCell cell = new TableCell();
            cell.Text = docList[i, j];
            row.Cells.Add(cell);
        }
        docTable.Rows.Add(row);
    }


}
```

Listing 21.7 Creating the .NET HTML Document Table

The `CreateOpendocCall` is used as a utility that creates an `OpenDocument` URL based on the CUID, logon token and document name that are all passed in as parameters.

The `String` variable `opendocCall` is a class variable used as a base from which to build the `OpenDocument` call.

```
private String opendocCall =
        "/OpenDocument/opendoc/openDocument.jsp?sIDType=CUID&";

private String CreateOpendocCall(String cuid, String token, String
docName)
    {
        return "<a href=" + opendocCall + "iDocID=" + cuid +
            "&token=" + token + ">" + docName + "</a>";
    }
```

You can now put all this together from the `Page_Load` method, which is called automatically when you call the parent page. The process is very simple. First retrieve the `infoStore` object you created on connection. Then get the `docList` using the `GetDocumentDetails` method. Finally, pass the `docList` array into the `AddDocTableRows` method and that should create your HTML document list.

```
protected void Page_Load(object sender, EventArgs e)
    {
        infoStore = (InfoStore)Session["InfoStore"];
        String[,] docList = GetDocumentDetails(
                            infoStore, "Average");
        if (docList != null)
        {
            AddDocTableRows(docList);
        }
    }
```

Now, you should have a fully functional application that allows you to log on to the SAP BusinessObject CMS, provides a list of clickable documents, and opens those documents into a viewer when clicked. Let's now look at simplifying the viewer.

21.3 Amending the Viewer with Extension Points

At this point, you've created a basic application. Let's assume that you also want to deliver only barebones viewer functionality because you want to keep the application as simple as possible for your user base. The obvious way to amend the viewer features is to use the Web Intelligence Interactive Viewing Extension and Integration Points API.

With this API, you should be able to achieve exactly what you need to do by simply editing two files. Both files are located in the web application directory structure of the application server. *They are* webiviewer.properties AND user.js. If you're using a default application with Tomcat, you'll find them in the following locations:

- <XIR31INSTALLPATH>/BUSINESSOBJECTS/YOURAPPLICATIONSERVERNAME/ WEBAPPS/ANALYTICALREPORTING/WEB-INF/CLASSES/WEBIVIEWER.PROPERTIES
- <XIR31INSTALLPATH>/BUSINESSOBJECTS/YOURAPPLICATIONSERVERNAME/ WEBAPPS/ANALYTICALREPORTING/VIEWERS/CDZ_ADV/CUSTOMIZE/USER.JS

> **Note**
>
> The location of the files, user.js and webiviewer.properties, will depend on what application server and what environment you're using. If you're not using a default application with Tomcat, check the SAP BusinessObjects documentation to locate them. However, you'll always find them in the same directory structure.

To inform Web Intelligence that you want to customize the viewer, you must first edit the webiviewer.properties file. Open this file in a text editor, locate the ALLOW_CUSTOMIZATION section, and then change the value to "yes."

```
#Allow customization [yes/no]
ALLOW_CUSTOMIZATION=yes
```

Next open the user.js file in a text editor, and add the following line:

```
hide_ui_element("ALL_EXCEPT_REPORT");
```

The `ALL_EXCEPT_REPORT` option will remove all aspects of the viewer with the exception of the report itself. You can see the output of a report viewer with toolbars, the status bar, and panels all removed in Figure 21.3.

If there are other lines in this file and you don't want to delete them, you can use the comment characters, `//` to remove a single line and `/*   */` to remove multiple lines. For example:

```
//hide_ui_element("REPORT_TABS");
/*
hide_ui_element("MENUBAR_DOCUMENT_MENU");
hide_ui_element("MENUBAR_ZOOM");
*/
```

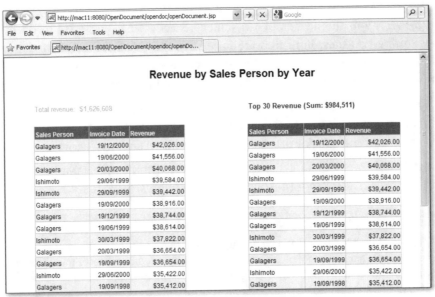

Figure 21.3 A Web Intelligence View with All Items Removed

If you decide that removing all features is overkill, then edit the user.js file so that only the items you require are visible. For example, to hide only the document menu and the left panel, set the options as follows:

```
hide_ui_element("MENUBAR_DOCUMENT_MENU");
hide_ui_element("LEFTPANEL");
```

You have quite a range of possibilities available to you in the user.js file, so experiment until you find the right combination.

21.4 Summary

In this chapter, we walked through the creation of a starter application designed to give you some idea of how to make use of the Web Intelligence SDKs and where Extension Points fit into the scheme of things. In this application, we only used the BOE SDK, with some code snippets in Java and .NET. When looking at the Extension Points, we only skimmed the surface of what you can do. Due to the very large number of potential uses and variety of development capabilities in the range of available SDKs, it's unrealistic to provide much more than a cursory glance at the possibilities.

If you want more information, check the SAP BusinessObjects Developer Library at *http://www.sdn.sap.com/irj/boc/sdklibrary*. There, you'll find full documentation on each of the current SDKs. You'll also find tutorials and more sample applications. Chapter 22 provides details for creating BI Widgets with Web Intelligence.

SAP BusinessObjects BI Widgets provides real-time access to your business intelligence content through widgets displayed on your desktop. Information is available at your fingertips to make informed decisions in a fast-paced environment.

22 Creating BI Widgets

The power of business intelligence (BI) is now available on your desktop without the need to log in to the InfoView portal. BI Widgets are components that reside on your desktop and can relay real-time business information in an easy to access format. Web Intelligence report parts and Xcelsius SWF files can be converted to BI Widgets. BI Widgets can also be integrated into the body of Microsoft Outlook emails. Figure 22.1 shows a sample BI Widget using a Web Intelligence report part.

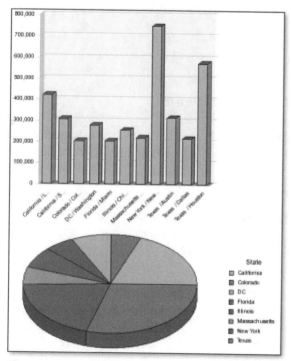

Figure 22.1 Sample BI Widgets

22.1   About BI Widgets

BI Widgets are defined as elements that perform a single function presented in a single, concise interface accessed through a desktop or email. Key features of SAP BusinessObjects BI Widgets include the following:

▶ Access to internal and external data via the SAP BusinessObjects Enterprise, Web Services, RSS feeds, and so on

▶ Simple drag-and-drop functionality for integration of SAP BusinessObjects Enterprise content

▶ Easy content search capabilities to locate BI content within the Enterprise environment

▶ Automated single sign-on (SSO) using user rights and security of SAP BusinessObjects Enterprise

▶ RSS Inbox integration with pop-up notifications of new feeds

▶ Instantaneous access to Web Intelligence report parts and Xcelsius SWF file content

▶ Windows Vista look and feel with transparency of windows

▶ Support for Windows Vista sidebar gadgets

▶ Ability to save and share widgets across the enterprise

22.2   Installation of BI Widgets Software

The BI Widgets desktop application must be installed on a user's computer. Access to the SAP BusinessObjects Enterprise environment is also necessary on the machine where BI Widgets are deployed. The following prerequisites are necessary for the installation of BI Widgets:

▶ Windows XP Service Pack 2, Windows 2003, or Windows Vista

▶ Microsoft .NET Framework 2.0 or later

▶ Flash Player 9 or later

▶ Connection to the SAP BusinessObjects 3.x repository

▶ Content search configuration and indexing set up (to use content search functionality)

Upon completion of the installation of BI Widgets, the connection to the repository must be set up to enable access to your BI content. Navigate to START • PROGRAMS • BUSINESSOBJECTS XI 3.1 • BI WIDGETS to access BI Widgets. The BI Widgets icon will appear on your Windows taskbar as shown in Figure 22.2.

Figure 22.2   BI Widgets Icon on Windows Taskbar

Right-click the icon to view the menu options available as shown in Figure 22.3. The options to make changes to your repository connection or to log on or log off of the enterprise are included in this menu.

Figure 22.3   BI Widgets Right-Click Menu

Select the Host and Login Preferences option to set your login properties or to add additional repository connections. The ability to access multiple repositories gives you access to all your BI content across the enterprise. Upon selecting the Host and Login Preferences option, the Host and Login Preferences dialog box appears as shown in Figure 22.4. The current connection set up during installation shows in the dialog box as well as any additional connections previously set up. From this dialog box, you can add new connections, remove connections, edit connections, or connect/disconnect a connection.

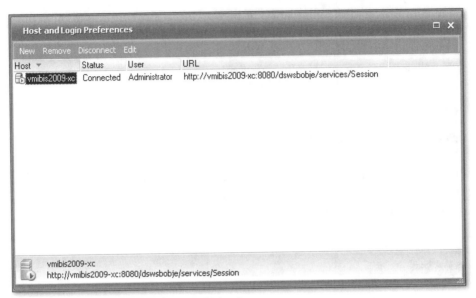

Figure 22.4 Host and Login Preferences Dialog Box

After you've logged in to your connection (or connections) to the SAP Business-Objects repository, you're ready to create BI Widgets to share on your desktop or across the enterprise.

22.3 Creating BI Widgets Using Web Intelligence

BI Widgets can be created with the simple drag and drop of your Web Intelligence report content using familiar, easy-to-use interfaces resembling Windows Vista dialog boxes. Although BI Widgets can be created using Xcelsius SWF as well as Web Intelligence report parts, for the purposes of this book, we'll discuss the inclusion of Web Intelligence content only. There are two ways to locate your Web Intelligence documents for inclusion: by using content search or by using the Document List Explorer.

22.3.1 Content Search

To use content search, your SAP BusinessObjects administrator must have already enabled the use of content search within your deployment. Also, the content indexing must already have been performed and scheduled for the search to have content to explore. If this functionality has been set up, then you can search for Web Intelligence documents within your enterprise by selecting Content Search from the right-click menu. Content search within BI Widgets works the same way as in InfoView. More information about performing content searches is contained within Chapter 11, Working Within InfoView.

22.3.2 Document List Explorer

Another method used to locate your Web Intelligence reports is to use the Document List Explorer. Select Document List Explorer from the right-click menu. A dialog box appears with a view resembling the document list within InfoView as shown in Figure 22.5. You can explore your documents by folders or categories. All your Web Intelligence documents and instances are contained within the Document List Explorer for selection.

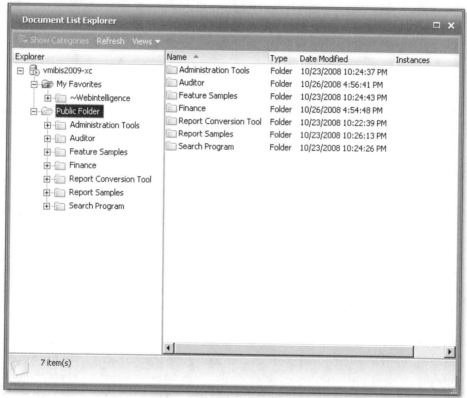

Figure 22.5 Document List Explorer

▸ Select the Web Intelligence document from the content search or Document List Explorer.

▸ Click, drag, and drop the Web Intelligence report part from the Web Intelligence Document Viewer (Figure 22.6) to your desktop.

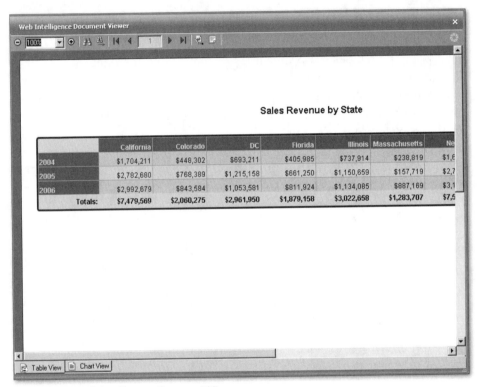

Figure 22.6 Web Intelligence Document Viewer

Remember that BI Widgets are small, concise elements that are displayed on the desktop. The size and content included in a widget should be limited to display the most information using the smallest space. Charts are often useful report content to include as BI Widgets. Also, using open document functionality as discussed in Chapter 15, Linking in Web Intelligence Reports, can be useful to provide further content when business questions arise without consuming too much space on your desktop. Open document functionality enables you to select a report part to open another report. Within a widget, this functionality can be used to open a more detailed Web Intelligence report in InfoView to explore the data further if the need arises.

22.3.3 Other File Types

Xcelsius SWF files can also be integrated as BI Widgets. Select Open Widget from Disk form the right-click menu to open a file browser to navigate to the appropriate SWF file to include as your BI Widget. You can also use the content search or Document List Explorer to search for Xcelsius SWF files to create desktop widgets.

When navigating within the Document List Explorer, you'll also be able to view other content contained within your InfoView environment outside of Web Intelligence documents and Xcelsius files. If you select one of these files types, the document will open in an Internet Explorer window and not display as BI Widget content.

22.3.4 Outlook Objects

Web Intelligence report parts can be included in Microsoft Outlook emails using the Web Intelligence Document Viewer to drag and drop the report part into the body of the email.

> **Note**
>
> To use BI Widgets with Microsoft Outlook, you must set your Outlook options to use Word as the Outlook text editor and HTML as the email format.

22.4 Setting BI Widget Properties

BI Widgets properties are defined for all widgets and for each widget individually. Individual widget properties are set within the Widget Options box for each BI Widget contained within your views. Program options are found within the right-click menu when selecting the BI Widgets icon on your Windows taskbar.

22.4.1 Widget Options

To set the properties for a BI Widget, select the Widget Options button on the right of the BI Widget residing on your desktop as shown in Figure 22.7.

Figure 22.7 Widget Options Button

From within the Widget Properties dialog box, you can define the refresh options for the BI widget. Refresh options include the following:

▶ **Retrieve data from the latest instance:** This retrieval is instantaneous to the time the new instance is generated. It will retrieve the latest instance of the document to feed data to the widget. You'll define how often BI Widgets will check for a new instance.

▶ **Refresh data directly from the database:** This retrieval may take additional time as it will perform a refresh from the database, so it will be limited by the speed of the database refresh time for the query. With this refresh type, you'll also define how often the database refresh will occur.

The export options for the BI Widget are also contained within the Widget Options dialog box as shown in Figure 22.8. You'll define the location to save the widget enabling you to share and distribute your BI Widgets across the enterprise.

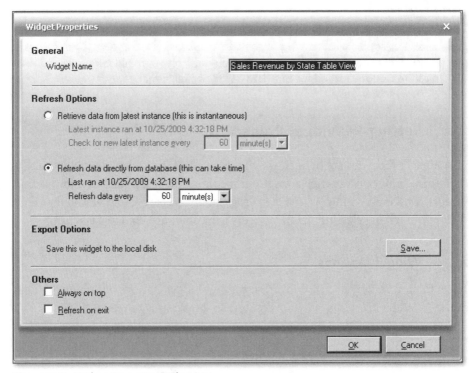

Figure 22.8   Widget Properties Dialog Box

The final properties available within the Widget Properties dialog box are to define how your widget will appear on your desktop. To make your widget appear on top of all other applications, select the Always on Top checkbox. To refresh the widget content upon exit of the BI Widget application, select the checkbox to Refresh on Exit.

22.4.2 Program Options

BI Widgets program options are defined through the options available in the right-click menu of the BI Widgets icon on the Windows taskbar as shown earlier in Figure 22.3. The following properties are available for definition on the right-click menu:

▶ **About:** Displays information about your current version of SAP Business-Objects Rich Client.

▶ **Show BI Widgets**: Enables the display of your BI Widgets on your desktop.

▶ **Open widgets from disk:** Opens a widget saved on your computer or network drive.

▶ **RSS Inbox:** Displays the RSS Inbox display to define any RSS feeds.

▶ **Widget Views:** Displays the Widget views box to create a collection of widgets for display on your desktop. The collection of widgets is defined as views (see Figure 22.9). New views can be added, renamed, opened, and closed from this view. Deselect the box next to the name of the widget to remove it from the view display.

Figure 22.9 Widget Views Box

▶ **Recent Widgets:** Shows the recently viewed widgets for a selection.

▶ **Document List Explorer:** Displays the Document List Explorer box to select Web Intelligence documents or Xcelsius SWF files contained within the repository.

▶ **Content Search:** Displays the content search box for creating searches upon the documents stored in the repository.

▶ **Host and Login Preferences:** Displays the Host and Login Preferences dialog box for definition of repository login information.

▶ **Login/Logout:** Logs in or out of the repository.

▶ **Quit BI Widgets:** Exits the BI Widgets program.

22.5 Summary

BI Widgets provide real-time access to BI content to aid managers and business users in making informed decisions in a time-sensitive manner. The sleek look and feel, ease of use, and incorporation of BI content across multiple environments gives BI Widgets an added edge in a competitive economy.

Appendices

Third-party tools fill a valuable niche by extending the SAP BusinessObjects Enterprise product suite with very innovative, powerful, and exciting new functionality. Third-party solutions allow you to maximize your return on investment with SAP BusinessObjects Enterprise XI 3.1.

A   Third-Party Vendors

There are currently several third-party vendors on the market that offer software products and tools to integrate with Web Intelligence and SAP BusinessObjects Enterprise XI 3.1. These products present many exciting capabilities that extend and complement existing SAP BusinessObjects XI deployments.

This appendix will alphabetically introduce twelve third-party vendors followed by a brief description of their product offerings and key features.

> **Note**
>
> This appendix includes any Web Intelligence and SAP BusinessObjects Enterprise XI 3.1 third party vendor the authors were aware of at the time of publication. There may be others that were not included. The inclusion and/or omission of a vendor from this appendix should not be seen as an endorsement or critique of their products and services.

Third-Party Vendors

► Antivia – *www.antivia.com*

► APOS Solutions – *www.apos.com*

► Business Intelligentsia – *www.businessintelligentsia.com*

► EBI Experts – *www.ebiexperts.com*

► GB & Smith – *www.gbandsmith.com*

► InfoBurst by InfoSol – *www.infosol.com*

► Integeo – *www.integeo.com*

► NOAD – *www.noadbi.com*

- Noetix – *www.noetix.com*
- Roambi by Mellmo – *www.mellmo.com*
- Teleran Technologies – *www.teleran.com*
- Tidal Software – *www.tidalsoftware.com*

A.1 Antivia

Antivia is an SAP Partner and currently offers three products that seamlessly integrate with SAP BusinessObjects XI. Their most notable offering is the Xcelsius Web Intelligence Integration Suite (XWIS).

XWIS is a product that allows you to integrate data from Web Intelligence reports into Xcelsius 2008 dashboards. This product also provides the capability of delivering drillable data grids from Universe drill paths. In addition, XWIS provides a fully interactive slice & dice panel for selecting dimensions and drilling into detail data.

Certified by SAP for its integration with SAP Business Objects, the products by Antivia are built on the Business Intelligence 2.0 framework and adhere to three fundamental concepts: usability, collaboration, and realization.

Antivia Product Offerings

- Xcelsius Web Intelligence Integration Suite (XWIS)
  - Integrates data from Web Intelligence directly into Xcelsius dashboards
  - Adds drillable Web Intelligence data with Universe drill paths
  - Bind Web Intelligence data with any Xcelsius component
  - Utilize a Slice & Dice panel for increased user flexibility
  - Add live collaboration to Xcelsius dashboards
- Scenario for BusinessObjects
  - Manage and manipulate hierarchies live within BusinessObjects reports
  - Easily save and share hierarchies with other users in the community
  - Instantly rearrange hierarchies to analyze data in 'what-if' scenarios
- Antivia Desktop
  - Community Insights – Social networking meets Business Intelligence

► Measure the value of reports by allow users to provide ratings

► Allow users to create polls and surveys on BI content

A.2   APOS Solutions

APOS Solutions is an SAP Partner and provides several powerful tools that extend the functionality of existing SAP BusinessObjects Enterprise installations. SAP Certified for integration with BusinessObjects, APOS offers six products that integrate with SAP BusinessObjects. These tools provide a wide variety of increased functionality and include products for administration, system monitoring, instance management, report bursting, and mapping with location intelligence.

APOS Solutions Product Offerings

► APOS Administrator: Advanced System Management for SAP BusinessObjects

  ► High-efficiency system administration consoles

  ► Rapid Response and failure recovery controls

  ► Automated report promotion and object management

  ► Power batch scheduling and rapid data source transition

  ► Bulk security and user preference management

► APOS Insight: System Monitoring and Analysis for SAP BusinessObjects

  ► Monitoring: Granular monitoring of system status and health

  ► Introspection: Predictive monitoring and failure prevention

  ► Governance: System and migration governance

  ► Auditing: Enhanced activity and security auditing, system metadata and structure analysis, content structure and usage analysis

► APOS Storage Center: Archive and Restore for SAP BusinessObjects

  ► Archiving – Business rules driven archive of report instances

  ► Backup and Versioning – Business rules driven backup of report instances, and report objects with versioning

  ► Selective Restore – Selective object restore without downtime

  ► Dynamic Exporting – Conversion of neutral format for long-term storage

  ► Intelligent Purging – Selective purging of instances from archive/backup

- APOS Publisher: Report Bursting and Distribution
  - Automated, business rules driven bursting of reports
  - Consolidation of custom packaging of reports
  - Enhanced statement generation and distribution
  - Enhanced destination and report distribution
  - Enhanced report security and encryption
- Microsoft Outlook End User Portal for SAP BusinessObjects
  - Simplified access to SAP BusinessObjects from Microsoft Outlook
  - View or schedule live reports
  - Download files for offline analysis
- ESRI GIS Integration – Location Intelligence
  - Location Intelligence for intuitive location analysis
  - Integrative visual mapping content with detailed reports and dashboards
  - Add reporting and context sensitive analysis to mapping applications
  - Simplified analysis from a location perspective

A.3   Business Intelligentsia

Business Intelligentsia is a third-party vendor offering a Scheduler Console for administrators experiencing difficulties managing an SAP BusinessObjects Enterprise XI environment.

They also offer a tool called Quick Audit XI used for extracting data from the CMS then making it available in a Universe.

Business Intelligentsia Product Offerings

- Scheduler Console
  - Powerful report rescheduling
  - Enhanced report schedule maintenance
- Quick Audit XI
  - Store data extracted from the CMS in a Universe

A.4 EBI Experts

EBI Experts strive to help organizations gain better insight into their business intelligence applications by improving agility, productivity, and return on investments.

Two products are currently being offered by EBI Experts that are intended to increase user satisfaction and help manage and measure SAP BusinessObjects deployments.

EBI Experts Product Offerings

▶ Enterprise Manager: Advanced SAP BusinessObjects Report Audit Solution

  ▶ Manage and measure the metrics of your SAP BusinessObjects deployment

  ▶ Combine with the auditing features in Web Intelligence to trace activity

  ▶ Delivers detailed graphic performance analysis

  ▶ Monitors user activity

▶ Version Manager: Smart Version Control Software Solution

  ▶ Comprehensive version control tool

  ▶ Manage, compare, and control multiple versions of universes and reports

  ▶ Designed for Web Intelligence and Crystal Reports

  ▶ Simple check-in/check-out features

  ▶ Compare content and structure of versions

  ▶ Web services based architecture

  ▶ Low entry cost

  ▶ View extended details of universes and reports

A.5 GB & Smith

GB & Smith currently offers four powerful and user-friendly tools to implement, manage, and document the security rights in your SAP BusinessObjects Enterprise XI and Edge deployments.

The tools by GB & Smith provide easy-to-use interfaces for managing complex SAP BusinessObjects deployments and enable you to see the entire 360 degree view of the security configuration.

GB & Smith Product Offerings

- ▶ 360View – SAP BusinessObjects Enterprise Security Solution
  - ▶ Powerful and intuitive web-based tool
  - ▶ Implement, manage, and document security
  - ▶ Use and manage security access levels
  - ▶ Import users and groups from Excel into the CMS
  - ▶ Manage universe overloads
  - ▶ Identify dormant user accounts
  - ▶ Provides user centric and object centric views
  - ▶ Visualize security
- ▶ 360Cast – Report Bursting Solution
  - ▶ User-friendly web-based tool for scheduling SAP BusinessObjects reports
  - ▶ Manage distribution lists for bulk report broadcasting
  - ▶ Create distribution lists from Excel files
  - ▶ Define several distributions lists, formats, and prompt values in each list
  - ▶ Visualize scheduled instances and tasks
  - ▶ Display all tasks, properties, and linked SAP BusinessObjects instances
- ▶ 360Plus – Repository Comparison Solution
  - ▶ Logon to several CMSs, manage repositories together
  - ▶ Compare reports, groups, and universes
  - ▶ Document every single element in your repository
  - ▶ Recycle unused user licenses
- ▶ Integrity – Control you SAP BusinessObjects Licenses
  - ▶ Works on any SAP BusinessObjects deployment
  - ▶ One click compliance

- ▶ Ensures license compliance
- ▶ Manage and audit your license costs effectively

A.6   InfoBurst by InfoSol

InfoSol has been a BusinessObjects partner for over ten years and provides a comprehensive range of information systems solutions, including consulting, education, and technical support.

InfoSol currently holds several SAP BusinessObjects certifications including the following:

- ▶ Authorized Education Partner
- ▶ Gold Partner
- ▶ Solution Provider Partner
- ▶ Migration Specialist
- ▶ Distributor Partner

In addition to its service certifications, InfoSol also provides a powerful solution known as InfoBurst for scheduling, bursting, and distributing reports to extend the reach of your SAP BusinessObjects deployment. InfoBurst is available in three different versions: InfoBurst, InfoBurst 2009, and InfoBurst Edge.

InfoBurst by InfoSol – Product Offerings

- ▶ InfoBurst – Enterprise publishing solution since 2002
  - ▶ Comprehensive Report Distribution – Unlimited distribution options
  - ▶ Intelligence Report Distribution – True report bursting
  - ▶ Versatile Report Scheduling – Supports external calendars
  - ▶ Secure Report Delivery – FTP and encrypted email support
- ▶ InfoBurst 2009 – The latest enterprise report distribution version
  - ▶ Platform for growth
  - ▶ Secure and traceable distribution
  - ▶ Intuitive user interface
  - ▶ Supports multiple connections

- Multi and single pass report bursting
- Flex-based user interface
- Plus over 25 additional features
- InfoBurst Edge – Report and dashboard distribution for the Edge series
  - True "refresh once" report bursting for Web Intelligence and Crystal Reports
  - Schedule and distribute Xcelsius dashboards
  - Dynamically refresh Xcelsius dashboards

A.7   Integeo – A Forge Group Company

Integeo, a FORGE group company and BusinessObjects Technology Partner, was founded in 2004 to develop and commercialize innovative Map Intelligence products, which offer a large range of visualization and analytical functionality for report developers and consumers that aim to eliminate the need for expertise in programming commonly associated with developing highly functional reports with mapping visualizations.

Integeo Product Offerings

- Map Intelligence for BusinessObjects
  - Create dynamic, web-based spatial applications within hours
  - No programming skills needed for developer or user
  - Visualize changes instantly
  - Filter and compare real-time and historic views
  - View outcomes based on different scenarios
  - Batch Geocoder converts addresses to coordinates
  - Two-way roundtrip between report and map

A.8   NOAD

NOAD is an SAP Partner and certified for integrating with SAP BusinessObjects and a software solution provider that enables companies to manage business Intelligence deployments securely and effectively.

NOAD's EQM4 solution integrates with SAP BusinessObjects and helps organizations effectively monitor, maintain, and manage the accuracy and integrity of their business intelligence systems.

NOAD Product Offerings

▶ NOAD EQM4 version 2.1 – SAP BusinessObjects Enterprise XI 3.1

  ▶ Change and Management

  ▶ Deployment Automation

  ▶ User Activity Monitoring

  ▶ Migration

  ▶ Compliance Management

A.9 Noetix

Noetix has been an SAP BusinessObjects technology partner for several years and in 2008 the Noetix Generator received the SAP certification for integrating with SAP BusinessObjects XI solutions. Noetix Generator automatically generates NoetixViews that accelerate access to Oracle E-Business Suite application data.

Noetix Generator reduces the effort of implementing BI applications by fully automating the integration of NoetixViews within the reporting tool's metadata layer, saving administrators resource costs in supporting a diverse reporting environment.

Noetix Product Offerings (Integrating with SAP BusinessObjects)

▶ Noetix Generator

  ▶ Automatic creation of SAP BusinessObjects classes and Objects

  ▶ Automatic population of SAP BusinessObjects Environment

  ▶ Automatic creation of SAP BusinessObjects security groups

  ▶ Descriptive NoetixViews content

  ▶ Intuitive organization of SAP BusinessObjects

  ▶ Predefined joins and view relationships

  ▶ Hundreds of answers "out-of-the-box"

- ▶ Key Features of Noetix Generator

  - ▶ Speeds the deployment of business intelligence (BI) applications

  - ▶ Automatically populates the reporting tool's metadata layer with Noetix views

  - ▶ Significantly reduces the development time and costs associated with deploying business intelligence solutions

  - ▶ Provides business professionals the freedom and flexibility to use their own reporting tools

A.10   MeLLmo, Inc.

MeLLmo, Inc., creators of Xcelsius, is a privately funded company founded in January 2008 to create new ways of accessing, displaying, and interacting with critical applications on mobile devices.

With efficient back-end algorithms and a patented small screen design, MeLLmo's SAP certified Roambi solution provides simple and secure mobile data visualizations for the iPhone. Mobile visualizations are easily created from a variety of data sources including Excel, CSV, and salesforce.com CRM reports.

meLLmo Product Offerings

- ▶ Roambi Lite: For Individuals – Data Sources

  - ▶ HTML Tables

  - ▶ CSV

  - ▶ Excel

  - ▶ *Salesforce.com* CRM Reports

- ▶ Roambi Pro: For Companies & Groups – Data Sources

  - ▶ HTML Tables

  - ▶ CSV

  - ▶ Excel

  - ▶ *Salesforce.com* CRM Reports

  - ▶ Google Spreadsheets

- Roambi ES: For Enterprise – Data Sources
  - HTML Tables
  - CSV
  - Excel
  - *Salesforce.com* CRM Reports
  - Crystal Reports
  - Web Intelligence

A.11 Teleran Technologies

Teleran Technologies, a provider of software for auditing, analyzing, and managing business intelligence enterprise applications, is an SAP partner and in 2009 achieved the SAP certification for integrating with SAP BusinessObjects. Their software suite fully integrates with SAP BusinessObjects XI 3.1 and provides performance, compliance, and cost control for SAP BusinessObjects customers.

Teleran Technologies Product Offerings

- iSight – Application Usage Auditing & Analysis
  - Continuously audit and analyze user, application, and database activity
  - Track user, report, and universe activity
  - Provides comprehensive visibility of SAP BusinessObjects environment
  - Capture information on query activity
  - Provide business policy monitoring, risk analysis, and compliance reporting
  - Alerts staff of inappropriate or suspicious activity
- iGuard – Usage Policy Management Improves Performance and Compliance
  - Provides business policy rules
  - Automatically protect the application and database from unauthorized reports and queries that violate business policies
  - Screens information requests from SAP BusinessObjects
  - Warn requestors of attempted policy violations

> ▶ Ensure consistency of active policies

> ▶ Creates new policies based on changing patterns

> ▶ Automatically maintain effective policies over time

A.12   Tidal Software

Tidal Software, now part of Cisco, is a member of the SAP partner program and provides an adapter solution that integrates with SAP BusinessObjects to enable information discovery, delivery, and management, as well as query, reporting, and sophisticated numeric and text data analysis capabilities.

Tidal Enterprise Adapter for SAP BusinessObjects XI Intelligence Platform is the interface between Tidal Enterprise Scheduler and the SAP BusinessObjects XI Intelligence Platform and Data Services. With this interface, users can define, launch, and monitor tasks within an SAP BusinessObjects environment.

Tidal Software Product Offerings

▶ Tidal Enterprise Adapter for SAP BusinessObjects

> ▶ Supports cross-application, cross-platform job dependencies, enabling integration of SAP BusinessObjects XI Intelligence Platform, Data Services, Web Intelligence, and Crystal Report solutions jobs with all other data flows

> ▶ Offers a single point-of-control for company-wide job scheduling through a Windows or web console

> ▶ Leverages existing technology and investment in SAP BusinessObjects for a complete enterprise solution

> ▶ Delivers industry-leading scheduling functionality, including GUI job definition and seamless handling of events, dependencies, resources, calendars, and output

> ▶ Provides exception-based management, scalability, role-based security, and enhanced manageability

> ▶ Eliminates scripting or command lines, dramatically reducing maintenance requirements and increasing ROI

A.13 Summary

Many third-party vendors exist in the market today to help users extend the functionality of their SAP BusinessObjects XI deployments.

The purpose of this chapter was to introduce and briefly describe the product offerings of the known third-party vendors that integrate with SAP BusinessObjects.

Third-party vendors provide many innovative tools and software solutions that help you increase your return on investment with SAP BusinessObjects and provide new functionality that does not exist with a standard deployment.

Service Pack 2 for SAP BusinessObjects Enterprise XI 3.1 provides many valuable improvements and enhancements to existing XI 3.1 deployments. Service Pack 2 extends the functionality of Web Intelligence with the addition of several new significant improvements.

B Web Intelligence XI 3.1 Service Pack 2

Service Pack 2 for SAP BusinessObjects Enterprise XI 3.1 introduces seven new enhancements to Web Intelligence XI 3.1.

The most significant enhancement is the addition of Input Controls, an easy-to-use set of report filtering tools that provide data analysts, report consumers, and report developers with the capabilities of producing reporting documents with components that offer guided analysis, with an assortment of content filtering and report personalization options.

This appendix outlines seven new features introduced with Service Pack 2 and contains a brief description of each new enhancement. Below is the list of enhancements to Web Intelligence included in Service Pack 2.

Enhancements to Web Intelligence

▶ Input Controls

▶ Fold/Un-Fold

▶ BI Services

▶ Query on Query

▶ Data Provider Extension Points

▶ Formula Language Extension Points

▶ Translation Manager

B.1   Input Controls

Input controls allow users to quickly navigate to the most relevant information for their needs by using on-report filters that can affect an entire Web Intelligence report or specific components within the report. The benefit of this feature is that all users are now able to utilize existing reports to access the information they need rather than having to create numerous reports with different hardcoded filters.

Ultimately, this leads to improved productivity and more confidence among report consumers. Input Controls allow guided analysis by providing a direction for report consumers to analyze the information displayed within a report.

Adding Input Controls to Web Intelligence Reports

Input Controls can be added to reports in the following scenarios.

- Viewing a report
- Editing a report
- Creating a report

Input Controls appear in a new tab in the Report Manager when editing or creating a Web Intelligence report. This fifth tab contains all Input Controls that have been added to the selected report and also contains a New and Reset button for creating new Input Controls and resetting the selection made with a control.

Input Controls are created by selecting a report object followed by choosing from a number of single-value and multiple-value control types. The next section lists the available Input Control types for dimensions and measures.

Single Value Control Types – For Dimension Objects

- Entry field
- Combo box
- Radio button
- List box

Multiple Value Control Types – For Dimension Objects

- Check box
- List box

Single Value – For Measure Objects

▶ Entry field

▶ Spinner

▶ Simple slider

Multiple Value Control types – For Measure Objects

▶ Double slider

Several properties are available for editing Input Controls. Below is a list of those properties. These properties can be easily edited when creating or editing controls.

▶ Label

▶ Description

▶ List of values

▶ Use restricted list of values

▶ Default value

▶ Operator

One of the most useful features of Input Controls is the flexibility to assign specific report elements to Input Controls.

> **Note**
>
> The report elements assigned to Input Controls appear in the Dependencies tab when editing an Input Control.

B.2   Fold/Unfold

The ability to either fold (hide) or un-fold (display) hierarchical content allows report consumers to quickly navigate to relevant information. Spend less time navigating from page to page or scrolling from top to bottom of a report and spend more time reviewing and analyzing company information.

The Fold/Unfold feature produces drill-like behavior by allowing a report consumer to click on a top-level report structure with an aggregate measure then viewing the details beneath that structure.

Combining the Fold/Unfold feature with the ability to track data changes and filter reports with Input Controls lends itself to producing reporting documents with additional guided analysis features.

The Fold/Unfold shortcut icon is located on the default toolbar located in the upper right corner of the report panel when viewing a report in InfoView. Toggle to folding or unfolding a reporting document by clicking the shortcut icon to select or deselect folding. This feature provides a method of collapsing and expanding the visual component in a reports structure.

B.3   Query on Query

The query on query feature allows report writers and power users to filter an existing query with another adhoc query. This is a useful way of combining corporate data with either another corporate data source or a personal data source.

For example, you could have a query that returns a list of customers that recently purchased SAP BusinessObjects products and the products they purchased. While looking at the report containing the results of this query, you may find it useful to combine the report data with personal Excel data with a list of customers that recently purchased SAP Business Warehouse.

The combination of these queries would provide a unique way to view the customers that are potentially considering querying SAP BW with SAP BusinessObjects products. This could lead to an increased number of proactive conversations to help the client drive value and increase their return on investment with SAP BusinessObjects.

B.4   BI Services

The new BI Services features provide report writers with the capability to publish entire reports or report parts as web services that can be consumed by any appropriate application or portal. This is a great mechanism for reusing Web Intelligence report content that contains tables, charts, complex calculations, and queries from multiple data sources.

With BI Services, the report metadata is exposed and allows users to see where the data is coming from and the definition of result objects retrieved by a query.

BI Services are available in Web Intelligence Rich Client and can be accessed by clicking a check box beside Show BI services in the upper right corner of Web Intelligence Rich Client. Web services can also be added to a Web Intelligence Rich Client document when creating a new report. Selecting other data sources as the data access type then enter or paste a WSDL into the provided box.

B.5 Data Provider Extension Points

The Data Provider Extension Points allow developers to connect to any structured data source by using an easy to understand API. This new feature allows deployments to access legacy data sources and also proprietary and obscure sources.

Query these data sources using SAP BusinessObjects Web Intelligence and combine with other data sources for deeper analysis.

B.6 Formula Language Extension Points

The Formula Language Extension Points functionality allows for custom functions to be added to the formula language and user interface with an easy to understand API.

This feature allows for business logic to be embedded directly within the UI. For example, if you have a field that contains encrypted data, you could write a custom function that automatically decrypts the data.

B.7 Translation Manager

The Translation Manager is a new feature that allows Web Intelligence reports to translate the report metadata plus several other areas in the reporting documents. This translation can be included in the following areas of a reporting document.

► Report content
► Query names

- ▶ Report names
- ▶ Static free-standing cells
- ▶ Alerter names
- ▶ Variable names

A single report can be translated into any supported language thereby reducing confusion and the number of reports created in the deployment.

B.8   Summary

Service Pack 2 for SAP BusinessObjects XI 3.1 provides many improvements to the Web Intelligence toolset. The new features in Service Pack 2 allow for more precise filtering of report data and provide the capability of fine tuning results for more actionable analysis.

C   The Authors

Jim Brogden is a software engineer, data analyst, award-winning technical author, and business intelligence consultant for Daugherty Business Solutions in Atlanta, Georgia. He combines a Masters degree in Information Technology and more than eight years of business intelligence development experience with a proven track record of delivering world-class business intelligence solutions to a number of fortune 200 clients. Jim has extensive experience with producing innovative Xcelsius 2008 visual presentations and countless hours of development using Web Intelligence, Desktop Intelligence, and Crystal Reports. He has been a Business Objects Certified Professional and Migration Specialist since 2006 and has performed several successful Business-Objects deployments and migrations. Jim is a graduate of the University of South Alabama

Heather Sinkwitz gained her expertise while working as a Business Intelligence Consultant specializing in BusinessObjects reporting solutions. She is currently employed as a Business Intelligence Developer for Rural/Metro Corporation. She is a certified instructor for the BusinessObjects Web Intelligence and Xcelsius tools. She brings her extensive background in the accounting field to the reporting process to aid in the completion of financial dashboards and reporting solutions. She enjoys presenting data in new and unique ways to aid companies in making informed decisions at a fast pace to remain competitive in today's market.

Mac Holden is currently working for Inovista Components, a small software house specializing in custom components for SAP's Xcelsius product in addition to Web Intelligence customization. Mac has over 15 years of software development and design experience, working primarily with web based technologies. He has 10 years of experience in using the various SDKs to create Web Intelligence applications for customers in many different locations and industries. He has also co-authored a number of books on Java Enterprise Development in addition to supplying articles for publications such as Java Pro. Mac is currently based in southern Spain and can be contacted at: *cmholden@inovista.com*.

Index

U

V

X

Y

Z